1994

Chaucer's *Troilus and Criseyde*

"Subgit to alle Poesye"

Essays in Criticism

MEDIEVAL & RENAISSANCE TEXTS & STUDIES

VOLUME 104

PEGASUS PAPERBOOKS

NUMBER 10

Chaucer's *Troilus and Criseyde*

"Subgit to alle Poesye"
Essays in Criticism

EDITOR

R. A. SHOAF

With the Assistance of Catherine S. Cox

Medieval & Renaissance texts & studies
Binghamton, New York
1992

Library of Congress Catalog Card Number:
92–61340 (cloth)
92–14323 (paper)

ISBN 0–86698–150–0 (cloth)
ISBN 0–86698–119–5 (paper)

This book is made to last.
It is set in Baskerville
and printed on acid-free paper
to library specifications

Printed in the United States of America

Contents

Preface

The essays in this collection demonstrate and are themselves examples of how *Troilus and Criseyde* is "subgit to alle poesye" (5.1790). Subject to poetry, *Troilus and Criseyde* also has poetry as its subject. *Troilus and Criseyde* is important, and these essays likewise, because, remarkable as the poem is in so many ways, it is perhaps most remarkable for its self-consciousness, what postmodernism would call its metatextuality: it knows itself as literature; it is writing about writing—but recursively, not redundantly. Great literature is most about the human when it is also, recursively, most about itself. These essays tell the story, each in its different way, of Chaucer discovering in *Troilus and Criseyde* that to tell a story about the human, it is necessary also to tell the story of telling the story, for this is the best way, the most economical as well as most faithful way, to represent the complexity of the human.

If the human differs from the rest of nature by virtue of the capacity for discourse, then this means that the human difference is difference itself, which is also difference from itself: human beings are human beings as and in the experience of non-self-coincidence, the experience of knowing themselves as other to themselves—"If no love is, O God, what fele I so?" (1.400). "I" is something I am only some of the time (recall Rimbaud's famous mot, "*Je est un autre*"). The experience of the characters Troilus and Criseyde is the experience of the otherness of self, to which each of them reacts in each's ownmost way: "Th'entente is al, and nat the lettres space," writes Criseyde, at the end (5.1630), when Troilus, in turn, wonders "I nevere wolde han wend, er this, / That ye, Criseyde, koude han chaunged so" (5.1682–83). The otherness of the self to itself is figured in part throughout the poem in Pandarus, the go-between, the mediator, who constantly reminds the self that it is other—"I . . . in my nece [have] yput this fantasie" (3.275). It is also figured in that other mediator in the poem, the Narrator, who puts "this fantasy" in us, Chaucer's readers, and who is increasingly conscious that this is just what he is doing—"Men seyn—I not—that she yaf hym hire herte."

If *Troilus and Criseyde* is "subgit to alle poesye" and if its subject is poetry, the subject of the poetry is subjectivity itself, the subjectivity of the self. The self is *sub-ject* to, "thrown under," the other, and the price of selfhood is the consciousness that selfhood has a price, that it is not freely given. However "modern" or even "postmodern" such a description may seem, it is also medieval—indeed, much that seems an invention of modern criticism is already closely anticipated if not predicted in medieval literary culture—and, just so, the following essays, in their different ways, teach us how Chaucer, the medieval poet, can teach us about our subjectivity. They are thus essays historicist in impulse; and that will be evident on even the most cursory reading. They are also, however, at the same time, theoretical essays, in the most important dimension of literary theory: the impulse to re-think the given, to interrogate its given-ness, and to seek alternative positions from which it can be comprehended. In this they continue even as they respond to one of Chaucer's deepest impulses in *Troilus and Criseyde*—the quest for "the forme of olde clerkis speche / In poetrie, if [we] hire bokes seche" (5.1854–55).

RAS & CSC
Gainesville, Florida
May 13, 1992

Acknowledgments

We would like to thank the individuals and institutions that helped to make this project possible. First and foremost, our publisher, MRTS, and its director, Mario A. Di Cesare, deserve our warmest thanks: without the Pegasus Paperbook Series and the commitments it represents, we could not have realized our initiative. Our desire to see *Troilus and Criseyde* figure more prominently in the undergraduate classroom would have remained unfulfilled without the commitment of Pegasus Paperbooks to affordable classroom materials.

We would like next to recognize the great patience and goodwill of our contributors who waited and worked alike with the utmost professional courtesy. The book, of course, is theirs, and it is only fitting to acknowledge how much and how collegially they contributed to its successful realization.

The secretarial staff of the Department of English in the University of Florida contributed their efficient and accurate services to many parts of the project, and we take this occasion to thank them warmly: Muriel Burke, Darla Wilkes, George Kingson, Joan Crawford. Also, the Faculty Support Center for Computing was instrumental in our work on the project. Last but not least, our Research Assistant in the Spring Term of 1992, Ms. Margit Wogowitsch, provided invaluable proof-reading services. We, of course, are responsible for any and all errors that remain.

Finally, several Chaucerians who do not figure directly in the final product nonetheless contributed to its realization. We would like to recognize and thank John A. Alford, Ross G. Arthur, Susan Crane, Judith Ferster, Allen J. Frantzen, Warren Ginsberg, Thomas Hahn, Lisa Kiser, Tim W. Machan, Glending Olson, Lee Patterson, A. C. Spearing, M. Teresa Tavormina, Eugene Vance, Mary Wack, Hope Weissman, and Winthrop Wetherbee.

RAS & CSC

Permissions

We gratefully acknowledge the following for permission to reprint material originally appearing under copyright in their publications.

Stephen A. Barney, "Troilus Bound," *Speculum* 47 (1972): 445–58; C. David Benson, *Chaucer's TROILUS AND CRISEYDE* (London: Unwin Hyman, 1990), Chapters 5 and 6; Sheila Delany, "Techniques of Alienation in *Troilus and Criseyde*," *The Uses of Criticism*, ed. A. P. Foulkes, Literaturwissenschaftliche Texte, Theorie, und Kritik 3 (Bern: Peter Lang, 1976), 77–95; Carolyn Dinshaw, "Reading Like A Man: The Critics, the Narrator, Troilus, and Pandarus," *Chaucer's Sexual Poetics* (Madison: University of Wisconsin Press, 1989), 28–64; John M. Fyler, "The Fabrications of Pandarus," *Modern Language Quarterly* 41 (1980): 115–30; J. P. Hermann, "Gesture and Seduction in *Troilus and Criseyde*," *Studies in the Age of Chaucer* 7 (1985): 107–35; David Wallace, *Chaucer and the Early Writings of Boccaccio*, Chaucer Studies xii (Woodbridge, Suffolk: Boydell & Brewer, Ltd., 1985), Chapters 5 and 6.

Some Notes on Using this Book

Certain features of our book should be brought to the attention of our readers. To save space and to simplify references, several lists of various data are appended at the beginning of the book. Readers should consult these lists before beginning to work with the book since they make it much more "user-friendly."

In the same spirit, each essay is preceded by a brief Prologue, written by the author of the essay, that serves to introduce the essay and its principal concerns and goals. By consulting the Prologue, readers can conveniently determine the relevance of a particular essay to their current interests. Further, instructors, by reading all 16 Prologues in any given semester, can refresh themselves as to the contents of the book while they are preparing their syllabi and lesson plans.

Material in foreign languages discussed in the essays is translated. If it is for illustrative purposes exclusively, we follow each contributor's decision either to cite the original only or a translation only.

Finally, we have occasionally intervened in the essays for one purpose or another (always in the footnotes), and our remarks are set off by italics plus the signature — *RAS & CSC*.

List of Frequently Cited Works

The works appearing in this list are cited in the essays in abbreviated form without further explanation. Full bibliographic information for each work follows the abbreviation we have selected for it. Several collections of essays are frequently cited for individual items they contain. These collections will be cited throughout our text by their editors' surnames—e.g., Lambert, "Criseydan Reading," in Salu (25).

Collections

Stephen A. Barney. Ed. *Chaucer's TROILUS: Essays in Criticism*. Hamden: Archon Books, 1980.

Jerome A. Mandel and Bruce Rosenberg. Eds. *Medieval Literature and Folklore Studies: Essays in Honor of Francis Lee Utley*. New Brunswick: Rutgers University Press, 1970.

Mary Salu. Ed. *Essays on TROILUS AND CRISEYDE*. Cambridge: D.S. Brewer, 1979.

Richard J. Schoeck and Jerome Taylor. Eds. *Chaucer Criticism*. 2 volumes. Notre Dame: University of Notre Dame Press, 1960.

Julian N. Wasserman and Robert J. Blanch. Eds. *Chaucer in the Eighties*. Syracuse: Syracuse University Press, 1986.

Individual Works

Aers, *Chaucer*. David Aers. *Chaucer, Langland, and the Creative Imagination*. London: Routledge, 1980.

Aers, *Community*. David Aers. *Community, Gender, and Individual Identity: English Writing 1360–1430*. New York: Routledge, 1988.

Anderson, "Theban." David Anderson. "Theban History in Chaucer's *Troilus*." *SAC* 4 (1982): 109-33.

Barney, "Troilus Bound." Stephen A. Barney. "Troilus Bound." *Speculum* 47 (1972): 445-58.

Benson, *Chaucer's T&C*. C. David Benson. *Chaucer's TROILUS AND CRISEYDE*. London: Unwin Hyman, 1990.

Bloomfield, "Distance." Morton W. Bloomfield. "Distance and Predestination in *Troilus and Criseyde*." *PMLA* 72 (1957): 14-26. Reprinted in Barney, 75-90.

Carton, "Pandarus's Bed." Evan Carton. "Complicity and Responsibility in Pandarus' Bed and Chaucer's Art." *PMLA* 94 (1979): 47-61.

Davis, *Glossary*. Norman Davis, et al. *A Chaucer Glossary*. Oxford: Clarendon, 1979.

Diamond, "Politics." Arlyn Diamond. *"Troilus and Criseyde*: The Politics of Love." In Wasserman and Blanch, 93–103.

Dinshaw, *Poetics.* Carolyn Dinshaw. *Chaucer's Sexual Poetics.* Madison: University of Wisconsin Press, 1989.

Donaldson, *Speaking.* E. Talbot Donaldson. *Speaking of Chaucer.* New York: Norton, 1970.

Fyler, "Fabrications." John M. Fyler. "The Fabrications of Pandarus." *MLQ* 41 (1980): 115-30.

Gordon, *Sorrow.* Ida L. Gordon. *The Double Sorrow of Troilus: A Study of Ambiguities in* TROILUS AND CRISEYDE. Oxford: Clarendon, 1970.

Havely, *Chaucer's Boccaccio.* N. R. Havely. *Chaucer's Boccaccio: Sources of "Troilus" and the "Knight's Tale" and "Franklin's Tale".* Chaucer Studies v. Cambridge: D. S. Brewer, 1980.

Howard, "Experience." Donald R. Howard. "Experience, Language, and Consciousness: *Troilus and Criseyde,* II, 596-931." In Mandel and Rosenberg, 173–92. Reprinted in Barney, 159–80.

Kaminsky, *Critics.* Alice Kaminsky. *Chaucer's* TROILUS AND CRISEYDE *and the Critics.* Athens: Ohio University Press, 1980.

Lambert, "Criseydan Reading." Mark Lambert. *"Troilus,* Books I–III: A Criseydan Reading." In Salu, 105–25.

Lewis, "What Chaucer Really Did." C. S. Lewis. "What Chaucer really did to the *Filostrato.*" *E&S* 17 (1932): 56–75. Reprinted in Barney, 37–54.

MacAlpine, *Genre.* Monica McAlpine. *The Genre of* TROILUS AND CRISEYDE. Ithaca: Cornell University Press, 1978.

Meech, *Design.* Sanford B. Meech. *Design in Chaucer's* TROILUS. Syracuse: Syracuse University Press, 1959.

Muscatine, *French Tradition.* Charles Muscatine. *Chaucer and the French Tradition.* Berkeley: University of California Press, 1957.

Payne, *Key.* Robert O. Payne. *The Key of Remembrance: A Study of Chaucer's Poetics.* New Haven: Yale University Press, 1963.

Pearsall, "Choices." Derek A. Pearsall. "Criseyde's Choices." *SAC. Proceedings* 2 (1986): 17-29.

Robertson, *Preface.* D. W. Robertson, Jr. *A Preface to Chaucer.* Princeton: Princeton University Press, 1962.

Rowe, *O Love!* Donald Rowe. *O Love! O Charite!: Contraries Harmonized in Chaucer's* TROILUS. Carbondale: Southern Illinois University Press, 1976.

Schless, *Chaucer and Dante.* Howard Schless. *Chaucer and Dante: A Revaluation.* Norman: Pilgrim Books, 1984.

Shoaf, *Currency.* R. A. Shoaf. *Dante, Chaucer, and the Currency of the Word: Money, Images, and Reference in Late Medieval Poetry.* Norman: Pilgrim Books, 1983.

Steadman, *Laughter.* John M. Steadman. *Disembodied Laughter:* TROILUS *and the Apotheosis Tradition.* Berkeley: University of California Press, 1972.

Taylor, *Chaucer Reads.* Karla Taylor. *Chaucer Reads* THE DIVINE COMEDY. Stanford: Stanford University Press, 1989.

Tatlock & Kennedy, *Concordance.* J. S. P. Tatlock and A. G. Kennedy. *A Concord-*

ance to the Complete Works of Geoffrey Chaucer. 1927; repr. Gloucester: Peter Smith, 1963.

Trimpi, *Muses.* Wesley Trimpi. *Muses of One Mind: The Literary Analysis of Experience and Its Continuity.* Princeton: Princeton University Press, 1983.

Wetherbee, *Poets.* Winthrop Wetherbee. *Chaucer and the Poets. An Essay on TROILUS AND CRISEYDE.* Ithaca: Cornell University Press, 1984.

Wood, *Elements.* Chauncey Wood. *The Elements of Chaucer's TROILUS.* Durham: Duke University Press, 1984.

Principal Editions and Translations

Our principal text of *Troilus and Criseyde* is that of A. C. Baugh as it appears in R. A. Shoaf, ed. *Troilus and Criseyde* (East Lansing: Colleagues Press, 1989). We have chosen this edition since the present collection, like it, is designed primarily for use in the undergraduate classroom.

All other citations of Chaucer's texts are taken from Benson, Larry D. (Editor), *The Riverside Chaucer*, Third Edition. Copyright © 1987 by Houghton Mifflin Company. Used with permission.

The following are cited throughout our text by surnames of the editors and translators unless a surname plus short title will help to prevent confusion.

apRoberts and Seldis. *Il Filostrato*. Trans. Robert apRoberts and Anna Bruni Seldis. Garland Library of Medieval Literature, vol. 53, series A. New York: Garland, 1982.

Barney. Stephen A. Barney. *Troilus and Criseyde. The Riverside Chaucer*. Gen. ed. Larry D. Benson. 3d ed. Boston: Houghton Mifflin, 1987. Pp. 471–585.

Branca. Vittore Branca. *Tutte le opere di Giovanni Boccaccio*. 12 volumes. Milan: Mondadori, 1964– .

Constans. Léopold Constans. *Le Roman de Troie par Benoît de Sainte Maure*. 6 volumes. Paris: Firmin Didot, 1904–12.

Donaldson. E. T. Donaldson. *Chaucer's Poetry*. 2nd ed. New York: John Wiley & Sons, 1975.

Mandelbaum. Allen Mandelbaum. *The DIVINE COMEDY of Dante Alighieri*. New York: Bantam, 1982–86.

Robinson. F. N. Robinson. *The Works of Geoffrey Chaucer*. 2nd ed. Cambridge: Houghton Mifflin, 1957.

Root. Robert Kilburn Root. *The Book of TROILUS AND CRISEYDE by Geoffrey Chaucer*. Princeton: Princeton University Press, 1926.

Singleton. Charles S. Singleton. *The Divine Comedy*. 3 volumes in 6 parts. Bollingen Series 80. Princeton: Princeton University Press, 1970–75.

Windeatt. Barry Windeatt. *Geoffrey Chaucer. TROILUS AND CRISEYDE: A New Edition of THE BOOK OF TROILUS*. London: Longman, 1984.

Abbreviations

1. Titles of Chaucer's Works Cited in this Volume

Anel	*Anelida and Arcite*
BD	*The Book of the Duchess*
Bo	*Boece*
ClT	*The Clerk's Tale*
CT	*The Canterbury Tales*
CYT	*The Canon's Yeoman's Tale*
FranT	*The Franklin's Tale*
HF	*The House of Fame*
KnT	*The Knight's Tale*
Lady	*A Complaint to his Lady*
LGW	*The Legend of Good Women*
MancT	*The Manciple's Tale*
MercB	*Merciles Beaute*
MerT	*The Merchant's Tale*
MilT	*The Miller's Tale*
MLT	*The Man of Law's Tale*
PardT	*The Pardoner's Tale*
ParsT	*The Parson's Tale*
PF	*The Parliament of Fowls*
Rom	*The Romaunt of the Rose*
SNT	*The Second Nun's Tale*
SqT	*The Squire's Tale*
T&C	*Troilus and Criseyde*
Thop	*Tale of Sir Thopas*
WBT	*The Wife of Bath's Tale*

2. Titles of Other Works—Ancient, Medieval, and Modern

Aen	*Aeneid*
Comm	*Commedia*
CP	*Consolation of Philosophy*
Dec	*Decameron*
Fil	*Il Filostrato*
Inf	*Inferno*
MED	*Middle English Dictionary*
MGH	*Monumenta Germaniae Historiae*
OED	*Oxford English Dictionary*
Para	*Paradiso*

Phars   *Pharsalia*
PN   *Poetria nova*
Purg   *Purgatorio*
RR   *Romance of the Rose*
Tes   *Teseida*
VN   *Vita Nuova*

Biblical Citations (with Douay–Rheims titles)

1 Tim   1 Timothy
2 Tim   2 Timothy
2 Pet   2 Peter
Eccl   Ecclesiastes
Isa   Isaias
Prov   Proverbs
Ps   Psalms
Rom   Romans
Rev   Apocalypse

3. Titles of Journals

Academy
AHDLMA *Archives d'Histoire Doctrinale et Littéraire du Moyen Âge*
AI   *American Imago: A Psychoanalytic Journal for Culture, Science, and the Arts*
ANQ   *A Quarterly Journal of Short Articles, Notes and Reviews*
AnM   *Annuale Mediaevale*
Archiv *Archiv für das Studium der Neueren Sprachen und Literaturen*
CL   *Comparative Literature*
ChauR   *Chaucer Review: A Journal of Medieval Studies and Literary Criticism*
CRCL   *Canadian Review of Comparative Literature*
Dante Studies
Diacritics
E&S   *Essays and Studies*
ELH   *English Literary History*
ELN   *English Language Notes*
EM   *English Miscellany: A Symposium of History, Literature and the Arts*
ES   *English Studies: A Journal of English Language and Literature*
ESC   *English Studies in Canada*
Exemplaria
HSELL   *Hiroshima Studies in English Language and Literature*
HumLov *Humanistica Lovaniensia*
IJP   *International Journal of Psychoanalysis*
JEGP   *Journal of English and Germanic Philology*
L&P   *Literature and Psychology*
M&H   *Medievalia et Humanistica: Studies in Medieval and Renaissance Culture*

MÆ	*Medium Ævum*
Mediaevalia	
MLN	*Modern Language Notes*
MLQ	*Modern Language Quarterly*
MLR	*Modern Language Review*
MP	*Modern Philology*
MQR	*Michigan Quarterly Review*
MS	*Mediaeval Studies*
Neophilologus	
NM	*Neuphilologische Mitteilungen*
PLL	*Papers on Language and Literature*
PMLA	*Publications of the Modern Language Association of America*
PQ	*Philological Quarterly*
Ren&R NS	*Renaissance and Reformation,* New Series
RBPH	*Revue belge de philologie et d'histoire*
RELat	*Revue des Études Latines*
RF	*Romanische Forschungen*
RomN	*Romance Notes*
RPh	*Romance Philology*
RS	*Research Studies*
SAC	*Studies in the Age of Chaucer*
SB	*Studies in Bibliography: Papers of the Bibliographical Society of the University of Virginia*
SHR	*Southern Humanities Review*
SMC	*Studies in Medieval Culture*
SoAR	*South Atlantic Review*
SP	*Studies in Philology*
Speculum:	*A Journal of Medieval Studies*
SR	*Studies in the Renaissance*
SBoc	*Studi sul Boccaccio*
SubStance:	*A Review of Theory and Literary Criticism*
TSLL	*Texas Studies in Literature and Language*
UTQ	*University of Toronto Quarterly: A Canadian Journal of the Humanities*
YIS	*Yale Italian Studies*
YJC	*Yale Journal of Criticism*

Troilus Bound*

STEPHEN A. BARNEY

Troilus's sorrows are of love, or what may be called the trammels of desire. The term "trammels," generalized to the idea of constraint and bondage, shifts the poem from a plot of twice-frustrated love to an investigation of providence and freedom. The agent of that shift is the philosophical, speculative, heightened if limited consciousness of the young prince. Primarily by way of his language, variously shaded and pointed and contravened by the other voices of the poem, we get access to how it feels to be imprisoned in figures paradoxically unsensuous and abstract. The shape of Chaucer's several uses of the imagery of bondage can be made out in others of his works, and within this complex framework Troilus seems a special instance of restricted potential. The confined spaces of the poem reinforce our sense that it suddenly explodes at the end: Troilus is released only in death.

> Man knoweth not his own end: but as fishes are taken with the hook, and as birds are caught with the snare, so men are taken in the evil time, when it shall suddenly come upon them.

The experience of reading the *Troilus* is like the experience of tightening a screw until at last something gives and the mechanism flies apart. The event can be looked on as a catastrophe or a relief, depending on the point of view. The effect is powerful and moving. Criticism of the poem should account for this effect, and indeed some brilliant work on the poem in recent times has given us various rewarding modes of apprehending what Joyce might have called the curve of the poem's emotion. We now see how the narrator's painful involvement and even more painful progressive detachment from the action of his own reported history work to control the reader's response. We see the function of the double pattern of time: the historical tempo and duration of events, which the narrator subverts when he can, and the underlying, seasonal pattern, expressed in metaphors, of fresh spring and dying winter, a pattern which reinforces the doom and hints finally at new life.[1]

---

* Originally appeared in *Speculum* 47 (1972): 445-58.
[1] See Donaldson, *Chaucer's Poetry*, 1129-44; Bloomfield, "Distance"; Henry W. Sams,

Analogous curves of activity can be made out in the principal characters. Pandarus changes from a garrulous and energetic figure, who always "com lepyng in atones," to a man who, like the Pardoner, silenced and still in sympathy and shame, "stant, astoned. . . . As stille as ston; a word ne kowde he seye" (2.939; 5.1728–29). Pandarus's whole body adds to his meaning. In the early books his gestures provide us with a constant parody of a father-confessor figure, and a parody of a celebrant of a sacrament in the consummation scene. But his flailing movements pass into utter quiescence as his eyes are opened, just as Chaucer seems to put behind him the elaborate parody of the religion of love when he draws near the climax.

Criseyde receives more than she gives. She is acted upon by Pandarus, by the stunning sight of Troilus ("Who yaf me drinke?"), by the song of true love which Antigone sings, by her own dreams, by—if we can trust the narrator—astrological powers, perhaps most deeply by the sweet song of a nightingale during those vulnerable moments between waking and sleeping, and finally by that most active instrument Diomede, who takes the reins, who is described in cruelly echoing terms as being "as fressh as braunche in May" (5.844; cf. 3.353). As Father Dunning writes, Criseyde "takes her colour from her company"; our knowledge of her is filtered through her circumstances and the point of view of her beholders.[2] She *seems* to change; that is, she is seen to change. She is, in fact, "slydynge of corage" (5.825); if one were to plot her development in the terms of mechanics, the vector representing her circumstances as a force would be long, and the vector representing her volition would be brief. When we see Criseyde alone, she is weighing alternatives; when we see Troilus alone, he is wishing.

It is Troilus, working as it were from within but in association with the poet, sometimes at odds with the narrator, who establishes the meaning of the events of the poem. If Pandarus excels, up to a point, in arranging circumstances, then Troilus excels—especially when larger forces take over from Pandarus—in contemplating and exposing the inner significance of events. Several qualities in his character account for this special capacity. Criseyde weighs the alternative future possibilities of her situation, then slides down the plane, inclined and oiled by Pandarus, of the first three books. Pandarus leaps from practical solution to practical solution, cheerfully contradicting himself. Even our narrator modifies his judgments, as if he were affected by the story he is telling. Troilus, in contrast, performs a mental activity that we may call thinking. Perhaps this is because he is young. Criseyde and Pandarus know the old dance of love, but Troilus is split in two at the outset of the poem. His intellect and his desire are at cross purposes, and he constantly complains—except when

---

"The Dual Time-Scheme in Chaucer's *Troilus*," *MLN* 56 (1941): 94–100, reprinted in Schoeck and Taylor, 180–85. Major and influential criticisms of the poem are in Muscatine, *French Tradition*, Chapter 5; Meech, *Design*; and Payne, *Key*, Chapters 6 and 7.

[2] T. P. Dunning, "God and Man in *Troilus and Criseyde*," *English and Medieval Studies Presented to J. R. R. Tolkien*, ed. Norman Davis and C. L. Wrenn (London: Allen & Unwin, 1962), 164–82.

he has his love—of disorientation. His language persistently voyages beyond the immediate situation and reaches for distant, final, absolute causes. He talks of Fortune, of Jove, of hell, of death.

In Book 2 we are presented with Criseyde's process of thought, her meandering attention from practical considerations of the affair, to Antigone's song, to the nightingale's song, and finally to sleep and the eagle dream.[3] With this depiction of her mental process we should compare Troilus's first moments alone after he is smitten with love (1.358–434). First he begins to "make a mirour of his mynde," that is, he speculates, and beholds the figure of Criseyde in his heart. He hopes he will "falle in grace" with her. He imagines that trouble, even the public exposure of his love, will be worth it. He decides to be secretive, aware of the consequences of "love to wide yblowe." He considers how to entice her, and immediately, we are told, he composes a song—at first we think it will be a wooing song. Our narrator renders it from his "auctor" Lollius (first mentioned here), and we know it is a translation of Petrarch's sonnet "S'amor non è."[4] The well-known "mistranslation" of the first phrase establishes my point: Petrarch means, "If this be not love"; Chaucer renders it, "If no love is." Troilus abstracts from Petrarch's abstractions. He had been considering his new love in fairly pragmatic, goal-directed thought, and now suddenly he complains of the nature of love itself, of its paradoxes, its "swete harm," its "quike deth." He is steerless in a boat at sea between constantly adverse winds. His song over, Troilus concludes the meditation commending his spirit to the God of Love, and formally plighting himself the God's and Criseyde's servant. Criseyde does not exactly think, but performs the operation Kingsley Amis once called "frowning and pondering." Troilus, perhaps in his youth and perhaps to his sorrow, tends toward the metaphysical.[5]

My purpose here is to pick out a strand of Troilus's thought that may generally be called the theme of bondage. Such terms as snare, prison, leash, trap, chain, bond, net, weir, bridle, rein, cage, and the ideas of captivity and thralldom run through the poem, and in correlation with the vegetation and animal imagery, the themes of Fortune, heaven, hell, religion, and death, the allusions to mythological figures, the narrative technique, the locale in space and time, the progress of events—in short, in correlation with all the elements of the poem that give it fullness, substance, and weight, this theme of bondage opens up for us the large and various landscape of Chaucer's meaning.

First we should consider briefly what kind of thinking about bondage was familiar to Chaucer. Fortunately we need not go far from *Troilus*; ample mate-

---

[3] Howard's excellent article—"Experience," 173–92—reinforces this position. Sister Mary Charlotte Borthwick, F.C.S.P., shows how the song Antigone sings systematically refutes Criseyde's timorous notions, "Antigone's Song as 'Mirour' in Chaucer's *Troilus and Criseyde*," *MLQ* 22 (1961): 227–35.

[4] Sonnet 88, *Rime* 132 or 133. See Patricia Thomson, "The 'Canticus Troili': Chaucer and Petrarch," *CL* 11 (1959): 313–28, and the references cited there.

[5] Payne, *Key*, Chapter 6, notices that eight of the ten lyric insets, the apostrophes which enrich and envalue the poem, are given to Troilus.

rial exists within Chaucer's work. Several *exempla* of snaring and imprisonment figure in his writings: Boethius; Mars ensnared by the love of Venus and then the net of Vulcan;[6] St. Paul;[7] and Satan.[8] These four figures may represent for us the four kinds of bondage towards which Chaucer's thought runs: imprisonment by Fortune (the world, nature, astral influence), by love, by evil (the devil, hell, sin, the flesh), or by Christ (God, the providential scheme of things).

The first kind of bondage, then, is the snare of things of this world, the things under the governance of created nature, of Fortune, and of the stars.[9] Boethius is informed of the binding power of nature, that things seek their proper course—it is a simple extension of the Aristotelian *locus proprius*. Lady Philosophy uses the imagery of binding, and one of her examples is the natural preference by birds of the hard woods over the easy cage (3 m. 2). Chaucer twice uses the same example, comically, as instances of a man's desire to leave his betrothed for a new lover, "Flessh is so newefangel."[10] As is his wont, Chaucer seems to take the bondage of our nature sometimes very seriously, sometimes not so seriously. The idea of the governing power of the stars occurs persistently in Chaucer. The astral influence of particular interest for us is Saturn's responsibility for real, not metaphorical, imprisonment. The planet-god tells us in the *Knight's Tale*, "Myn is the prison in the derke cote" (2457).[11] Troilus worries that he may have had "Aspectes badde of Mars or of Saturne."[12] The *Knight's Tale*, like *Troilus* based on Boccaccio, is in many respects a companion-piece to the *Troilus*. Each tale erects a superstructure of Boethian philosophy on Boccaccio's plot, and in the *Knight's Tale* the theme of bondage emerges as both metaphor and event. Palamon and Arcite were real prisoners, and they were also aware of their metaphorical bondage in the reign of Fortune.[13]

Chaucer's characters often designate the chances or apparent necessities of their situations by the general term Fortune, and refer to Fortune's power as

---

[6] KnT 2389.

[7] ParsT 344; Rom 6774–76.

[8] Apoc. 20:1–3; MLT 360–61; MLT 634–35; Buk. The categories of the theme of bondage that I have discerned in Chaucer nearly (and independently) coincide with those of Pierre Courcelle, used in his study of the body-prison theme from Plato to the twelfth century, "Tradition platonicienne et traditions chrétiennes du corps-prison (Phedon 62b; Cratyle 400c)," *RELat* 43 (1966 for 1965): 406–43.

[9] See Howard R. Patch, *The Goddess Fortuna in Mediaeval Literature* (Cambridge: Harvard Univ. Press, 1927), 82–83.

[10] MancT 163–74; 187–95; SqT 606–20.

[11] See also KnT 1328–29; LGW 2597–98.

[12] 3.716. The rain was caused by a conjunction of Jupiter, Saturn, and the moon in Cancer: 3.624–25.

[13] See Kiichiro Nakatani, "A Perpetual Prison—The Design of Chaucer's *The Knight's Tale*," *HSELL* 9 (1963): 75–89 (available from the MLA bibliography center at Pennsylvania State Univ.); KnT 1084–89; 1488–90; 1815–18; 3094–95; and esp. 2987–93, 3059–61, and Arcite's definitions, 1224–37.

a snare, a chain, a cage: the imagery is Boethian.[14] I believe it would be safe to generalize upon these cases: that when Chaucer's characters, including "Boece," the type of the prisoner of Fortune, complain of nature or the stars or Fortune as the determinant of their plight, they are wrong, and simply do not have a large enough vision to get at the real causes. In its comic aspect, these ignorant misjudgments of causes amount to more or less feeble attempts to rationalize a bad situation, and to free the speaker from personal guilt. In its more serious aspect, the failure to perceive causes beyond the natural scheme and Fortune is that ignorance of providence which is pagan and can be damning. Chaucer the poet, god-like, can dispose events in his poems so as to reveal to us the ignorance and the real motives of the people in his fictions. Sometimes, and Theseus in the *Knight's Tale* is the great example, the true vision of things is given to a character *in* the story; more often we are left to judge for ourselves.

The second type of bondage, the bondage of love, is represented in Chaucer in various forms: as the travail and woe of sexual attraction, as marriage, and as the harmonious linkages of the universe. These three kinds of love can be seen as reflections of one another, with the sacrament marriage mediating between sexual desire and divine order. I take the figure of Mars, whom Chaucer says Venus "brydeleth in her manere," as the type of the bondage of love.

In Proverbs, Wisdom is contrasted with a harlot who entangles a man.

> Immediately he followeth her as an ox led to be a victim, and as a lamb playing the wanton, and not knowing that he is drawn like a fool to bonds. Till the arrow pierce his liver: as if a bird should make haste to the snare, and knoweth not that his life is in danger.[15]

This is gloomier than the tone Chaucer strikes, but our poet does frequently image forth the bond of love between humans as bridle, snare, chain, or prison.[16] These metaphors are so prevalent in medieval love poetry that one could not speak of a source, but Chaucer surely found ample precedent for this bittersweet language of love's bondage in the *Romance of the Rose*, in which the theme of love's imprisonment has both metaphorical and literal presentation: the God of Love locks the lover's heart, and Jealousy imprisons Fair Welcome in a donjon.[17] The moral burden of the verses from Proverbs seldom applies

---

[14] KnT 1490; FranT 1356; Bo 5 pr. 2; 2 pr. 8.

[15] Prov. 7:22-3, Douai trans.

[16] See, e.g., Anel 183-84; 233; 284; KnT 1815-18; Thop 784-86.

[17] Rom 2087-95, 2028-29; 2767; 3177-78; 3533; 3648; 5126-27; 3918-19; 3944-46; 7527; 1620-24; 1642-48; 1469-71. For some idea of the prominence of the theme of the bondage of love, see James Wimsatt, *Chaucer and the French Love Poets* (Chapel Hill: Univ. of North Carolina Press, 1968), 34-35, and esp. the poems by Baudouin de Condé, "Li Prisons d'amours," *Dits et contes de Baudouin de Condé et de son fils Jean de Condé*, ed. Auguste Scheler (Brussels: Victor Devaux, 1866), 1:267-377 and Froissart, "La Prison Amoreuse," (*Œuvres* 1:304-6).

to Chaucer's use of the figure. My favorite example of his light touch on this theme is from a poem doubtfully ascribed to Chaucer, "Merciles Beaute": "Sin I fro Love escaped am so fat, / I never thenk to ben in his prison lene" (37–38). The nearest Chaucer comes to condemning the bondage of desire is quiet admonitions, foreshadowings of danger in places like the Legend of Cleopatra in *The Legend of Good Women,* in which Antony is "so narwe bounden" in the snare of love "that al the world he sette at no value" (599–602).

If Chaucer is usually light-hearted with regard to the leash of sexual attraction, he is overtly and notoriously funny on the subject of the bond of matrimony. Of marriage he insists in "Lenvoy de Chaucer a Bukton" that "I wol nat seyn how that yt is the cheyne / Of Sathanas, on which he gnaweth evere," and that one would rather be captured in Friesland (disgusting Friesland!) "than eft to falle of weddynge in the trappe" (9–10, 24). Bukton is about to marry, and Chaucer urges him to take counsel from the Wife of Bath in the matter. Her husband of course will be both "dettour" and "thral"; St. Paul had written, in the *second half* of the verse I Corinthians 7:4, that the wife has the power over the husband's own body.[18] Both Miller and Merchant call marriage a snare; the Miller endures it, but the Merchant vows, "Were I unbounden, ... / I wolde nevere eft comen in the snare."[19] On the contrary, the Knight at the end of his *Tale* refers seriously to "the bond / That highte matrimoigne or mariage" (3094–95).

The *Knight's Tale* concludes on a Boethian note, in the powerful speech of Theseus. He begins:

> "The Firste Moevere of the cause above,
> Whan he first made the faire cheyne of love,
> Greet was th'effect, and heigh was his entente.
> Wel wiste he why, and what thereof he mente,
> For with that faire cheyne of love he bond
> The fyr, the eyr, the water, and the lond
> In certeyn boundes, that they may nat flee."[20]

This is nearly the Empedoclean love, the Platonic idea of the relation of the things of this world to the One. For Boethius, and for Theseus, the idea of the cosmic bond of love is primarily of value to humans as consolation for the perceived mutability of creatures. Theseus needs to argue "that thilke Moevere stable is and eterne" (3004). We shall see that the idea fails as consolation for Troilus.

We have glanced at the bondage of Fortune and nature, and at the bondage of love. I shall be briefer with the bondage of sin, the flesh, and the devil. Again, the metaphor is commonplace: Chaucer might have picked it up from

---

[18] Pro WBT 154–61. She glides over the first half of the verse.
[19] MilT 3231–32; Pro MerT 1226–27; cf. MilT 3224; MerT 1285; CIT 143–47.
[20] KnT 2987–93. Boethius uses imagery of cosmic order as the bond of love esp. in 2 m. 8; 3 m. 9, 4 pr. 6, m. 6.

the Epistles or from Boethius.[21] The Second Nun, addressing Mary, speaks of her soul as in prison (71–74), and the Parson paraphrases St. Paul on the "prisoun of my caytyf body."[22] The devil will ensnare a man, say both the Friar (1659–60) and the Second Nun:

> For he [the feend] that with his thousand cordes slye
> Continuelly us waiteth to biclappe,
> Whan he may man in ydelnesse espye,
> He kan so lightly cache hym in his trappe,
> Til that a man be hent right by the lappe,
> He nys nat war the feend hath hym in honde.   8–13

Finally, the Parson calls hell a prison (311). From the bondage of our sin, from the devil, from hell, Christ is the deliverer. Chaucer presents this good news through the characters of Saint Cecilia, Custance, and the Parson.[23] It is clear that Chaucer sets the ideas of bondage to and delivery from sin mainly in the mouths of his pious characters. The one exception I have noted is the Friar's reference to the bondage of the fiend, but his tale has been *about* the fiend, and in any case we expect piety at the end of a tale.

Equally pious are the few references in Chaucer to Satan's own bondage and Christ's role as gaoler. This last of our four categories is supported only by two references in the *Man of Law's Tale*, and the one joking reference to Satan's chain which I have already quoted from "Lenvoy a Bukton."[24] However, we should include here the image of the cosmic bond, when it is perceived as the rein of providence instead of Fortune. One God holds the bonds of Nature.

My hope is that this excursus on Chaucer's theme of bondage has provided a context sufficiently broad in scope and various in texture to account for the versions of the theme we find in the *Troilus*. I said earlier that Troilus collaborates with the poet in exploring the meaning of his action. For the remainder of this paper I wish to examine Troilus's ideas on the subject of bondage in the context of the other characters' and the narrator's statements about it.

Troilus first touches on the subject in his first speech, in which he twits his companions for their folly in loving. I shall dwell on this passage at some length, because I think that it is especially instructive. Among other inconveniences of love, Troilus tells his friends, "And whan youre prey is lost, woo and penaunces" (1.201). This metaphor, based on the commonplace topic of the

---

[21] See, e.g., 2 Pet. 2:19; Rom. 7:24; 1 Tim. 3:7; 2 Tim. 2:26; Bo 1 m. 4, 18–22; 2 pr. 6, 105–9; 2 pr. 7, 152–57; 3 m. 10, 1–4; 3 m. 12, 2–3; 4 m. 2; 5 pr. 2, 27–43. See also *Aen.* 6:730–4; Eccl. 9:12 (quoted at the head of this paper). See the article by Courcelle, note 8 above, and the many references collected by Albert S. Cook, ed., *The Dream of the Rood: An Old English Poem Attributed to Cynewulf* (Oxford: Clarendon, 1905), 38–39, and Robert W. Frank, Jr., *PIERS PLOWMAN and the Scheme of Salvation* (New Haven: Yale Univ. Press, 1957), 82–83.

[22] ParsT 344; see also ParsT 144–50, Rom. 7:23–4.

[23] SNT 345–47; MLT 570–71; ParsT 277, 1072.

[24] MLT 360–61; 634–35; Apoc. 20:2–3. The Biblical basis for the idea of Christ as redeemer from a snare or prison may be found in Ps. 90:3; 123:7; and Isa. 61:1.

hunt of love, is the seventh in a significant series of metaphors, similes, and personifications found after the prologue to the poem. The similes compare Criseyde to a "thing inmortal" and the first letter "A" in beauty; the personifications are of Fortune and Veer; the other metaphors compare Criseyde to a bright star under a cloud, and compare looking at women to feeding ("baiten"). Seven occurrences of these figures in 150–odd lines is not frequent, but the pace of action and the rapid shifting of narrative perspective in these opening lines more than compensate for rhetorical sparseness. The density of foreshadowing event and commentary at the beginning of the poem is echoed by the even more compact, almost confusing sequence of culminating actions and narrative reflections on the poem at the end.

With Troilus's words the narrative pace swiftly grinds to a halt, as our narrator enters upon sixty lines of comment, most of which elaborates images drawn from Troilus's own speech. The gist of the comment is that a man is likely to fall in love, but the high rhetorical framework makes it seem as if great tragedy were taking place—it is the technique of the *Nun's Priest's Tale*. Troilus is shot by the spiteful God of Love, and plucked like a peacock. He has been proud, but now he is "kaught." He has climbed the stair, now he must descend. He is like Bayard, thinking to prance free, but realizing he must endure "horses lawe." Troilus has waxed "sodeynly moost subgit unto love," is thrall to love which binds all things, "For may no man fordon the lawe of kynde." The narrator then turns to his audience and tells us, "Refuseth nat to Love for to ben bonde, / Syn, as hymselven liste, he may yow bynde."

Here the idea of the bondage of love is fully presented, with ornate apostrophe, and reference to the mythology of the divinity of love, natural law, the changes of fortune and the fall of pride. The extended simile comparing Troilus to the horse Bayard teaches us how to read this little *planctus*. The primary tenor of the simile proposes that both Bayard and Troilus are subject to the "lawe of kynde," but the secondary tenor links Bayard's foolish pride to Troilus's. The expression of Bayard's pride carries the burden of the simile. He wishes to skip out of his path "so pryketh hym his corn," until the whip corrects him, and he is "first in the trays, ful fat and newe shorn." The horse is goaded from within, by his "corn," and from without by the lash; yet he seems to take pleasure in himself. It is from the horse's point of view that we learn that he is fat and newly shorn—in fact the image is presented as *cogitatio recta*, as Bayard's own thought. These are, I think it will be agreed, oddly unheroic values to be attached, however indirectly, to a "worthy kynges sone" at the outset of the poem. We infer that Troilus himself is "kaught" between interior drives and exterior attractions, and further that he is as innocent of these forces as Bayard. The attitude we are left with is of tired and essentially comic human wisdom, fully sensible of the limited range of possibility for the will.

A glance at Chaucer's source reinforces this view. Chaucer added the Bayard simile entire, and perhaps more interesting he changed the metaphor of Troilus which initiated this whole sequence. Boccaccio has his more experienced Troiolo refer three times to fetters and ensnarement in his first speech;

in each case the reference is to a *man's* being "kaught." Chaucer reverses this, and has Troilus speak of woman as man's prey. Chaucer's method here resembles his treatment of many of his sources in other works—for instance the *Clerk's Tale* and the *Man of Law's Tale*—in that the changes tend to intensify the emotions and disparities present in the source. Troilus uses the bondage metaphor more aggressively than Troiolo, and yet since Troilus is clearly less experienced in the ways of love than his Italianate counterpart, the transition from pride to fall is sharper.

This first image of bondage typifies Chaucer's management of the theme throughout the poem. The protagonist himself introduces the theme, unaware of its reversed application to himself. The narrator, in comic horror, elaborately apostrophizes the protagonist's blindness, and inappropriately universalizes his response: "O blynde world, O blynde entencioun!" (1.211). The reader is left with a vague sense of the potential seriousness of the theme, and at the same time with an acute sense of the all-too-human, gentle, comic quality of the bondage of love. Love, like flesh, is with us; it is the donnée of the poem. Chaucer twists more comedy from the situation in another divergence from Boccaccio, by depicting his Troilus's love as little fleshly as seems possible.[25] This alteration is partly responsible for the enormous critical red herring of "courtly love" which has been dragged across the poem.

Troilus himself seems most conscious of his limitations. Chaucer often expresses Troilus's sense of his own bondage by the vehicle of the animal imagery which patters through the poem.[26] During his first sorrow, Troilus says of himself, "O fool, now artow in the snare. . . . Now artow hent, now gnaw thin owen cheyne!" (1.507–9) and "I pleyne, ikaught, ye, nevere wight so faste'!" (1.534). In Book 3 Troilus apostrophizes Criseyde's eyes as he is about to embrace her, calling them "humble nettes," and wondering "How koude ye withouten bond me bynde?" (3.1355, 1358). During his poignant tour about Troy in the fifth book, when Troilus recalls the landmarks of his love, he speaks of the temple where "Me kaughte first my righte lady dere" (5.567). In one important instance in which Troilus assumes the role of hunter instead of prey, when he embraces Criseyde and tells her, "Now be ye kaught," she deflates his prowess: "Ne hadde I er now, my swete herte deere, / Ben yold, ywis, I were now nought heere!" (3.1210–11). In one place Boccaccio likened Troiolo to a falcon; Chaucer alters the simile, and compares Criseyde to the falcon (3.1782–85). Troilus really feels free only once, during his double sorrow, when he first hears good news from Pandarus, and exults: "For I am hool, al brosten ben my bondes" (2.976). From the long view, this seems sadly wrong.

Troilus's deprecating descriptions of himself are heightened in effect by the

---

[25] See the brilliant article by C. S. Lewis, "What Chaucer Really Did to *Il Filostrato*."

[26] See Meech, *Design*, "The Brute Creation," 320–32. [In the original printing of this essay a list of passages in T&C containing animal imagery was given here. It is pointless and I have deleted it.]

other characters' contrasting use of the snare metaphors. In Book 2 Criseyde asserts that Troilus will never boast of her, and in her legalistically flavored language says, "he shal me nevere bynde in swich a clause" (2.728), and that she stands "unteyd in lusty leese" (2.752). She talks of catching her father "withouten net" in Book 4 (1371), and claims for herself, in Boethian terms as we have seen, a natural right to freedom: "For who may holde a thing that wol awey?" (4.1628). Not until she recovers a part of her vision in the last book does she speak in other than these aggressive terms. At last she says,

> "On tyme ypassed wel remembred me,
> And present tyme ek koud ich wel ise,
> But future tyme, er I was in the snare,
> Koude I nat sen; that causeth now my care."[27]

Pandarus is more overt in his use of these hunting metaphors, and more cynical. At one point he tells Troilus to hold to his "triste" and he will "the deer unto thi bowe dryve" (2.1534–35); on the other hand, he tells Criseyde she has "fisshed fayre" if she kills both Troilus and himself with disdain, and later that she has done well to catch Troilus "withouten net" (2.328; 583). About his own affairs Pandarus is less confident. He has no cause, he says, to soar like a hawk, and he compares himself to Phoebus "bounden in a snare" by love (1.670–71; 663). The most aggressively venereal language is, as we should expect, connected with Diomede. When he receives Criseyde, he "by the reyne hire hente" and "ledde hire by the bridel."[28] Later he considers "How he may best ... Into his net Criseydes herte brynge.... To fisshen hire, he leyde out hook and lyne" (5.774–77).

These images of the bondage of love serve the double function of expressing the moods of trammeled limitation or aggressive confidence of the characters, and of commenting on the nature of the force, the motive love, which is driving the action. From the most cynical point of view the love is bestial, Bayardian. The hunting and snaring metaphors throughout the poem affect our view just as did the single elaborate simile of Bayard, by requiring us to look at Troilus's love from within a framework—animal imagery—which has built into it negative and deprecating opinion. This is however not the whole story, but only the Mars-Venus part of it, the humiliating, dehumanizing aspect of love's bondage. Even so the humiliation exists, and Troilus can express it best because he not only feels it but can see it; Pandarus jokingly and Diomede harshly only make clearer and purer a quality of love which Troilus's analytical imagination has distinguished at the outset.

The paired alternative to the bondage of animal, sexual love is the bondage of cosmic love, invoked in the Proem to Book 3 in the person of Venus—as goddess, planet, and natural principle—who "a lawe han set in universe."[29]

---

[27] 5.746–49. Cf. Criseida's different view in the *Filostrato*, where she speaks of the bondage of love, which holds things "serrata forte e stretta con gli artigli" (3.48).

[28] 5.90; 92. See 5.873, and Robertson, *Preface*, 497.

[29] 3.36. Boccaccio paraphrased part of Boethius in a hymn to love which he gave to

Troilus calls love the "holy bond of thynges" (3.1261) in a brief prayer while he
is in bed with Criseyde, but the locus classicus of this bondage is his hymn at
the end of Book 3, based on a poem in Boethius's *Consolatio*. The hymn praises
love as the binding force of nature, which "halt peples joyned," which "knet-
teth lawe of compaignie," which makes discordant elements "holden a bond,"
that "constreyneth" the sea, that keeps a bridle on "al that now loveth." In
conclusion, Troilus prays God (3.1766-68)

> "That with his bond Love of his vertu liste
> To cerclen hertes alle, and faste bynde,
> That from his bond no wight the wey out wiste";

that He make cold hearts love, pity sore hearts, and keep those who are true.

Troilus is obviously in a manic state here. The narrator has described him as
leading his life "in suffisaunce, in blisse, and in singynges," keeping around
him "a world of folk ... The fresshest and the beste he koude fynde" (3.1716,
1721). No other woman can unbind even one knot of Criseyde's net around his
heart, "he was so narwe ymasked and yknet" (3.1734). Bound by love of
Criseyde, Troilus sings of cosmic love. He goes into a garden with Pandarus to
sing his hymn. The setting is very different from that of his first hymn, "If no
love is," which Troilus sang on his bed; but the setting does resemble that of
the complaint which Pandarus tells Criseyde he overheard, "In-with the paleis
gardyn, by a welle" (2.508): we suspect this garden setting is an adroit fiction
of Pandarus's, who conceals Troilus's real moony condition. Troilus's confident
assertions about the regulation of the universe, and the providential power of
God, are very much tempered by the mood of the moment. The hymn is
colored by its context, the gay festiveness of Troilus described before it, and,
with sharp irony, the reference to "the townes werre," the exemplum par
excellence of strife over against love, which follows the hymn. At this point,
Troilus's reason and his will seem to be working in harmony, and he can speak
cheerfully of his desire for his heart to be encircled and bound fast. The
succession of events which looked before like miserable Fortune is now seen as
happy, virtually sacred design. The reader knows that this Boethian melody will
change.

When Troilus experiences his second and final woe, the loss of Criseyde, he
turns to the darker aspects of the theme of bondage, the bondage of flesh and
the bondage of Fortune seen as fate. The constant analogy to being trapped in
flesh is death, a death for which Troilus wishes during both his woes.[30] When
Troilus is first smitten, the narrator tells us "sodeynly hym thoughte he felte
dyen, / Right with hire look, the spirit in his herte" (1.306-7). A part of him
is already dead, as he acknowledges in the song from Petrarch, "O quike deth

---

Troiolo. Chaucer made this hymn the proem to Book 3, and gave Troilus another hymn, this
time based directly on the same passage in Boethius (2 m. 8; Tr 3.1744-71).

[30] See, for interesting examples from many more instances of Troilus's death wish, 1.572;
4.163; 250; 501-18; 1081; 5.41, 205.

..." (1.411). Pandarus as usual takes Troilus's deeply felt, self-analytical, and rhetorically expressed perceptions and uses them as arguments with Criseyde; he tells her, "I se him deyen, ther he goth upryght" (2.333) and urges her to be gracious and spare him. The narrator couches Troilus's relief from his desire for death, at the consummation of his love, in terms of rescue, almost of resurrection:

> And right as he that seth his deth yshapen,
> And dyen mot, in ought that he may gesse,
> And sodeynly rescous doth him escapen,
> And from his deth is brought in sykernesse,
> For al this world, in swych present gladnesse
> Was Troilus, and hath his lady swete.
> With worse hap God lat us nevere mete!   3.1240–46

Troilus's desire for death reaches furthest when he expresses the tormenting separation of flesh and spirit which he had felt, in different modes, from the beginning. A complaint in Book 4 summarizes this: Troilus laments that Fortune has not taken Priam, or one of his brothers, or even himself, "I, combre-world, that may of nothyng serve, / But evere dye and nevere fulli sterve." He senses that he is blind, and will end his life "as Edippe, in derknesse." He begs his "wery goost, that errest to and fro" to flee from his body, and his soul to flee from his heart. Finally, addressing Criseyde, he says that when his heart and body die, his spirit will rush to her (4.274–322). For Troilus, death will not only end his woe, but disencumber his spirit, now bound to his "wofulleste / Body," to fly to Criseyde.[31]

Another topic of Troilus's constant surveillance of the last things, the language of heaven and hell, is less directly connected to the theme of bondage, but we need to glance at it in order to get at another view. Things in the poem *are* heaven and hell, not just comparable entities: the narrator says it *is* heaven to see Troilus, to hear Antigone's voice, to consummate love, to hear Troilus's praises of Criseyde;[32] and Troilus corroborates these metaphors, on the hellish side, telling Criseyde her absence is hell.[33] After the consummation of his love, he tells Pandarus that "Thow hast in hevene ybrought my soule at reste / Fro Flegetoun, the fery flood of helle" (3.1599–1600). Such a state is especially desirable for Troilus, who constantly laments the flux and unfixity and steerlessness of his emotional state, the "fery flood," and who longs for a pole star, a rudder, a fixed point or a stable ground, a love of steel which he believes he has found in Criseyde.[34] Hence when he loses her to the Greeks,

---

[31] See also 4.470–76. Criseyde thinks, it seems, of death as "bittre bondes": 3.1116.

[32] 2.637, 826; 3.1204; 1251; 1322; 1742. See Meech, *Design*, 266–268, on heaven and hell.

[33] 5.1376, 1396. The names of Ticius, Cerberus, Amphiorax, the Furies, Pluto, Tantalus, Flegetoun, Athamante, Styx, Ixion, and Alceste color the poem: 1.786; 859; 2.105; 436; 3.592; 593; 1600; 4.1539; 1540; 5.212; 1532.

[34] On marriage as stability see Sister Anne Barbara Gill, *Paradoxical Patterns in Chaucer's*

the description of him is especially poignant: "To bedde he goth, and walweth ther and torneth / In furie, as doth he Ixion in helle."[35]

Bondage to a wheel, Ixion's damnation, may be taken as one image for Troilus's whole progress.[36] He undergoes two complete revolutions before his death: he "is clomben on the stair" in his pride, at the beginning, and he descends in the pain of love; he mounts again in Book 3, to fall once more. Especially under Pandarus's tutelage he perceives these revolutions as the doing of Fortune, and can even complain in Book 4 with the experienced tone of the narrator at the end, "O ye loveris, that heigh upon the whiel / Ben set of Fortune ... God leve that ye fynde ay love of stiel."[37] Early in the poem Troilus had complained how Fortune "pleyeth with free and bonde" (1.840). This sense of his bondage to Fortune Troilus augments by what must have been in Chaucer's mind his most wrongheaded opinion, setting character at greatest remove from author: Troilus argues in the notorious "tough" speech in Book 4 that "al that comth, comth by necessitee" (4.958–1078). Troilus is trapped by love, constrained in his body, bound to the wheel of Fortune, and enmeshed in the cloth of destiny.

Some events in the poem reinforce the theme of bondage, affecting us in roughly the way an acted image can on the stage. Troilus constantly finds himself in confined spaces: his bed within his chamber, the temple in which he meditates, the closet from which he issues to meet Criseyde, the walls of Troy itself. The sickbed chamber at Deiphebus's house is described as cramped (2.1646). When he learns of Criseyde's exchange for Antenor, Troilus goes immediately to his bed. The narrator, conflating bondage and vegetation imagery, speaks of him as "Ibounden in the blake bark of care," and Troilus proceeds to enclose himself:

> He rist hym up, and every dore he shette
> And wyndow ek, and tho this sorwful man
> Upon his beddes syde adown hym sette,
> Ful lik a ded ymage, pale and wan....[38]

TROILUS: An Explanation of the Palinode (Washington: Catholic Univ. of America, 1960), 72, and CIT 663.

[35] 5.211–12. Pandarus makes two joking comparisons of Troilus's bed to a sepulchral place: 2.1310–11; 1638. Patch, *The Goddess Fortuna*, 167, shows that Ixion's and Fortune's wheels were associated. In Baudouin's poem (n17 above) the prison of love contains a wheel of Fortune.

[36] The excellent article by Gerry Brenner is the fullest account to date of the various structuring devices in the *Troilus*: "Narrative Structure in Chaucer's *Troilus and Criseyde*," *AnM* 6 (1965): 5–18. See also Charles A. Owen, Jr., "The Significance of Chaucer's Revisions of *Troilus and Criseyde*," *MP* 55 (1957–58): 1–5, reprinted in Schoeck and Taylor, 2:160–66.

[37] 4.323–5. Charles Berryman, in "The Ironic Design of Fortune in *Troilus and Criseyde*," *ChauR* 2 (1967): 1–7, suggests that what Troilus sees as Fortune is an inevitable result of human nature: "Each character is bound to the movement of Fortune's wheel by the involuntary acting out of his own nature" (3).

[38] 4.232–35. In the *Filostrato*, Troiolo's friends had closed the windows.

He goes on to batter himself and the chamber walls, like a fatally wounded bull.[39] These stanzas manage to depict in external gestures Troilus's wish to be bound, that is to live in a world whose constancy matches his own, and at the same time to be free from his own desires, from his body, from Fortune's turning. He wallows in his bed like a man lost at sea.

In Book 5 Troilus lingers at the walls of Troy, looking out toward the Greek camp, hoping for Criseyde's return. Many critics have noticed that the fate of Troy and the fate of Troilus contain parallel movements.[40] The triumphant entries of Troilus through the gates of Dardanus into Troy and into Criseyde's heart are narrated as a single event; so his loss of Criseyde is experienced at the walls of the besieged town. Diomede assures Criseyde that "the folk of Troie, as who seyth, alle and some / In prisoun ben" (5.883–84), and the narrator tells us that, just as Troilus had been plucked like a peacock by the God of Love (1.210), so Fortune "gan pulle awey the fetheres brighte of Troie" (5.1546). The town's walls are a borderline between this world and that, the world of Pandarus and the bedroom, and the world of Diomede and the field of battle. The town is a citadel against chaos, as is the citadel of Cyprus in *Othello*; in both works we follow closely what goes on within, and respond with distant terror to the without, the Greeks or the Turks. Climactic actions take place on the ramparts or in the bedrooms, and the citadel is cloistered, feminine, or adolescent. In the *Troilus* what *happens* is often at a far remove from what is *said*: the best example is the action of Book 3, which is bedroom farce, and the language of the book, which is ... not. But when Troilus stares from the walls of Troy, action and language become one.

The last event of the poem is Troilus's death, as "His lighte goost ful blisfully is went" (5.1808). He looks down on "this litel spot of erthe" and laughs, as had Boccaccio's Arcite, Dante, Scipio, Lucan's Pompey, and Prudentius's St. Agnes before him.[41] The seldom noticed passage in *Boece* which corresponds to Troilus's final revelation uses bondage imagery:

> And yif the soule, which that hath in itself science of gode werkes, un-bownden fro the prysone of the erthe, weendeth frely to the hevene, despiseth it nat thanne al erthly ocupacioun; and [usynge] hevene rejoys-eth that it is exempt fro alle erthly thynges?   2 pr. 7, 152–57

---

[39] The simile (4.239–245) is borrowed from Boccaccio, derived from Virgil and Dante: *Fil.* 4:27; *Inf.* 12:22–24; *Aen.* 2:223–24.

[40] See, for example, Kittredge, *Chaucer and His Poetry*, 117, 120–21; Walter C. Curry, "Destiny in Chaucer's *Troilus*," *PMLA* 45 (1930): 135; Curry, *Chaucer and the Mediæval Sciences*, rev. ed. (New York: Barnes & Noble, 1960), 285–86; T. A. Stroud, "Boethius's Influence on Chaucer's *Troilus*," *MP* 49 (1951–52): 1–9, reprinted in Schoeck and Taylor, 2:133; and most fully John P. McCall, "The Trojan Scene in Chaucer's *Troilus*," *ELH* 29 (1962): 263–75. For an opposing view see Robert O. Mayo, "The Trojan Background of *Troilus and Criseyde*," *ELH* 9 (1942): 245–56.

[41] Boccaccio, *Teseida* 11:1–3; Dante, *Par.* 22:124–38; Cicero, *De Re Pub.* 6:16–20; Lucan, *Pharsalia* 9:1–14; Prudentius, *Peristephanon*, 14:91–99. See John W. Clark, "Dante and the Epilogue of the *Troilus*," *JEGP* 50 (1951): 1–10; and Morton W. Bloomfield, "The Eighth Sphere: A Note on Chaucer's *Troilus and Criseyde*, V. 1809," *MLR* 53 (1958): 408–10.

This finally is Troilus's freedom from bondage, from the *terreno carcere* and "al oure werk that foloweth so / The blynde lust." The wheeling, cycling, constrained movement of the poem finally opens out, and in the last paradox, which Dante had exploited before Chaucer, we see the protagonist eternally wheeling in the sphere of the fixed stars at the same time that he is at last fixed and oriented in "pleyn felicite." When man is out of time, as we learn from the *Paradiso*, the circular and the linear, and the free and the bound, become one.

I hold with E. Talbot Donaldson that Troilus's

> *trouthe*, his integrity, ... the quality that he will not surrender even to keep Criseyde with him, is the one human value the poem leaves entirely unquestioned: it is because of it that Troilus is granted his ultimate vision.[42]

The integrity which is comic naiveté at first becomes tragic delimitation at the end. The poem is comic because it is human, and tragic because it looks at the end of humanity. The title of this paper is meant to suggest my sense of Troilus as in some way Romantic and Promethean. Troilus is a natural man, and liable to love; he is likewise a man of purity of heart and of speculative intellect, and liable to frustration and sorrow. When we in these days wonder at the wisdom of holding to what we can see of the truth, come hell or high water, we might look to Troilus as a model of heroic steadfastness and tragic incapacity. He is bound to the truth and bound by the truth. To be true is to be vulnerable to death; Chaucer directs our attention at the end of the poem to the other man, bound to a cross, "that sothefaste Crist, that starf on rode," who rose and redeemed. This is the archetype of the bondage that frees. The last stanza tells us that God is "uncircumscript, and al maist circumscrive."

Afterword

Some twenty years after its first composition, I look on this essay with the doting affection of a father toward the child of his youth. Out of respect for the stability of history, and out of laziness, I have revised very little—only some stylistic matters I no longer stomach.

In a few places the essay makes the judgment that Chaucer is wise. I think he is, but I also think that only the wise can judge rightly of wisdom, and hence I think these opinions presumptuous.

In these decades feminist criticism has become prominent. This essay is not, I think, antifeminist (and surely Chaucer is the most feminist of medieval authors), and it claims to be about Troilus, not about her whom Alceste names as the sole title character, Criseyde (LGW F 441, G 431); still, I would phrase things differently if I wrote today. But I do not think the character of Troilus can be read as silly, feeble, corrupt, or even remarkably blind, given what

---

[42] Donaldson, *Chaucer's Poetry*, 1138.

Chaucer presents as his historical circumstances. If I did, the pain of the poem would vanish, and it would be worthless.

The conclusion of this essay strikes a homiletic tone that I now think unearned. It was written in New Haven during the riotous scenes accompanying the "Black Panther trials" in that city, when I was witness to brave and encouraging and just behavior, and to craven and frightening and vile behavior. The homily was addressed to myself. Its ground is religious, and I am now not minded so much to deny its purport as to regret that I couldn't then, and probably still can't, do it better. It appeals where it should demonstrate, and its heightened rhetoric is a telling sign of its sliding of courage. It would be worthwhile to examine the religious stance embedded in Chaucer's work—not Chaucer's "beliefs"; surely these are unknowable, surely he had no expressible theology—but that would be another, more difficult task.

The Opaque Text of Chaucer's Criseyde[*]

C. DAVID BENSON

Criseyde has always been recognized as one of Chaucer's greatest creations. Critics have shown how much more complex she is than her model in Boccaccio's FILO-STRATO, but few have discussed the deliberate opaqueness of her characterization. Chaucer repeatedly keeps us from access to Criseyde's inner self. Like the narrator, Hector, and Troilus in Book 1, each reader must construct a Criseyde from the limited, exterior information provided by the poem. Throughout TROILUS, Chaucer incites us to speculate about what his heroine is thinking and feeling while pre-venting us from certain knowledge. Her famous soliloquy in Book 2 provides little more than the illusion of interiority; we watch as she reviews her options but are never allowed to know what she herself wishes. A careful examination of the scene during which Troilus rides under Criseyde's window, including her famous state-ment, "Who yaf me drynke?" further demonstrates her elusiveness. Here and else-where each reader is provoked to interpret from a few public and partial clues the process by which Criseyde falls in love, while the private experience itself remains hidden. The opaqueness of Chaucer's Criseyde makes her an open text capable of generating multiple fictions; though this may seem particularly modern, it was probably inspired by Benoît de Sainte-Maure's twelfth-century ROMAN DE TROIE. Unlike many male writers then and now, Chaucer never claims to be omniscient about his heroine, and he is unique among medieval authors in not condemning her. His job is narrative, any judgments must come from us.

Although she plays only a secondary role in the first and last books of Chau-cer's *Troilus and Criseyde*, Criseyde has always been the poem's most fascinating character. Robert Henryson chose her as the protagonist for his powerful con-tinuation of Chaucer's story in the *Testament of Cresseid*, and David Daiches calls her "the first truly complex heroine in post-classical European literature."[1] English poets of the sixteenth-century understood her possibilities: although they often portray her as an inconstant whore, they also show her as an ideal sweetheart and pitiable victim.[2]

---

[*] Originally appeared in *Chaucer's TROILUS AND CRISEYDE* (London: Unwin Hyman, 1990), Chapters 5 and 6, in a different form.

[1] Daiches, *A Critical History of English Literature*, vol. 1 (London: Secker and Warburg, 1961), 100.

[2] Hyder E. Rollins, "The Troilus-Cressida Story from Chaucer to Shakespeare," *PMLA* 32

Modern critics have acknowledged the subtlety of the characterization of Criseyde, although most still emphasize only one or two of her many traits in order to produce a coherent interpretation. But the best analyses are those that insist on how much more various Chaucer's heroine is than her model in Boccaccio's *Filostrato*. Charles Muscatine demonstrates that she speaks one way with Troilus and another way with Pandarus, Richard A. Lanham refers to her "multiple self," and Robert W. Frank, Jr., notes that Chaucer has made her at once more sensitively emotional and calculatingly controlled.[3] Her most sympathetic interpreter in this century, E. Talbot Donaldson, calls her "a mystery," which each reader will solve differently. Donaldson is right, though I want to argue that she is more radically elusive than the "paradox" he defines.[4]

Criseyde is not so much a collection of discrete traits, however diverse, as an endlessly protean figure who must be created anew with each reading. The thoughts and actions of almost all literary characters can be interpreted in different ways, but with Criseyde we must first decide what it is that she, in fact, thinks and does. Although allusions to Criseyde's psychology occur repeatedly in the poem, the exact nature of her inner self is kept from the reader. Many male critics claim that they have fallen "in love" with Criseyde, but her real fascination is less erotic than literary. Her textuality dominates her sexuality. Criseyde may have no children, but she is an endlessly generative fiction.

Chaucer transforms the woman he found in Boccaccio's *Filostrato*. The Italian Criseida is much like Troiolo: they share the same worldly values, and the reader is fully informed about the urgent desires of both. Any difference between the two, such as Criseida's initial discretion, is the result of her social position (as a woman and non-royal) and not an innate quality. The English lovers, however, are given contrasting traits, and, of most importance, they are portrayed in radically different ways. Concerning Troilus's thoughts and emotions, Chaucer provides even more information than had Boccaccio, but he tells us much less about Criseyde's mental life. At crucial moments in the story, he is silent or reports only her public speech, forcing each reader to imagine what she is really thinking and feeling. It is precisely this deliberate and suggestive opaqueness that makes the English Criseyde so fascinating.

Book 1 of Chaucer's *Troilus and Criseyde* shows us how we must read its heroine by portraying her at a distance through the eyes of a series of male spectators, who create their own individual Criseydes. Her public appearance and actions are fully available to these observers, but her inner being, whose depth

---

(1917): 383–429; and C. David Benson, "True Troilus and False Cresseid: The Descent from Tragedy," *The European Tragedy of Troilus*, ed. Piero Boitani (Oxford: Clarendon Press, 1989), 153–70.

[3] Muscatine, *French Tradition*, 153ff.; Lanham, "Game, Play, and High Seriousness in Chaucer's Poetry," *ES* 48 (1967): 21–22; Frank, "*Troilus and Criseyde*: The Art of Amplification," in Mandel and Rosenberg, 163.

[4] The specific words come from Donaldson's "Chaucer in the Twentieth Century," *SAC* 2 (1980): 7–13; but see also his *Chaucer's Poetry*, 967–71, and the several articles on Criseyde in his *Speaking of Chaucer*.

is repeatedly insisted upon, remains largely hidden from view and thus subject to multiple interpretation. The very first mention of Criseyde in *Troilus* adds a few lines to *Filostrato* about her "drede" and indecision after Calchas's desertion (1.94–98; see also 108), but the stanza-length portrait that follows is entirely exterior (1.99–105). The Criseyde seen, or rather created, by the narrator is a transcendent, almost divine being: "lik a thing immortal" whose beauty is "aungelik."

In the following stanza we are shown a second Criseyde from the perspective of Hector to whom she goes for protection:

> In widewes habit large of samyt broun,
> On knees she fil biforn Ector adown;
> With pitous vois, and tendrely wepynge,
> His mercy bad, hirselven excusynge.   1.109–12

Criseyde's dress and actions (kneeling, weeping) are emblematic and observed from afar. In response to her appearance and in keeping with his character, Hector takes her to be the very model of the innocent, young widow: "[He] saugh that she was sorwfully bigon, / And that she was so fair a creature" (1.114–15).

Our next view of the heroine is through the eyes of Troilus ("His eye percede, and so depe it wente, / Til on Criseyde it smot" [1.272–73]); this third male observer perceives a third Criseyde: not an angel or widow but a desirable, courtly being.

> She nas nat with the leste of hire stature,
> But alle hire lymes so wel answerynge
> Weren to wommanhode, that creature
> Was nevere lasse mannysh in semynge.
> And ek the pure wise of hire mevynge
> Shewed wel that men myght in hire gesse
> Honour, estat, and wommanly noblesse.   1.281–87

The distant point-of-view is insisted upon with words like "semynge," "shewed," and "gesse." In contrast to a full account in the following stanza of what Troilus is feeling (1.288–94), Criseyde's emotions are largely inaccessible. She appears as a beautiful, distant object, whose true character can only be imaged by her admirers. Like them, each of us must construct our own Criseyde from the deliberately limited exterior information provided in the poem.

Criseyde's lack of identity and dependence on others for definition may be a result of her gender. In a pioneering article, David Aers argues that Criseyde is a victim of male oppression and that the inferior condition of women in Trojan society denies her any chance to become a genuine individual.[5] Such a feminist analysis, which continues to be developed in contemporary criticism,

---

[5] Aers, "Criseyde: Woman in Medieval Society," *ChauR* 13 (1979): 177–200; reprinted with some changes in his book *Chaucer*.

is persuasive.[6] Criseyde can easily be seen as a victim of her father, Pandarus, the Trojan parliament, and Diomede. She achieves some measure of security only during the love affair with Troilus, which happens during her father's absence. Once Calchas demands her back, however (his paternal rights in no way abrogated by his long neglect), Criseyde is again described as his daughter (4.92, 663), as she has not been since early in Book 1 (94), signalling both a renewed dependence ("And stood forth muwet, milde, and mansuete" [5.194]), and her coming victimization by the predatory Diomede.

The understandable indignation of feminist readings of Criseyde does not, however, deny her triumph as a literary character. Chaucer is sensitive to the social marginality of women, but he uses that historical condition to create a heroine of extraordinary fictional power. Her silence and lack of self-assertion, reflecting the traditional political position of women, open an artistic space for readers to create their own Criseydes. Leo Braudy notes something similar in film, whose characters, while more limited and distantly portrayed than those in the standard realistic novel, are not necessarily inferior: more easily than novelistic characters, "film characters can leave their plots and inhabit our dreams, so free because they are so elusive."[7]

In passages added to *Filostrato*, *Troilus and Criseyde* repeatedly incites us to wonder what its heroine is thinking and feeling while preventing us from certain knowledge. For instance, soon after Criseyde is first told that she is loved by Troilus, Pandarus looks to a future time:

"Whan ye ben his al hool, as he is youre:
Ther myghty God yet graunte us see that houre!"   2.587–88

Criseyde's spoken response is provocative—

"Nay, therof spak I nought, ha, ha!" quod she;
"As helpe me God, ye shenden every deel!"   2.589–90

—but we are told nothing about her private thoughts. At least one critic, however, is confident that Criseyde now fully understands that Pandarus's intent is to bring the proposed affair to a physical union.[8] This is a plausible interpretation, but by no means the only one. Criseyde's opaqueness incites speculation even as it prevents certainty.

Other crucial scenes also keep readers at a distance from Criseyde's deepest thoughts. When Pandarus brings his niece to speak with Troilus for the first time, he begs her to act boldly and secretly to cure her lover's pain (2.1730–50). Immediately before her uncle's words, we are told that Criseyde is "Al innocent of Pandarus entente" (2.1723), but we are told nothing of her

---

[6] See, for example, Diamond, "Politics," in Wasserman and Blanch, 93–103; and Carolyn Dinshaw, "Readers in/of *Troilus and Criseyde*," *YJC* 1 (1988): 81–105 (*included in this volume*).

[7] Leo Braudy, *The World in a Frame* (Garden City: Doubleday, 1976), 184.

[8] Murray F. Markland, "Pilgrims Errant: The Doubleness of *Troilus and Criseyde*," *RS* 33 (1965): 74.

response once that intent has been made clear. Later in the same scene, Pandarus puts the lovers on notice that he will soon summon them for a longer private meeting at his house. Troilus eagerly responds "How longe shal I dwelle, / Er this be don?" (3.201–2), but the text again tells us nothing about Criseyde's reaction to her uncle's promise.

The most famous instance in which the narrator explicitly bars us from Criseyde's mind occurs just after Pandarus finally does invite Criseyde to his house, though ostensibly only for dinner. When Criseyde asks whether Troilus will be there, Pandarus says that he will not be, but adds that she would have nothing to fear even if he were. The narrator then addresses us directly:

> Nought list myn auctour fully to declare
> What that she thoughte whan he seyde so,
> That Troilus was out of towne yfare,
> As if he seyde therof soth or no;
> But that, withowten await, with hym to go,
> She graunted hym, sith he hire that bisoughte,
> And, as his nece, obeyed as hire oughte.   3.575–81

Many have assumed that they know precisely what "she thoughte." William Dodd suggested that "on the whole, the poet subtly makes us feel that Pandarus's reassurances are sufficient to allay the heroine's suspicions, and that she went to his house in innocence," but his contemporary George Lyman Kittredge expressed what has become the majority view, "Pandarus lies, of course, but it is perfectly clear that she does not believe his protestations."[9] The lines themselves support neither opinion, or rather they support either—and several others as well. The only interpretation offered in the text itself is purely conventional (if slyly humorous) and exterior: Criseyde obeyed her uncle as a niece should. Yet even though the passage keeps us in ignorance, we cannot dismiss the problem of what Criseyde really thought because the lines provoke us to seek an answer. The "auctour" invoked at the beginning of the stanza is no help, for the scene is original with Chaucer. Once again it is each individual reader who is left "fully to declare" what lies behind Criseyde's public words and behavior.

My claim that the reader is frequently excluded from Criseyde's inner being is not the generally accepted view. Although a few critics have noted, without detailed analysis, our lack of access to Criseyde's mind, as in Robert O. Payne's important observation that "we are always moved outside her at critical moments," many excellent Chaucerians have argued that one of the poet's great achievements is allowing us to see clearly into the heroine's mind and heart.[10] For instance, Jill Mann writes that "we are introduced to the minute-by-minute workings of her mind, to a complex notion of her psychological pro-

Her mind (handwritten marginal note)

---

[9] Dodd, *Courtly Love in Chaucer and Gower* (Boston: Ginn, 1913), 170; Kittredge, *Chaucer and His Poetry* (Cambridge: Harvard Univ. Press, 1915), 132.

[10] Payne, *Key*, 201; see also Donaldson, *Chaucer's Poetry*, 969.

cesses. . . ."[11] In an influential essay on Criseyde's soliloquy alone in her closet after Pandarus tells her of Troilus's love, Donald Howard argues that "the reader is allowed to participate in Criseyde's mental life," and that "we are able to *feel* her feeling just as we are able to think her thoughts." He concludes that "for a space of some four hundred or more lines in Book 2, I have *been* Criseyde, have experienced the world as she experienced it, have had my mind and being subsumed in her."[12] Howard's view that we intimately share Criseyde's consciousness in this section has been often endorsed by others.[13] In contrast, I would maintain that Chaucer reports Criseyde's superficial calculations during this scene rather than the deepest recesses of her heart and mind. Her soliloquy provides little more than the *illusion* of interiority: we simply do not know what she truly feels and must ourselves decide her commitment to the various possibilities she reviews.

Criseyde's soliloquy on whether to accept Troilus's love (2.687–812) is certainly more intricate and believable than its source in *Filostrato*, but the topics she considers remain detached from her feelings. She weighs the social consequences of different actions, such as the advantages and disadvantages of being loved by a member of the Trojan royal family (2.703–14), without addressing her own personal desires. The simple opposition in the corresponding debate of Boccaccio's Criseida between the pleasures of hidden sensuality and the difficulties of keeping the affair alive and secret (2.68–78) becomes in Chaucer's reshaping a tangle of conflicting motives and forces open to a variety of interpretations by individual readers.[14]

Criseyde first declares that she ought not grant Troilus her love (2.703–04), and then goes on to consider the possible trouble if she angered the king's son (2.704–14), the need for moderation (2.715–21), the prince's virtues (2.722–28), the impossibility of stopping others from thinking what they will about a love affair (2.729–35), the honor (well-deserved she thinks) of having been chosen over all other women in Troy (2.736–49), and her freedom to do what she likes in love (2.750–63). Then, negative thoughts occurring to her (2.764–70), she considers the danger to her freedom that love poses (2.771–84), the treachery of lovers (2.785–98), and the malice of gossips (2.799–804). What Criseyde never says during this remarkable speech is whether she actually loves Troilus. Her arguments remain hypothetical. Although declaring that she has

---

[11] Mann, *Chaucer and Medieval Estates Satire: The Literature of Social Classes and the General Prologue to the Canterbury Tales* (Cambridge: Cambridge Univ. Press, 1973), 199. John Bayley, *The Characters of Love* (New York: Basic Books, 1960), 91, compares Chaucer's thorough exploration of Criseyde's consciousness with Henry James's method in the first part of the *Golden Bowl.*

[12] Howard, "Experience," in Mandel and Rosenberg, esp. 174, 178, 191.

[13] David Aers, *Chaucer* (Brighton: Harvester, 1986), 97; for a recent, and quite subtle, reading of Criseyde in the Howard mode, see Pearsall, "Choices," 17–29; for the opposite argument, which is nevertheless different from mine, see Robert apRoberts, "The Growth of Criseyde's Love," *Medieval Studies Conference Aachen 1983: Language and Literature*, ed. Wolf-Dietrich Bald and Horst Weinstock (Frankfurt: Lang, 1984), 131–41.

[14] Citations to Boccaccio's *Filostrato* are from the edition of Branca.

the right to love "in cas if that me leste" (2.758), we never learn if that is indeed what she does wish. For all our exposure to her calculations, Criseyde's deepest being eludes us.

At other stages in the wooing, the text is equally silent about Criseyde's feelings. Boccaccio's Criseida reads Troiolo's ardent first letter eagerly, vowing to find a time and place to "quench this fire" ("spegner questo foco," 2.114–15). In contrast, Chaucer's account is almost impudent in its refusal to tell us anything important about his heroine's response:

> Avysed word by word in every lyne,
> And fond no lakke, she thoughte he koude good;
> And up it putte, and wente hire in to dyne.   2.1177–79

We assume that Criseyde is here feeling many things in addition to approval of Troilus's epistolary style, but we are not told what these are.

The subtlety of the process by which Criseyde falls in love, and the way that Chaucer keeps much of the process hidden, while provoking our interpretation, are demonstrated by an episode original with the English poet just before Criseyde's soliloquy. After retiring to her closet, she sees the prince himself ride by under her window (2.610–86). In contrast to the full account of Troilus's feelings when he first sees Criseyde, Chaucer makes it more difficult than is usually recognized to understand what his heroine is thinking and feeling at this parallel moment of her experience. We know that she has been affected in some way, but must ourselves decide precisely how and why. The scene deserves to be examined carefully.

The first stanza of the episode deliberately moves from Criseyde ("But as she sat allone and thoughte thus, / Ascry aros at scarmuch al withoute" [2.610–11]) down into the street to report the voice of Trojan citizens as they notice Troilus's return from battle: "Se, Troilus / Hath right now put to flighte the Grekes route!" (2.612–13). The account remains objective in the next stanza (2.617–23). We hear the conclusion of the townspeople's speech, and then, in the narrator's voice, a factual description of Troilus and a general statement ("men seyn") about necessity. The third stanza (2.624–30), which describes Troilus's appearance more particularly, remains in the third person, though the previous objectivity gives way to a more personal response:

> But swich a knyghtly sighte, trewely,
> As was on hym, was nought, withouten faille,
> To loke on Mars, that god is of bataille.   2.628–30

Yet it remains unclear who is supposed to be looking at this "sighte." Presumably it is the townspeople, whose observation of the prince had been previously emphasized, or perhaps it is the narrator himself, though his observation could only be an act of the imagination.

The most serious difficulties with perspective begin in the following stanza (2.631–37). Admiration for Troilus becomes much warmer, and the suggestive phrase

> For bothe he hadde a body and a myght
> To don that thing, as wel as hardynesse   2.633–34

has been understood as Criseyde's admiration for Troilus's potential prowess
as a lover, apparently on the principle that whenever a word or phrase is
ambiguous in English ("to don that thing") it must be sexual. Certainly many
modern readers, perhaps most, assume that the next statement, which can also
be taken erotically, is Criseyde's:

> So fressh, so yong, so weldy semed he,
> It was an heven upon hym for to see.   2.636–37[15]

These lines *might* indeed describe what the heroine is thinking (their special
intensity is an argument in favor), but nothing identifies them as such. The text
signals no return to Criseyde, though some have assumed that the whole scene
is meant to been seen through her eyes.[16] The only voices that have been
clearly established within the scene, however, are those of the narrator and the
townspeople, either of whom might be thought to have such thoughts about
Troilus, especially if the words are not read sexually. In fact, both perspectives
are reaffirmed in the very next stanza (2.638–44), which provides an objective
description of what Troilus has suffered in battle ("His helm tohewen was in
twenty places" [2.638]) and then reports more speech from the people in the
street: "Here cometh oure joye, / And, next his brother, holder up of Troye!"
(2.643–44). The text hints that the sight of Troilus's wounded but physically
powerful body might have been one of the forces that impelled Criseyde to
accept his love, but we cannot be certain that this is what she feels. The scene
is deliberately constructed to leave the experience open.

Before Criseyde is mentioned again, attention switches briefly to Troilus, as
he blushes in response to the townspeople's praise (2.645–46), and then to an
unidentified viewer:

> That to byholde it was a noble game,
> How sobrelich he caste down his yën.   2.647–48

When the narration finally returns to Criseyde, we are shown her conscious-
ness, as usual, only opaquely:

> Criseÿda gan al his chere aspien,
> And leet it so softe in hire herte synke,
> That to hireself she seyde, "Who yaf me drynke?"   2.649–51

Something has happened to Criseyde, but what exactly? We are told that she
sees Troilus's blushing face and that she lets that sight, which is not further
analyzed, slip into a heart that remains hidden. We are left with her magnifi-

---

[15] E. Talbot Donaldson, "Cresseid False, Criseyde Untrue: An Ambiguity Revisted," *Poetic
Traditions of the English Renaissance*, ed. Maynard Mack and George de Forest Lord (New
Haven: Yale Univ. Press, 1982), 70–71.

[16] Karla Taylor, e.g., in *Chaucer Reads*, 123.

cently enigmatic question, "Who yaf me drynke?" Despite the drama of these words, they are only an exterior expression of Criseyde's response. Chaucer forces us to imagine exactly what drink she is referring to. Is it a powerful poison, strong liquor, or just a little white wine? Older editors glossed "drynke" as "love potion," but the recent (and wiser because less prescriptive) practice has been to take it as "any intoxicating beverage."[17] Although Criseyde's words will immediately suggest to most readers the irresistible love potions of medieval romance (which may be the way Criseyde wishes to explain the experience to herself), the context of *Troilus* makes us aware, as John Bayley notes,[18] that whatever the apparent similarities, Criseyde's experience is fundamentally *different* from that of lovers like Tristan and Isolde, even as their sudden, overwhelming passion is evoked. For Criseyde there is no fatal potion, no one irrevocable moment when love becomes an absolute, as there is for Troilus.

Criseyde blushes and withdraws her head from the window after seeing Troilus ride by, but she appears less moved by passion than by self-regard and pity. The narrator declares that although she ponders his "prowesse," "estat," "renown," "wit," "shap," and "gentilesse," she favors him most because "his distresse / Was al for hire" (2.659–64). The narrator then disputes those who would accuse Criseyde of having "so lightly loved Troilus" at "firste syghte"; on the contrary, he insists that she only "gan enclyne / To like hym first," after which Troilus's own good service began to undermine ("myne") her resistance, helped by the favorable influence of the planet Venus (2.666–86). Some modern critics read this statement as Chaucer's clever way of raising questions about Criseyde's motives while claiming to defend her, but Jill Mann persuasively resists such a cynical, reductive interpretation.[19]

The narrator's remarks accurately define how Criseyde falls in love. It is a long, contingent, mysterious process. Many different forces, in addition to the sight of Troilus and the stars, bring Criseyde to accept love, including Pandarus's incessant arguments and threats, her own deliberations, Antigone's lovely, idealistic song in praise of love (2.827–75), and the haunting dream of the eagle painlessly snatching her heart away (2.925–31). All make their contribution, but, despite the attempts of different critics to see one or another of these moments as decisive, Chaucer does not himself define the relative importance of each as Criseyde falls in love. Specific evidence that Criseyde has fallen in love appears only much later when she is in later in bed with Troilus and in response to his declaration that she is caught, she replies,

> "Ne hadde I er now, my swete herte deere,
> Ben yold, ywis, I were now nought heere!"   3.1210–11

Yet even here Criseyde remains opaque; we hear her intriguing spoken words

---

[17] *The Riverside Chaucer*, 1033.
[18] *The Characters of Love*, 93.
[19] Mann, "Troilus' Swoon," *ChauR* 14 (1980): 323.

but are kept from her inner thoughts. If she claims to have previously fallen in love with Troilus, we are not allowed to know when, as A.C. Spearing shrewdly notes,[20] nor are we told exactly why or how. Later still, as the lovers are about to part, Criseyde insists that she loved Troilus only because of his "moral vertu" (4.1667–73). We need not assume that Criseyde is deliberately lying to recognize this as one more public and partial explanation for a private experience beyond our knowledge.

Our distance from Criseyde's heart and mind is especially pronounced during her betrayal of Troilus in Book 5. Although Chaucer provides some of her public words and actions, he continually makes us guess what is occurring within. Soon after her arrival in the Greek camp, Criseyde states her resolve to return: "To Troie I wole, as for conclusioun" (5.765). The narrator then informs us that before two months were over she was very far from such an intention and had let both Troy and Troilus "knotteles thorughout hire herte slide" (5.766–70), but he never shows how and why that change occurred.[21] The closest he comes to an explanation is a single stanza describing her response after Diomede has both predicted the utter destruction of Troy and offered to serve her in love:

BKS

> Retornyng in hire soule ay up and down
> The wordes of this sodeyn Diomede,
> His grete estat, and perel of the town,
> And that she was allone and hadde nede
> Of frendes help; and thus bygan to brede
> The cause whi, the sothe for to telle,
> That she took fully purpos for to dwelle.   5.1023–29

The stanza is more of a list than an analysis, in which is it difficult to determine the relative significance of the various forces mentioned. For instance, is Criseyde's fear of the fall of Troy more or less important than the attractions of the forceful, high-born Diomede? Furthermore, this rare insight into the heroine's consciousness is severely limited. These thoughts are only an early stage in her change: they only "bygan to brede" the reason that she decided to dwell among the Greeks, and they say nothing directly about how she comes to love Diomede, if, in fact, she ever does.

The narrator earnestly tries to makes sense of and mitigate blame for Criseyde's actions in the Greek camp, but his bafflement only underlines the elusiveness of her character. Like a good semiologist, the narrator examines the signs provided by other accounts (her giving Diomede a sleeve as a pennon and weeping over his wounds), but he admits that he has no authoritative access to her truest feelings: "Men seyn—I not—that she yaf hym hire herte"

---

[20] Spearing, *Chaucer: Troilus and Criseyde* (London: Arnold, 1976), 19.

[21] For a somewhat different analysis of this scene and of the lack of psychological believability in Chaucer's character, see the important article by Arthur Mizener, "Character and Action in the Case of Criseyde," *PMLA* 54 (1939): 65–81.

(5.1050). Her heart remains hidden. Criseyde then disappears from the narrative except for her final letter to Troilus, which is so cold and in such bad faith that we realize that we no longer have any idea what Criseyde is doing in the Greek camp, let alone what she is really feeling and thinking (5.1590–1631). She has become totally opaque.

On one of the few occasions that we are allowed any access into Criseyde's mind during Book 5, she imagines her future as a text of falseness:

> "Allas! of me, unto the worldes ende,
> Shal neyther ben ywriten nor ysonge
> No good word, for thise bokes wol me shende.
> O, rolled shal I ben on many a tonge!"   5.1058–61

Criseyde fears that she will be made into a negative *exemplum*: everything said about her until the end of the world will be only bad ("no good word"). This is an accurate description of how her character appears in most other versions of the story, but not in *Troilus and Criseyde*. Chaucer's Criseyde is an open text. The same lack of consistent identity ("slydynge of corage" [5.825]) that Criseyde knows will bring her moral condemnation is used in *Troilus* to produce a brilliant literary success. Using the familiar terminology of Roland Barthes, we might see Chaucer's Criseyde as a supreme example of a *scriptible* rather than a *lisible* text. She does not represent a unified or even complex authorial statement of meaning, but instead challenges each reader to make her new.

My claim that Chaucer's Criseyde is an open text who is capable of generating multiple fictions may seem inappropriately modern, but there is some evidence for it in the work that first told of her love for Troilus: Benoît's twelfth-century *Roman de Troie*. In the long final speech of his heroine, Benoît has her utter a series of contradictory statements, which he makes no attempt to resolve: she says nothing good will ever be said about her, that she acted wrongly and stupidly in abandoning Troilus, that she was ruined by listening to Diomede's speeches, that she has brought disgrace upon womankind, that she had the best lover a woman ever had, that there is no reason to repent, that she should be true to the valiant and worthy Diomede, that she never would have deceived Troilus if she had remained in Troy, that she has conquered her lonely state in the enemy camp and achieved contentment, that one should never suffer because of what people might say, that she is now both happy and sad, that she wishes Troilus well, that she must grant Diomede all that he wishes to keep him in love with her, and finally that she hopes to achieve joy and happiness (ed. Constans 20237–340).

The speech in Benoît does not characterize a single person; instead it provides an anthology of different responses to what has happened (fearful, hopeful, repentant, triumphant, opportunistic, satisfied, deceived, conflicted, nostalgic, scheming, and proud), every one of which has the potential to be developed into the portrait of a different kind of women. In addition to supplementing Boccaccio with individual lines from this powerful speech, which is not reproduced in *Filostrato*, Chaucer seems to have been inspired by its variety to create his special Criseyde in *Troilus and Criseyde*. Although Benoît eventually draws the standard moral about female unfaithfulness, the words he gives to his heroine suggest an infinite number of narratives. Chaucer does not himself write these stories (what single author could?), but they remain latent within his text.

The traditional mystery and otherness of women, which is one of the results of their political marginalization in patriarchal societies, is used by Chaucer to construct a Criseyde who challenges every reader to rewrite her opaque text. Like most medieval literature, *Troilus* exists within a masculine aesthetic that can only gaze on women from afar, but it is Chaucer's particular achievement to exploit, rather than attempt to deny, this limitation. He never pretends that he knows what Criseyde is thinking or feeling. He is neither omniscient author nor omnipotent male. His is also the only medieval version of the love story that refuses to draw a lesson that condemns the heroine. Chaucer understands that it would be futile to legislate the final meaning of Criseyde: his function is to use his literary skills to involve individual readers with her in order that they may create their own Criseydes. His job is narrative, any judgments must come from us.

Techniques of Alienation in Troilus and Criseyde*

SHEILA DELANY

TROILUS is a subtly but fundamentally ideological text whose controversial epilogue is anticipated throughout by a number of narrative techniques which create esthetic distance. In our century such techniques have been articulated by Bertolt Brecht in his theory of alienation (A-effect), but they have been practiced in other genres than drama, and by other medieval authors than Chaucer. This esthetic frame accounts for many of the stylistic peculiarities of Chaucer's romance.

Four operations of A-effect displayed in TROILUS are: 1) The audience is not encouraged to identify with the central characters but rather to evaluate their actions and opinions. 2) The work of art attempts to defamiliarize the "normal" by offering a viewpoint different from the one usually adequate to the genre. 3) The artist exposes his/her own role and the artificiality of the medium or genre in which s/he works. 4) Crucial questions are asked and answers given directly, whether by artist, narrator or dramatis personae.

The reading suggests that "alterity" does not necessarily obviate the use of modern critical categories for medieval art and that subversive literary techniques (such as alienation) may serve either a historically progressive or a historically conservative ideological purpose.

The principle of alienation in art, or esthetic distancing, has been in our time most clearly articulated by the German communist poet and playwright Bertolt Brecht. Brecht wrote frequently about alienation (A-effect) in art, and one of his most succinct definitions of it comes from a brief essay on acting:

> The A-effect consists in turning the object of which one is to be made aware, to which one's attention is to be drawn, from something ordinary, familiar, immediately accessible, into something peculiar, striking, and unexpected. What is obvious is in a certain sense made incomprehensible, but this is only in order that it may then be made all the easier to comprehend. Before familiarity can turn into awareness the familiar must be stripped of its inconspicuousness; we must give up assuming that the object in question needs no explanation. However frequently recurrent,

*Originally appeared in *The Uses of Criticism*, ed. A. P. Foulkes, Literaturwissenschaftliche Texte, Theorie und Kritik 3 (Bern: Peter Lang, 1976): 77–95.

modest, vulgar it may be it will now be labelled as something unusual.[1]

Yet alienation in art was not invented by Brecht. It was rather a discovery or even a recovery, for deliberate esthetic distancing has been practiced in various arts of different historical periods. There is nothing specifically twentieth-century about it, though it will be in any given period a "modern" technique. It will be useful to any artist in any medium who wants his or her work to be actively evaluated rather than passively received according to formal convention.

Indeed the purpose of alienation technique can be said to be: to undercut the conventional forms on which an audience habitually relies as a cue to response. The danger in automatic or habitual response (and it is of course culturally conditioned) is that the audience may fail to understand two things about the work of art. First, the audience may neglect substantive intellectual issues—whether moral, religious or political issues—which the artist considers essential to the work. Second, the audience may ignore or minimize the degree of deliberate shaping that informs the work, its individual, made quality. Hence techniques of alienation call into question both the received forms and the responses that are usually adequate to them. By jolting the audience out of easy reliance on received forms, alienation reasserts the importance of consciousness. The primacy of the artist's conscious aim is reasserted, and so is the necessity for the audience to understand the work of art through an act of conscious will. The desired response is not a passionate swoon, but a passionately correct esthetic and moral judgment.

I should like to give a few examples of how A-effect operates in a given work of art. Afterward I shall offer a reading of *Troilus and Criseyde* as a work in which Chaucer uses A-effect in order to goad the audience toward critical judgment of the conventions of medieval romance, and of character and action in the poem. Such judgment is not, of course, an end in itself, but the means toward an ideological end: that the audience should understand and accept the rigorous Augustinian doctrine which Chaucer makes explicit in the so-called "epilogue" but which has been adumbrated all along precisely by alienation techniques. Chaucer uses devices which, in Brechtian terms, "[turn] the object ... from something ordinary, familiar, immediately accessible, into something peculiar, striking, and unexpected." The ordinary is made for the moment incomprehensible, but only so that another viewpoint, the orthodox Christian, may enter and eventually dominate: once we permit that to happen, comprehension is restored, albeit on a new level. I hope that the non-Chaucerian examples I give will expand my reader's notion of A-effect so that Chaucer's esthetic purpose will become the more apparent.

For Brecht, one of the best exemplars of A-effect was the traditional Chinese theatre. Here a number of devices were used to create an impression of

---

[1] "Short Description of a New Technique of Acting which Produces an Alienation Effect" (1940); in *Brecht on Theatre*, trans. and ed. John Willett (New York: Hill and Wang, 1974), 143–44.

strangeness. Among them is the decorous, controlled and ritualistic quality of the acting, an apparent coldness which "comes from the actor's holding himself remote from the character portrayed." This style of acting contrasts with the conventional western mode where the actor tries to become the figure he portrays, tries to lose himself in the dramatic character. Another alienation device in Chinese theatre is the candor of stage business. Props are handed the actor while he performs, the setting is changed in full view of the audience. There is no attempt to "create an illusion," hence no fear of breaking one. And above all, Brecht writes,

> the Chinese artist never acts as if there were a fourth wall besides the three surrounding him. He expresses his awareness of being watched.... The audience identifies itself with the actor as being an observer, and accordingly develops his attitude of observing or looking on.[2]

It is beyond the scope of this paper to discuss the ideological purpose of these devices in the Chinese theatre itself, but in western theatre the dramatic function of A-effect, in Brecht's view, is to reveal the abnormality of the normal—that is, of life under capitalism—and to make it impossible for the audience to accept as natural or inevitable the events they see on stage.

Brecht was also alert to A-effect in painting, especially in the works of Breughel, who, as Brecht remarks, "deals in contradictions." Breughel is able to explore the fullest meaning of the events he depicts not by presenting them in magnificent, sentimental and unrealistic isolation but rather by locating those events very solidly in the real world where they occurred. Thus

> In *The Fall of Icarus* the catastrophe breaks into the idyll in such a way that it is clearly set apart from it and valuable insights into the idyll can be gained. He doesn't allow the catastrophe to alter the idyll; the latter rather remains unaltered and survives undestroyed, merely disturbed.... The characters turn their backs on the incident. Lovely picture of the concentration needed for plowing. The man fishing in the right foreground, and his particular relationship to the water.... Special beauty and gaiety of the landscape during the frightful event.[3]

Similarly with Breughel's painting *The Tower of Babel* (158–59):

> The tower has been put up askew.... Delivery of the building materials is a very laborious business; the effort is obviously wasted.... Powerful oppression prevails, the attitude of the men bringing up the building materials is extremely servile, the builder is guarded by armed men.

What Breughel forces us to acknowledge, then, is the depth and the dialectical complexity of human existence at any given moment: its physical, social and mythic components and the often disjunctive relation among them.

---

[2] "Alienation Effects in Chinese Acting," ibid., 91–92.
[3] "Alienation Effects in the Narrative Pictures of the Elder Breughel," ibid., 157.

Let us turn to literature, in fact to medieval romance, for Chaucer was by no means the only poet to exercise a critical perspective on courtly love and romance. When Gottfried von Strassburg composed his great verse romance *Tristan* during the first few years of the thirteenth century, he stressed two intentions. One was to follow the old authoritative source of the Tristan legend as closely as possible; the other was to show Tristan and Isolde not as fairy-tale creatures but as real flesh-and-blood lovers in a hostile society. Unfortunately the two aims were not always consistent, for early versions of the romance contained motifs that caused Gottfried some discomfort. Among them was the motif of the dragon that must be killed in order to obtain the hand of the princess Isolde. Gottfried permits himself the dragon, but at the same time he exposes the absurdity of promising one's daughter to whoever kills a dragon. He does this mainly through dialogue, especially in such an exchange as the one that occurs between Isolde and her mother when a false steward claims to have killed the dragon:

> "Oh, no, my pretty daughter. Gently," her mother Isolde said to her, "do not take it so to heart! For whether it was done by fair means or foul, we shall see that nothing comes of it! ..."
>
> "Oh, mother," said the lovely girl, "my lady, do not dishonor your high birth and person! Before I comply, I will stab a knife through my heart! I shall take my own life before he has his pleasure of me! ..."
>
> "No, sweet daughter, have no fear of that. Whatever he or anybody says, it is of no importance at all. He shall never be your husband, not if all the world had sworn it!"

And when it comes to the old motif of a swallow bringing one of Isolde's golden hairs back to England, Gottfried rejects it outright:

> Did ever a swallow nest at such inconvenience that, despite the abundance in its own country, it went ranging overseas into strange lands in search of nesting materials? I swear the tale grows fantastic, the story is talking nonsense here! It is absurd, too, for anyone to say that Tristan, with a company, sailed the seas at random and failed to attend to how long he was sailing or where he was bound for, nor even knew whom he was seeking!—What old score was he settling with the book, who had this written and recited? The whole lot of them, the King, who sent his council abroad, and his envoys (had they gone on a mission in this style) would have been dolts and fools.[4]

In short, Gottfried asks us all along to decide: not to be taken in automatically by romance conventions and motifs, but to retain the same critical perspective that he does. As befits his artistic self-consciousness, however, Gottfried does not hesitate to employ such an "unrealistic" motif as the little multicolored dog Petitcrieu as a polysemous symbol. The principle Gottfried argues for, then, is

---

[4] *Tristan*, trans. A. D. Hatto (Middlesex: Penguin, 1960), 154–55: Chapter 11, "The Wooing Expedition."

the artist's freedom to choose, reject or manipulate material for his own conscious aims.[5]

Closer to home, the music of Pharaoh Sanders shows a powerful and witty use of A-effect. His saxophone speaks like a voice or blows like wind. The artist as shaman conjures spirits down from the sky or up from earth with bells, makes the ancient ram's horn shriek, exorcises. You are entirely caught up in the power of the ceremony, its eros and thanatos—until eventually the band breaks into a facile waltz: the old English tune "Greensleeves." Everyone is stunned for a moment, the audience laugh, they are surprised and restored. The artist has taken you out of the work as masterfully as he put you into it. Partly the shock of contrast and perspective shows us how far we had entered into the shamanistic experience; it demands that we know why, and what it means about our lives. But the contrast also says something about the innocuous, familiar "Greensleeves" as well: that it too is art; as much as the ram's horn, it is material to be used by someone who has the genius to use it new.

I would suggest, then, that there are four general hallmarks of alienation effect in literature. First, the audience is discouraged from identifying with the central characters, and is encouraged instead to evaluate them, their actions and their opinions as correct or incorrect. Second, the work of art tries to illuminate the peculiarity of the everyday by offering a different point of view from the one usually adequate to the particular medium or form. Third, there is on the artist's part a clear awareness of his or her own role and of the artificiality of medium or form. Fourth, the crucial questions are not asked, nor the crucial statements made, subtly or indirectly at the risk of their being ignored or minimized; they are asked or stated openly and directly, whether by artist, narrator, or *dramatis personae*.

Let me turn now to *Troilus* to show how Chaucer deliberately introduces these techniques of alienation into his version of the medieval romance. Many of the stylistic features of *Troilus* that I shall use have already been noticed, listed, and in varying degrees of thoroughness discussed by other writers. I shall not retrace their steps in detail, but instead will attempt to show that there is a connection between the many stylistic peculiarities of *Troilus*, for the poem does indeed make sense as an esthetic whole if we apply appropriate esthetic standards. Nor do I intend to give an exhaustive reading: *Troilus* is a work of staggering richness, and I hope here to add another way of approaching it, as valid and as partial as any other.

---

[5] It should be added, though, that eventually Gottfried fails to sustain his dual purpose, for the conscious critical perspective he turns on romance is turned more and more searchingly on Tristan and Isolde themselves. In showing us their human reality Gottfried also demonstrates their capacity to be vicious, manipulative and opportunistic. By the end of his work (and it is unfinished) the reader finds it difficult to admire Tristan and Isolde at all.

1. *The audience is not encouraged to identify with the central characters, but is encouraged to evaluate their actions and opinions as correct or incorrect.*

It has long been one of the commonplaces of Chaucer criticism that Chaucer is "half in love with Criseyde"—much as Alexander Pope, according to Cleanth Brooks, is charmed with Belinda in the *Rape of the Lock*.[6] I believe that Chaucer is tougher on his heroine than many critics acknowledge, and that if we sympathize with her or Troilus by the end of the poem it is despite Chaucer's best efforts to disengage us. It seems to me that both figures become, during the course of the poem, increasingly lucid and, simultaneously, more difficult to accept in their own terms as Chaucer pushes them to act out the furthest implications of their characters and opinions, placing them (in Turgenev's phrase) in relations that bring them out.

In the delineation of character Chaucer uses several means to distance us from his hero and heroine. One aspect of style that helps to provide a critical perspective is the imagery associated with them, particularly the two prominent and sustained image-clusters of animals and of fire or heat. Lists of these images have been compiled by others, and I shall not repeat the effort:[7] more to the point here is the effect of imagery. Both image clusters are associated predominantly, though not only, with Troilus; both imply a view of him which is at odds with, and belittles, his own professions of noble motives and good in-

---

[6] See "The Case of Miss Arabella Fermor" in *The Well-Wrought Urn* (New York: Harcourt Brace, 1947). I have argued against Brooks's position in "Sex and Politics in the *Rape of the Lock*," *ESC* 1 (1975): 46–60, reprinted in *Weapons of Criticism: Marxism in America and the Literary Tradition*, ed. Norman Rudich (Palo Alto: Ramparts Press, 1975), and in my *Writing Woman: Women Writers and Women in Literature, Medieval to Modern* (New York: Schocken Books, 1983).
This is not to say that the Narrator may not be charmed by Criseyde. The crucial distinction between Chaucer and his narrator is kept before us especially by E. T. Donaldson; see "Chaucer the Pilgrim," "Four Women of Style," and "Criseyde and Her Narrator," all reprinted in *Speaking of Chaucer*; see also his commentary on *Troilus* in *Chaucer's Poetry*.

[7] For example, Beryl Rowland, "The Horse and Rider Figure in Chaucer's Works," *UTQ* 35 (1966): 246–59 and "Aspects of Chaucer's Use of Animals," *Archiv* 201 (1964): 110–14. The most thorough compilation is in Meech, *Design*. Since Meech's primary concern is with overall structure and patterns of design, he rarely gives a close analysis of the images he lists. Though this doesn't diminish the importance of his work, I would suggest that a close reading sometimes leads to a conclusion at odds with Meech's own position, which is that Chaucer "means to build sympathy for [Troilus] and even admiration" (404). Even without a close reading of imagery, however, Meech's view of Troilus seems inconsistent. On the same page he writes that Chaucer, in giving freedom of will to Troilus, renders him, like the other characters, "praise or blameworthy." But if Troilus can be judged blameworthy, in what sense is he sympathetic or admirable? These responses to Troilus are not necessarily mutually exclusive, but the categories do require some further adjustment.
For other comments on Chaucer's animal imagery, see John Spiers on the Fox in *Chaucer the Maker* (London: Faber and Faber, 1951), 67; Mary Griffin, "The Pekok . . ." in *Studies on Chaucer and His Audience* (Hull, Quebec: Les Éditions 'L'Éclair', 1956); and D.W. Robertson's illuminating discussions of animal iconography in his *Preface*.
As Meech points out, "The instances of figurative linkage with animals in the *Troilus* not only outnumber those in the *Filostrato* but are more diverse than they and more vividly particular" (323). Images of fire are fewer than in Boccaccio, and used somewhat differently (353).

tentions. If Troilus is as proud as a peacock (1.210), timid as a snail (1.300) or a mouse (3.736), as needy of control as Bayard the horse (1.218-24), trapped like a bird (1.353), as frustrated as a bear gnawing its chain (1.509), as unresponsive to reason as an ass to the harp (1.731), if he is an ape of God like every other lover (1.913)—all this suggests the animal nature of Troilus and of mankind: that aspect of his nature which he wilfully ignores but which is forcefully brought home to us. Nor is the point conveyed only indirectly, but in a narrative interjection:

> But O Fortune, executrice of wyrdes!
> O influences of thise hevens hye!
> Soth is, that under God ye ben oure hierdes,
> Though to us bestes ben the causes wrie.   3.617-20

The image anticipates a line from Chaucer's later lyric "Truth"—"Forth, beste, out of thy stal!"—a lyric which develops the Christian ideology implicit throughout *Troilus* and stated clearly in the "epilogue."

We may consider too a more ironic use of imagery:

> What myghte or may the sely larke seye,
> Whan that the sperhauk hath it in his foot?   3.1191-92

The next stanza tells us that it is Criseyde who "felte hire thus itake" (1198). Yet the lines occur just after the extremely awkward and nearly pornographic prelude to the lovers' union. It is a section of the narrative in which Troilus has swooned from either sorrow or fear; he has been accused of cowardice by both Pandarus and Criseyde, and Criseyde has had to take the physical initiative. By the time we come to the conventional image of pursuer and prey we wonder who is the hawk and who the sely lark. Since Chaucer's management of the narrative has virtually destroyed the conventional romance (and social!) sex-role allocation, the image is exposed as rigid and trite; simultaneously, it exposes the deficiencies of human reality.

The imagery of fire seems to serve a similar purpose. The fire of lust and the fires of hell are too intimate a part of the medieval imagination and the medieval iconographic tradition to be irrelevant here: again they suggest, however indirectly, a system of values against which Troilus must be weighed and found wanting.

Another means of alienating the characters appears with the portraits of Troilus, Criseyde and Diomede that are placed so oddly near the end of the poem (5.799-840). The portraits have drawn assorted critical comment, some writers viewing them as belated and inept, others as entirely appropriate.[8] My view is that they are both: their placement is awkward and unexpected from

---

[8] Meech (448n7) gives a brief resumé of the controversy. For his own view see pages 112-13; also A. C. Spearing, "Chaucer as Novelist" in *Criticism and Medieval Poetry* (London: Edward Arnold, Ltd., 1964), 98; Claes Schaar, *The Golden Mirror* (Lund: Gleerup; reprinted 1967), 191-92; and Donaldson, *Speaking*, 57-58.

the point of view of conventional romance narrative, and the descriptions are jarringly formal in contrast with the psychological depth and realism to which the poem has accustomed us; nonetheless they are appropriate to Chaucer's aim. They force us suddenly to see the three from afar, no longer living persons but static iconographical figures in a stained-glass window, as they will go down in tradition. This abrupt perspective prepares us for the cosmic distancing and the moral placement that become explicit at the end of the poem.

Finally, the behavior of Troilus and Criseyde provides the most direct and powerful means by which Chaucer encourages a critical view of his characters. It is somewhat inaccurate to call this process a progressive degradation or degeneration of character, as this implies a radical decline from some earlier peak of virtue. I tend here to agree with Arthur Mizener when he writes,

> Chaucer's characters do not change or develop under the impact of experience; they display various aspects of an established set of characteristics as the progress of the narrative places them in varying circumstances.[9]

Pandarus offers little difficulty to most critics: the immorality implicit in his cynicism is revealed when he approves Troilus's love though it were adulterous and incestuous (1.676–79); when he offers Troilus his sister (1.860–61); when he slanders Poliphete in order to bring Troilus and Criseyde together (2.1615–21); confesses himself to be a pander (3.253–55); and lies to Criseyde (3.786–91 and elsewhere).

With Troilus, self-pity, self-deception and passivity become more and more prominent traits of character, to the point where his taking to bed after hearing of Criseyde's exchange for Antenor comes across as a piece of comedy—a predictable reflex, like a nervous tic. As J. S. P. Tatlock noted, "A modern man is excusable for thinking him a poor stick who gets from Criseyde when she is exposed to Diomed, no more than his deserts."[10] It may be difficult (even Tatlock finds it difficult) to extend such traits into a critical judgment. But when Troilus descends to Pandarus's level by offering any one of his sisters in exchange for services rendered (3.407–13), we can scarcely avoid such a judgment. Similarly we can only feel that something is seriously amiss when Troilus wishes his father, brothers or himself dead rather than Criseyde exchanged (4.274–80).

With Criseyde, the problem of evaluation is somewhat more difficult. I cannot help thinking that part of the difficulty comes from a subtle kind of sexism: that gentlemanly critics, seeing in Criseyde qualities they are taught to accept as "feminine," are as reluctant to deplore these qualities in Criseyde as they would be with any real woman. But Criseyde's character—her very "femininity"—includes conscious and manipulative self-presentation, coyness, calcula-

---

[9] "Character and Action in the Case of Criseyde," reprinted in Chaucer, *Modern Essays in Criticism*, ed. Edward Wagenknecht (New York: Oxford Univ. Press, 1959), 351.

[10] "The People in Chaucer's *Troilus*," in Wagenknecht, 336.

tion, egocentricity, self-pity, self-deception, fear and passivity. To be sure, these traits are understandable in context of Criseyde's tenuous social position, just as they are understandable today in real women for the same reasons. What is the weight of social circumstance relative to individual will? No Catholic can afford to privilege the former so heavily that it outweighs the latter: nor does Chaucer. For him, finally, as for any Catholic, the moral will is determinative and (though we might not agree) in some sense untouched by circumstance. If we want a sense of what Chaucer considers an ideal of femininity we have only to read his portrait of "good fair White" in *Book of the Duchess*: a woman governed not by fear but by prudence, self-confidence, honesty and the conscious choice of virtue.

A few passages will suffice, I hope, to indicate the basis of my response to Criseyde. When Pandarus first comes to Criseyde she employs a flirtatious feminine strategy: the claim that she has only recently dreamt of her visitor (2.89–90). It is the same strategy that the Wife of Bath's gossip advised her to use in order to entrap the young clerk Jankin. Criseyde continues to play up to Pandarus's superior masculine knowledge of the affairs of war, but when she asserts "I am of Grekes so fered that I deye" (2.124) I become rather uncomfortable with her milking the feminine role. When Pandarus begins to speak of love, "With that she gan hire eighen down to cast"—another bit of conscious self-presentation. In defending her morality Criseyde says to her uncle that surely he would have chastised her had she loved "outher hym [Troilus] or Achilles, / Ector, or any mannes creature" (2.416–17). Hector and Troilus yes— but Achilles, an enemy hero? Does she know herself already so opportunistic, or is she merely thoughtless?

Criseyde's egocentricity emerges as she continually credits herself with power of life and death over Troilus—if she refuses to love him he will surely die of sorrow or commit suicide. Repeatedly she uses this misperception to justify her action (e.g., 2.459–60, 663–65, 1590–94). Pandarus is able to play on this idea, so flattering to any woman's concept of herself (cf. 2.1127, 1279–81 and 1736); and when the same motive is given for her wish to comfort Diomede (5.1042), though he has displayed no sorrow, its shallowness is at last painfully obvious.

The famous line "Who yaf me drynke?" (2.651) has been made to yield assorted fruit. I see in it another instance of Criseyde's passivity, and a theatrical assumption of the posture of the traditional romance heroine. In his parodistic balade, "To Rosemounde," Chaucer presents himself as a lovelorn "trewe Tristan the secounde." Criseyde has just been reading a romance with her women; perhaps her reference to a love-potion is meant to identify her as a new Isolde.

Like Pandarus, Criseyde can talk up any argument that serves her purpose; if it serves her purpose to slander her father (4.1366–1407), so be it. And, like her uncle, she is always prepared to find reasons after the fact for her actions: reasons for loving Troilus (2.701ff.), reasons for leaving Troy (4.1528ff.) and finally reasons for not returning to Troy (5.689–707, 1023–29).

As I read the poem, then, Chaucer has taken some pains to distance us from Troilus and Criseyde. Of course there must be in any great literature some sense on the spectator's part of *sua res agitur*. Yet it is not always through consistent positive identification that this is best accomplished. Nor is some degree of identification incompatible with moral judgment if the author's aim is to enable us to judge ourselves. I am by no means immune from empathy with the story of Troilus and Criseyde, yet the net effect, I feel, is well conveyed by a statement that Brecht made about two of his plays:

> The spectator's "splendid isolation" is left intact; . . . he is not fobbed off with an invitation to feel sympathetically, to fuse with the hero and seem significant and indestructible. . . . A higher type of interest can be got from making comparisons, from whatever is different, amazing, impossible to take in as a whole.[11]

2. *The work of art tries to illuminate the peculiarity of the everyday by offering a different point of view from the one usually adequate to the medium or form.*
  In an essay on acting, Brecht writes that

> The object of the A-effect is to alienate [that is, to externalize or objectify] the social gest underlying every incident. By social gest is meant the mimetic and gestural expression of the social relationships prevailing between people of a given period.[12]

To which one can add that it is precisely in exposing the underlying social gest that the so-called normality—the real peculiarity and relativity—of a given action or opinion becomes apparent. As the *Troilus* is not a drama but a narrative poem, exposure is achieved through the resources of style. Chaucer's main vehicle here is his narrative persona, but he is also able to use equivocal language and religious imagery with devastating effect, and to give the work a sociopolitical background which provides a constant touchstone for evaluation.
  E. Talbot Donaldson's phrase "deliberate mystification" best summarizes Chaucer's narrative stance in the *Troilus*: a device whereby the Narrator's questions or assertions force us to challenge what we would otherwise have taken for granted or accepted as a normal convention of romance. Some of these *loci* have been analyzed by Donaldson, primarily in relation to Criseyde: I shall consider a few others. One is the Narrator's comment after he describes Criseyde's social status:

> But wheither that she children hadde or noon,
> I rede it naught, therfore I late it goon.   1.132–33

To this point we have naturally assumed that Criseyde had no children. Yet she is a widow, we are reminded, and might have had children. If so, where are they; if not, why not? It is of course easiest for narrative purposes to have Criseyde childless; if this is the reason why she is traditionally childless, then we

---

[11] Notebook entry on *Baal* and *Dickicht*, Willett, 9.
[12] "Short Description," in Willet, 139.

are forcibly reminded of the artificiality of romance itself—its freedom from the encumbrances of normal social life.

Or again, when Troilus suffers the pangs of unrequited love and claims to have a fever, the Narrator remarks:

> But how it was, certeyn, kan I nat seye,
> If that his lady understood nat this,
> Or feynede hire she nyste, oon of the tweye;
> But wel I rede that, by no manere weye,
> Ne semed it as that she of hym roughte,
> Or of his peyne, or whatsoevere he thoughte.   1.492-97

It would scarcely have occurred to us to think that Criseyde knew of Troilus's love before her interview with Pandarus in Book 2. But the Narrator raises that possibility under guise of denying it—or at least of judging by appearances—and with it the possibility of a Criseyde as capable of manipulating Pandarus as she is of being manipulated by him.

After Criseyde's interview with Pandarus, the latter requests a more private conversation:

> And everi wight that was aboute hem tho,
> That herde that, gan fer awey to stonde,
> Whil they two hadde al that hem liste in honde.   2.215-17

What is "al that hem liste"? Why do we need to be excluded from the conversation along with the women in waiting, especially when we have heard every detail of what has just preceded? The narrator tells us in the next stanza that the subject of their conversation was "hire estat and hire governaunce"—but why is special privacy suddenly required, and what is the particular meaning here of "estate" and of "governance": social position merely, or moral conduct? And what is the relation between uncle and niece anyway: how frequent a visitor is he, has he been a lover, why does Criseyde flirt with him?

After Criseyde and Troilus have been brought together, but before their union is consummated, the Narrator tells us that she was no longer afraid—"I mene, as fer as oughte ben requered" (3.483). But what, precisely, is the requisite degree of fear in such a case? Chaucer deftly allows his Narrator to remind us that there is another stage to the romance; and while Criseyde may feel no fear at the moment, she is of course virtuous and modest enough to feel some fear of the potential sexual bond if she should think of it. The technique resembles that in an earlier passage where, assuring us that Criseyde did not fall in love too quickly (2.666ff.), the Narrator causes us to wonder whether she did not, after all, do exactly that. How consciously does Criseyde participate in her own deception? Two further examples suggest that she may have been a willing victim. The Narrator does not know whether Criseyde believed Pandarus's lie about Troilus being out of town (3.575-81), nor can he say with any certainty whether, in the bedroom scene, she tolerated Troilus's familiarity out of sorrow or social obligation or some other motive (3.967-73).

Besides the ambiguity of the narrative voice, the entire linguistic texture of

the Troilus abounds with equivocation. A general syntactic ambiguity pervades
the poem, as in stanza two of the first book:

> To the clepe I, thow goddesse of torment,
> Thow cruwel Furie, sorwynge evere yn peyne,
> Help me, that am the sorwful instrument,
> That helpeth loveres, as I kan, to pleyne.   2.8–11

The phrase "sorwynge evere yn peyne" could apply, syntactically, either to
"thow" or to "I"; "to pleyne" could be attached to "help me" or to "that
helpeth lovers"; "kan" means either can or know. 1.623 depends heavily on
punctuation, hence on editorial discretion, for its meaning: "how devel
maistow brynge me to blisse?" or "How, devel, maistow brynge me to blisse?"
with emphasis on the ironic contrast between devil and bliss. When Criseyde
first looks at Troilus, armed and mounted, from her window, we are told that
he had "a body and a myght / To don that thing" (2.633–34). The verb is not
specified, presumably it is to fight, for he is just come from battle; or is it to
make love, inasmuch as Troilus is being observed by Criseyde as her future
lover? Soon after, we learn that Troilus wrote frequently to Criseyde:

> Fro day to day he leet it nought refreyde,
> That by Pandare he wroot somwhat or seyde.   2.1343–44

What is the exact weight of "by Pandare he wroot"—that the letter was de-
livered by Pandarus, or that the letter was composed by Pandarus, or both? Still
further on, Pandarus exhorts Criseyde:

> "Sle naught this man, that hath for yow this peyne!
> Fy on the devel! thynk which one he is,
> And in what plite he lith; com of anon!
> Thynk al swich taried tyde but lost it nys.
> That wol ye bothe seyn, whan ye ben oon."   2.1736–40

The first "he" has an indefinite antecedent (devil/man), though the sense of
the next line makes clear that the subject is Troilus; "seyn" can be read as
either see or say; "oon" may mean either when the pair is alone together or
when they are sexually united.

Donaldson notes another linguistic habit of the narrator: his use of the qual-
ifier "as":

> All but the very simplest uses of *as* to express equivalence cause a
> distancing between the things compared. . . . But in the last two books of
> *Troilus* Chaucer rarely if ever permits the narrator to say in his own per-
> son, and in so many words, that Criseyde loved Troilus. There is always a
> distancing device, if only one so seemingly negligible as the little *as*. Yet
> the cumulative effect of such devices may well weaken one's confidence
> that what is said to be real is real.[13]

---

[13] *Speaking*, 71.

Similar in effect to syntactic ambiguity and qualifiers is another form of equiv-
ocal language: pun. Again it isn't my purpose to compile an exhaustive list of
puns in Troilus,[14] but rather to indicate a stylistic tendency. Probably the two
best-known puns in Troilus occur when we see the "makeless" (Matchless/
unmated, 1.172) Criseyde, and when Troilus apostrophizes the house of the
absent Criseyde as a lantern "of which queynt is the light" (quenched/cunt,
5.543). To these we may add the "stuwe" (closet/brothel, 3.601) in which
Troilus is concealed at Pandarus's house; the narrator's indignation at anyone
who might "lye on" (tell lies about/be recumbent upon, 4.20) Criseyde; his
regret for the laughter "men" (people/males, 4.866) used to find in Criseyde;
and Troilus's agonized self-interrogation about why he does not help to his
own "cure" (benefit/salvation, 5.49).

All of these stylistic features are confusing on the surface and are intended
to be so; my argument is that they illuminate by confusion, thus leading deeper
than the surface. Through pun, ambiguity and the rest, the familiar becomes
unfamiliar, the reliable phrase, feeling or concept becomes unreliable, the in-
conspicuous word becomes conspicuous, and a conventional idea is made to
yield unconventional associations. Once again the reader is jolted out of easy
expectations and made to confront other possibilities. It is a technique favored
by the French surrealists too—to use language in such a way as to demonstrate
the artificiality of our conditioned expectations. While I am far from claiming
Chaucer as a proto-surrealist, I would suggest he had a similar purpose in
mind.

That same process of illumination by confusion is evident in Chaucer's han-
dling of religious imagery in *Troilus*. Early on in the poem the religious
imagery seems quite in the tradition of courtly lyric and romance as Chaucer
develops the "religion of love" in scrupulous detail with its god, its prayers, its
servants, saints and martyrs, its heaven, its hope, despair and grace (1.15-51).
He allows Troilus to develop it further in baiting lovers, just after his own
"conversion" (1.330-50). But gradually the congruence dissolves. The juxta-
position of religion and love becomes so strained, incompatible and finally out-
rageous—"yoked by violence together" as Dr. Johnson remarked of Donne's
imagery—that we must see the two value systems as finally hostile. The follow-
ing sequence will illustrate this development.

The first intrusive note is sounded when Pandarus, describing the valor of
Troilus, calls him "shield and life for us": there is the briefest disjunction in
which we remind ourselves that it is not a prayer, nor is Jesus being described,
but Troilus. The gap widens when we find that Troilus trivializes religious devo-
tion by using it as his cover for amorous pursuit (3.533-46). Later, Criseyde's
body is referred to as "this hevene" (3.1251). Apart from the obvious Jan-

---

[14] Some of Chaucer's puns have been listed by H. Kökeritz, "Rhetorical Word-Play in
Chaucer," *PMLA* 69 (1954): 937-52, and by Paull F. Baum, "Chaucer's Puns," *PMLA* 71
(1956): 225-46, and "Chaucer's Puns: A Supplementary List," *PMLA* 73 (1958): 167-70. For
others in *Troilus*, and a more detailed discussion, see Sheila Delany, "Anatomy of the
Resisting Reader," *Exemplaria* 4 (1992): 7-34.

uary-like overtones of the image, the phrase occurs after we have been nearly stifled by the sultry atmosphere of this first consummation, with its voyeurism, reversal of sex-roles, petulance and manipulation and near-pornography: an atmosphere resembling that of the Temple of Venus in the *Parliament of Fowls*: and this is Troilus's heaven. But the climax of bad taste is reached with the Narrator's comment on Criseyde's attitude toward Pandarus's interference: "What! God foryaf his deth, and she al so / Foryaf..." (3.1577–78). Here it is no longer possible to hold the two systems in equilibrium; they have parted company for good.

The social dimension provided by the Trojan background also offers a perspective on the love-story: not only as an allegorical parallel to it, as John McCall shows[15] but also as a larger reality which Troilus and Criseyde are willing to trivialize for their own needs, much as they trivialize religion. Pandarus does it first, when the arrival of a Greek spy provides the occasion (or excuse) for Pandarus to deliver Troilus's first letter to Criseyde (2.1111–15); Troilus repeats it by reducing the war and negotiations as nothing more than a backdrop to their romance (4.1286–1358). We discover via Calkas that the fate of Troy is sealed in its origins: a labor dispute (albeit with the gods): "Bycause he [King Lameadoun] nolde payen hem here hire, / The town of Troie shal ben set on-fire" (4.125–26). And the tragic history of Thebes is also kept before us in the romance read by Criseyde's ladies, as well as in Diomede's antecedents. These, the historical, political and economic realities, Troilus and Criseyde try to insulate themselves from. By conventional romance standards they are perfectly justified in doing so, but in offering this touchstone of judgment Chaucer again exposes not only the artificiality of romance convention but also what Brecht calls "the underlying social gest."

3. *There is on the artist's part an explicitly stated awareness of his/her own role and of the artificiality of medium or genre.*

Here again narrative voice is the primary vehicle conveying the awareness of the artist observing himself being observed, or, in Robert O. Payne's formulation, "art so unconcealed as to demand the reader's continual consciousness of it as a process symbolic of its own content."[16] Though it is naturally in the four prologues that the artist-narrator is most explicitly conscious of his role, his voice intrudes throughout the poem, whether he is establishing his personal relation to love (1.8–56, 3.1319–20), or reminding us of the painstaking scrupulosity with which he uses old material (1.393–99, 4.1415–21, 5.799, 834, 1044, 1051). He may call our attention to the artificiality of rhetoric by translating it for us into everyday terms: "The dayes honour, and the hevenes yë, / The nyghtes foo—al this clepe I the sonne" (2.904–5). Sometimes he reminds us of the mechanics, the bare bones, of his narrative (1.1086,

---

[15] John P. McCall, "The Trojan Scene in Chaucer's *Troilus*," *ELH* 29 (1962): 263–75.
[16] Payne, *Key*, 217.

3.491–505, 531–32, 4.1127). Or, using the conventional modesty trope, he may assert his incompetence to do justice to a particularly moving scene (4.799–805, 5.267–73).

Perhaps the most striking use of A-effect through authorial intervention occurs in five stanzas toward the very end of the poem (5.1765–99). Having just told us of Troilus's death, the poet proceeds to remind us that his real subject is love, not war; sends us to the relevant sources if we wish to pursue the theme of war; sends us to other books treating of Criseyde; restates his purpose and defines his audience; apostrophizes his book; and concludes with a brief digression on the condition of the English language and its potentially destructive effect on his work. This remarkable passage forces us to see, if we have not already absorbed the point, that the story could have been told differently, and that the present version is the result of conscious effort and selection. The passage also distances us in another way. By reminding us of deliberate craft, it reintroduces an intellectual perspective. This not only helps us to overcome the nearly unbearable tension and pathos of the last book, but also prepares us for the *moralitas* with which the poem ends.

4. *Crucial questions are asked, and statements made, directly, whether by artist, narrator or* dramatis personae.

Not every question in a work of art constitutes an effort toward A-effect. Questions play an important role, for instance, in Wolfram's *Parzival*, as an index to the hero's naiveté; and "Who's there?"—the opening words of *Hamlet*— poses the problems of mistrust and mistaken identity that are so important in the play. Such questions as these do not exist for the sake of their answers, but rather for what they mean in themselves. I am speaking here, however, of questions that transcend the immediate literary context—indeed that transcend art itself, leaping out of the work of art as permanently important questions about why we live as we do. These questions, moreover, are not only answerable, they are answered in the work of art.

An example of such questions appears in the rice-merchant's "Song of Supply and Demand" from Brecht's *The Measures Taken*:

> Down the river there is rice
> In the provinces up the river people need rice:
> If we leave the rice in the warehouses
> The rice will cost them more.
> Those who pole the rice-barge will then get less rice
> And rice will be even cheaper for me.
>> What is rice actually?
>> Do I know what rice is?
>> God knows what rice is!
>> I don't know what rice is
>> I only know its price.
>> . . . . . .

What is a man actually?
Do I know what a man is?
God knows what a man is!
I don't know what a man is
I only know his price.

The series of questions and answers takes us through a rapid course in basic dialectics: not only supply and demand, but theory of value, labor-power as commodity, alienation and class consciousness.

In *Troilus* there is an infrastructure of precisely such heavily-charged questions and their eventual answers. "If no love is," asks Troilus,

"O God, what fele I so?
And if love is, what thing and which is he?
If love be good, from whennes cometh my woo?" 1.400–402

Though there are specific passages that could be taken as answers to this group of questions about love (e.g., 3.1744–71), the fullest answer is the entire poem with epilogue, for only on finishing the poem do we learn what love is in its human and divine manifestations, and whence comes Troilus's woe.

Rather petulantly, Criseyde asks another key question just before her first sexual encounter with Troilus: "Is this a mannes game?" (3.1126). The subject of manliness or manhood is raised several times in the poem, at four different levels of meaning. In the courtly-love tradition, Troilus is "her man"—the devoted servant of his mistress (as in 1.468 and 4.447). Criseyde's question suggests three other levels as well. Its surface reference is to courage ("be a man"), while the obvious ironic reference is to sexuality. At the same time we can ask the question "What is it to be a man?" of any person, humanity at large (as it is used, e.g., in 2.1501 and 3.10). Thus Criseyde's question leads far beyond its immediate dramatic context and invites us to consider what it is, after all, to be most fully human. This question, like the other, has a dual aspect which requires for its real answer both the dramatic action and the epilogue: Troilus's fear, weakness and lust truly express the limitations of human nature, while his eventual transcendence expresses what humanity is capable of at its Christian best.

Troilus poses a third question, which strikes at the heart of the poem: "Whi nyl I helpen to myn owen cure?" (5.49). In the immediate context Troilus is contemplating some drastic action to rescue Criseyde. Yet the question opens almost dizzying vistas of meaning—the paralytic disease of his own character, human nature at large, the question how far our will is free, the abuse of free will if we have it, etc. It then contracts as rapidly again as we are deftly returned to the dramatic context.

Probably the most important question in the poem—the tropological question "Quo tendas?" ("Where are you heading?")—is asked thrice by Criseyde. It is couched in at least twenty occurrences throughout the poem of the word "fyn" (goal or purpose), so that the questions themselves emerge with startling clarity to illuminate more than their immediate narrative context. Reproaching

Pandarus for suggesting the idea of loving Troilus, Criseyde says, "Is al this paynted proces seyd, allas! / Right for this fyn?" (2.424-25). It is not the only "painted process" we encounter in the poem: her question might as well apply to the words of Troilus or Diomede, or to her own professions of love: what are, after all, the real aims or motives of the speakers? Just after Criseyde has decided to love Troilus she repeats the question: "To what fyn lyve I thus?" and a few lines later confesses her ignorance of ultimate ends: "To what fyn is swich love I kan nat see" (2.794). Later, lamenting her departure from Troy she exclaims, "To what fyn sholde I lyve and sorwen thus?" (4.764). To what end—her love, her life, anyone's life, human life. With Troilus's ironic laughter in the eighth sphere, the answer finally appears in the magnificently orchestrated stanza that concludes the narrative proper:

> Swich fyn hath, lo, this Troilus for love!
> Swich fyn hath al his grete worthynesse!
> Swich fyn hath his estat real above,
> Swich fyn his lust, swich fyn hath his noblesse!
> Swich fyn hath false worldes brotelnesse!   5.1828-32

Though the reading of *Troilus* that I have just presented is not specifically a Marxist reading, it has some methodological relevance for those who are committed to Marxist, historicist or other contemporary criticism and esthetics. If I have succeeded it indicates, first of all, that the application of modern critical categories to older literature is not necessarily a Procrustean effort. On the contrary, the validity of a theory like Brecht's lies precisely in its ability to illuminate art for which it was not specifically designed: the art of earlier periods and of other cultures. Much of this work remains to be done, though we may look for examples to the pioneering studies of Max Raphael on prehistoric cave painting, of George Thomson on Greek tragedy, or of Norman O. Brown on the evolution of Greek myth. In short, alterity, too, has its limits.

This is perhaps my most evident theoretical conclusion, but I want to mention two others. First, I think we can agree that alienation is a subversive technique inasmuch as it undercuts traditional art forms, conventional responses or associations, and some received ideas. In this sense it is legitimate to consider Chaucer a "subversive" poet. Yet the case of *Troilus* shows that subversive art, as technique, is not necessarily subversive in the ideological sense, for it may subvert a current art form in order to revalidate an obsolescent ideology. What Chaucer shows us in *Troilus* is the subversion of courtly romance, in the service of a Christian ideology which had already begun to crumble under the weight of history. The failure of the Crusade movement, the great schism in the Church, the impact of Aristotelian rationalism and the development of nominalism in Europe had begun the process that would be continued in the revolutionary religious movements of eastern Europe, especially the Hussite and Taborite movements in Bohemia. It would culminate a century after Chaucer's death in the Anabaptist movement and, afterward, the Protestant Reformation. A similar case in our own century is Ezra Pound. Pound was a brilliant and innovative poet, not least in his subversion of conventional poetic technique in the *Cantos*, yet the subversion returns us to Renaissance bourgeois concepts of order, national unity and individual heroism. Style and ideology are not necessarily isomorphic in any period: innovation in the one guarantees nothing in the other.

Second, it is hardly necessary at this stage in the development of Chaucer scholarship to be reminded once again of Chaucer's conscious sophistication. More to the point is our willingness or ability to see Chaucer as a poet who reflects the stress and contradictions of his time. The ambivalence of Chaucer's narrator is something we have all experienced, and if we can no longer look to Christian ideology to resolve it, we can perhaps find in the work of revolutionary poets like Brecht a resolution more appropriate to ourselves. In the tradition of medieval writing about love, *Troilus and Criseyde* is a devastating attack on *La Vita Nuova*, on the conviction that human love can lead to divine love. In love Troilus and Criseyde find their object of worship, and in each other. To this Chaucer says no, because God sits in judgment in heaven; whereas if we are moved to deny *La Vita Nuova* it is because for us god is nowhere.

Reading Like a Man: The Critics, the Narrator, Troilus, and Pandarus[*]

CAROLYN DINSHAW

This essay is concerned to situate literary acts in large structures of medieval social organization, and to suggest that the gendered structure of literary acts in the late Middle Ages has deeply informed our own signifying practices in the present day, forming a patriarchal tradition of understanding language and literary activity. The essay begins with two modern-day critics of TROILUS AND CRISEYDE whose approaches to the text differ sharply and famously: E. Talbot Donaldson and D. W. Robertson, Jr. I suggest that their critical strategies in fact not only converge but repeat the reading strategy Troilus is represented in the poem as adopting. I argue that this reading strategy is shown, both in the poem and in its critics, to be gendered masculine. I then look at two readers represented in the poem who provide crucial denaturalizing perspectives on this masculine reading: Criseyde offers a hint of what it might be to read like a woman, and Pandarus suggests that men don't have to read like men. Given that masculine reading, in this poem, proceeds by unacknowledged exclusion, elimination, and constraint, the prospect that neither women nor men have to read like men is an immensely liberating one, and one that proved abundantly fruitful in Chaucer's later creations—among them the Wife of Bath and Griselda.

I want to begin this analysis of *Troilus and Criseyde* by considering two famous readings of the poem, famous in themselves and famously at odds with each other. These are the readings of E. Talbot Donaldson and D.W. Robertson, Jr., whose methods and conclusions have formed the poles of critical controversy over this poem and in medieval literary studies in general. The two critics base their readings on diametrically opposed theoretical principles: Donaldson eagerly participates in the emotional vicissitudes of the narrative, even implying that such response constitutes the emotionality of the text's characters, whereas Robertson urgently resists such subjectivity as he tries to escape solipsism—the blight of modernity, in his view—via medieval literature. But as the near interchangeability of their names felicitously suggests, these two "sons" are in fact

---

[*] Originally published in *Chaucer's Sexual Poetics* (Madison: Univ. of Wisconsin Press, 1989), 28–64. This essay has been abbreviated for inclusion in the present collection: omitted material is signalled by ellipses in square brackets—[. . . .] (*RAS & CSC*).

in accord with one another in making the same critical moves: as I hope to demonstrate, they both impose firm control on the dangerously "slydynge"—women and texts—in constructing their readings of *Troilus and Criseyde*.

Such a general and fundamental agreement between critics who are explicitly and vociferously divided on theoretical issues is significant, I find, because it is symptomatic of a larger, more pervasive literary structure subtending and informing their contrasting literary projects—New Criticism and patristic exegesis, respectively. This structure is the patriarchal structure of literary activity; I am interested in analyzing each critic as he articulates patriarchal discourse in his critical practice, and, further, I am interested in detailing the culturally pervasive, gendered understanding of literary activity that motivates this critical practice. Each critic, I shall suggest, reads "like a man": each defines the disruptive Other in, and of, the text as feminine and limits it, turns away from it, in order to provide a single, univalent textual meaning fixed in a hierarchical structure. Each shaping the course of Chaucer criticism, these major critical articulations by Robertson and Donaldson thus perform "masculine" readings (as Donaldson initially refers to his own) while each critic implies that his reading is finally neuter and normative—"humanistic" in Donaldson's case, "objective" in Robertson's. [. . . .]

It is crucial to understand that "reading like a man," as I analyze it here, is not necessarily the destiny of male anatomy. I am interested in this kind of reading as a gendered response, socially constructed, and I want to focus on the fact of its constructedness. Such a denaturalization of the masculine response constitutes the first step in any feminist analysis: it sees that the dominant perspective isn't given, natural, or universal and that there can therefore be other perspectives. The first step toward the formulation of alternatives to a monistic reading strategy is to recognize the existence of such a strategy. . . . And, in fact, I suggest that Chaucer provides us with precisely such a denaturalizing perspective on the act of reading in *Troilus and Criseyde*, in the figures of readers in the narrative. The narrator, Pandarus, and Troilus are all characterized as readers of feminine texts. After looking at the two modern critical readers—Donaldson and Robertson—I shall analyze these three male readers in Chaucer's text; all three, I suggest, turn away from the feminine in their final responses to the affair gone bad. But Pandarus, unlike the other two, is only acting—is thus reading precisely *like* a man—and thereby opens up the suggestion that there are other ways to read *as* a man. [. . . .]

But to return to Robertson and Donaldson: it must be remarked here that each of these critics did much to advance the academic careers of women scholars. My analysis is not meant even to insinuate otherwise. I am concerned with a cultural phenomenon, a general understanding of literary activity that is articulated through these two critics, as it were. But the discrepancy is itself significant and needs to be theorized. . . . Troilus is caught in an analogous position: as an individual man, he is deeply attached to, deeply believes in the uniqueness and singularity, the free and individual subjectivity, of a woman; but he is simultaneously implicated in, indeed complicit in, a larger societal attitude that sees women as mere counters in a power-asymmetrical patriarchal

social structure. There is a difference, of course, between this fictional charac-
ter's position and modern readers': whereas one is stuck forever, the others,
along with society, can indeed change. This possibility is what Chaucer's cri-
tique of "reading like a man" can finally suggest to us.

1

Donaldson was in love with Criseyde. He had been for years, from his earliest
declarations in the 1950s (in lectures later collected in *Speaking of Chaucer*) to
his last avowal in *The Swan at the Well: Shakespeare Reading Chaucer* (1985).[1]
"Enchanted" by Criseyde (53), in his writings he offers a reading of the poem
that is a "masculine response" to this "attractive" woman (64); like Troilus and
the narrator, he is one of "those who love Criseide." Indeed, he claims that "al-
most every male reader of the poem" (9) falls in love with her, and he explicitly
fashions his analysis as a reenactment of the stages of the narrator's falling in
and out of love (92):

> In . . . this paper I shall be following the narrator in his endeavor to avoid
> [the "moralitee" of *Troilus*], and indeed shall be eagerly abetting him in
> trying to avoid it, and even pushing him away when he finally accepts it.

[. . . .] Finding Criseyde "charming" (53 and passim), albeit enigmatic and
finally incapable of providing lasting fulfillment, Donaldson openly embraces
his vicarious response to the poem. He exuberantly declares that his reading is
subjective, an expression of his masculine desires. Amorous behavior provides
metaphors for much of Donaldson's criticism and, indeed, for his conceptual-
ization of the foundational enterprise in medieval literary studies, the editorial
setting of texts: in "The Psychology of Editors of Middle English Texts,"
printed in *Speaking of Chaucer*, he likens the selection of one manuscript read-
ing over another to the selection of a wife. The text is a woman—a bride, in
fact; the editor, a restless husband; and textual editing, a metaphorical court-
ship and marriage, fraught with "powerful charms," allurements, and disen-
chantments (109, 112).

But such unabashed amorousness is the last thing that D.W. Robertson, Jr.,
would think appropriate to critical analyses of medieval literature. Whereas he
has characterized modern literature as appealing to parts of us "below the

---

[1] E. Talbot Donaldson, "The Masculine Narrator and Four Women of Style," "Criseide
and Her Narrator," and "The Ending of 'Troilus'," in *Speaking of Chaucer*—hereafter cited by
page number in the text; "Criseyde Becoming Cressida: *Troilus and Criseyde* and *Troilus and
Cressida*," in *The Swan at the Well: Shakespeare Reading Chaucer* (New Haven: Yale Univ. Press,
1985). See also his "Cressid False, Criseyde Untrue: An Ambiguity Revisited," in *Poetic
Traditions of the English Renaissance*, ed. Maynard Mack and George deForest Lord (New
Haven: Yale Univ. Press, 1982), 67–83; "Briseis, Briseida, Criseyde, Cresseid, Cressid:
Progress of a Heroine," in *Chaucerian Problems and Perspectives*, ed. Edward Vasta and Z. P.
Thundy (Notre Dame: Univ. of Notre Dame Press, 1970), 1–12; and *Chaucer's Poetry*.

belt," reading medieval literature, Robertson contends, is essentially an intellec-
tual experience, and he denies that any merely emotional response forms a
valid basis for a reading.[2] Following Augustine in *De doctrina Christiana*,
Robertson takes a certain pleasure in the text, in the decoding of its figurative
language—in the challenge of passing through the *littera* of the text to the
sententia (of *caritas*) beneath. But this "pleasure" Augustine finds quite inexpli-
cable,[3] and Robertson insists that it is very limited—it is strictly an "intellec-
tual" pleasure. Solving the puzzle of the *littera* inspires the mind with a love of
the *sententia* found within—a love that itself originates in God, not in human
feelings. The "emotional" or "subjective" are Romantic and post-Romantic lit-
erary preoccupations; thus he bases his analyses on the gap between the mod-
ern sensibility and the medieval mind. Medieval people were not like us, and
we are mistaken to see ourselves in medieval literature, he maintains: "If we
impose our own terms on it, we might as well be studying ourselves rather than
the past" ("Method," 80). Robertson's Middle Ages of "quiet hierarchies"
(*Preface*, 51) is founded on Augustine and Boethius, and his medieval aesthetic
is derived essentially from *De doctrina Christiana* and the Christian exegetical
tradition.

Augustinianism thus dominates his discussion of *Troilus and Criseyde* in *A
Preface to Chaucer*. To begin, Robertson points to the distinction between medi-
eval and modern concepts of tragedy (*Preface*, 473–74):

> Medieval tragedy is, of course, very different from modern tragedy, in
> which the suffering protagonist becomes an emblem of humanity crushed
> by the mysterious iniquities of a strangely recalcitrant world. But to the
> medieval mind, that hostile world of fortuitous events was an illusion gen-
> erated by misdirected love.... To attribute a modern conception of trag-

---

[2] Robertson['s] [. . . .] major statement of his critical method is his *Preface*, hereafter cited
in the text. See, further, his "Historical Criticism" (1950); "Some Observations on Method
in Literary Studies" (1969), hereafter cited as "Method" in the text; and "The Allegorist and
the Aesthetician" (1967)—all reprinted in his collection, *Essays in Medieval Culture* (Princeton:
Princeton Univ. Press, 1980)—for briefer, specific statements of method.

There have been many critiques of Robertson's method, in various forms (lectures, book
reviews, introductory chapters of critical studies); I do not attempt a full critique here. For
a few of the most cogent, see Donaldson, "Patristic Exegesis in the Criticism of Medieval
Literature: The Opposition," in *Critical Approaches to Medieval Literature: Selected Papers from
the English Institute, 1958-1959*, ed. Dorothy Bethurum (New York: Columbia Univ. Press,
1960), 1–26; R.S. Crane, "On Hypotheses in 'Historical Criticism': Apropos of Certain
Contemporary Medievalists," in his *Idea of the Humanities and Other Essays Critical and
Historical*, 2 vols. (Chicago: Univ. of Chicago Press, 1967), 2:236–60; Donald R. Howard,
review of *Fruyt and Chaf*, by Robertson and B. F. Huppé, *Speculum* 39 (1964): 537–41; David
Aers, *PIERS PLOWMAN and Christian Allegory* (London: Arnold, 1975); Paul Theiner, "Robert-
sonianism and the Idea of Literary History," *SMC* 6/7 (1976): 195–204; and, most recently,
Lee Patterson, "Historical Criticism and the Development of Chaucer Studies," in *Negotiating
the Past: The Historical Understanding of Medieval Literature* (Madison: Univ. of Wisconsin
Press, 1987), 3–39.

[3] See Augustine, *De doctrina Christiana* 2.6.7–8, ed. J. Martin, CC 32 (Turnhout: Brepols,
1962), 35–36.

edy to Chaucer would be to deny his faith in the providential order and to make him, in his cultural environment, a shallow fool.

Troilus is a medieval tragedy whose characters are motivated by *cupiditas*, misdirected love. Its "moralitee" is simple and absolute: love of earthly things for themselves (not in service of love for God) is sinful and destructive.[4]

The simplicity and absoluteness of this "moralitee" are a reflection of the simplicity and absoluteness of the Middle Ages as a cultural whole. In essay after essay, Robertson assiduously defends that cultural whole from the historical imperialism of modern readers ("Method," 77):

> The integrity of past structures must be respected. . . . Above all, it seems obvious that we shall need to exhibit far greater reluctance than we have usually shown to impose our own formulations . . . as though they were universal truths.

But perhaps this protection of the past exceeds scholarly historical concern: the diction of his analysis of *Troilus*, as well as of his other analyses, suggest that the discrepancy he formulates between the modern period and the Middle Ages is invested with deep feeling which goes explicitly unacknowledged (see *Preface*, 3–51, esp. 30–33, 38–44, 51). As he puts it in the passages quoted above, the modern age deals in "mysterious iniquities," "strang[e] recalcitran[ce]," "crushed" humanity, "suffering"; in the Middle Ages, such a "hostile world of fortuitous events" is only, comfortingly, "an illusion." And if the modern age is not seen as mysteriously terrifying (the exaggerated diction here suggests parody, even cynicism), the suggestion is that it is silly—"shallow," foolish—in comparison to the Middle Ages. Most of all, the modern age is characterized by solipsism, Robertson insists time and time again; by looking at the literature of another age in its own terms, we might be able to extricate ourselves from "that rancid solipsistic pit into which the major tendencies of post-romantic thought have thrust us" ("Method," 82).

Striking, then, in his analysis of *Troilus* is his focus on Troilus as modern man (*Preface*, 497): the suffering Troilus of Book 5 becomes

> the "aimlessly drifting megalopolitan man" of the modern philosophers, the frustrated, neurotic, and maladjusted hero of modern fiction, an existentialist for whom Being itself, which he has concentrated in his own person, becomes dubious.

Troilus, whose mind is a "mirour" (1.365), whose love of Criseyde Robertson sees as only narcissistic, only solipsistic, becomes in effect a figure of the bad literary critic who reads his own modern attitudes into the medieval work—the critic who, as Robertson puts it at the beginning of his book, turns "history into a mirror which is of significance to us only insofar as we may perceive in it what appear to be foreshadowings of ourselves" (*Preface*, 3). Only after his

---

[4] For the latest extended statement of this position, see Wood, *Elements*.

death and ascension into the eighth sphere does Troilus attain a fuller view of earthly life and detachment from that solipsistic self—the same sort of "equanimity and detachment" that Robertson recommends to the literary critic ("Method," 84)—and laugh at "all those who take a sentimental attitude toward such love as that between Troilus and Criseyde" (*Preface*, 501). That is, Troilus, redeemed critic, laughs at *us*, modern readers culturally steeped in sentimentality.

So *Troilus and Criseyde* provides a corrective for the post-Romantic critical sensibility. Although this is in part merely to say that Robertson sees the function of the poem and of medieval literature in general as didactic, it might also serve to suggest that there is a good deal of self-loathing in his reading. Robertson would want to identify himself with Troilus the redeemed critic, of course, but he also must see himself as that condemned solipsistic figure; he is constantly working to get out of that "pit" in which he thinks we all live in the modern age. Such disgust with the modern self is registered most often in Robertson's writings as a disgust with sexuality. For, in Robertson's eyes, Chaucer's main literary preoccupation—his "o sentence"—is the analysis and condemnation of cupidity, most often bad love in amorous relationships; and of all the kinds of love the Middle Ages knew, we as moderns know only "that carnal impulse which, as Virgil says, we share with the animals" (*Preface*, 462). Chaucer's works would seem to exist to condemn the very urges that, according to Robertson, identify and define us as modern people.

Thus Troilus's erotic impulses—modern man that he is—are seen as entirely bestial; the Boethian hymn he sings at the end of Book 3 is blasphemous. We know what Troilus really wants, and it's a "deed of darkness" (*Preface*, 492): when Troilus exclaims, "O paleys desolat, / O hous of houses whilom best ihight, / O paleys empty and disconsolat, / O thow lanterne of which queynt is the light" (5.540–43), Robertson suggests that "the ironic pun on 'queynt' is a bitter comment on what it is that Troilus actually misses" (*Preface*, 500). The bitterness of Robertson's own comment here suggests that his continual preoccupation with and condemnation of sexuality may be at bottom a recoil from the female body. It is telling that although both lovers come off badly in Robertson's view—both are cynical, nasty, and brutish—Troilus, I believe, is seen with the lesser compassion throughout the analysis. And, tellingly in Robertson's hierarchical scheme, Troilus is the one who resigns his princely status and enslaves himself to a demeaning passion for a woman. The unhinging, destabilizing effects of the woman—finally, of her "queynt"—on Troilus are what is to Robertson most abhorrent in the poem.

Troilus does finally achieve the properly hierarchical view of fleshly love, of course, and it's the desire for that "queynt" that must be put in its place. Chaucer's urgent admonition in the poem's Epilogue is, Robertson maintains, his "o sentence" in all the major poetry. Robertson concludes the analysis, and his book (*Preface*, 503), by lamenting that

In our own society, although a few poets like Mr. Eliot continue to emphasize the value of love in Christian terms, the urgent need for a love that is neither lust nor avarice has now become the affair of psychologists and sociologists.

Robertson's reading of the literature of the Middle Ages is informed by a nostalgia for a prior, perfect time—a time of orderly and rational love, a time when sexuality was fully governed by the reason, a prelapsarian time such as Augustine imagined Eden to be.[5] Robertson flees from the unfulfilling, the disorderly, the unsettling in modern experience—excessive emotionality; irrational sentimentality; rampant eros; and sexuality, especially of the female "queynt"— and embraces totality. In a process which Lee Patterson calls "ruthless totalizing,"[6] Robertson's construction of a monolithic intellectual structure that is the literature of the Middle Ages recovers a unity lost circa 1400 and restores the sexuality of people to its fully human—not bestial—realm, thus fulfilling the "urgent need for a love that is neither lust nor avarice."

While Donaldson gleefully announces his emotional entrance into the text, then, Robertson does not. One way of characterizing differences in the styles of these two critical approaches (picking up on Robertson's expressions of distrust, his suspicions of modern critics' "concealed self-study" ["Method," 821])[7] is to invoke Paul Ricoeur's contrast between the "hermeneutic of suspicion" and the "hermeneutic of recovery." The hermeneutic of suspicion— reductive, demystifying—reveals the essential "poverty" of our natures; the hermeneutic of recovery discovers a "full[ness]" of meaning.[8] Robertson posits and reads against a sense of modern spiritual emptiness and sheer carnality; Donaldson discovers a rich complexity of lived experience. "Willingness to suspect, willingness to listen; vow of rigor, vow of obedience"—Ricoeur's aphorism (27) captures the feeling of the two critics at work: Robertson, vigorously demonstrating that the text—no matter what it *says*—always carries the message of *caritas*; and Donaldson, patiently following, even imitating, the text. Like psychoanalytic interpretations, from which Ricoeur derives the hermeneutic of suspicion, Robertson's readings aren't "falsifiable," as R.S. Crane has seen; since the text can always mean something other than what it says, the exegesis can't be proven wrong.[9] This exegesis that is always "right," that has all the answers, is very different from Donaldson's hesitancy in front of the text (*Chaucer's Poetry*, 966):

Things are difficult to see steadily for more than a short period, re-appear

---

[5] Augustine discusses prelapsarian sexuality fully in *De civitate Dei* 14.10–26, ed. Bernardus Dombart and Alphonsus Kalb, CC 47 (Turnhout: Brepols, 1955), 430–50.

[6] Patterson, *Negotiating the Past*, 34.

[7] In "The Allegorist and the Aesthetician" (101), Robertson links post-Romantic aestheticism with Mussolini, Hitler, and Stalin.

[8] Paul Ricoeur, *Freud and Philosophy: An Essay on Interpretation*, trans. Denis Savage (New Haven: Yale Univ. Press, 1970), 27.

[9] Crane, "On Hypotheses in 'Historical Criticism,' " esp. 254–58.

in changed shape, become illusory, vanish; as the poem progresses one finds oneself groping more and more in a world where forms are indistinct but have infinite suggestiveness.

Donaldson delights in the text's indistinctness, its "infinite suggestiveness." And Criseyde, ever fascinating, never completely understood (83), focus of desire in the narrative, is for him the emblem of that textual indeterminacy. But for all his delicate nurturing of poetic complexity, for all his understanding of the erotic instabilities of the text and his alertness to critical involvement in those textual erotics, I finally sense a desire for order, a desire to control a threateningly uncontrollable libido, in Donaldson's analysis not entirely unlike that in Robertson's. Despite his claims of identification with the narrator and Troilus as lovers of Criseyde, Donaldson is not, as are they, betrayed by the lady. The critic can see farther than the limited narrator and Troilus, who learn the hard way that Criseyde is a thing of this unstable world. Indeed, this critical vision makes him as all-seeing as the poet himself, and we might suggest that Donaldson identifies most deeply with that omniscient poet whom he formalistically posits as locus of creative power and textual control. The critic's own plain speaking, his simple-but-elegant style, and his ability to work language on several different levels (all epitomized in the title of his collected essays, *Speaking of Chaucer*), are intimated in his description of the omniscient Chaucer: he speaks (47) of

> Chaucer's ability to describe things simultaneously from several distinct points of view while seeming to see them from only one point of view, and thus to show in all honesty the complexity of things while preserving the appearance of that stylistic simplicity which we feel to be so honest and trustworthy.

This could be, as well, the lucid and honest Donaldson. (And we note in passing that, like the poet, he includes a "retraction" at the end of a new and risky work: concluding "Chaucer the Pilgrim," he remarks that "it is now necessary to retract" some earlier comments about the Prioress [11].)

Donaldson is fascinated by Criseyde precisely because he sees her as the essential indeterminacy of the text. In this way he associates textual "slydynge" as well as erotic errancy with the feminine. But he has Criseyde's potentially disruptive "corage," and therefore the poem's "infinite suggestiveness," under control.[10] "Attractive women" such as Criseyde, he states, have the power to make fools of "us male critics," as do beautiful and difficult poems; some measure of "complexity," "ambiguity," "slydynge" is nice, but some control is also necessary to reduce the threat of real disruption that unlimited "slydynge"

---

[10] For a major study of the poem in which similar moves to control the female character are made, see Winthrop Wetherbee, *Poets*. But Wetherbee is, significantly, aware that his focus on Troilus must inevitably lead him to read Criseyde *in malo*; see chapter 6, "Character and Action: Criseyde and the Narrator." McAlpine (*Genre*, 230–33) also analyzes critical control of Criseyde.

poses to the reader who values a New Critical poetic whole. It is Donaldson's formalism, in this sense functioning like Robertson's historicism, that provides the structure for this delimitation and control. Donaldson's is less obviously a totalizing enterprise than is the essentially positivistic historicism of Robertson; nevertheless, the totalizing is there: Donaldson's criticism can entertain some ambiguity and indeterminacy because it has already, in an analytically prior move, posited an author to whom all signifying responsibility can be referred as "the origin, and the proprietor of [the text's] significance," as Patterson puts it.[11]

It may be, further, that such a concept of an omniscient poet can itself be seen as part of a patriarchal literary project: with its concern to authorize, legitimate, and, finally, delimit meanings, the concept of an author as all-controlling locus of meaning promotes patriarchal values of final authority, fidelity, and legitimacy.[12] Certainly, as Donaldson invokes it, the formalistic model of omniscient poet manipulating his characters not only establishes the poet as firm center of meaning in the poem but particularly emphasizes that poet's manipulation and control of the female character. . . . "You can never understand a woman" is a way of understanding her. Criseyde becomes a sign of instability, compared to and subsumed by Heavenly stability, and the poem's totality is asserted and assured.

Donaldson began, we recall, by characterizing his response as a "masculine" one, and carefully stated that "*almost* every male reader" falls in love with the lady. This leads to intriguing questions: What about the female reader of this text? Will she love Criseyde, too? Or, as Criseyde herself fears, will women hate Criseyde most of all? What about that male reader who *doesn't* fall for her? Is he not sufficiently "masculine," or is he just a churl? It would have been interesting to hear Donaldson approach these questions, as aware as he was of the subjectivity of the critic and the importance of gender; but he seems in fact to have forgotten about the gender-specificity of his claims. By the end of his analysis he has universalized and naturalized *his* response so as to make it the basis of *everyone's* response, speaking of "human love, and by a sorry corollary everything human" (92).

---

[11] Patterson, *Negotiating the Past*, 24, writing specifically about Charles Muscatine's criticism. [. . . .]

[12] Some feminist literary theory, especially French feminist theory, has focused on critical categories such as unity, realism, filiation, authorial omniscience, and critical mastery of the text, as loci of patriarchal criticism. A few particular examples include Shoshana Felman, "Women and Madness: The Critical Phallacy," *Diacritics* 5 (1975): 2–10, for a critique of realism and unity; Barbara Johnson, "Teaching Ignorance: *L'École des femmes*," *YFS* 63 (1982): 165–82, on pedagogical mastery, which can be extended to the "single authoritative teacher" (182) that is the omniscient poet of the New Critics; Hélène Cixous and Catherine Clément, *The Newly Born Woman*, trans. Betsy Wing (Minneapolis: Univ. of Minnesota Press, 1986), especially "A Woman Mistress," concerning mastery in the transmission of knowledge; and Luce Irigaray, *This Sex Which Is Not One*, trans. Catherine Porter with Carolyn Burke (Ithaca: Cornell Univ. Press, 1985), indicting the logic of discourse and attempting to discover how to speak a language of the female body, undoing representation altogether.

So Donaldson and Robertson, theoretically antagonistic, in practice make very similar critical moves: a vigorous limitation of the disturbing, a rigorous structure controlling the unstable and threateningly destabilizing, are the foundations of both approaches.[13] [....] In both cases the delimitation of the text's meaning is achieved through a rejection or containment of what is constituted as feminine.

How are we to explain this phenomenon—the fact that the opposite sides of this critical dispute over reading the poem seem to converge, and that they do so around the issue of the feminine? A clue is perhaps found in Donaldson's explicitly fashioning his reading as a sort of reenactment of the narrator's response to the story of Troilus and Criseyde. For the narrator is a reader, too, a translator who reads, comments on, and questions "Lollius" and other "olde bokes." This is, as the narrator stresses, a Latin text, a pagan fable, written in a strange language and depicting the unfamiliar customs of the ancients. It is, in other words, that captive alien woman of Deuteronomy 21:10–13 who provides the model for Saint Jerome's Christian hermeneutics. [....] Just as the alien woman must be stripped, taken as the spoils of battle, and prepared for the bridal, made ready to marry the triumphant Israelite warrior and become a matron of his household, so, says Jerome, must the classical text be stripped of its eloquent, seductive letter to reveal its naked truth, the wisdom that can be put to Christian use.[14]

The Christian narrator of *Troilus and Criseyde* might be expected to strip this alien woman of her garments of captivity, to pare her nails, shave her head, and scrub her down with niter—that is, to remove the pagan fable, its eloquence and mores, and discover underneath the fecund body of truth. He does not, however; the narrator at the outset of the poem suggests instead that the Christian "charite" in which he lives can be itself enhanced by the telling of the pagan tale of Troilus's woe (1.49). But not having divested this text of its feminine seductiveness, he responds in his reading to its carnal delights, the delights represented in the love story as well as the delights of narrative description and pacing—all the pleasures of the letter. And not having been divested, she remains an alien woman; the narrator does not domesticate her and, consequently, finds that her seductive *littera* won't issue in any fruitful *sententia*. It is only then, at the very end of the poem, that he strips and reclothes the woman, marries and properly domesticates her, and addresses his future progeny. He derives the "moralitee" in a critical move that closely parallels the one both Robertson and Donaldson make, a rigorous control of the dangerous feminine. And as we'll see, this containment of or turning away from the feminine also de-

[13] Richard Waswo, in "The Narrator of *Troilus and Criseyde*" (*ELH* 50 [1983]: 1–25), in a keen argument about irony and the Epilogue to the poem, demonstrates that critics who ostensibly oppose Robertson's reading nonetheless agree with and proceed according to his basic contention that the Epilogue is a seamless part of the whole poem, and that there are no essential contradictions in the poem.

[14] See letter 70, to Magnus, in *Epistulae*, ed. I. Hilberg, CSEL 54 (Vienna: F. Tempsky, 1910), 1:702.

scribes Pandarus's verbal rejection of the female character in the "text" that he has created and that he "reads"—the "old romaunce" of Troilus and Criseyde.

By figuring the role of the reader in the narrative, Chaucer makes the act of critical reading a major preoccupation of the entire poem. *Troilus and Criseyde* in fact provides a powerful analysis of reading—of masculine reading—and I take the convergence of these two disparate but masculine critics, Robertson and Donaldson, to be a precise corroboration of this analysis. Masculine reading in *Troilus and Criseyde* is dominated at last by a desire to contain instability, carnal appetite—those things that [. . . .] medieval writers (and their descend- ants, modern critics) associate with *femina*. The narrator, Pandarus, and Troi- lus, too, all characterized as readers of feminine texts, turn away at last from the disruptive feminine toward orderly, hierarchical visions of divine love in which desire is finally put to rest. Such efforts at containment, Chaucer shows in the poem, are urgent emotional responses to the rough disillusionments of carnal involvement, of involvement with the feminine.

Seen from a larger perspective, however, these efforts are ironically unneces- sary, even redundant. The "slydynge" of Criseyde's "corage," as we shall see, turns out to work in conformity to masculine structures of control, to work as a function of her structural role as woman in Troy's patriarchal society.[15] Feminine "slydynge," as we'll see, does not actually threaten the power struc- tures in this narrative. Pandarus, alone of all our masculine readers, recognizes this, and thus his response to Criseyde, expedient and tactical as it is, provides a perspective within the poem on "reading like a man."

But let us turn first to the narrator, to trace the arc of his pleasure in the letter of his text, in the garb of that alien woman.

2

The narrator presents himself at the outset of the poem as the uninvolved translator of the old, approved story of Troilus and Criseyde, emotionally, geo- graphically, and temporally removed from his "matere." Time and again he avows his strict fidelity to his *auctor*—in a tone, though, that indicates something beyond strict fidelity. The narrator's *own* action of relaying the auctorial mes- sage is signaled at such times, of course: our awareness is drawn to the narrator as he tells us he's reading and retelling. But further, he seems to take pleasure in what he doesn't read: with delight he draws attention to what his *auctor* doesn't say. The unknown detail is provocative, suggestive, perhaps even mildly titillating: the presence of the unknown—whether Criseyde has children or not,

---

[15] For an analysis of the poem that reads Criseyde in relation to the exigencies of Trojan society, see David Aers, "Chaucer's Criseyde: Woman in Society, Woman in Love," in *Chaucer*, Chapter 5. [. . . .] Aers argues throughout his book against readings that would de-psychologize Criseyde; I set Criseyde's subjectivity in the larger frame of her structural function within patriarchy, which itself de-emphasizes her psychological value.

what exactly the lovers' letters say—is not disruptive of the incipient love affair or the narrative but is itself generative, exciting.

"The pleasure of the text," writes Roland Barthes, describing a model of reading more appropriate to the narrator's choices here than models of *stripping* the body of the text (in Macrobius, Jerome, Augustine, Richard of Bury), "is not the pleasure of the corporeal striptease or of narrative suspense," which would lead directly to full revelation. Rather, "it is the very rhythm of what is read and what is not read that creates the pleasure of the great narratives." Not totality but "intermittence" is the figure of pleasure in reading, as Barthes puts it:

> The intermittence of skin flashing between two articles of clothing (trousers and sweater), between two edges (the open-necked shirt, the glove and the sleeve); it is this flash itself which seduces, or rather: the staging of an appearance-as-disappearance.[16]

Immediate revelation of the whole body of wisdom is not what the Barthesian reader or the narrator of *Troilus and Criseyde* seeks. The garb itself—the unfolding narrative—is the site of bliss.

Thus the narrator's careful pacing of the love affair's unfolding reveals his progressively escalating personal interest, a growing emotional involvement. He skips over details extrinsic to the love affair (1.145–47); he stops the flow of narrative to tell "every word" of the *Canticus Troili* (1.393–420), and he hastens the progress of the courtship in Book 2, telling not every word this time, but "th'effect, as fer as I kan understonde" (2.1220) of Criseyde's first letter to Troilus. Such narrative moves suggest the narrator's incipient interest in the text's own surface eloquence.

So although the narrator's reading and retelling of Lollius purports to be a straightforward, disinterested rendering of the Latin text into English, it turns out to be a record of the narrator's gradual seduction by the text's letter, by its feminine charms. His involvement with the carnality of this text is apparent not only in these rhythms of the disposition of the narrative, the text's eloquent surface; it is thematized as vicarious erotic response to the love story itself. Without a lover of his own, he takes pleasure in the reading and rendering of others' pleasures; he substitutes their pleasures for his own. Erotic substitution—vicariousness—indeed defines his whole poetic project in *Troilus and Criseyde* as he sets it out in the proem to Book 1: he will take pleasure in the advancement of the "causes" of lovers in his audience; he substitutes their amorous successes for his lack of amorous action. Further, the act of translation is itself both the substitution of one language for another, and, in the terms of classical rhetoric, the substitution of an "improper" term in the place of a "proper" one.[17]

---

[16] Roland Barthes, *The Pleasure of the Text*, trans. Richard Miller (New York: Hill and Wang, 1975), 10. [. . . .]

[17] *Translatio*, according to Quintilian and Donatus, denoted trope or figure of thought

We can see that the narrator's act of translation is itself eroticized both as it engages the surface of the narrative and as it finds a locus in the fable for his substitute erotic identification—his vicarious pleasures. His protestations that he is making a faithful translation of his author, simply a straightforward substitution of English for Latin, serve in fact to cover up the deeper substitutions he has made. Such protestations are abundant in the first part of the poem: let us consider, for example, his remarks about his rendition of the *Canticus Troili*:

> And of his song naught only the sentence,
> As writ myn auctour called Lollius,
> But pleinly, save oure tonges difference,
> I dar wel seyn, in al that Troilus
> Seyde in his song, loo! every word right thus
> As I shal seyn; and whoso list it here,
> Loo, next this vers he may it fynden here.   1.393–99

Lollius as source is mentioned for the first time in the poem here, and the narrator asserts that he is in accord with that source. In fact, he is *more* than absolutely faithful: the narrator gives the particular words of a song of which his *auctor* gives only the "sentence."[18] Where *did* the words of Troilus's song come from? The narrator suggests that he can know exactly what Troilus said *without a source*: Lollius is cited but at the same time seems to be unnecessary, superfluous. It seems that the narrator must have some channel of direct communication with Troilus: the parallel syntax brings the two characters into close relation: "al that Troilus seyde ... I shal seyn." The narrator's claim of historically faithful, word-for-word translation here works as a cover for his

---

in general, as well as allegory, metaphor, metonymy, and other tropes in particular. That substitution is the mechanism of *translatio* is apparent in Quintilian (*Institutio oratoria* 9.1.4–5, ed. and trans. H. E. Butler, Loeb Classical Library [Cambridge: Harvard Univ. Press, 1969], 348–51):

> Est igitur tropos sermo a naturali et principali significatione translatus ad aliam ornandae orationis gratia, vel, ut plerique grammatici finiunt, dictio ab eo loco, in quo propria est, translata in eum, in quo propria non est. ... Quare in tropis ponuntur verba alia pro aliis.

> The name of *trope* is applied to the transference of expressions from their natural and principal signification to another, with a view to the embellishment of style or, as the majority of grammarians define it, the transference of words and phrases from the place which is strictly theirs to another to which they do not properly belong. ... Therefore the substitution of one word for another is placed among *tropes*.

See also Donatus, *Ars grammatica* 3.6, ed. Henricus Keil (Hildesheim: Georg Olms, 1961), 4:399. Geoffrey of Vinsauf's discussion of *ornatus difficilis* also makes it clear that poetic trope depends on the substitution of one signifier's attributes for another (*Poetria nova*, lines 765–67a [in *Les Arts poétiques du XIIe et du XIIIe siècle*, ed. E. Faral (Paris: Honoré Champion, 1958), 221]). See Eugene Vance, "Chaucer, Spenser, and the Ideology of Translation," *CRCL* 8 (1981): 217–38, later expanded in his *Mervelous Signals: Poetics and Sign Theory in the Middle Ages* (Lincoln: Univ. of Nebraska Press, 1986), 311–51. [. . . .]

[18] I follow the punctuation of this stanza in F. N. Robinson, *Works of Geoffrey Chaucer*, 2nd ed. [. . . .]

deeper involvement, his deeper substitution: it masks his identification with the lover of the woman, Criseyde.

But even when the narrator claims that he can't follow his *auctor* strictly, word for word—can't "tellen al . . . of his excellence"—his act of *translatio* expresses his carnal delight in the text. While describing the scene of the consummation of Troilus and Criseyde's love, the narrator pauses to make his literary intentions explicit:

> But soth is, though I kan nat tellen al,
> As kan myn auctour, of his excellence,
> Yet have I seyd, and God toforn, and shal
> In every thyng the grete of his sentence;
> And if that ich, at Loves reverence,
> Have any word in eched for the beste,
> Doth therwithal right as youreselven leste.   3.1324–30

Translation, according to medieval translators, could proceed either by rendering "every word right thus," a process the narrator alludes to in his rendition of Troilus's song, or by rendering "the grete of (var. "al holly") [the] sentence," as he states here. Jean de Meun, for example, makes this distinction in the preface to his translation of Boethius's *De consolatione*;[19] and Jean de Hareng, in the afterword to his *Rettorique de Marc Tulles Cyceron*, a translation of the anonymous *Rhetorica ad Herennium* and two books of the *De inventione*, states that sometimes he translates word for word, but more often he tries to achieve the "sentence." A word-for-word translation is not adequate for rendering obscure passages, he claims, and in translating these, he must "sozjoindre et acreistre"—just as the narrator, here in Book 3, suggests that he has "in eched" (added in) a word or two "for the beste," in achieving his author's "sentence."[20]

Fidelity to the authorial sentence is typically emphasized in medieval discussions of translations.[21] But *this* protestation of fidelity is not only a conventional

---

[19] Jean de Meun writes in his preface that he took as a commandment Philip IV's suggestion that he express "la sentence" of the author without following too closely "les paroles du latin." He explains that a word-for-word rendering of the Latin into French would still have been too obscure to those readers who do not know Latin well. See "Boethius' *De consolatione* by Jean de Meun," ed. V.L. Dedeck-Héry, *MS* 14 (1952): 168.

[20] Jean de Hareng shows himself to be very sensitive to the particular character of each language (Latin and French), and his sense of the difficulty of translation comes through in his afterword. As closely as he can, he states, he follows the author's manner of treatment of the subject, but it is not possible to follow it absolutely, since properties of diction and syntax vary from language to language. Consequently, the translator must know the peculiarities of each language, writes Jean, and he will find that sometimes it is appropriate to translate "parole por parole," more often "sentence por sentence," and sometimes, because of the obscurity of the "sentence," it is appropriate to add and subtract. See Jean's afterword in "Notice sur la *Rhétorique de Cicéron*, traduite par Maître Jean D'Antioche, ms. 590 de Musée Condé," by Leopold Delisle, in *Notices et extraits* (Paris: Klincksieck, 1899), 36:261; and in "Humanisme et traductions au Moyen Age," by Jacques Monfrin, *Journal des savants* (1963): 169.

[21] On the model of *translatio studii*, medieval translation was seen as the handing down

statement: the narrator's act of translation is an expression of his carnal love. Thus we see that his strategy of "eching in" is enunciated at the moment of the lovers' highest bliss. Just as the idea of word-for-word translation is used in the service of his own identification with Troilus as lover of a woman, the idea of relaying his author's sentence is expressed at the moment of his deepest vicarious response to the tale. [....] Using fidelity as a translator to cover for his erotic engagement, he protests that, having told of the weary trials of the lovers, he must continue to follow his auctor in relating their joys (3.1191–97). And just after Criseyde cries to Troilus, "Welcome, my knyght, my pees, my suffisaunce!" and we are told that the lovers that night "felten in love the grete worthynesse," the narrator bursts out:

> O blisful nyght, of hem so longe isought,
> How blithe unto hem bothe two thow weere!
> Why nad I swich oon with my soule ybought,
> Ye, or the leeste joie that was theere?   3.1317–20

Then follows, at this climactic time for the lovers, the stanza in which the narrator confesses that he *might* have "in eched" a word or two; and, following that, there is a further stanza yet about his act of translation ("For myn wordes, heere and every part, / I speke hem alle under correccioun" [3.1331–36]). The narrator's *translatio* is not merely flat fidelity to the sentence; it combines the textual eroticism of intermittence with vicarious pleasure in the love affair. The act of translation is *his* version of consummation. Reading and relaying the fable, adoring the seductively clad woman, is a substitute activity with a very real erotics of its own.

But the delights of intermittence, like the pleasures of Troilus and Criseyde's love, are short-lived. We note that the narrator's delight in what he does not read and in auctorial hints lessens as he comes to Criseyde's betrayal. As we have seen with the critics, particularly Donaldson, instability and uncertainty in the fable are centered in Criseyde; the necessary qualifications of the worth of the fable stem from dissatisfactions with the female character. The feminine, again, is the letter's uncontrollability—both its ambiguous or uncertain details and its final, unalterable outcome—especially as it is concentrated in Criseyde. The pleasurable rhythm—"I read on, I skip, I look up, I dip in again"[22]—is replaced by strain and discomfort, aloofness, doubt, and disagreement with his "olde bokes." In fact, we see in the narrator's treatment of Criseyde throughout the narrative a tendency to fill in the blanks where she is concerned, a nervousness that tends to foreclose the pleasure that those seductive gaps might afford. We have seen that an uncertainty early on, in Book 1, opens up

---

of authoritative sentence from past to present: the received idea was transferred to a contemporary context, historical differences unnoticed in the service of sentence. See Douglas Kelly, "*Translatio Studii*: Translation, Adaptation, and Allegory in Medieval French Literature," *PQ* 57 (1978): 287–310, esp. 291, for a discussion of *translatio* as a literary method of transferring received ideas. [....]

[22] Barthes, *The Pleasure of the Text*, 12.

regarding Criseyde's maternity and that it is left open, apparently unproblem-
atic; indeed, not to know all is even tantalizing. But the narrator's interjection
in Book 2, his defense of Criseyde against potential detractors, functions to
close gaps that haven't even opened: it is a massive explanatory effort, designed
to answer questions before they have arisen (that is, questions that begin to nag
the narrator himself): "Now *myghte* som envious jangle thus" (2.666; my empha-
sis). If some uncertainties are still pleasurable in Book 3 (why Criseyde didn't
ask Troilus to rise, for example), they become uncomfortable in Book 4; and
by Book 5 these lacunae have become dark pools where doubts spawn. Vicari-
ous participant in the affair, the narrator wants to believe in Criseyde; he tries
rather desperately to control those gaping holes, rushing in with a "But trewely
. . ." after nearly every ambiguous or difficult detail that occurs to him:

> Tendre-herted, slydynge of corage;
> *But trewely*, I kan nat telle hire age. 5.825–26 (my emphasis)

> Men seyn—I not—that she yaf hym hire herte.

> *But trewely*, the storie telleth us,
> Ther made nevere woman moore wo
> Than she, whan that she falsed Troilus.
>   5.1050–53 (my emphasis)

Even as the narrator tries to interpret matters to Criseyde's benefit, however,
new vagueness and uncertainties proliferate.

> "But al shal passe; and thus take I my leve."

> *But trewely*, how longe it was bytwene
> That she forsok hym for this Diomede,
> Ther is non auctour telleth it, I wene. . . .
> For though that he bigan to wowe hire soone,
> Er he hire wan, yet was ther more to doone.
>   5.1085–92 (my emphasis)

Pleasurable intermittence is indeed long gone; suspicion and distrust instead
govern his response. Far from taking pleasure in what his books don't mention,
the narrator suggests that the *auctores* might be lying or suppressing informa-
tion (4.15–21; 5.1089–90). He holds himself aloof from them as he writes:
"Men seyn—I not." And when he has finally related Criseyde's betrayal, he
asserts that he would still prefer to defy the tradition and excuse her "for
routhe" (5.1099). But the lady and the fable have disappointed him; the fem-
inine here proves out of his control.

It is at this point, the point at which the seemingly uncontrollable feminine
threatens to destroy masculine lives and masculine projects (the female charac-
ter threatens Troilus's sense of himself; the feminine letter threatens the possi-
bility of deriving any moral worth from this), that the narrator strips off the
fable, in the Epilogue, to reveal the poem's moral message. When the alien
woman isn't stripped, the narrator falls for her carnal charms, but still she

remains Other, alien; undomesticated, she will not become a matron of Israel. That is, the classical fable itself does not impart wisdom that can be appropriated for Christian purposes: it does not provide a strong secular model for imitation. Consequently, the narrator removes the covering, the veil, the tale itself, gradually but completely, at the end of the poem. He apologizes to women for having written this story at all; it is distasteful, and its intent isn't exactly clear ("N'y sey nat this aloonly for thise men, / But moost for wommen that bitraised be / Thorugh false folk" [5.1779-81]). He would rather, he claims, undertake to translate classical texts whose fables are themselves useful for Christian imitation, tales of Penelope and Alceste. And if the tragic has proved unsatisfying, he sends it off, hoping to write a comedy next; "som comedye" (5.1788), with its Dantean divine intimations, would be more useful for Christian readers. He then removes the action from the classical battlefield, elevates the "lighte goost" of Troilus into the heavens, changes the perspective (Troilus's "lokyng") to that of divine Providence, and has Troilus damn his own story—"al oure werk" (5.1823).[23] The fecund body is available only when the feminine seductiveness of the alien woman is distanced and finally removed, only when the narrator separates himself from the possibility of erotic involvement by getting rid of the tale. It is then that the "moralitee" of the tale, as the narrator reads it, can emerge: all is "vanite / To respect of the pleyn felicite / That is in hevene above" (5.1817-19); the joys of the world are brittle, unstable, transitory. When the letter itself is done away with—when the classical "forme of olde clerkis speche" is cast aside—this proper Christian spirit is revealed.

> Lo here, of payens corsed olde rites!
> Lo here, what alle hire goddes may availle!
> Lo here, thise wrecched worldes appetites!
> Lo here, the fyn and guerdoun for travaille
> Of Jove, Appollo, of Mars, of swich rascaille!
> Lo here, the forme of olde clerkis speche
> In poetrie, if ye hire bokes seche!   5.1849-55

The "moral" and "philosophical" spirit of the text is then offered to the correction of Gower and Strode. That spirit will be productive, as the letter has not been: the narrator addresses directly his progeny here. From the alien woman now domesticated by the narrator as reader will issue guidance for "yonge, fresshe folkes" (5.1835).

The spirit underneath the letter has nothing to do with "slydynge" earthly

---

[23] As Wetherbee observes (*Poets*, 236-37), the syntax of the stanza renders unclear who, exactly, is speaking line 1825: it could be the completion of Troilus's thoughts or of the narrator's own, effectively damning his own poetic project:

> And in hymself he lough right at the wo
> Of hem that wepten for his deth so faste,
> And dampned al oure werk that foloweth so
> The blynde lust, the which that may nat laste,
> And sholden al oure herte on heven caste.   5.1821-25

love "that passeth soone as floures faire" (5.1841); it is founded on an insist-
ence on solidity, security, "circumscription" (5.1865). This is an unexception-
able Christian "sentence," and its intention is to increase and multiply the faith
in others. But the alternating vehemence and desperation, the emotional
careening of the narrator in the last ten stanzas of the poem [. . . .] suggest that
Chaucer means to represent this movement toward unity, solidity and closure
as an intense, emotional urgency. As I shall suggest in a moment, *everyone*
needs some such solidity and closure; but after the narrator's amatory partici-
pation in the preceding narrative, his concluding response can well be consid-
ered a markedly gendered one, a masculine response under the pressure of
what he construes as feminine. Chaucer's critique reasons not the need but a
misogynistic formulation and fulfillment of it.

3

If the narrator's act of encountering the letter is erotic, Pandarus's vicarious
love act of bringing Troilus and Criseyde together is represented as literary.
There are in fact many parallels between these two figures: both take vicarious
pleasure in the lovers' pleasure, for example, as many critics have noted.[24]
Most apposite to my purposes, both are characterized as readers. Pandarus's
actions are in fact thoroughly paralleled to the narrator's—climactically, likened
to reading an old romance—and, as a consequence, reading as an activity with
a gendered valence is more fully developed in the poem. Looking at Pandarus
will enable us to determine, finally, *why it matters* that reading be understood in
gender terms: the figure of Pandarus will allow us to perceive this masculine ac-
tivity in relation to the larger social organization of patriarchy of Troy or of any
patriarchal society. But let us first observe the extent of the parallels between
the narrator and Pandarus, and therefore the thoroughness with which Chau-
cer associates reading in *Troilus and Criseyde* with masculine control of the fem-
inine.

The narrator is not the only excited onlooker in the consummation scene in
Book 3: Pandarus, too, is loudly present. His presence is obtrusive, his vicari-
ous enjoyment almost obscene. He has, of course, contrived the entire event;
throughout the first three books of the poem, his self-interest and pleasure are

---

[24] Various parallels between the narrator and Pandarus have been noticed by critics: see,
for example, Waswo, "The Narrator of *Troilus and Criseyde*"; Nevill Coghill, *The Poet Chaucer*
(1939; reprint London: Oxford Univ. Press, 1950), 75–76; Donaldson, "Criseide and Her
Narrator" and "The Ending of 'Troilus'"; Rowe, *O Love!*; and Carton, "Pandarus' Bed." And
several critics have specifically focused on Pandarus's function as "makere," among them,
Donaldson, "Chaucer's Three 'P's': Pandarus, Pardoner, and Poet," *MQR* 14 (1975): 282–
301; Thomas A. Van, "Chaucer's Pandarus as an Earthly Maker," *SHR* 12 (1978): 89–97; and
Rose A. Zimbardo, "Creator and Created: The Generic Perspective of Chaucer's *Troilus and
Criseyde*," *ChauR* 11 (1977): 283–98. My reading of Pandarus owes much to Muscatine, *French
Tradition*, 137–53.

clearly noticeable in his constant references to the affair that use the first person plural possessive adjective: he speaks of "oure joie." And now, bustling around the lovers in this climactic scene, as he has earlier shuttled to and fro between the lovers, his energy is frenetic, sexual, as the language suggests: "But Pandarus, that so wel koude *feele* / In every thyng, to *pleye* anon bigan" (3.960–61; emphasis mine). Pandarus arranges the scene: he tells the lovers where to kneel and what to say; he even tosses the faint Troilus into Criseyde's bed. Finally he takes his cue to leave the bedside, but he apparently does not even leave the room. The narration of his lying down to sleep immediately follows upon Troilus's taking Criseyde in his arms: the three of them are packed into the stanza as they are into the chamber.[25]

Pandarus's activity, like the narrator's act of translation, provides its own erotic satisfactions. It keeps him physically active, breathless, and sweaty: he leaps, he perspires, he moves back and forth between the two lovers (2.939; 2.1464). Both of these mediating acts, pandering and translating, are substitutes for amorous action—Pandarus and the narrator are both, by their own admission, unsuccessful in love—and both activities yield vicarious pleasures. It's no coincidence that the two characters should describe themselves in the same terms: Pandarus likens himself, as unsuccessful lover advising a would-be-lover, to a whetstone: "A wheston is no kervyng *instrument*, / But yet it maketh sharpe kervyng tolis" (1.631–32; my emphasis). The image allies Pandarus's vicarious amorous role with the narrator's poetic role—it is from Horace's *Ars poetica*, where Horace (ironically) describes his vicarious role as teacher of the poetic art: "So I'll play a whetstone's part.... Though I write naught myself, I will teach the poet's office and duty."[26] And the narrator, in turn, sees himself as the "sorwful *instrument*, / That helpeth loveres, as I kan, to pleyne" (1.10–11; my emphasis).[27]

These lexical links make the amatory charge of literary activity in this poem all the clearer. "Matere," "purpos," and "werk" are used to describe the affair (in a figure taken from Geoffrey of Vinsauf's *Poetria nova*) and the poem (1.1062–71; 1.53; 1.5; 2.16). Critics have noted that Pandarus, in creating his "werk," is much like a poet creating a text, inventing scenes, planning dialogue, "shaping" (2.1363) the plot—a poet being a "shaper" (*scop*) in Old English. But what interests me most is that he reads a thoroughly eroticized text, just as the narrator does: at the consummation scene,

---

[25] And on the morning after, if Pandarus does not actually enjoy Criseyde firsthand he certainly replays a *version* of Troilus's enjoyment of her the night before: Troilus "sodeynly" takes her in his arms (3.1186), and Pandarus "sodeynly" thrusts his arm under her neck (3.1574) as he jokes, pokes, and finally kisses her.

[26] See *Ars poetica*, lines 304–6 (ed. and trans. H. Rushton Fairclough, Loeb Classical Library [Cambridge: Harvard Univ. Press, 1955], 474–77):

> ergo fungar vice cotis, acutum
> reddere quae ferrum valet, exsors ipsa secandi;
> munus et officium, nil scribens ipse, docebo.

[27] It is only a step away from these eroticized "instruments" of literary creation to the "sely instruments" of the Wife of Bath and her husbands.

> with that word he drow hym to the feere,
> And took a light, and fond his contenaunce,
> As for to loke upon an old romaunce.   3.978–80

Pandarus withdraws from the lovers, sits himself down near the fire, and reads the lovers' persons as characters in a script he has himself written—reads them as if *they* constituted "an old romaunce." [....]

Pandarus's final response to the ultimately disappointing affair is, as well, very similar to the narrator's, in verbal form and in emotional dynamics.[28] The extravagance of the emotional expression is shared: Pandarus cries, "I hate, ywys, Criseyde; / And, God woot, I wol hate hire evermoore!" (5.1732–33); the narrator's tone and syntax ("Lo here!", "Swich fyn!") become obsessive. The one rejecting Criseyde, the other doing so and calling on the only unblemished earthly woman, the Virgin, both appeal ultimately to providential order in response to the destabilizations and dissatisfactions of involvement with the feminine—woman and the letter of the text.

There is, of course, another masculine reader of a feminine text in the poem: Troilus. We might see him as a gracious reader of Criseyde, taking the spirit *in bono* even when he cannot understand the letter. In Book 3, for example, in his most explicit equation of woman and text, he suggests that though the "text" of mercy is not easy to read in Criseyde's eyes, it is that kind message that he knows is there and that he will persevere in seeking:

> This Troilus ful ofte hire eyen two
> Gan for to kisse, and seyde, "O eyen clere,
> It weren ye that wroughte me swich wo,
> Ye humble nettes of my lady deere!
> Though ther be mercy writen in youre cheere,
> God woot, the text ful hard is, soth, to fynde!
> How koude ye withouten bond me bynde?"   3.1352–58

Earlier, when he reads her first letter (the exchange of letters constitutes the lovers' intercourse at that point in the affair), he "took al for the beste" (2.1324–27). Even when he senses some "chaunge" in her last letter—the letter being, again, a substitute for Criseyde's body—"fynaly, he ful ne trowen myghte" (5.1632–35). He is unwilling to draw conclusions until he sees the irrefutable ocular proof; and when he does see it, he wails in anguish at the sight: "I ne kan nor may ... unloven yow a quarter of a day!" (5.1696–99). But as I shall suggest more fully in a moment, we might rather see his readings as interpretations attending less to the words or signs and more to what he wants to see—turning away from the difficult, the resistant, or the recalcitrant in making some sense of the text; and he, at last, turns away from earthly woman's love from his vantage on high. Looking down at this little spot of earth, he

---

[28] See Donaldson, "The Ending of 'Troilus,'" 95; and Robert B. Burlin, *Chaucerian Fiction* (Princeton: Princeton Univ. Press, 1977), 131–33. [....]

condemns "blynde lust, the which that may nat laste" and appeals to the surpassing, ever-fixed love in Heaven. In this totalizing impulse—the desire to eliminate instability, adjudicate difficulties, secure a clear moral structure and enduring rest—enacted as a turning away from a woman, Troilus is finally joining the others in reading like a man.

The connection between closure and masculine reading thus comes into clear focus in the Epilogue. To "read like a man" in this poem is to impose a structure that resolves or occludes contradictions and disorder, fulfills the need for wholeness. It is to constrain, control, or eliminate outright the feminine—carnal love, the letter of the text—in order to provide a single, solid, univalent meaning firmly fixed in a hierarchical moral structure. Donaldson, Robertson, the narrator, Pandarus, Troilus all read like men: they invoke structures of authority in order to order the disorder, to stop the restless desire represented in and enacted by their texts, to find rest.

Everyone needs such rest, of course, not just men. The issue is not whether a text should be left open or should be closed—indeed, I turn away from complications and recalcitrant details in creating a whole, unified reading of the poem—but how that rest is achieved, whether the costs and sacrifices of closure are understood, acknowledged, problematized. Such rest and closure are what every ideology provides; but the problem with "soothing and harmonious ideologies" is that they achieve their vision of wholeness by unacknowledged exclusion, elimination, constraint.[29] And the problem with this particular ideology, this masculine ideology activating "reading like a man," is that it achieves its harmonious rest by constituting the feminine as disruptive Other, constraining, and finally turning away from it.[30] This is a high price to pay for order and stability, and the high cost is made clear in the reductiveness of the Epilogue. The Epilogue takes back the whole project, at last, of *Troilus and Criseyde*. [....] To read like a man, to turn away from the feminine (the letter, the woman) constituted as disruption, radically limits all human experience in the world.

4

But if that's "reading like a man," what might it be to "read like a woman"? Is there any alternative to this masculine reading response suggested in the poem? Is there such a thing in this work as a feminine response? To begin to answer these questions, we must turn now to Criseyde, for she is not only a text read but is herself a reader.

At the beginning of this romance, in a city under siege, Criseyde reads a

[29] Burlin quotes Erich Fromm, *Man for Himself* (New York: Rinehart, 1947), on the flight into "soothing and harmonious ideologies," in the chapter on *Troilus and Criseyde* in his *Chaucerian Fiction*, 133. I am indebted to Burlin's view of the end of the poem.

[30] For varied discussions of precisely this point, see *Feminist Theory: A Critique of Ideology*, ed. Nannerl O. Keohane, Michelle Z. Rosaldo, and Barbara C. Gelpi (Chicago: Univ. of Chicago Press, 1982).

romance about a city under siege—Thebes (2.78–84).[31] Thebes was associated
in the medieval imagination with an unending cycle of violence and familial
transgression. Likewise, romance narrative, considered generically, itself pro-
ceeds by dilation, delay, incessant deferral.[32] The very book, then, that she
reads is one that in itself problematizes closure. But further, the romance she's
reading adumbrates the outcome of her romance: it tells the ancestry of her
future lover, Diomede. It tells her of the events that ultimately place him in the
Greek camp, available and eager to win her love. Diomede will eventually in
fact narrate these very events to her in Book 5, as he convinces her to forget
Troilus and give her love to him. And Cassandra (another woman reader) will
narrate these very events to Troilus, who will, at length, accept them, recognize
Criseyde's betrayal, and seek his own death.

That is, that romance *would* tell Criseyde of her own story if she were
allowed to finish it. It would then enact a kind of narrative impossibility: Cri-
seyde would be reading her own narrative. But Pandarus interrupts Criseyde's
reading (alluding to the twelve books already written on this matter) before she
can ascertain *her* romance's origins and begins to work on *his* "text"—a ro-
mance of his own creation, which he will soon sit back and "read." It is as if,
in this inaugural moment in the affair of Troilus and Criseyde, Criseyde
threatens to know too much, to get ahead of the narrative, to read things im-
possible for her to read, things that must remain hidden from her. Cassandra
(the other major female reader in the poem, as I've just mentioned) not only
threatens to but does indeed know too much. Troilus explicitly scorns her read-
ing of his dream. We might suggest that, in this text, feminine reading seems
to male readers to be excessive: it goes beyond licit or proper awareness; it is
potentially disruptive of orderly, logical, linear narratives that have well-de-
limited boundaries; and it is therefore curtailed, kept in check.

Criseyde herself seems to be aware of such constraints imposed upon her as
reader. When Pandarus cuts off her reading, insisting instead that she get up
and dance with him, "And lat us don to May som observaunce" (2.112),
Criseyde refuses, in what sounds like mock shock:

> "I? God forbede!" quod she. "Be ye mad?
> Is that a widewes lif, so God yow save?
> By God, ye maken me ryght soore adrad!
> Ye ben so wylde, it semeth as ye rave.
> It sate me wel bet ay in a cave

---

[31] Also noticing the *mise en abyme* of the text here, and analyzing the text's plurality,
especially in reference to gesture, is John P. Hermann, "Gesture and Seduction in *Troilus
and Criseyde*," *SAC* 7 (1985): 107–35 *(included in this volume)*. David Anderson traces the
Theban subtext of the poem; see "Theban History in Chaucer's *Troilus*," *SAC* 4 (1982): 109–
33.

[32] Lee Patterson commented on the "central recursiveness" of Theban history in a
lecture on *Anelida and Arcite* (Univ. of California at Berkeley, Spring 1985). See Patricia
Parker, *Inescapable Romance: Studies in the Poetics of a Mode* (Princeton: Princeton Univ. Press,
1979), on the "dilation" of romance.

To bidde and rede on holy seyntes lyves;
Lat maydens gon to daunce, and yonge wyves." 2.113–19

She knows that she, as widow, as woman without a husband, should be reading saints' lives—uniform, unambiguous narratives based on the repetition of one life on earth.[33] Criseyde's tone suggests here that everyone knows the reading appropriate to a woman without a man is the reading of perfectly closed narratives whose letter is itself worthy of imitation. And if Criseyde feels the constraints on her own reading activity, she is also aware of herself as the future victim of masculine reading: she knows that her literary reputation as a traitor is in fact set, that she'll be interpreted only one way, by male *auctores* who write "thise bokes" and by "wommen" who will believe them:

She seyde, "Allas! for now is clene ago
My name of trouthe in love, for everemo!
For I have falsed oon the gentileste
That evere was, and oon the worthieste!

"Allas! of me, unto the worldes ende,
Shal neyther ben ywriten nor ysonge
No good word, for thise bokes wol me shende.
O, rolled shal I ben on many a tonge!
Thoroughout the world my belle shal be ronge!
And wommen moost wol haten me of alle.
Allas, that swich a cas me sholde falle!

"Thei wol seyn, in as muche as in me is,
I have hem don dishonour, weylaway!
Al be I nat the first that dide amys,
What helpeth that to don my blame awey?"   5.1054–68

It is in fact these "wommen" whose rancor Criseyde dreads most. Male *auctores*—this narrator included—who write "thise bokes" present readers with final castigations of Criseyde: literary tradition represents Criseyde as a traitor to be turned away from;[34] and "wommen" have no access to her other than

---

[33] Here, it will suffice to quote Gregory of Tour's oft-cited remark (*Gregorii episcopi Turonensis Liber vitae patrum*, ed. Bruno Krusch, in MGH, Scriptores rerum merovingicarum [Hannover: Hahn, 1885], 1:662–63; trans. Charles W. Jones, *Saints' Lives and Chronicles in Early England* [Ithaca: Cornell Univ. Press, 1947], 62):
Unde manifestum est, melius dici vitam patrum quam vitas, quia, cum sit diversitas meritorum virtutumque, una tamen omnes vita corporis alit in mundo.

[It is better to talk about the life of the Fathers than the lives, because, though there may be some difference in their merits and virtues, yet the life of one body nourished them all in the world.]

[34] For an excellent review of Criseyde's literary history, see Gretchen Mieszkowski, "The Reputation of Criseyde, 1155–1500," *Transactions of the Connecticut Academy of Arts and Sciences* 43 (1971): 71–153.

through this authoritative lens, as Criseyde well knows. Their view of Criseyde is thus "immasculated," to use Judith Fetterley's felicitous term, and such immasculation turns women away from women.[35] Or, in the terms of my analysis, they are reading like men. Rather than being sex-determined, masculine reading as the totalizing imposition of control is indeed constructed, a behavior rather than a "natural" biological destiny.

When Criseyde is left alone, though, or remains uninterrupted in the company of women, she performs acts of reading that suggest—just hint at—a positive alternative to constricting masculine reading. The problem with "reading like a man" is that it totalizes, that it not only insists on a unified reading but construes as feminine and consequently excludes whatever does not accord with that whole. In contradistinction, the emphasis in Criseyde's response to Antigone's song in Book 2 is on her absorbing, taking in every word, without any excisions or occlusions. After she has talked with Pandarus at the beginning of Book 2, she thinks about their conversation, then walks out into the garden with her three nieces and a "gret route" of her women; she hears Antigone's song and, in an attempt to interpret it, to "read" it, she inquires about the author and comments on the experience of "thise loveres" that might yield such "faire" verses.

> But *every word* which that she of hire herde,
> She gan to prenten in hire herte faste,
> And ay gan love hire lasse for t'agaste
> Than it dide erst, and synken in hire herte,
> That she wex somwhat able to converte.
>
> 2.899–903 (my emphasis)

This passage describes her initial impression ("She gan to prenten in hire herte faste"); it doesn't describe her further process of interpretation, her choices and eventual exclusions. But I want to point to another instance of her reading in which the emphasis is again on this sense of the entire text, every word of it: when Pandarus boldly delivers Troilus's first letter (by shoving it down her front), she retires to her chamber, away from that uncle, "Ful pryvely this lettre for to rede"; she "Avysed word by word in every lyne, / And fond no lakke" (2.1176–78). In contrast, in a passage I have already quoted above, Troilus reads Criseyde's first letter as allegorical and concludes with a general reading, without reference to the particulars:

> But finaly, he took al for the beste
> That she hym wroot, for somwhat he byheld
> On which hym thoughte he myghte his herte reste,
> Al covered she the wordes under sheld.   2.1324–27

This contrast is based on slender evidence, admittedly, and is dependent on the

---

[35] Judith Fetterley, "Introduction: On the Politics of Literature," in *The Resisting Reader* (Bloomington: Indiana Univ. Press, 1978), xi–xxvi.

unknowable words of each letter; but I want to pursue it, tentatively, a little further. Certainly, critics have noted time and again that Criseyde deliberates, ponders, carefully considers every word in her early encounters with Pandarus and Troilus (the narrator in fact is the first to make this kind of point [2.666–79]). This is again in contrast to Troilus, who falls in love in an instant; in private Criseyde "every word gan up and down to wynde / That he had seyd, as it com hire to mynde" (2.601–2) after her uncle has dropped the big news about the prince. Perhaps this slight emphasis in Criseyde's responses indicates not the mere scheming of a woman—a negative judgment that has been made often enough—but, rather, hints at a kind of (reading) response that keeps the whole in view—every word of it.

Considerable arguments might be mounted against Criseyde as reader, particularly in the latter books of the poem; she could easily be seen as preemptive and self-serving, for example, distorting the text and creating interpretations for her own benefit. But these early reading acts, foundational to her identity in the love affair, do contain a consistent, delicate emphasis and appear to suggest something of a contrast to the men reading in the narrative. I suggest that Criseyde's reading acts here adumbrate alternatives to misogynistic, totalizing reading, alternatives most fully developed in the Wife of Bath and Griselda. Such strategies upsetting totalizing literary acts are associated, I suggest, with the feminine in Chaucer's texts, and this slight emphasis on "every word" in Criseyde's depiction as she reads alone or among women may in fact point to them.

If Criseyde leads us to a perspective on masculine reading, there is a further awareness yet in the poem of "reading like a man" in the figure of Pandarus—a man who reads like a man. Such an awareness is an especially powerful demonstration of the constructedness of the masculine response: if Criseyde suggests that women can and do read like men, Pandarus suggests that men don't have to read like men. [. . . .]

5

[In a long section of my original argument, I examine patriarchal social structure's use of the female character and female desire as a trafficking in women, a trafficking that in many ways in the poem—including Troilus's own words to Pandarus (3.407–13), even though he at other times deeply affirms Criseyde's autonomy and uniqueness—is suggested to be constitutive of Trojan society.]

Pandarus, from his perspective as trafficker in women, sees that because women are treated as mere objects of trade in this society, their hearts must by necessity be "slydynge." He knows Criseyde and never thinks for a moment that she will return. He knows that heart, that is, not only because he knows his close relative but because he is a pander.

"Ye, haselwode!" thoughte this Pandare,

> And to hymself ful softeliche he seyde,
> "God woot, refreyden may this hote fare,
> Er Calkas sende Troilus Criseyde!"
> But natheless, he japed thus, and pleyde,
> And swor, ywys, his herte hym wel bihighte
> She wolde come as soone as evere she myghte.   5.505-11

This issue is less that Calkas won't let Criseyde go (5.508) than that Criseyde herself won't come (5.511). Pandarus is aware that she will never return, and he only keeps up appearances for Troilus's sake:

> Pandare answerde, "It may be, wel ynough,"
> And held with hym of al that evere he seyde.
> But in his herte he thoughte, and softe lough,
> And to hymself ful sobreliche he seyde,
> "From haselwode, there joly Robyn pleyde,
> Shal come al that that thow abidest heere.
> Ye, fare wel al the snow of ferne yere!"   5.1170-76

Pandarus's final rejection of Criseyde in Book 5—his reading her like a man, turning away from the feminine—is an act performed for the benefit of Troilus. These angry last words, furious, excessive, final, cannot really be an expression of his own disappointment or disillusionment. He is acting *like* a man—rejecting the feminine—and soon Troilus and the narrator will do the same. But from the fact of Pandarus's expedient behavior we can extrapolate an idea of considerable importance: reading *like* a man is a behavior that can be adopted in specific circumstances; there are thus other ways to read *as* a man. This is a principle with deep and broad implications: literary history, tradition, hermeneutics—although they are represented in male-dominated society as, and indeed proceed by, a containment or occlusion of the feminine—do not necessarily have to be structured according to this dynamic. The literary enterprise need not be constituted by opposition, by exclusion, by oppressive mastery and consequent constriction. The fiction of the *Legend of Good Women* picks up precisely this point: a tradition alternative to the one Criseyde is aware of, a tradition that does not proceed by constraining the feminine viewed as disruptive Other, is urgently needed.

There may not have appeared to be alternatives in the 1950s to Robertson's and Donaldson's assumptions about reading. But *Troilus and Criseyde* itself is a corrective to that apparent reality; it suggests that a first step toward finding alternatives in literary practice to containing and rejecting the feminine is an awareness that this "natural" literary practice is not natural, that it is, precisely, a fabricated strategy—that of reading like a man. Chaucer suggests just such a larger view through the characters of Criseyde and Pandarus. They are the characters who understand constrained necessity; and they are the characters with whom Chaucer, after all, had much in common. Chaucer, too, as a bourgeois in the aristocratic court, was constrained by dominant (masculine) power, as were aristocratic women. And Chaucer, like Pandarus, was responsible for its various traffics, as Waswo also observes: we recall that he served as messenger for Prince Lionel; as esquire, transacted Edward III's business; monitored commercial traffic in the Port of London as Controller of Customs; managed royal property as Clerk of the Works; even participated in negotiations regarding Richard II's marriage.[36] The connection between Chaucer and Pandarus seems to have been picked up, in fact, by Deschamps, in his famous lyric to Chaucer: a crux in his *ballade* (probably written in the 1390s) can be explicated in these terms. Calling England the "Kingdom of Aeneas," Deschamps lauds Chaucer as a translator, a linguistic go-between as, precisely, "Pandras."[37]

It is evident that fourteenth-century readers, apparently women in particular, responded to the upsets, the disruptions, the discomforts of *Troilus and Criseyde* by wanting soothing, harmonious, unified narratives: it is no coincidence that the palinode for the poem, the *Legend of Good Women*, is written in the form of saints' lives, those rigorously controlled narratives such as Criseyde ought to be reading. But [. . . .] this response is again an "immasculated" one; it is gendered as masculine in the legends themselves. The very masculine narrator, increasingly restive, immobilizes female characters and keeps a tight grip on the letter of his pagan texts. And the consequences are drastic: the series breaks off mid-sentence. If the feminine is too rigorously constrained—if people keep reading *like* men—poems indeed stop.

---

[36] For the suggestion that Pandarus has an autobiographical relevance to Chaucer, see Waswo ("The Narrator of *Troilus and Criseyde*"), who also comments that Chaucer, "constrained by necessity" as a bourgeois in an aristocratic court, had much in common with the aristocratic ladies as well (14). For Criseyde as an autobiographical figure, see Lambert, "Criseydan Reading," in Salu, 105–25.

[37] As Gretchen Mieszkowski suggests in " 'Pandras' in Deschamps' Ballade for Chaucer" (*ChauR* 9 [1975]: 327–36), "pandras" is a probable reference to the character in Chaucer's *Troilus and Criseyde*. Eugen Lerch proposed this reading in "Zu einer Stelle bei Eustache Deschamps" (*RF* 62 [1950]: 67–68), arguing against the prevailing reading established by Paget Toynbee in "The Ballade Addressed by Eustache Deschamps to Geoffrey Chaucer" (*Academy* 40 [1891]: 432), of "pandras" as Pandrasus, a character in Wace's *Brut*. Lerch's hypothesis went unnoticed until Mieszkowski resuscitated it and argued for it.

Pandarus's "Unthrift" and the Problem of Desire in Troilus and Criseyde

ROBERT R. EDWARDS

For most readers of TROILUS AND CRISEYDE, *the key interpretive problem is to explain how the poem represents the erotic attachment between its two protagonists. Chaucer's narrator and his characters offer various formulations, among them courtly love, charity, mutual affection, celestial love, and natural appetite. This essay begins by analyzing one especially troubling definition and then considers the implications for our understanding of the poem. In a speech to Troilus in Book 4, Pandarus seems to define Troilus's love as mere desire and "casuel plesaunce." Both Troilus and the poem's narrator subsequently reject Pandarus's characterization, but the speech is thematically rich in its nuances and clearly linked to other parts of the poem. Close study of Chaucer's changes and additions to the original passage in Boccaccio shows that Pandarus's speech demonstrates how desire remains an imperfectly resolved element in the poem. The source of this abiding contradiction is Chaucer's conscious reinscription of the* CONSOLATION OF PHILOSOPHY *and the* ROMAN DE LA ROSE, *works that Boccaccio used as sources but whose influence Chaucer greatly intensifies. These sources create a paradoxical effect, for as philosophical systems they integrate desire with other notions of love while impoverishing it as a topic of moral speculation. Consequently, they introduce ethical and aesthetic limitations that shape the problematic ending of the poem. The extent and kind of these limitations may be seen by contrasting Dante's discussion of desire in* PURGATORIO 17 *and* 18.

> "This town is ful of ladys al aboute;
> And, to my doom, fairer than swiche twelve
> As evere she was, shal I fynde in som route,
> Yee, on or two, withouten any doute.
> Forthi be glad, myn own deere brother!
> If she be lost, we shal recovere an other."   4.401–6

In Book 4 of *Troilus and Criseyde*, just after Troilus learns that the Trojan parliament has decided to exchange Criseyde for Antenor and thereby unwittingly seal the fate of both the love affair and the city, Pandarus hastens to comfort his distraught friend. In a seven-stanza speech, he offers Troilus what seems a cynical and detached sort of consolation; the passage quoted above stands at

the center of that speech (4.379–427), which frames an argument covering half
a dozen points. Pandarus begins by describing Troilus's loss as a shift in For-
tune: "Who wolde have wend that in so litel a throwe / Fortune oure joie wold
han overthrowe?" He quickly points out, however, that Fortune's gifts are
"comune" rather than vested in individuals and goes on to admonish Troilus,
"thi desire al holly hastow had, / So that, by right, it oughte ynough suffise."
Then, in a compressed and elliptical sentence, he argues Troy is replete with
beautiful and desirable women. Without discounting Criseyde's beauty, he
promises Troilus a capable and speedy replacement. In support of that propos-
al, he contends further that all virtues cannot be contained in one person:
"God forbede alwey that ech plesaunce / In o thyng were, and in non other
wight!" New love replaces old, he says, and "syn it is but casuel plesaunce, /
Som cas shal putte it out of remembraunce." Thus new love will alleviate
Troilus's pain, and Criseyde's absence will at length remove her from his heart.

Pandarus's speech is remarkable for its thematic richness as well as its ap-
parent cynicism and sudden estrangement from Criseyde. Delivered in Troi-
lus's darkened chamber by an empathetic friend himself nearly undone "[f]or
verray wo" (4.357), it is a piece of skillful and dispassionate reasoning about
the nature of passion. In Boccaccio's *Filostrato* the corresponding speech oc-
cupies only four stanzas. Chaucer amplifies his source in ways that bring new
meaning to the text. In the *Filostrato*, Troiolo complains, "Fortuna insidiosa se
ne 'l mena, / e con lui 'nsieme il sollazzo e 'l diporto" ("Envious fortune leads
[my sweet comfort] away, and with it my solace and pleasure" [4.45.5–6]).
Chaucer removes this vague reference to Fortune from Troiolo and assigns it
to Pandarus, and he gives it a philosophical rather than courtly meaning.
Pandarus advises, in lines added by Chaucer, "Ne trust no wight to fynden in
Fortune / Ay propretee; hire yiftes ben comune" (4.391–92). He thus associ-
ates the "hap" of Troilus's love with the doctrine in Boethius's *Consolation of
Philosophy*, which denies "that ever any mortel man hath resceyved ony of tho
thynges to ben hise in propre" and asserts instead that man is put "in the
comune realme of alle" (Bo 2 pr. 2.10–12, 84–85). He also draws on the view
of earthly love expounded in the *Roman de la Rose*, specifically in the speeches
of Reason and Ami in Jean de Meun's continuation of the poem.[1]

The shift in speaker and reference is paralleled by a second enhancement of
meaning. Pandarus clearly identifies Fortune's gifts as Troilus's desire (4.395),
and the equation of common gifts and desire points in turn toward the Old
Woman's famous remarks about sexual appetite in the *Rose*. She contends that
every man and every woman hold their love commonly and that desire oper-
ates across the species without differentiating individuals except on the basis of
gender. Her speech plays rhetorically on grammatical and gender distinctions
(*touz / toutes, commun / commune, chascun / chascune*) which connect rather than
divide men and women in a single appetite.

---

[1] Dean S. Fansler, *Chaucer and the ROMAN DE LA ROSE* (New York: Columbia Univ. Press,
1914), 209; Barney, *Riverside TROILUS* 1046.

> Ains nous a fait, biau fix, n'en doutes,
> Toutes por touz et touz pour toutes,
> Chascune por chascun commune
> Et commun chascun por chascune.[2]

Pandarus's formulation of desire is another substantial change wrought in the speech. Boccaccio's text describes Troiolo as the intending subject and author of his desire; Pandaro tells him, "Ciò che disideravi avuto l'hai" ("You have had what you desired" [4.47.3]). The line is recast by Chaucer, however, so that Troilus's desire becomes identical to the object of his desire: "thi desire al holly hastow had."[3] Desire is hypostatized, removed from the domain of fantasy to a social realm where it is both sign and referent. At the same time, the *Filostrato*'s aristocratic social vision of Troy as a city "piena di belle donne e graziose" ("full of beautiful and gracious ladies") acquires a new structure and function. Troy is besieged on the outside and Hector has just told the Trojan parliament, in another passage of Chaucer's invention, "We usen here no wommen for to selle" (4.182). The city's encirclement and isolation serve, however, to define it as the site for a closed system of domestic exchange. Pandarus envisions an economy of desire internal to Troy, in which men, bound to each other by friendship and kinship (the two are convertible for Pandarus), lose and regain Troy's beautiful women.[4] In Boccaccio this exchange involves surplus and increments. Pandaro tells his friend, "però se noi perdemo / costei, molte altre ne ritroveremo" ("Thus if we lose this one, we shall find many others" [4.48.8]). Chaucer's version calls for an erotic equilibrium in Troy: "Forthi be glad, myn own deere brother! / If she be lost, we shal recovere an other" (4.405-6). This circulation also permits, as Pandarus says in a stanza added to the original, the distribution of specific qualities associated with different women.[5] In this way, as in Ovid and Andreas Capellanus,[6] "newe love" and "newe cas" work against the declining arc of desire by permitting "newe avys" (4.416)—that is, a continuation of desire and appetite by

---

[2] *Le Roman de la Rose*, ed. Félix Lecoy, 3 vols. (Paris: Champion, 1966-74), 13885-88. I cite the translation by Charles Dahlberg, *The Romance of the Rose* (Princeton: Princeton Univ. Press, 1971): "Instead, fair son, never doubt that [Nature] has made all us women for all men and all men for all women, each woman common to every man and every man common to each woman" (238).

[3] MED cites the passage under the sense of "Fulfillment of (one's) wish, desire, passion, or urge." OED comes closer in its transferred sense: "object of desire; that which one desires or longs for." This sense also appears at 1.465 and 4.199. In *Troilus and Criseyde*, "love" undergoes a similar extension of meaning from a state of loving to "love object" or "lover."

[4] Carolyn Dinshaw (*Poetics*, 58-64—*included in this volume*) discusses the relation between exchange and patriarchy; see pp. 71-73. Windeatt notes that Pandaro says Troiolo will not find unwilling women; Pandarus makes them beautiful women (*Troilus* 375).

[5] Pandarus's disingenuous fear that all virtues might be located in a single woman ironically echoes the remark that Criseyde makes to him when he praises Troilus's virtues in Book 2: "For gret power and moral vertu here / Is selde yseyn in o persone yfere" (2.167-68).

[6] Barney, *Riverside TROILUS* 1046 and Windeatt, *Troilus* 375.

finding new objects of contemplation and thought.[7]

Pandarus's speech is notable, too, for its links to other parts of the poem. Structurally, it is the final element of a sequence (public event, private response, and interview) that parallels the action in Book 1.[8] Thematically, Pandarus makes the same argument about Fortune in Book 1, when Troilus sees Fortune as his foe and Criseyde as an unobtainable object. There Pandarus reminds his friend "that Fortune is comune / To everi manere wight in som degree" (1.843–44). Just as joys pass away, he assures Troilus, so do sorrows. And after the lovers' consummation in Book 3, the same argument about love and Fortune reappears (3.1622–38), amplifying Pandaro's laconic counsel of restraint in the *Filostrato*: "che ponghi freno alla mente amorosa" ("curb your amorous intent" [3.60.5]). Pandarus warns that the "worste kynde of infortune" is to have been in prosperity and remember it when it is lost. On both these occasions as in Book 4, Chaucer adds to Boccaccio's text to let Pandarus make the same point: Fortune is by turns the mechanism of comedy and tragedy.

Pandarus's speech is, of course, repudiated no sooner than it is uttered. The narrator, in lines that have no counterpart in Boccaccio, assures us and the audience of court lovers to whom he addresses his work, "Thise wordes seyde he for the nones alle, / To help his frend" (4.428–29).[9] A substantial body of criticism has shown how much of the poem's drama and meaning reside in the narrator, and here, as so often in the poem, the narrator intervenes in order to put things in the best light. Nonetheless, it is a curious intervention, for the narrator seeks to regulate the meaning of a speech that the poet has rendered and then consciously amplified. The speech thus creates a moment in which the text breaks the illusion of seamless representation to uncover its contradictions, its multiplicity of voices, its conflict of perspectives.

The issue, we should remember, is not that Pandarus might actually persuade Troilus to adopt his vision of an economy of desire operating inside Troy's city of "friends." Boccaccio's Troiolo refuses to commit "un tale eccesso" (4.50.4), and for Chaucer's Troilus, the advice literally goes in one ear and out the other (4.434). When Troilus recovers himself, he offers a lengthy refutation (4.435–516) of Pandarus's advice. Ida Gordon says that Pandarus's words raise the problem of "what constitutes 'trouthe' in love," when such love is a gift of fortune.[10] R. A. Shoaf contends that Troilus finally elects death over Pandarus's version of love.[11] At this point in the poem, however, the chief concern is that the narrator does not want his readers and audience to credit Pandarus's speech as a plausible understanding of the story. He dismiss-

---

[7] Later in the scene Boccaccio's Troiolo makes the point that love may diminish in time (4.59.4–8). Chaucer omits this stanza.

[8] Wetherbee, *Poets*, 206–7.

[9] A parallel example of the phrase (1.561) appears in Pandarus's first interview with Troilus.

[10] Gordon, *Sorrow*, 97.

[11] Shoaf, *Currency*, 122.

es it as an "unthrift" (4.431), an impropriety.[12] He intrudes here as he intrudes earlier in the poem to say that Criseyde did not give her love suddenly (2.666–79) and as he will intrude later to refuse to blame her fully for abandoning Troilus for Diomede (5.1086–99). Yet it is precisely as an "unthrift," a transgression or scandal that we must understand Pandarus's speech, for here he reveals the fixed and narrow conception of desire that has driven the poem thus far and to which the poem's action will return in succeeding events, namely the replacement of Troilus by Diomede.[13] Troilus may imagine that he has succeeded in redefining and even refining desire as a "newe qualitee" (3.1654), but at the point where the poem makes its decisive turn and destiny takes over, Pandarus suggests that another motive has been driving events all along.[14] In fact, Pandarus's description of the love affair as "casuel plesaunce," blunt and uncompromising as it is, looks forward to the perspective the narrator will adopt at the end of the poem.[15]

The poetic effect of Pandarus's "unthrift" depends on an extravagant gesture of disclosure and on the confirmation later afforded by retrospect. The explanatory power of the speech derives from Chaucer's ability to combine sources in a richly allusive intertextuality. Chaucer translates and extends Boccaccio's text by connecting the narrative action of the *Filostrato* to the views of love expounded in the *Consolation* and the *Rose*. Both these texts are independent sources for the *Filostrato*.[16] In addition, Jean de Meun, as John V. Fleming points out, translated Boethius twice, once in his *Boece* and then in the *Rose*,

---

[12] "Impropriety" is Shoaf's gloss for *unthrift* (*Troilus* 195). OED also cites the passage in the sense of "dissolute conduct, loose behavior, impropriety." Davis, *Glossary*, glosses the term as "nonsense, foolishness"; Francis Henry Stratman as "folly," *A Middle English Dictionary*, rev. Henry Bradley (Oxford: Clarendon, 1891). The contrasting term *thrift* appears clearly at 2.582, 2.847, 2.1687, 3.947, 3.1249, 4.1630; it is part of an asseveration ("by my thrift") at 2.1483 and 3.871.

[13] John Fyler notes that Diomede's "courtship in Book 5 echoes Troilus' in Book 2, but as tragedy or farce" ("Fabrications," 127—*included in this volume*). Theodore A. Stroud says that Diomede's boorish nature illustrates the principle, maintained in Pandarus's speech, that Fortune is indiscriminate in distributing her goods—see "Boethius' Influence on Chaucer's *Troilus*," MP 49 (1951–52): 1–9; reprinted in Schoeck and Taylor, 2:122–35, at 131.

[14] Richard F. Green suggests that the "newe qualitee" is *trouthe*, which keeps the stylized game of love from becoming anarchy—see "Troilus and the Game of Love," *ChauR* 13 (1978–79): 201–20. When Troilus finally reproves Criseyde at the end of the poem, he asks, "Where is youre feith, and where is youre biheste? / Where is youre love? where is youre trouthe?" (5.1675–76).

[15] See Fyler for a discussion of the ways in which Pandarus's fabrications become real in the poem.

[16] Robert Hollander discusses the borrowings from the *Consolation* in Boccaccio—see *Boccaccio's Two Venuses* (New York: Columbia Univ. Press, 1977). Barney (*Riverside TROILUS*), Fansler, Windeatt (*Troilus*), and Wood (*Elements*), have shown how often Chaucer cites or alludes to the *Rose* in retouching and amplifying Boccaccio. Fleming believes that "the early Boccaccio is absolutely riddled with the *Roman de la Rose*" and that Chaucer found in the *Filostrato* a historical application of the *Rose*'s erotic doctrines to the classical past—see John V. Fleming, "Smoky Reyn: From Jean de Meun to Geoffrey Chaucer," *Chaucer and the Craft of Fiction*, ed. Leigh A. Arrathoon (Rochester: Solaris Press, 1986), 1–21, at 5. In the *Legend of Good Women* (F 328–34 and G 254–66) the God of Love will remonstrate against the poet for translating the *Rose* and writing *Troilus and Criseyde*.

where "he examined sexual love from the perspective of Boethian analysis."[17] The intertextuality is further intensified for Chaucer because he used Jean's translation of the *Consolation* for his *Boece*. Chaucer's innovation is to reinscribe the *Consolation* and the *Rose* in his translation of Boccaccio, deepening their influence and enhancing the poem's meaning. He does so by associating the two texts in a language that conveys the experience of desire that Pandarus treats as the defining characteristic of the love story. This reinscription is deeply ambivalent and problematic. Pandarus's dictum that all men and women must "suffren loves hete, / Celestial, or elles love of kynde" (1.978–79) is an emblem of the tensions involved in trying to join the two sources. I shall try to explain later how the connection constrains and impoverishes the poem. But it is a connection made early in the story and confirmed throughout the ascendancy of Troilus's good fortune.

The scene in Book 1 where Troilus first glimpses Criseyde presents one of several examples in which Chaucer combines the *Consolation* and the *Rose* in order to rewrite Boccaccio's text. Troilus encounters Criseyde at the springtime festival honoring the image of Pallas Athena, Troy's protectress. Boccaccio makes it apparent that the renewal of the landscape celebrated by the feast extends through the domain of sentient creatures, including mankind: "gaio diviene ogni animale, / e 'n diversi atti mostra suoi amori" ("Every animal becomes lusty and shows its love in different acts" [1.18.3–4]). Chaucer likewise associates the renewal of "lusty Veer the pryme" (1.157) with the festival attended by "so many a lusty knyght, / So many a lady fressh and mayden bright" (1.165–66). The setting thematically connects the erotic appetites of the vegetative and animal souls in the natural world to the worship of images and even images in a doomed cause.

In the first part of the scene, Troilus disparages Love's power, and his mocking prepares for Love's revenge in the ensuing action. Chaucer emphasizes vengeance by adding seven stanzas (1.218–66) on the theme of Love's overwhelming power. The narrator draws the lesson from this vengeance for his audience, reminding them, "Love is he that alle thing may bynde, / For may no man fordon the lawe of kynde" (1.237–38). Love's power is a commonplace of courtly poetry, stated most emphatically in the *Rose*. But the phrasing here is clearly Boethian, evoking the rational ordering of the world by divine providence: "al this accordaunce [and] ordenaunce of thynges is bounde with love" (Bo 2 m 8.13–15). We have, then, a conscious doubling of sources. Like the dreamer in the *Rose*, Troilus is taken as a thrall whose will to resist Love disappears and remains inaccessible to reason. Coevally, the Boethian terms anticipate the Proem and "Canticus Troili" of Book 3.

Chaucer carefully plots the moment in this scene when desire is constituted

---

[17] Fleming, 4. Alastair Minnis shows that Jean's engagement with Boethius includes as well the commentators on the *Consolation*, notably William of Conches—see "Aspects of the Medieval French and English Traditions of the *De Consolatione Philosophiae*," *Boethius: His Life, Thought and Influence*, ed. Margaret Gibson (Oxford: Blackwell, 1981), 312–61, at 315–34.

for Troilus. In Boccaccio, Troiolo jokes with his men and casts his glance among the various women, when by chance his gaze penetrates to where Criseida stands. Chaucer revises the details to accentuate the subjectivity of the moment and to cast Troilus as the intending subject. Troiolo's roaming gaze (*l'occhio suo vago*) penetrates to a place, but Chaucer depicts an act in which the gaze is directed specifically at Criseyde and fixes on her as its object:

> And upon cas bifel that thorugh a route
> His eye percede, and so depe it wente,
> Til on Criseyde it smot, and ther it stente.
>
> And sodeynly he wax therwith astoned,
> And gan hir bet biholde in thrifty wise.   1.271–75

Both Boccaccio and Chaucer depend here on the *Rose*, specifically on the scene in which the dreamer looks into the Mirror of Narcissus, the paradigm of erotic attraction and appetite. Troilus's gaze occurs by chance (*cas*), it falls on one figure out of a group (*route*), and it produces compulsive desire. In the Middle English translation of the *Rose* commonly ascribed to Chaucer, the same elements and sequence appear:

> In thilke mirrour saw I tho
> Among a thousand thinges mo,
> A roser chargid full of rosis,
> That with an hegge about enclos is.
> Tho had I sich lust and envie. . . .   Rom 1649–53

Chaucer supplements Boccaccio's text in order to make explicit the connection between sight and desire, and he does so by again evoking the *Consolation* and *Rose* together:

> And of hire look in him ther gan to quyken
> So gret desir and such affeccioun,
> That in his hertes botme gan to stiken
> Of hir his fixe and depe impressioun.   1.295–98

Like the dreamer's entrapment in the "mirrour perilous" (Rom 1601; cf. 1642), Troilus's desire is constituted in "his fixe and depe impressioun" of Criseyde.[18] The precise nature of that impression is indicated by the *Consolation*. In Book 5, meter 4 Boethius presents the Stoic contention that "ymages and sensibilities . . . weren enprientid into soules fro bodyes withoute-forth" (Bo 5 m 4.6–10) much like letters written on parchment or figures reflected in a mirror. The soul, "nakid of itself" as Nicholas Trivet says in his gloss to the passage, receives the sense impressions brought to it whether by chance or de-

---

[18] Fansler cites Love's instruction of the dreamer (Rom 2523–37) as a possible source (152), but the passage in the *Rose* is not about the lover's experience so much as the conduct he ought to display.

sign. The limitation of this view, as Boethius points out, is that it allows the soul no capacity for knowledge or for moral discrimination. The mechanism of desire that Chaucer elaborates and ascribes to Troilus comes from a position that Boethius discredits.[19] Thus seen in the context of Chaucer's sources, the Trojans' festive worship of the image of Pallas is recreated in Troilus's idolatrous and solipsistic desire.

Chaucer's fusion of the *Consolation* and the *Rose* in this passage provides a framework for understanding other representations of desire in the poem. Boccaccio initially describes Criseida along the lines of the *donna angelicata* of the Dolce Stil Nuovo, an objectified and luminous presence who signifies divine intervention—in short, a miracle. Like the *stilnovisti*, Boccaccio portrays her through metaphors that assert her independent reality and place in the external, natural world: "quanto la rosa la vïola / di biltà vince, cotanto era questa / piú ch'altra donna, bella" ("as much as the rose overcomes the violet in beauty, so much was she more beautiful than any other lady" [1.19.3–5]).[20] Chaucer retains part of this description, notably in the image of Criseyde as a bright star under a black cloud (1.175). But the thematic stress in *Troilus and Criseyde* falls on the blackness. Chaucer fashions Boccaccio's phrase "sotto candido velo in bruna vesta" ("under a white veil in a black habit" [1.26.8]), itself an echo of Beatrice's approach to Dante in *Purgatorio* 30,[21] into a space of negativity that Troilus's desire penetrates, much as the dreamer in the *Rose* arbitrarily fixes his desire on a bud in the rose bush. Criseyde is dressed in "widewes habit blak" (1.170), she stands near the door of the temple "in hir blake wede" (1.177), and "[s]he, this in blak, likynge to Troilus / Over al thing, he stood for to biholde" (1.309–10).

Troilus's love begins with his eye piercing the darkness and seizing an image. The source of the image, as the poem makes clear, is not in itself passive, for Criseyde strikes a confident pose and asserts her right to stand where she wishes. Nonetheless, she is experienced throughout the passage as an object seen, an image imprinted on the soul from without. The narrator undertakes to recreate Troilus's subjective experience for us, telling us that Criseyde is "so

---

[19] Chaucer presents the same false argument in the *Book of the Duchess*; for discussion, see Robert R. Edwards, *The Dream of Chaucer: Representation and Reflection in the Early Narratives* (Durham: Duke Univ. Press, 1989), 86–87.

[20] Bonagiunta of Lucca and Guittone d'Arezzo attack Guido Guinizelli for the audacity of his comparisons between his lady's beauty and the natural world. For them the comparisons represent a transgression of faith and literary propriety. In the sonnet "Voi, ch'avete mutata la mainera," Bonagiunta accuses Guinizelli of seeking to surpass other poets through his "sottiglianza" and obscure language, and Guittone counsels him, "A Good man, when he praises, separates praise from worth, / Honoring the laws of the wise and not the foolish" (*The Poetry of Guinizelli*, ed. and trans. Robert R. Edwards [New York: Garland, 1987], 65; see discussion pp. xliii-xlv). The stilnovistic portrayal of Criseida early in the *Filostrato* is supplemented by Boccaccio's extensive references to the *Vita Nuova*; it is contrasted by the portrayal of her intense sexual appetite in Part 3 of the *Filostrato*, which Chaucer suppresses in Book 3 of *Troilus and Criseyde*.

[21] See *Il Filostrato*, ed. Branca, 2:849.

good a syghte" (294), that "hire look" (295) kindles desire and makes Troilus
feel that his spirit dies in his heart (307). Afterwards Troilus returns to his
palace like the dreamer in the *Rose*: "Right with hire look thorugh-shoten and
thorugh-darted" (325). Even the brief physical description of Criseyde in this
scene (281–87) contributes to the experience of seeing. Chaucer renders the
descriptive passage shorn of Boccaccio's stilnovist rhetoric and artfully frames
it as if it were a moment of attention suspended within Troilus's gaze. In that
specular moment, her graceful limbs answer to womanhood, and she moves in
such a way "that men myght in hire gesse / Honour, estat, and wommanly
noblesse" (286–87). It is this figure of his subjectivity that Troilus subsequently
contemplates, as he sits waking in his bed:

> ... his spirit mette
> That he hire saugh a-temple, and al the wise
> Right of hire look, and gan it newe avise.
>
> Thus gan he make a mirour of his mynde,
> In which he saugh al holly hire figure.   1.362–66

The phrasing "make a mirour of his mynde" appears in Love's description of
Swete-Thought.[22] But in the *Rose* Love specifies that Swete-Thought evokes
the memory of past events to assuage the lover's pain (2801–3, 2815–20).
Troilus as yet shares no history with Criseyde from which he might draw
memories. It is, rather, the Boethian overtone in the passage that conveys the
essential idea: the figure is insubstantial, its arrival analogous to the execution
of a text on a neutral medium—"ryght as we ben wont somtyme by a swift
poyntel to fycchen lettres emprientid in the smothnesse or in the pleynesse of
the table of wex or in parchemyn that ne hath no figure ne note in it" (Bo 5 m
4.16–20).

A parallel scene repeats and complicates this portrayal of desire. In Book 2,
Troilus rides into town triumphantly just after Pandarus has been pleading his
case with Criseyde. The scene is largely of Chaucer's invention, though later in
the *Filostrato* Troiolo rides by Criseida's house. What makes the passage partic-
ularly interesting is that Chaucer here rewrites the scene in the Palladion, this
time from the vantage point of Criseyde's experience with Troilus as the object
of her sight. As Jill Mann has observed, both scenes occur by chance.[23] Like
Criseyde, Troilus is presented as an object seen. The narrator says he is "swich
a knyghtly sighte, trewely" (2.628) and seems to be "[s]o lik a man of armes
and a knyght" (2.631). For the physical description of Criseyde in Book 1, we
are given the visual image of Troilus's heroically battered helmet and shield.

---

[22] Rom 2804–08; Alfred David, *Riverside Chaucer* 1109, Barney, *Riverside TROILUS* 1027,
and Windeatt, *Troilus* 109.

[23] Jill Mann, "Chance and Destiny in *Troilus and Criseyde* and the *Knight's Tale*," *The
Cambridge Chaucer Companion*, ed. Piero Boitani and Jill Mann (Cambridge: Cambridge Univ.
Press, 1986), 75–92, at 76–77.

Like Criseyde in the temple, the hero modestly lowers his eyes. In the earlier scene the "fixe and depe impressioun" of Criseyde sticks to the bottom of Troilus's heart. Now his bearing affects her, and she lets his image "so softe in hire herte synke" (2.650). Criseyde acts with more resistance to love than Troilus, blushing at her own "thought" (652, 660). But "thought" in this context means the visual image that Criseyde produces and contemplates; it is the same kind of figure that Troilus, alone in his chamber, calls forth when he "gan it newe avise" (1.364) and that Pandarus will later call "newe avys" (4.416).[24] The narrator hastens to assure us that Criseyde does not give her love suddenly and that at this point she only inclines toward liking him. Yet the scene, which Chaucer added to the poem, suggests that she starts with a more complicated but fundamentally similar model as Troilus's desire for her.

Desire in *Troilus and Criseyde* begins from these two points and undergoes a rich thematic elaboration, especially through Pandarus's mediation. The letter Pandarus urges Criseyde to write increases Troilus's desire (2.1335, 1336) and leads him "to desiren moore" (2.1339). In Book 3, consummation leads to renewed desire. As he prepares to depart in the morning after their love making, Troilus tells Criseyde, "Syn that desir right now so biteth me, / That I am ded anon, but I retourne" (3.1482-83). The narrator remarks, "So harde hym wrong of sharp desir the peyne / For to ben eft there he was in plesaunce, / That it may nevere out of his remembraunce" (3.1531-33). The process, he says, is internal and self-driven: "And verraylich of thilke remembraunce / Desir al newe hym brende, and lust to brede / Gan more than erst, and yet took he non hede" (3.1545-47). Troilus makes the same observation when he speaks to Pandarus: "And ay the more that desir me biteth / To love hire best, the more it me deliteth" (3.1651-52). Barry Windeatt points out that here "Troilus's delight grows in proportion to the urgency of desire."[25] Chaucer's phrasing in the passage suggests, too, that desire impels him to love.

The representation of desire in these passages and elsewhere stands beside other claims in the poem about the nature of erotic attachment. In Book 3, Criseyde admires Troilus's governance of his desire (3.470-83). In the consummation scene, pagan and Christian elements are apparently joined in Troilus's exclamation, "O Love, O Charite!" (3.1254); but Love's mother, he quickly adds, is Venus, and the "Benigne Love" (3.1261) he addresses is Cupid translated simultaneously into religious and courtly traditions.[26] Cupid is the referent, too, when he praises "the heighe worthynesse / Of Love" (3.1609-10) to Pandarus. Criseyde, before she leaves for the Greek camp, tells Troilus that "moral vertu, grounded upon trouthe" (4.1672) first disposed her toward him

---

[24] The limitations of the internal images in these passages become apparent at the end of the poem when Troilus achieves "ful avysement" (5.1811): "And down from thennes faste he gan avyse / This litel spot of erthe" (5.1814-15). Chaucer borrows the passage from the *Teseida*, where Boccaccio's verbs are *ammirare* and *rimirare*. Comparison of the texts shows that Chaucer obviously took care to have the later passage echo the earlier ones in his poem.

[25] *Troilus*, 333.

[26] Schless, *Chaucer and Dante*, 122-23.

and that his "resoun" has since governed his appetite. These terms seem consistent with her response to Troilus as she observes him in Book 2, contemplating the inner and outer man and admiring Troilus's "excellent prowesse, / And his estat, and also his renown, / His wit, his shap, and ek his gentilesse" (2.660–62). She is won over, however, by being the object of his desire: "But moost hire favour was, for his distresse / Was al for hire" (2.663–64). A similar duality is apparent in Troilus's description of himself as a man "with desir and reson twight" (4.572). Stephen Barney proposes that Troilus alone of the poem's characters is concerned with speculating about final causes, but a key passage like his hymn to cosmic love at the end of Book 3 "is colored by its context, the gay festiveness of Troilus described before it, and, with sharp irony, the reference to 'the townes werre,' the exemplum *par excellence* of strife over against love, which follows the hymn."[27] Throughout the poem, the characters speak of love as service and a means of ennoblement largely in their public address; the private speech between Troilus and Pandarus and the interior monologues uttered by Criseyde display a different array of motives. Appetite, fear, curiosity, and pleasure guide their conduct and actions. Criseyde perfectly expresses the dichotomy of public and private speech when she admonishes Pandarus and Troilus, "So werketh now in so discret a wise / That I honour may have, and he plesaunce" (3.943–44). If Chaucer has reconceived the thinly disguised, though fictitious, allegory that Boccaccio wrote to spark desire in his beloved ("Proemio" 23), the noble sentiments and philosophical trappings do not entirely change or conceal the erotic dimensions of the narrative.

The nature of desire remains, then, a fundamental and imperfectly resolved problem in *Troilus and Criseyde*. I want to suggest that the problem of desire is structured and constrained by the sources Chaucer brings to his treatment of the poem. By combining the *Consolation* and the *Rose*, he has brought two discursive systems to bear on the representation of desire. These are, moreover, powerfully reductive systems that seek to integrate and unify erotic experience under divine love. The *Consolation* urges transcendence of desire, Fortune, and the world. Lady Philosophy groups desire with "false goodes" (Bo 3 pr. 2) and says that "delyces of body" are bestial (Bo 3 pr. 7.12–16). The *Rose*, for all its courtly trappings and Neo-Ovidian satire, reduces desire to mere creaturely appetite and consummation to consumption. The dreamer takes possession of the rose as the culmination of a narrative and thematic movement beginning with Nature's confession and Genius's speech. As in Alan of Lille's *De planctu Naturae*, Nature regenerates the species by outstripping death in the grisly race ("trop fiere chace" [15947]) of propagation against mortality. She allies herself with Love and Venus, and enjoins all who have her tools to use them; Genius excommunicates those who do not perform Nature's offices.

Boethius and the *Rose* are radical extensions of the same formulation about spirit and matter. Neither allows ontological or moral status to the sensual and

---

[27] "Troilus Bound," 455 (*included in this volume*).

corporeal dimensions of human experience. Separately and together, they in-
tensify Chaucer's poem, bringing a rigorous analytical framework to courtly
narrative. But they also impoverish desire as an object of moral deliberation. In
the end, the poem submits to the logic of these positions, and celestial love
takes over from natural love, charity superceding creaturely appetite. Most
readers, even those eager to salvage aesthetic ambiguity or an elegiac tone of
regret, agree that this is a plausible way of looking at pagan antiquity from the
perspective of a fourteenth-century Christian. Yet it is not the only way. We can
gain a deeper understanding of the problem of desire in Chaucer's poem and
of the terrible candor of Pandarus's "unthrift" by looking at Dante's handling
of desire in the *Commedia*.

In *Purgatorio* 17 and 18, Vergil offers Dante an exposition of love that con-
nects love, pleasure, and cognition. Neither Creator nor creature, Vergil ex-
plains, was ever without love (17.91–92), and he goes on to distinguish natural
from elective love (*amore naturale* and *amore d'animo*). Natural love is "the de-
sire each creature has for its own perfection,"[28] and it is by definition without
error. Elective love involves free will; it can err by having a wrong object ("per
malo obietto") or by being pursued with too much or too little vigor, but it
avoids being the cause of sinful pleasure ("mal diletto") when it is directed to
the Primal Good (God) or to secondary worldly goods in moderation ("ne'
secondi sé stesso misura" [17.98]). Thus, Vergil concludes, love is the cause of
every virtue or vice in man (17.103–5). In canto 18, these distinctions ramify
into an analysis of the ethics of desire. Vergil asserts that the mind is naturally
drawn to what pleases it and that its abstractive powers create an image toward
which the mind inclines. This first inclination, he says, is love (*amor*), and pleas-
ure reinforces it. From it follows a spiritual movement of desire (*disire*) toward
the object, and after desire comes joy (*gioire*).[29] By this means, different kinds
of love may be distinguished, and the mind (in contrast to the Stoic formula-
tion in Boethius) is not a captive of its pleasures and objects of desire. The
source of natural love, Vergil explains, remains inaccessible, but free will
operates innately in human reason: "Quest' è 'l principio là onde si piglia /
ragion di meritare in voi, secondo / che buoni e rei amori accoglie e viglia"
("This is the principle wherefrom is derived the reason of desert in you,
according as it garners and winnows good and evil loves" [18.64–66]).

My purpose in invoking Dante here is not to suggest that Chaucer is careless
in formulating the theme of desire, nor is it to suggest that Chaucer's poem,
suffused as it is with Neoplatonic influences, must be judged by the Aristo-
telian-Thomistic distinctions of the *Commedia*. Pandarus's conception of "loves

---

[28] Singleton, 2:2:392.

[29] The exposition of Dante's doctrine here is taken from Singleton's commentary
(2:2:414); see also Edward Moore, *Studies in Dante*, Second Series: Miscellaneous Essays
(Oxford: Clarendon, 1899), 204. James L. Shanley quotes *Purgatorio* 17 to show that Troilus
had free will but used it unwisely, since no human pleasure is sufficient for complete
happiness—see "The *Troilus* and Christian Love," *ELH* 6 (1939): 271–81; reprinted in
Schoeck and Taylor, 2:136–46, at 142–43.

hete" differs categorically from Dante's notion of love extending to Creator and creatures alike. Similarly, "love of kynde" and celestial love do not correspond to Dante's natural and elective love, both of which have spiritual ends.[30] The point, rather, is that Dante works within a system that allows him to portray desire as an object of moral deliberation and knowledge.[31] We are moved, Vergil says, by those things we desire and so come to know them, and in knowing them we reach judgments about their properties, utility, and ends. As he remarks to Dante, employing an evocative image of cognition, "non ciascun segno / è buono, ancor che buona sia la cera" ("not every imprint is good, although the wax be good" [18.38–39]). Particularly in earthly matters, man's "innata libertate" (18.68) allows him to distinguish good and evil objects. This is the basis of what Vergil describes with the encompassing term "moralità" (18.69).

By contrast, Chaucer's poem formulates desire in such a way as to allow no complex or sustained reflection on such matters. The "secondary goods" that form our worldly experience and much of our moral life devolve to creaturely appetite or spiritual transcendence, to Pandarus's "casuel plesaunce" or Troilus's disembodied laughter from the heavens. As he rewrites the *Filostrato*, Chaucer abandons not only its doomed pagan world but also the secular world. Though the poem is able somewhat to recuperate Troilus's *trouthe* as an ethical value, it must abandon the virtuous actions to which desire leads him in Book 3 (3.425–27) and by which Criseyde quells her fears (3.470–88).[32] It loses the concrete sense, too, of Pandarus's initial description of Criseyde as a "lady vertuous" (1.898), "a worthy place to love" (1.895). More than the rhetorical figure of *diminutio* is involved when the narrator, translating Boccaccio's euphemistic phrase "d'amor sentiron l'ultimo valore" ("they experienced the highest power of love" [3.32.8]), finds himself unable to speak of "the grete worthynesse" (3.1316) of carnal love or of the shared felicity by which "eche of hem gan otheres lust obeye" (3.1690). The constraints imposed by Chaucer's sources finally become thematic and aesthetic limitations.

The palinode dismisses "thise wrecched worldes appetites" (5.1851) along with temporal goods. The narrator, like Troilus in the eighth sphere, has a Boethian perspective, as he appeals to his audience to choose celestial love in the form of Christ's redemption. Whether with fervent devotion or mixed emo-

---

[30] Schless, 112–14.

[31] Kenelm Foster shows how Dante balances the unifying belief that "all human desires *are* radically one" with the particularity of experience needed to claim that our desires can be the objects of moral deliberation—see *The Two Dantes and Other Studies* (Berkeley: Univ. of California Press, 1977), 37–55.

[32] Siegfried Wenzel contends that in Book 4 Troilus is a figure who becomes the perfect representative of a flawed, worldly view of love—see "Chaucer's Troilus of Book IV," *PMLA* 79 (1964): 542–47. Windeatt's comparisons between Chaucer and Boccaccio on the issue of sensuality give a sense of the area of philosophical reflection about desire that the borrowings from Boethius and the *Rose* effectively close off in Chaucer's poem—see "Chaucer and the *Filostrato*," *Chaucer and the Italian Trecento*, ed. Piero Boitani (Cambridge: Cambridge Univ. Press, 1983), 163–83, at 175–78.

tions, he has detached himself from the world of his poem. But the "yonge, fresshe folkes" in his audience, who are the "loveres" addressed at the beginning, still seek the "plesaunce" of worldly love. So, too, does the audience of his next poem—"Ye lovers that kan make of sentement" (LGW F 69). For this audience, the courtly world he addressed in virtually all his writing before the *Canterbury Tales*, social models and institutions come from "the forme of olde clerkis speche / In poetrie" (5.1854–55), which the narrator rejects. In this respect, they have not escaped pagan history, for the constrained and ultimately futile choices that hang over doomed Troy apply to them as well. By defining desire as Boethius and the *Rose* prescribe and as Pandarus reveals in his "unthrift," the poem leaves them implicated in tragic history without the means to deliberate fully on the objects of their erotic and moral experience.

"Our owen wo to drynke": Loss, Gender and Chivalry in Troilus and Criseyde

LOUISE O. FRADENBURG

Cultures differ in the ways in which they practice violence and in the ways in which gender differences become involved in the practice of violence. The most important premise of this essay is that women and men–"feminine" and "masculine" subjects–are not born to inflict or endure violence in the ways that they do, but rather must be acculturated or "constructed" for certain patterns of violence. This essay accordingly explores how TROILUS AND CRISEYDE both participates in, and analyzes, cultural practices of violence in the later fourteenth century. TROILUS AND CRISEYDE is a poem that in some ways asks us to see the problematic nature of "honorable" violence, and in other ways asks us to turn a blind eye to it. The poem engages in the shaping of masculine and feminine subjects for violence, and in the "occlusion"–the concealment–of the frequently dishonorable consequences of being chivalrous. But TROILUS AND CRISEYDE also asks us to see the importance of those medieval practices and discourses that "heroize" suffering– make it glamorous, "manly," morally authoritative–and "deheroize" mere survival, making the wish to live seem a humiliating (feminine) weakness of character. The poem asks us to analyze the heroization of suffering in part through the poem's revisions of courtly love motifs, and thereby through its portrayal of how the "feminine chivalric subject"–Criseyde–is constructed for a particular experience of violence. In so doing the poem performs a kind of cultural work similar to that provided by psychoanalysis in twentieth-century culture: it asks us to see how and why subjects might be constructed to "consent," in fact to desire, their own jeopardy, if such jeopardy is a significant aspect of their culture's practice of violence.

> "Therto we wrecched wommen nothing konne,
> Whan us is wo, but wepe and sitte and thinke;
> Oure wrecche is this, our owen wo to drynke."
> —Criseyde[1]

There are histories of suffering and of violence. The interdependence of such histories must seem obvious, yet their links can be, and have been, obscured

---

[1] *T&C* 2.782–84.

often enough because of the political inarticulacy of those who suffer and because those who commit violence rarely remind us of what it is like to suffer, except insofar as they rewrite the suffering of others as their own capacity to suffer gloriously *"for"* lord, king, nation.[2] Such a heroization of suffering *for*, in the history of the West, typically devalorizes actual suffering, and devalorizes those who attempt to avoid it as well as those prohibited from inflicting it. For the heroic ideal, survival is a non-noble goal; it is ignoble to complain of physical pain; those not categorically permitted to wound others have no honor in themselves, but only through relations of dependence on those who bear arms.

The heroization of suffering *for* has in fact been one of the chief means of occluding the history of suffering and its relation to the history of violence. The foregrounding and idealization of an *intentional* relationship to violence has, for example, made it difficult to treat the effects of disease, war, dispossession, rape, and psychic trauma as potentially related "patterns of suffering" constructed, at least in part, by "theory, action, and perception," and endured by "embodied" selves.[3] The heroization of suffering has also played a central part in the development of what Marcuse called "the ideology of death"—the inculcation of the acceptance of death as the ground for all forms of domination, the inculcation of "compliance with the master over death."[4] In what ways has consent to the "transvaluation" of death—to its transformation from that which ends our lives into that which gives meaning to our lives—been solicited? How have subjects been brought to serve as "arms of the state"? Moreover, if the primary site of the construction of the subject's consent to sacrificial violence is (however diversely formed) the "family," or "household," what relations might we imagine between familial practices of violence as well as of desire, on the one hand, and violence practiced by community or nation?[5] Finally, if there are rhetorics that speak and produce violence, how have "literature" and literary study participated in the violence of glorification, the politicization of loss, the domination of "the scene of writing" itself?[6]

---

[2] See Elaine Scarry's chapters on "The Structure of Torture" and "The Structure of War" in *The Body in Pain: The Making and Unmaking of the World* (New York: Oxford Univ. Press, 1985).

[3] See David Michael Levin's argument for a "cultural epidemiology" in *Pathologies of the Modern Self: Postmodern Studies on Narcissism, Schizophrenia, and Depression* (New York: New York Univ. Press, 1987), 5, 7.

[4] Herbert Marcuse's essay "The Ideology of Death," in *The Meaning of Death*, ed. Herman Feifel (New York: McGraw-Hill, 1959), 64–76, analyzes the relations between the treatment of death in Western philosophy and larger cultural strategies of domination.

[5] Teresa de Lauretis argues that "violence is en-gendered in representation"; "violence between intimates must be seen in the wider context of social power relations; and gender is absolutely central to the family." See "The Violence of Rhetoric: Considerations on Representation and Gender," in *The Violence of Representation: Literature and the History of Violence*, ed. Nancy Armstrong and Leonard Tennenhouse (London: Routledge, 1989), 240–41.

[6] For an analysis of the rhetoric of violence in Italian humanist texts, see Stephanie Jed, "The Scene of Tyranny: Violence and the Humanistic Tradition," in *The Violence of Representation*, 29–44, at 29, 41.

These questions are important ones for readers of *Troilus and Criseyde* because it is a poem in which both violence and its occlusion have in some ways been very successful.[7] Its apparent preoccupation with "intimate desires" and with psychic trauma, with private spaces and secret conversations and innermost thoughts, has by and large, and not at all surprisingly, been replicated in a critical tradition more concerned with the vicissitudes of love than war. Given that the occasional appearances made by psychoanalytic criticism within this tradition (as within studies of mourning in general) have tended to confirm the irrelevance of communal violence to desire and loss, what might readers of *Troilus and Criseyde* have to gain by exploring psychoanalytic discourses on loss?[8] How could attention to such discourses help us think more deeply about the patterning of violence and suffering in and around Chaucer's poem? And is it, further, possible that *Troilus and Criseyde* might in turn contribute importantly to our understanding of rhetorics of loss?

Here I can do little more than suggest a few ways of approaching these questions. When we consider psychoanalytic theories of mourning in terms of histories of suffering, such theories seem to emerge in a cultural "place" once occupied by the exaltation of the masculine chivalric subject's *capacity* to confront and endure infinite loss, and by the depreciation of the feminine chivalric subject's claims to reparation. Psychoanalytic theory seems to occupy this cultural location partly because some of its developments are implicated in the heroization of suffering, as is suggested by the derivation of the Oedipal paradigm from classical tragedy, the association of the Oedipal paradigm with mourning through the theory of identification, and the frequent recurrence in Freud and elsewhere of nostalgic, archaicizing allusions to bygone elites.[9] Julia Kristeva's work in *Black Sun* offers a way of bringing out some aspects of a psychoanalytic rhetoric of violence relevant to *Troilus and Criseyde*.

Kristeva writes:

---

[7] Three helpful discussions of these issues are Diamond, "Politics"; Sally Slocum, "Criseyde among the Greeks," *NM* 87 (1986): 365–74; and David Aers's discussion of Criseyde in *Chaucer*. I differ from Aers's account and from Diamond's chiefly in my stress on *TC*'s *recuperation* of aristocratic loss.

[8] For an analysis of the elegy, and of studies of grief, in this connection, see my essay "Voice Memorial: Loss and Reparation in Chaucer's Poetry," *Exemplaria* 2 (1990): 170–202, esp. 184–85.

[9] The importance of the activity of identification in mourning, and in the construction of the psychoanalytic subject, was pointed to by Freud in passages like the following from "Mourning and Melancholia": "all the time the existence of the lost object is continued in the mind. Each single one of the memories and hopes which bound the libido to the object is brought up and hyper-cathected"; Freud's further association in that essay of the process of mourning with the formation of the superego helped to situate mourning and identification within the Oedipal trajectory. On the contribution made by "Mourning and Melancholia" to the theory of identification, see Jean Laplanche, *Life and Death in Psychoanalysis*, trans. Jeffrey Mehlman (Baltimore: Johns Hopkins Univ. Press, 1976), 79; see also Julia Kristeva, *Black Sun: Depression and Melancholy*, trans. Leon Roudiez (New York: Columbia Univ. Press, 1989), 11.

The child king becomes irredeemably sad before uttering his first words; this is because he has been irrevocably, desperately separated from the mother, a loss that causes him to try to find her again, along with other objects of love, first in the imagination, then in words.[10]

Black Sun is Kristeva's tragic *Poetics*, a lamentation for irredeemable grief, irrevocable separation, the exposed and abandoned male child, the disinherited heir, kinged finally through struggle; her collocation of the irredeemable with the "triumph" of sublimation—of creativity in the form of art—is in the mode of tragedy. In her chapter "Psychoanalysis—A Counterdepressant," we move from the irrevocable and desperate and apparently unwanted separation of the Oedipal child king from his mother to the revelation of "matricide" as "our vital necessity," and the "inversion of matricidal drive into a death-bearing maternal image," the "bloodthirsty Fury": "For man and for woman the loss of the mother is a biological and psychic necessity, the first step on the way to becoming autonomous." Though Kristeva sees loss as a necessity for woman as well as for man, however, there is no child queen in this chapter.[11] The "peculiar" difficulty of the feminine subject's travail in separating from the mother does not, unlike that of the masculine subject, produce *in and of itself* the triumph of creativity. As happens so often in the rhetoric of loss, "good" and "bad" mourning are gendered.[12] The grief of men leads in a relatively straightforward renunciatory path, an *ascesis*, away from the maternal object, through identification with the "father," to sublimation and "poetic form."[13] In contrast the grief of women remains inglorious, inarticulate, its object encrypted—"Our wrecche is this, oure owen wo to drynke," says Criseyde—"[u]nless," writes Kristeva (30),

> [*another*] massive introjection of the ideal succeeds ... in satisfying narcissism with its negative side *and* the longing to be present in the arena where the world's power is at stake.

Moreover, when lack—valued by some psychoanalytic theory as enabling the construction of the subject—is given in some privileged way to the "father," the "mother" *is* lacked, but cannot generate the kind of "creative" lack that constructs a subject; thus while the mother may be granted a role in biological repro-

---

[10] Kristeva, *Black Sun*, 6.

[11] On sublimation, see Kristeva, 22. Kristeva contends (*Black Sun*, 27–30) that because woman, unlike man, must identify with the mother *as* woman, but also must separate from her, it is more difficult for the feminine subject to turn affect into symbol, "matricidal drive" into a "death-bearing maternal image": "Indeed, how can She be that bloodthirsty Fury, since I am She ... She is I?" The result of the woman's travail is her "constant tendency to extol the problematic mourning for the lost object ... not so fully lost, and it remains, throbbing, in the 'crypt' of feminine ease and maturity."

[12] On the distribution of "good" and "bad" mourning according to gender, see Fradenburg, "Voice Memorial," 185.

[13] The "father" has some complicated meanings in this connection which are explored by Kristeva at pages 23–24 in her discussion of "symbolic lineage."

duction, she is granted no role in the process of the social birth of the subject.[14]

Kristeva's invocation of matricide thus brings out the potential for violence in the psychoanalytic rhetoric of mourning: the destruction of the "mother" by her daughters as well as by her sons. Whether daughter or son is involved, rescue—in the form of cultural participation—arrives in the form of the father, who exacts a price, demands the sacrifice of the mother in order for the process of "substitution" to begin. The consequences of such a narrative imperative for the feminine subject seem to be, in Kristeva's thought, the uncertainty of her participation in culture—her identity somehow doubly uncertain, problematic. The submission of the masculine subject is also demanded, if he is to inherit, if nothing else is to be taken from him: he is threatened with isolation if he continues to grieve unremittingly, and is bought off for his renunciation with promises of future wealth, life, power, art. There is a strict economy in such rhetorics of mourning—in their inculcation of the consent to death, their offers of compensatory cultural glories. Discourses of loss—some psychoanalytic theory among them—have coercive designs on, and coercively design, the course of the subject's desire, and they embed those designs in the formation of the subject's gender identity. At the same time it is unquestionably true that such violence works to substantiate and further masculine privilege.

And yet is there something psychoanalytic theory can contribute to the understanding of mourning besides permitting us to decipher within some of its manifestations the presence of an accommodation of violence?[15] Juliana Schiesari's recent work stresses the potential productivity of mourning for female solidarity and community, a productivity achieved not through triumph or mastery over an irrevocably lost maternal object but through a continued relationality with the figure of the mother and hence with female communities.[16] Other work that has been done on the productive agency of the mother in the cultural as well as biological construction of the subject would include Sara Ruddick's argument that one aspect of the practice of mothering is precisely the conforming of a child to the "rules" of its culture.[17] There is also,

---

[14] Maurice Bloch's "Death, Women, and Power" in *Death and the Regeneration of Life*, ed. Maurice Bloch and Jonathan Parry (Cambridge: Cambridge Univ. Press, 1982), 211–30, shows how women—perhaps because of their association with biological birth, and certainly because of their cultural devaluation—can be made to stand, in funeral rituals, for division, death, and sorrow, whereas men will be associated with rebirth into, and of, the community.

[15] Freud himself, as Lorraine Siggins puts it, repeatedly affirms "that a loved object is never really relinquished"—see "Mourning: A Critical Survey of the Literature," *IJP* 47 (1966): 14–25, at 17, where she cites Freud's "Letter to Binswanger," in *Letters of Sigmund Freud*, ed. E. L. Freud (New York: Basic Books, 1960). I have argued elsewhere ("Voice Memorial," 182–83) that such an understanding might provide a basis for the revaluation rather than the punishment of mourning, for the rethinking of problematic concepts like "substitution" for the lost object and "mastery of grief."

[16] Schiesari, "Appropriating the Work of Women's Mourning: The Legacy of Renaissance Melancholia," *Working Paper* No. 2, Univ. of Wisconsin-Milwaukee Center for Twentieth-Century Studies (1990–91), 10.

[17] See Sara Ruddick, "Maternal Thinking," in *Mothering: Essays in Feminist Theory*, ed. Joyce Treblicot (Totowa: Rowman and Allanheld, 1984), 213–30; and *Maternal Thinking:*

in Melanie Klein's work, a powerful analysis of the infant's experience of maternity as anticipating any and all future dialectics of lack and fullness that might be thought fundamental in the construction of subject-positions; and in Laplanche's analysis of "maternal care" the mother, far from contributing only the figure of an object of nostalgia, becomes herself a bearer of

> intrusion into the universe of the child of certain meanings of the adult world. . . . The whole of the primal intersubjective relation—between mother and child—is saturated with these meanings. . . . In the final analysis the complete oedipal structure is *present from the beginning*.[18]

Psychoanalysis has offered languages with which to talk in detail about the historicity, the artifactuality, of the subject, and therefore about the role of loss in the subject's construction (not, again, as an experience to be "mastered" or "triumphed" over but as what Marcuse might call an external fact to be grieved). Psychoanalysis thus allows us to think about "fantasy" (which does not mean that something is "unreal" or has never happened, but means rather that whether or not it "actually" happened it inhabits one's psyche in a specifically elaborated way) in connection with the practice of violence. Once psychoanalysis has historicized for us the mourning subject, war can no longer so easily be posited as a privileged "reality" to which all other experiences must measure up if they are to be taken seriously, nor can attempts to articulate the experience of suffering so readily be undermined as doubtful, mere artfulness.[19] To this extent psychoanalytic theory has enabled the very critique of its own complicities with the rhetoric of violence which we have been at pains to examine, and in thus exposing the very strategies of isolation in which it sometimes participates, furthers a shareable political discourse about loss and desire.

If the interiorized and interiorizing tragedy of the subject becomes one of the chief modes whereby psychoanalytic discourse en-genders loss and heroizes masculine suffering, and if the historicizing of the mourning subject becomes the chief psychoanalytic countertext to sacrificial melancholy, what connections useful to a reading of *Troilus and Criseyde* can we make between these figurations of the subject and earlier rhetorics of loss? Tragedy, Aristotle insisted long ago, is about great men, and Kristeva wants to remind us also of "the relationship philosophers have maintained with melancholia . . . black bile (*melaina kole*) saps great men."[20] Is there a philosophical articulation of greatness in re-

---

Toward a Politics of Peace (Boston: Beacon Press, 1989).

[18] Laplanche, *Life and Death in Psychoanalysis*, 44–45. Klein's work is easily available in *The Selected Melanie Klein*, ed. Juliet Mitchell (New York: The Free Press, 1986).

[19] In the Preface to *Images of Women in Peace and War: Cross-Cultural and Historical Perspectives*, ed. Sharon Macdonald, Pat Holden and Shirley Ardener (Madison: Univ. of Wisconsin Press, 1987), xvii, Pat Holden and Shirley Ardener note that the definition of "war" itself is always problematic and is itself an object of contestation. And yet "war" is repeatedly used rhetorically as a touchstone for reality; see my chapter on "Soft and Silken War" in *City, Marriage, Tournament: Arts of Rule in Late Medieval Scotland* (Madison: Univ. of Wisconsin Press, 1991). On doubt and pain, see Scarry, *The Body in Pain*, 4.

[20] Kristeva, *Black Sun*, 6–7.

lation to melancholia during the later Middle Ages? What, during the later Middle Ages, did the work of, or occupied the cultural location, now taken by psychoanalysis? There were, for example, traditions on *tristitia* and despair that provided powerful narrative models for the production of "truth" through valorization of suffering both physical and psychic, creating for the soul an experience of interiority *through* suffering that may well have helped to make the place of the tragic subject of Kristevan psychoanalysis: "Without a bent for melancholia there is no psyche, only a transition to action or play."[21] The Middle Ages also saw the elaboration of extremely powerful models for the valorization of suffering: the Crusades, the chivalric orders, spectacular punishment, penitential theory and practice, the centering of communal and individual piety around the Passion, the melancholy of the courtly lover. The rhetoric and practices of loss characteristic of the warrior culture of the medieval aristocracy will be the particular concern of the following discussion of *Troilus and Criseyde*.

Troilus and Criseyde is a poem about loss, communal as well as private; the poem is centrally concerned with the construction of the aristocratic subject *for* loss, for the delectation and transvaluation of loss, and with the production of an aristocratic poetry whose future is figured as equally uncertain. *Troilus and Criseyde* examines the production of a heroic attitude which *prepares for* rather than obstructs the *ascesis* of military endeavor at the end of the poem (the futility of Troilus's search for Diomede), so that even the masculine chivalric subject's loss of the ability to assert his honor through violent confrontation with his double contributes to the honoring, as it were, of his infinite capacity to inhabit the space of loss. That the reward is a vision of the littleness of the earth, of the absurdity of mourning, is, from the standpoint of aristocratic culture, merely a raising of the stakes, one which *enables* the communalization and spiritualization of Troilus's trajectory, making the most transcendent meanings of all—Christian ones—for "yonge, fresshe folkes, he or she" (5.1835), *out of* Troilus's loss: *Troilus and Criseyde*, I would argue, shows how the aristocracy of the later Middle Ages substantiated itself partly *through* its melancholic embroidering of embarrassment, rejection, humiliation, betrayal, defeat, valorizing them as a means of preventing their implications from posing radical questions about the heroization of suffering.[22]

Thus by the end of the poem, we might say, Troilus dies, but his honorable fate—honorable *through* psychic agony, through the very exhaustion of his chances, through his reduction to a desire completely incapable of achieving its aims and finally suffused with a sense of the vanity even of the attempt—acquires discursive power just at the moment when the text is flooded with metapoetic concerns. Criseyde, by contrast, dishonorably survives, and knows that she will be destroyed by books—"thise bokes wol me shende" (5.1060)—and

---

[21] Susan Snyder, "The Left Hand of God: Despair in Medieval and Renaissance Tradition," *SR* 12 (1965): 18–59; Kristeva, *Black Sun*, 4.

[22] See "Sovereign Love" and "Soft and Silken War" in *City, Marriage, Tournament* for a fuller discussion of this issue.

that she is powerless to affect her reputation. Does this mutually exclusive dis-
tribution of life and good literary reputation mean that Chaucer writes com-
pletely from the point of view of the aristocratic delectation of loss, desirous
perhaps of the power of such an affective strategy for his "litel . . . tragedye"?
(5.1786) Does his text (also) activate counter-strategies that perform cultural
work similar to those psychoanalytic insights that actually enable mourning *not*
in the service of the transcendentalization of violence? Can we suggest what
those strategies might have been for such a poet writing in the later Middle
Ages? The lynchpin here is precisely the contrast between Criseyde and Troi-
lus. Does *Troilus and Criseyde*, while displaying with extraordinary fullness the
aristocratic power to recuperate loss for the practice of violence, ask us at the
same time to deheroize suffering and to grant to "mere" survival, not a mirror-
ing heroic privilege, but more simply the depth of our desire for it, and the ul-
timately political power of the possibility that survival, as ideology and as prac-
tice, might go unpunished? Does Criseyde become the bearer of a valued abil-
ity to mourn in a way that makes a future, permits survival, without celebrating
renunciation and legitimating violence? Or does the suppression of Criseyde's
grief by Pandarus in Book 4—"So lef this sorwe, or platly he wol deye. / And
shapeth yow his sorwe for t'abregge, / And nought encresse, leeve nece
swete!" (4.924–26)—mean that once again woman's mourning leads nowhere
unless to a man's greatness, that Criseyde will become the bearer not of a
valued wish to live on, but of "inconstancy"? And what might be the relation
between the feminization of survival in *Troilus and Criseyde* and heroic constan-
cy in *The Legend of Good Women*, on the one hand, and, on the other, of
Chaucer's own need to survive the vagaries of a political career?

These are difficult questions to answer, partly because Criseyde's capacity for
survival itself bears to some extent the marks of a fantasy, that fantasy being
that only men die in war, that women are less subject to physical violence than
men during either peace or war, that men risk their bodies to protect those of
women ("youre body shal men save," says Hector to Criseyde [1.122]); women
prove their honor, if they prove it at all, through the difficulty of their choices,
through the heroic preservation of their chastity, not through the practice of
arms—i.e., they prove their honor through tests of faith, trials of consent.[23]

Though we can have no hope of cataloguing with any fullness here the role
of violence in late medieval women's lives, it is worth pausing to call a few facts
and images to mind. We know that both noble and non-noble women were
"unofficially" engaged in the practice of warfare when, as was often the case,

---

[23] See Sharon Macdonald, "Drawing the Lines—Gender, Peace and War: An Introduc-
tion," 1–26, in *Images of Women in Peace and War*, esp. page 4 on the role played "in the
creation of a well-ordered [martial] ideology, [of] dualities such as all women as potential
mothers and all men as potential warriors." See also *Society at War: The Experience of England
and France During the Hundred Years War*, ed. C. T. Allmand (Edinburgh: Oliver and Boyd,
1973), 26–27, for an example of an oath "to maintain the honour of womanhood, . . . and
to do this with our bodies, if need be," on the part of a military order founded by the Duke
of Bourbon.

husbands were absent or dead, and they had frequent occasion to defend themselves from rape, injury and death during times of peace as well as in times of war. In one local study, moreover, Kathryn Gravdal describes "life" as it appears in the records of the Abbey of Cerisy in Normandy during the time of the Hundred Years' War and the difficulties women faced in seeking reparation for violence inflicted on them:

> We find a picture of poverty, broken family structures, quotidian sexual violence, incest, demoralization, and social instability. The court is notably lax in sentencing, practically flaunting canon law. The names of the jurors in any given sitting frequently include those of men convicted of criminal behavior in the preceding sessions.[24]

In one of the rape cases tried by this court, the accused man was convicted and fined for rape, and the woman in question fined three times as much for allowing him to have carnal knowledge of her (Gravdal 213). And the *Registre Criminel de la Justice de Saint-Martin-des-Champs a Paris*

> clearly suggest[s] that women, who commit far fewer crimes, receive the death penalty three times more frequently than men;

their punishments were burial alive (in order to shield their modesty from hanging) for "lesser offenses," as when in 1342 Ameline La Soufletiere is buried alive for the theft of a man's purple cloak, and burning at the stake for "grave" offenses;[25] when Criseyde is introduced in Chaucer's poem, and the town, angered by her father's betrayal, wants to burn her—"al his kyn"—"fel and bones" (1.91), this is no fantasy of pagan barbarism. Shulamith Shahar writes in *The Fourth Estate* that women died "by the cruellest methods of execution known to the cruel society of the Middle Ages." As Gravdal remarks of medieval French law: "Slow to protect and quick to punish, this society gives every sign that it values female life less than male."[26]

Gravdal also remarks that widows (Criseyde's station in life) were the most frequent victims of rape because they were "unprotected" by father or husband (Gravdal 217). Her research suggests at the same time that relatives and guardians and friends and acquaintances could as easily be the source of violence as of protection. So, perhaps, does evidence from Chaucer's own life: of the witnesses present on Chaucer's behalf at Cecily Champain's well-known release of Chaucer from "*omnomodas assiones tam de raptu meo tam*[sic] *de aliqua alia re vel causa*—actions of whatever kind either concerning my rape or any other matter"—Donald Howard remarks of the witnesses who were present on

---

[24] Kathryn Gravdal, "The Poetics of Rape Law in Medieval France," in *Rape and Representation*, ed. Lynn A. Higgins and Brenda R. Silver (New York: Columbia Univ. Press, 1991), 211.

[25] Gravdal 215–16; Shulamith Shahar, *The Fourth Estate: A History of Women in the Middle Ages*, trans. Chaua Galai (London: Methuen, 1983), 21.

[26] Gravdal, 216. For a broad review of the treatment of rape in medieval law, see Shahar, *The Fourth Estate*, 16–17.

Chaucer's behalf that they were "some very big guns indeed, which means he thought the matter grave"; if Cecily is to be identified as the stepdaughter of Alice Perrers, who had been the mistress of Edward III,

> it means that Chaucer raped or seduced the stepdaughter of an old friend who had done him many favors.... Or it means that his old friend's step-daughter brought against him a vindictive accusation.[27]

The vulnerability of women to intimate violence is also registered in the late fifteenth-century theologian John of Ireland's commentary on the Annunciation in his *Meroure of Wyssdome*, in which he warns ladies to eschew "worldly plesance" in the form not only of the company of strange men, but also that of kinsmen and friends, because "gret perell js ... to be allane with [th]ame jn sacret placis and tyme."[28] And Georges Duby has argued of medieval France that incest was not a stigmatized aberration nor even an overlooked occasional vice, but rather a central practice and sign of seigneurial power.[29]

Troilus and Criseyde was written during the Hundred Years' War, during the period of decline in England's fortunes and glory. The poem's interiorization and spiritualization of loss and its apparent rejection of the meaningfulness of mortal combat with one's enemy (Troilus is not allowed a battle to the death with Diomede) refigure late fourteenth-century disappointment in the prowess of chivalry, in its powers of protection. Such disappointment would have been exacerbated by the demoralization of civilians during the Hundred Years' War. C. T. Allmand notes that

> one of the biggest changes in warfare which occurred at this period was the way in which, as the scale of war continued to expand, this expansion was made to embrace larger proportions of the populations of both England and France than ever before.[30]

The war made on the civilian population was most grievous in its effects in France, whose "unhappy fate" it was "to provide the battleground for much of the war," as Chaucer himself well knew, having participated in the 1359 campaign;[31] but England was raided frequently during the latter part of the fourteenth century, when England's fortunes turned for the worse, and there was great fear of invasion (Allmand 9, 11)—a fear of perforation which seems, in

---

[27] Donald R. Howard, *Chaucer: His Life, His Works, His World* (New York: E. P. Dutton, 1987), 317, 318.

[28] *The Meroure of Wyssdome ... by Johannes de Irlandia*, ed. Charles Macpherson, vol. 1 (Edinburgh: William Blackwood and Sons, for the Scottish Text Society, 1926), 137.

[29] See his chapter on "Incest, Bigamy and Divorce among Kings and Nobles," in *Medieval Marriage: Two Models from Twelfth-Century France*, trans. Elborg Foster (Baltimore: Johns Hopkins Univ. Press, 1978). Critics who argue that Chaucer could not possibly even have dreamed of implying that Pandarus may have had incestuous desires for Criseyde should reconsider the family history of the period.

[30] *Society at War*, ed. Allmand, 9.

[31] See Howard, *Chaucer*, 69–73.

Chaucer's poem, to be displaced onto Criseyde in the form of her anxieties, her ambiguous loyalties, her uncertain nationality, the general fragility of her borders. For England as well as for France, "war was a form of human activity which had by now come to pervade all the ranks of those societies in or between which it was being fought" (Allmand 13). Though Allmand does not expound on them, the consequences for women must have been terrible; during the English siege of Limoges in 1370, Howard notes, Edward the Black Prince, "borne in on his litter, watched while the soldiers, on his orders, ran about killing the citizens—men, women, and children."[32]

Thus, when Pandarus arrives at Criseyde's house to tell her about Troilus's love for her, and she says "is than th'assege aweye? / I am of Grekes so fered that I deye" (2.123–24), we might reasonably conclude that her fears—here and at any other moment in the poem—are more than justified. But many of her critics have wanted to see Criseyde as unheroic, concerned "only" with survival; they have isolated her anxieties from the historical contexts that explain them (as indeed do some her interpreters within the poem itself), positing those anxieties as part of an essential character and thereby perpetuating fantasies of male rescue and feminine weakness. C. S. Lewis wrote that Chaucer

> so emphasized the ruling passion of his heroine, that we cannot mistake it. It is Fear—fear of loneliness, of old age, of death, of love, and of hostility; of everything, indeed, that can be feared. And from this Fear springs the only positive passion which can be permanent in such a nature; the pitiable longing, more childlike than womanly, for protection, for some strong and stable thing that will hide her away and take the burden from her shoulders.[33]

To treat fear as a characterological matter where Criseyde is concerned is of course to fail to analyze the extent to which the question of violence done to Criseyde, and its role in the construction of her desires, is constantly both raised and occluded in *Troilus and Criseyde*, a poem which represents only chivalrous knights as braving actual violence: Troilus goes off to fight the war and comes back with arrows hanging off him, an image treated as erotic as well as heroic: "Who yaf me drynke?" says Criseyde (2.651). But, again, inside Troy, inside those private Trojan spaces in which love is pursued, the potential for violence against Criseyde is brought before us even as it is made to disappear.

There are, to begin with, the threat of Criseyde's being burned to death for her father's treachery; her fear of the Greeks; the forcefulness of some of Pandarus's gestures towards her ("And in hire bosom the lettre down he thraste," 2.1155); the coerciveness of his rhetoric ("And therfore, er that age the devoure, / Go love," 2.395–96). When Book 2 opens, Pandarus, who has been feeling "his part of loves shotes keene" (2.58), is awakened to his "grete em-

---

[32] Howard, *Chaucer*, 128.

[33] C. S. Lewis, *The Allegory of Love: A Study in Medieval Tradition* (New York: Oxford Univ. Press, 1958), 185; cited in Kaminsky, *Critics*, 145–46; for bibliography on the question of Criseyde's fear, see Kaminsky, 200nn58 and 59.

prise" by the song of the swallow Procne; the allusion is rendered in such chill-
ingly neutral tones that it is difficult to believe either that Chaucer expected his
audience to draw the inference or that he did not: Procne

> so neigh hym made hire cheterynge,
> How Tereus gan forth hire suster take,
> That with the noyse of hire he gan awake.   2.68–70[34]

In a further tableau which itself seems to allude to the tableau of Pandarus's
awakening, Criseyde listens to the song of Procne's raped and mutilated sister,
Philomela, in the form of the "nyghtyngale"—here described by Chaucer as
male, and as singing *"Peraunter* . . . a lay / Of love" (2.921–22; my emphasis)—
just before she falls asleep and dreams (2.925–31) of the eagle who painlessly
rips out her heart and leaves his behind—a simultaneous evocation and denial
of violence, an image at once of overwhelming invasive power and of apparent
reciprocity ("herte lefte for herte").[35] Book 2—the book in which Criseyde is
brought to desire—is thus marked by a series of allusions to invasive violence
and rape whose import is nonetheless rendered completely ambiguous. But this
doubleness is at work everywhere in *Troilus and Criseyde*'s poetics of violence.

One of the most important moments that stage what Lynn A. Higgins and
Brenda R. Silver refer to as the "elision of the scene of violence" characteristic
of literature about rape is the consummation scene in Book 3.[36] Here the
specter of rape is raised by Troilus himself—"Now yeldeth yow, for other bote
is non!" (3.1208)—and is then made to vanish when Criseyde utters the words
that might seem to confirm her consent, not only to her "capture" at this
moment, but to the entire course of the affair:

> "Ne hadde I er now, my swete herte deere,
> Ben yold, ywis, I were now nought heere!"   3.1210–11

But just previous to this moment, the narrator has posed the following rhetori-
cal question:

> What myghte or may the sely larke seye,

---

[34] The story is told in Ovid's *Metamorphoses* 6 of how Tereus, married to Procne, raped
her sister Philomela, subsequently imprisoning her and cutting out her tongue so that she
could not accuse him of his crime. Philomela weaves a tapestry telling her story and sends
it to her sister; they revenge themselves upon Tereus and are turned into a swallow (Procne)
and a nightingale (Philomela). The story is also told in Chaucer's *Legend of Good Women*; he
leaves out the sisters' revenge against Tereus. For a brilliant reading of this myth that is
relevant to my concerns in this essay, see Patricia Joplin, "The Voice of the Shuttle is Ours,"
in *Rape and Representation*, 35–64.

[35] Images of coupling, of "twoness," that suggest both reciprocity and dominance,
consent and coercion, reappear elsewhere in the poem, indicating again the extent to which
the abjection of the later fourteenth century's experience of the war is being both recalled
and denied in *Troilus and Criseyde*; fear of violation is at once expressed and suppressed. See,
e. g., the irony of Troilus's use of the expression "we tweyne" just when he informs Criseyde
"Now be ye kaught" (3.1207), and the pastoral image of the "wodebynde" twisting about its
tree (3.1230–31).

[36] "Introduction: Rereading Rape," in *Rape and Representation*, 5.

Whan that the sperhauk hath it in his foot?   3.1191–92

He adds that "Criseyde, which that felte hire thus itake, / ... / Right as an aspes leef she gan to quake" (3.1198, 1200). A picture of maidenly modesty? Or are we indeed to question what the innocent, helpless and possibly foolish lark is supposed to say when the sparrowhawk has it in its foot? Possibly "Ne hadde I er now, my swete herte deere, / Ben yold, ywis, I were now nought heere"?[37]

But what of the fact that the exquisite pastoral images used to describe the lovers' pleasure in Book 3 (1226–32) are followed immediately by a simile that compares Criseyde's *language* to that of the nightingale?

> And as the newe abaysed nyghtyngale,
> That stynteth first whan she bygynneth to synge,
> Whan that she hereth any herde tale,
> Or in the hegges any wyght stirynge,
> And after siker doth hire vois out rynge,
> Right so Criseyde, whan hire drede stente,
> Opned hire herte, and tolde hym hire entente.   3.1233–39

Are we to hear behind Criseyde's (to us) inaudible voicing of her "entente" the mutilated mouth of Philomela? The poem at this moment recalls for us the oc-clusion of the voice of the survivor—Philomela, Procne, and Criseyde are all women who survive to tell their stories but whose voices are in various ways rendered inaudible or ambiguous. The possibility of Criseyde's rape can be spoken only through a kind of intertextual haunting. Is Book 3, then, like the garden in Book 4 of *Daphnis and Chloe*, what John Winkler has called "a micro-cosm of the pastoral world—protected, fertile, flowering, with a structure of recollected violence in the center"? Do Troilus and Criseyde discover here that "sexual violence is not merely an unhappy accident that might be avoided, but is a destiny written into the very premises of socially constructed reality?"[38] It seems likely that they do, though not in such a way as to become "aware" of their circumstances.

This moment of consummated love, of overheard but inaudible privacy, is itself both a preservation and a violation of inner space; the presence of such a silence at the structural core of *Troilus and Criseyde* bespeaks the extent of the poem's fixations on violence that cannot be articulated, and explains as well its fascination with the uncertainties of speech, its defensive garrulities (the Narra-tor and Pandarus, for example). The consummation scene is written to produce an ambiguity that *cannot be resolved* through interpretation; we cannot "decide" whether Criseyde has consented or not, whether she has been raped or not. We can only see that the possibility has been raised and then made unde-

---

[37] Aers (*Chaucer*, 127–28) recognizes that "male domination" makes the question of desire very problematic in this scene; but even he posits a "genuine love" that can be distin-guished from "social practice and ideology."

[38] John J. Winkler, "The Education of Chloe: Erotic Protocols and Prior Violence," in *Rape and Representation*, 15–34, at 25.

cidable; and this suggests that for a woman in Criseyde's position sexual vio-
lence may *be* what she has for love, may *be* the medium of her consent. It sug-
gests also that such ambiguity is in part designed to protect the delectation of
invasive violence, and is talismanic for the masculine chivalric subject—who by
means of such occlusion may retain the conviction both of his masculinity and
of his honor.

We could of course argue that part of what Chaucer is trying to achieve in
Troilus and Criseyde—this would perhaps be true of some of his sources as well—
is an avoidance of rape, an attempt to avoid tragic repetition of the circum-
stances of Helen's abduction (elopement? rape?). Certainly Book 4 presents
Troilus, Criseyde, and Pandarus attempting to imagine solutions to their pre-
dicament that have not already proved destructive, and may suggest that their
failure to do so is "tragic"—not because they lack imagination, but because
their culture provides no real alternatives (see, for example, 4.547–609). So
that, though they avoid the "ravyshhyng" of women, Criseyde is apparently
doomed to repeat her reliance on the ambiguities of male "protection," and
Troilus to turn his rage and sorrow inward. But is Troilus heroized *because* he
refuses rape? To what extent is the refusal of rape a recuperation of the war-
rior ideal in *Troilus and Criseyde*, part of Troilus's ennobling *ascesis*?

Or is the undecidability of Chaucer's text designed not just to occlude vio-
lence but to make us "see" its occlusion? For it may be that "seeing" the oc-
clusion of violence (that is, seeing the trace of what has been màde to disap-
pear) was about as far as Chaucer was able to go by way of a deheroization of
suffering. Further, it may be that the value placed at the end of the poem on
vision rather than effective action marks the presence of an ideological *cul-de-
sac* in which nonetheless a real struggle over the value of "survival" is taking
place—one which would break out again with the *Legend of Good Women*, a
poem also centrally concerned with the workings of gender in the heroization
of suffering and the devalorization of survival, and one in which the Chauceri-
an narrator is himself somewhat accommodating and obedient. Chaucer's own
career, after all, was not one in which heroism was easily affordable.[39]

This in itself raises another set of complex issues; for the poem's privileging
of vision cannot be unrelated to the voyeurism (apparent voyeurism? does he
watch, or does he deflect the voyeuristic gaze by reading, and what has the
world gained by his so doing?) of Pandarus's behavior in Book 3—"And with
that word he drow hym to the feere, / And took a light, and fond his conte-
naunce, / As for to looke upon an old romaunce" (3.978–80). The poem's priv-
ileging of vision might therefore also be related to the coy, prurient ambiguity
of yet another moment of undecidability that follows on the morning after
Troilus and Criseyde's first night together: the moment that *might* be read, but
I would argue could never *definitively* be read, as Pandarus's incestuous dalli-
ance with Criseyde:

> With that she gan hire face for to wrye

---

[39] See Paul Strohm, *Social Chaucer* (Cambridge: Harvard Univ. Press, 1989).

> With the shete, and wax for shame al reed;
> And Pandarus gan under for to prie,
>
> . . .
>
> I passe al that which chargeth nought to seye.
> What! God foryaf his deth, and she al so   3.1569-76

From the pastoralization of violence, to the avuncularity of incest? Chaucer's poem indeed treads the finest of lines between the perception of the occlusion of violence and the desire to participate in it. And yet I think it is a line that can be read: it may be, in Chaucer's poem, what there is in the place of an awareness willing to read the strength of the wish for survival, willing in particular to read the ways that, in cultures committed to the uses of death, the wish for survival constructs the subject to desire where there is no desire, and to deny desire where it might be. The simultaneous detachment and curiosity of Chaucer's narrators seems to tread this line; they look on, but change nothing, and so perhaps can be said neither to do violence nor to prevent it, neither to hurt nor to rescue; what they desire is never clear, though it is always clear that they desire something, that they are "in it" for something, even if it seems that they are "in it" only for "protection." The close intercalation in Book 3 of Pandarus as go-between and of the *Galeotto* of canto 5 of the *Inferno* is relevant here—does he merely look on or does he make desire happen where it would not? is he responsible for sexual violence, has he tried to cover up its traces? "kep the clos" (3.332); and yet Chaucer doesn't take himself off the hook by putting anyone in hell, and doesn't much glamorize his own search for "vision."[40] We should question, however, whether unheroic avuncularity—"erand" rather than "grete emprise" [2.72-73]—is preferable to heroization. While Chaucer's refusal to heroize Pandarus, or the narrator of *Troilus and Criseyde*, may inscribe a sense of the kinds of contributions a courtier must make to the glorification of his betters' losses—while Chaucer's apparent neutrality, his ambivalence, his devotion to "both sides," may be a problem rather than an intention—such ambiguities are perhaps there in the first place because, as the Prologue to *The Legend of Good Women* attests, he sees in ways that bring out conflict and danger, even if the screen of ambiguity breaks out afresh each time we seem ready to see the scene of violence done to as well as by desire. Criseyde's survival may be read as a countertext to the heroization of suffering, but only when it is read alongside of the narrator's preoccupation with the question of whether he can do anything to "rescue" her, and thus to that small degree asks a question about whether he has maintained "the honour of womanhood," has helped "widows, virgins and ladies."[41]

If the question of engendered consent to violence impels the narrative of *Troilus and Criseyde*, then one of the crucial things that does the work of psy-

---

[40] See Karla Taylor's fine chapter on "A Text and Its Afterlife" (*Chaucer Reads*, 50-77), which charts the intercalation I have just mentioned.

[41] *Society at War*, ed. Allmand, 27.

choanalysis in this poem is precisely the poem's reconsideration of the motifs of courtly love, and the resulting fullness of attention given to the construction of subjects of desire; the ways in which the procedures involved enforce the experiential transformation of what Pierre Bourdieu calls "coerced relations" into "elective" and "reciprocal" ones;[42] and the difficulties posed thereby for the notion of consent. It is well-known that Chaucer in effect brought out Criseyde's consent *as a problem*, whereas in Boccaccio she is more straightforwardly eager and in charge of the narrative that brings about the fulfillment of "her" desires, "double" only in an *intentional* difference between depth and surface; and Chaucer calls attention to this issue also when he counterpoises the incredible, if powerfully handled, conventionality of the way Troilus falls in love—the subtle streams of her eyes, and so on—with the songs and dreams and interventions of the gaze and the promptings and coercions of Pandarus that characterize the way Criseyde falls in love. Chaucer, moreover, pushes the point of the contrast upon us with the following:

> Now myghte som envious jangle thus:
> "This was a sodeyn love; how myght it be
> That she so lightly loved Troilus,
> Right for the firste syghte, ye, parde?"
> Now whoso seith so, mote he nevere ythe!
> For every thing, a gynnyng hath it nede
> Er al be wrought, withowten any drede.   2.666–72

Book 2 begins with the narrator's famous meditation on change; it is also in this book that Criseyde remarks, "That erst was nothing, into nought it torneth" (2.798), and it is no accident that once again Criseyde is made the bearer of an examination of the historicity, as opposed to the melancholy, of desire, given subsequent events. But nonetheless the departure taken here by Chaucer allows us to read an important construction of the feminine subject of chivalric culture.[43]

In Book 2, long before the completion of the trajectory that reveals Criseyde's story to be partly that of the feminine chivalric subject, a subject produced *for* consent—that is, for an enervation of will/desire refigured as the paradox of an obedient choice—Criseyde ponders the (for her, as feminine chivalric subject) defining irruption of an "other" desire into the disciplined camouflage of her survival as a traitor's daughter in Troy—a situation in which that other desire that comes to claim her will do so as the desire of something that is *not* other, but is rather at home in Troy, surrounded by brothers and parents, she living in Troy, after all, chiefly on the *grace* of the masculine chivalric subject.

---

[42] Pierre Bourdieu, *Outline of a Theory of Practice*, trans. Richard Nice (Cambridge: Cambridge Univ. Press, 1977), 171.

[43] The "feminine chivalric subject" I describe below does not exhaust the possibilities for the subject-positions of aristocratic medieval women, but it was one of the most powerfully enforced and culturally-validated of such positions.

Now, where Book 1 is concerned, while Hector's grace in intervening for Criseyde's life by definition can ask for nothing in return without departing from the economy of honor, Criseyde's meditations in Book 2 on whether or not to allow Troilus to take over and serve as a more intimate "protector" suggest that such grace will count for nothing in the absence of a deheroized feminine practice of calculation, quietude, survival. Thus the disappearance of the betraying, abandoning, imperfect human father, Calcas, clears the stage for the heroizing of the masculine chivalric subject's paternal powers: Hector's "grand" gift of her life to her, grand because of its apparent positioning beyond any possible return that she could make to Troy's best warrior, grand also because of its willingness to risk, to stake itself on her innocence, to refuse to read a difference between her surface and her depths.

Criseyde is generously deracinated, defathered—"Lat your fadres treson gon / Forth with meschaunce, and ye youreself in joie / Dwelleth with us, whil yow good list, in Troie" (1.117-19)—so that she may be, as feminine subject, "rescued" for, taken by, called to, the ideality of chivalric culture, as object of its lavish and absurd expenditures of trust and effort. The scene of her entry into the ideality of chivalric culture, which is also the scene of her entry into Chaucer's poem, is one of two moments in *Troilus and Criseyde* that does not seem in any way to ironize the genre of chivalric romance—the other also being Hector's intervention, also a refusal of ignoble exchange, of the "charge" of that "natural" father whose own choice had, after all, been survival: "Syres, she nys no prisonere"; "I not on yow who that this charge leyde"; "We usen here no wommen for to selle" (4.179-82). Criseyde is thus prepared, through the fact of her paternity, as exclusively *for* the desire or at least purposes of the masculine chivalric subject, by honorably cutting her loose from her history, thus marking her with the "chance" of honor, the opportunity to provide "aventure" for the masculine chivalric subject, making her as adventitious as the damsels of uncertain identity encountered in the pages of Malory's own obsessive work on rescue and threat.

The fantasy—and the lethal message—is that the "life" of the feminine chivalric subject has no history of its own, is owed not even to the paternity (let alone the maternity) of blood or to the participation of that subject in social relationships, but rather is refounded upon the nature of the masculine chivalric subject's desire with respect to her, at least when they meet in those romance encounters and exchanges that structure the meaning and even the possibility of identity. Where the chivalric fantasy of rescue is concerned—and I am arguing that this is a founding fantasy for the construction of the gendered aristocratic subject in the later middle ages—the lineage, history, origin of the romance heroine acquires meaning only through the arrival of desire from the place of the masculine subject, in the sense that she will be his "aventure," she will seem to break in upon his life with the force of a risk, a chance, that founds his honor. And as in the *Knight's Tale* as well this founding moment remakes conquest and takes the form, for her, of an appeal to him, that is, of a request, a question, a wish—in Hector's speech the terms of Criseyde's residence in Troy will be "whil yow good list." The wish is, ultimately, for life, or to put it another way, for a life free of the threat of violence, but since the figure who grants this wish does so through his possession of a superior power of violence [violence being the medium that gives risk its honorable meanings— he may choose either to rape or to rescue, to slay tyrants (Theseus) or be one (Creon), to wage war against women (Theseus) or to save them from the effects of war (Theseus)]—the appeal is for a life figured as free of the threat of death, but only by gift of the other, and therefore as not free at all. Thus the power of death gives meaning to, makes possible, the life of the feminine chivalric subject; and her appeal inscribes her as desiring the intervention of the male subject, as consenting to the loss of the meaning of her history, even as his desire defines her. Moreover, since violence is the medium that gives risk its honorable meanings, the wish to live or to be free from violence, posited as proper to the feminine chivalric subject, places her *as subject* outside the very chivalric ideality that takes her in and on which she is brought to depend. The consensual desire of the feminine chivalric subject is thereby constructed, through loss and violence, for domination: for "compliance with the master over death," for the acceptance of death as the condition whereby life may be refigured as the gift of the ruler. Since she is not recognized as having any capacity in herself to give this kind of symbolic, culturally valorized gift of life, moreover, it is not such a far distance for the feminine chivalric subject to become the bearer of death for the masculine subject, hence wielder of violence from a very different kind of place.

Thus the feminine chivalric subject is constructed to enter the "symbolic order" of chivalric culture through the renunciation of all desire that does not take the form of an appeal for a life free of violence, hence through an erotization of borrowed power, of bonded freedom, of forgiven debt. When she gains entry into language, she will articulate an appeal for freedom to love, for the right of consent to love, as with the formel eagle in the *Parliament of Fowls*; but as the obvious limitations on the choices available to the formel eagle make clear, that very appeal will be predicated on the constitution of an authority whose power of protection and rescue, whose power to rape and kill, may be petitioned.

The profound role of loss and violence in the construction of the feminine chivalric subject, in particular of that subject's gendered relation to bodily suffering, is brought out by Criseyde in the lines that I have used as the epigraph to this essay:

> "Therto we wrecched wommen nothing konne,
> Whan us is wo, but wepe and sitte and thinke;
> Oure wrecche is this, our owen wo to drynke."   2.782–84

When, that is, the masculine rescuer turns out to be the seducer, traitor, rapist (as happens repeatedly in *The Legend of Good Women*), appeal fails and there is no further recourse to be had from chivalric ideality: that is, *feminine* "complaint," as opposed to appeal, must inevitably fall upon deaf ears as there is no feminine subject-position within chivalric ideality from which complaint can be spoken, from which losses can be articulated. Chaucer's poetry—*Anelida and*

Arcite, The Legend of Good Women, The Squire's Tale, Alcyone in *The Book of the Duchess*—repeatedly stages, indeed comes to grief upon, the scene of the inefficacy of any feminine complaint addressed, as it were, to the "rescuer" about *himself,* in his guise of thief or rapist or abandoning lover of "novelrie" (in the case of Ceys it is a matter of his death, when he can no longer offer protection but only unheeded advice spoken by a simulacrum);[44] and these are possibly the circumstances of patronage as well, as the Prologue to *The Legend of Good Women* seems to attest. That, in Chaucer's poetry, this kind of attempt at communication is repeatedly made—and equally repeatedly not only broken off but apparently implicated in the breaking off of the narrative of which it is a part—clearly demonstrates that complaint is the impotent obverse of those founding moments of successful feminine appeal (and thereby of consent to the transvaluation of death) in the beginning of works like *The Knight's Tale* and *Troilus and Criseyde.* Narrative begins as it does in *Troilus and Criseyde* and in *The Knight's Tale* because each work situates the masculine interlocutor of the female subject as rescuer and not as tormentor; as a result the question that is asked, the appeal that is made, can produce a future, "new life," a media success as it were, in the form of narrative. But Criseyde's lines about women's woe hint at that narrative paradigm wherein the coincidence of rescuer and tormentor in the same person turns the feminine subject's affect—her "wo"—into body: she is language-less, somatized, and figured as the source of her own unpleasure: "our owen wo to drynke." Once again loss will turn the language and affect of woman's woe back into the body unless a renunciation of the lost object intervene—the heroism of which renunciation, for the feminine subject, will in turn be depreciated by all the factors we have just established as constituting her petitionary position in chivalric culture, to the point that renunciation of the lost object becomes a renunciation of the subject's right even to hope for reparation.

---

[44] See Fradenburg, "Voice Memorial," 171–72.

The Fabrications of Pandarus[*]

JOHN M. FYLER

The character and function of Pandarus are Chaucer's major addition to the story of Troilus. As the expert in the Ovidian "ars amatoria" he is, like the poet, an artificer of situations, a devisor of fictions to bring Troilus and Criseyde together. Like the poet he proclaims on a grand scale the rhetorical strategy of the aubade: he uses the events of the Trojan War as stage props for his private drama. But in two episodes, entirely of Chaucer's invention, Pandarus invents fabrications that unwittingly foreshadow what will happen in fact. The supposed threat to Criseyde's property by Polyphete, which he uses as a pretext for the lovers' first meeting, foreshadows her betrayal by the Trojan parliament; and the pretense that Troilus is jealous of Horaste forces Criseyde to defend herself against a fictional charge that will soon enough be true. These scenes, especially the first, have multiple ironies and several effects. Pandarus is punished for his artistic presumption when Fate in effect quotes his fabrications and makes them come true. But Pandarus's fabrications also point to and in large part define the most important issues in the poem: our increasing questions about the substantial nature of reality itself; our growing revulsion at all artifice, coupled with our awareness of its necessity and even beauty, in a contingent world.

One of the most powerful and disturbing qualities of *Troilus and Criseyde* is its insistence that we remain uneasy about things in experience that we usually take more or less for granted. The poem jars loose our normal sense of the substantiality and palpable texture of events. It does so most obviously by forcing us to remain suspended between involvement in the lives of its characters and detachment from their fates. As Morton W. Bloomfield pointed out some years ago, this suspension derives in large part from the historical distance of the Troy story, a distance doubly felt because the Trojan War belongs to a pagan, foreign past.[1] Our looking back in time has, in fact, much in common with Troilus's cosmic retrospect at the end of the poem. From the eighth sphere, or from the analogous distance of several thousand years, can historical truth be any more real to us than fiction? Can the waking reality of Troy be any more substantial to us than a dream?

This blurring together of illusion and reality occurs in the details of Chau-

---

[*] Originally published in *Modern Language Quarterly* 41 (1980): 115–30.
[1] Bloomfield, "Distance," 14–26.

cer's narrative as well as in its framing perspectives. Its primary agent is Pandarus, whose character and function are Chaucer's major addition to the story he inherited from Boccaccio. In the *Filostrato* Troiolo has more lines of speech than all the other characters together; Chaucer makes Pandarus the most talkative, with twice as much to say as his counterpart Pandaro.[2] His increased volubility signals a shift in emphasis, most clearly apparent in the scenes Chaucer invents for the go-between. Pandarus operates as love's strategist, the expert in the Ovidian *ars amatoria*. He is an artificer of situations, a deviser of fictions to bring Troilus and Criseyde together. Like the narrator of the poem, he suspends himself, usually with comic self-consciousness, between the real and the fictional, and between sympathetic involvement and amused detachment. He can comically lament, with apparent sincerity, the hectic schedule of his activity: "O verray God, so have I ronne! / Lo, nece myn, se ye nought how I swete?" (2.1464–65); but he can also, within a hundred lines, so advise Troilus on how to feign illness: "For hym men demen hoot that men seen swete" (1533).[3] Pandarus is also akin to the poet in his role as artificer. He deliberates on the best way to approach Criseyde, just as an architect plans a house before he begins to build it (1.1065–71). In Geoffrey of Vinsauf this image describes the poetic, not the amatory art; its source, moreover, is Boethius's portrayal of *Deus artifex* (Bo 4, pr. 6, 82–89).[4] There are the makings here, in other words, of a comparison between the divine Creator and his human epigones.[5] And in fact, the disparity between their powers becomes evident in the flawed artifices of the go-between.

Although at one moment of high comedy we are told that God and Criseyde forgive Pandarus for his trickery (3.1577–78), God's instrument Fate is witty, and gives the human artificer a lesson. For his precarious constructions, like those of the narrator of the poem (1.141–47; 5.1765–71), choose to ignore the

---

[2] The statistics have been assembled by Meech, *Design*, 9.

[3] The echo is doubly noticeable because of the rareness of the word *sweat* in Chaucer's poetry. It appears thirteen times in various forms, according to the Tatlock-Kennedy *Concordance*. Of these, three are in Book 2 of *Troilus*. The only other works with more than one occurrence are *MilT*, with two, and the *CYT*, with four. As these contexts imply, the word has connotations of crass comedy.

[4] *The Riverside Chaucer*, 451. Noted by Root in his edition of *Troilus and Criseyde*, 430.

[5] Bloomfield presents this argument in miniature (26n14). See also Robert W. Hanning, "The Theme of Art and Life in Chaucer's Poetry," in *Geoffrey Chaucer*, ed. George D. Economou (New York: McGraw-Hill, 1975), 19; Donald R. Howard, introduction to *TROILUS AND CRISEYDE and Selected Short Poems*, ed. Donald R. Howard and James Dean (New York: New American Library, 1976), xxiv; and especially E. Talbot Donaldson, "Chaucer's Three 'P's': Pandarus, Pardoner, and Poet," *MQR* 14 (1975): 282–301.

The comparison of God, Nature, and human artificers is a conventional one; see the quotations from William of Conches and Daniel of Morley in Brian Stock, *Myth and Science in the Twelfth Century: A Study of Bernard Silvester* (Princeton: Princeton Univ. Press, 1972), 254 and 265. On Nature the *artifex*, whose patterns human artists copy, see Jean de Meun's *Roman de la Rose*, ed. Félix Lecoy (Paris: Champion, 1966), 2:15975–16218. The traditional sources of this comparison are outlined by Etienne Gilson, "La Cosmogonie de Bernardus Silvestris," *AHDLMA* 3 (1928): 22n1. Also see Joseph Anthony Mazzeo, "The Analogy of Creation in Dante," *Speculum* 32 (1957): 706–21.

Trojan War in order to focus on Troilus's love affair. Pandarus uses the events of the war as stage props for his private drama. He quotes a few innocuous lines from Oenone's letter to Paris, which Troilus claims not to have read (1.654ff.); the rest of *Heroides* 5 forecasts the fall of Troy. He tells Criseyde that his news for her is not that the Greeks have sailed away, but something five times better (2.126); he uses the arrival in Troy of a Greek spy as a pretext for privacy on his second visit (2.1112-13). His joking diverts Criseyde's attention from the story of Thebes: "Is it of love? O, som good ye me leere!" (2.97; also 106-12); Cassandra will make clear its relevance to current events when she explains Troilus's dream in Book 5 (1456ff.). Most astonishingly, Pandarus uses the conjunction of Saturn and Jupiter in Cancer, which we are almost certainly to understand as an omen of the fall of Troy,[6] merely for its predictable and convenient heavy rainstorm. But the events of the war frustrate his efforts to create an ordered, private lovers' world. The two, of course, prove not to be separable: Criseyde is traded for Antenor; Troilus's possibilities of moral action are circumscribed by what his brother Paris has already done (4.547-53). The sweep of history takes events beyond the power of Pandarus's control.

What Pandarus does, in other words, is to proclaim on a grand scale the rhetorical strategy of the *aubade*. He pretends, until it is no longer possible to do so, that the "real" world is an illusion, and that the little world of the lovers is all that is real. The pretense is not ignoble: a public weal that requires fighting on Helen's behalf or treating Criseyde like chattel, as the Trojan council does when it hands her over to the Greeks, demands no high allegiance. But if Pandarus quotes Fate unknowingly to foster his illusion, the harsher world outside claims its due. For Fate, in return, answers Pandarus's misappropriation of his historical setting by quoting some of his more ingenious ideas. His fabrications—illusions convincing enough to be believed real by the other characters —become, in only slightly altered form, part of the substance of history. Two episodes of Chaucer's invention reveal Pandarus's uncanny knack for devising fictions that foreshadow what will happen in reality. His final ruse for getting Troilus into Criseyde's bedroom, the invention of a fictional rival Horaste, forces the guiltless heroine to defend herself against a charge that will soon enough be true. This dramatic irony, which plays on the audience's foreknowledge[7] of the rest of the story, shifts our sympathy back and forth between

---

[6] Robert Kilburn Root and Henry Norris Russell, "A Planetary Date for Chaucer's *Troilus*," *PMLA* 39 (1924): 62. Also see John J. O'Connor, "The Astronomical Dating of Chaucer's *Troilus*," *JEGP* 55 (1956): 556-62.

[7] I am deliberately skirting two related problems in defining the response of Chaucer's audience to *Troilus*. The first is theoretical, and arises in any instance of dramatic irony: do we have to know the details and outcome of a story before our first reading of it? The answer must be that the meaning of ironic foreshadowings, as of other elements of structure, becomes more apparent each time we reread a narrative. Indeed, one mark of the way in which we know more than the actors in a story is precisely our ability to relive their experience vicariously time after time, and to puzzle out, from our detached vantage point, the significant patterns that must forever remain obscure to them.

The second problem is specific, and concerns Chaucer's fourteenth-century audience: how

Criseyde and Troilus, the one tricked by a seduction ploy, the other—as that ploy reminds us—soon to be betrayed. If the balance of our sympathy here comes to rest with the hero, another fabrication complicates our response by reminding us that Criseyde is a victim too. Pandarus's excuse for the gathering at Deiphebus's house—a pretext for Troilus to speak with Criseyde for the first time—is an invented threat against her property by Polyphete. The choice of a villain is more plausible than its chooser can know. Criseyde's response, that Polyphete would not dare act without the backing of his friends Antenor and Aeneas (2.1474), puts him in the bad company of the men who will betray Troy, and reminds us of the central irony of the poem: that Criseyde will be exchanged for Antenor, for the supposed public good. There are even more direct foreshadowings of that trade. Pandarus asks Deiphebus, Helen, and the others to bolster his niece's precarious position. Support for her is freely and quickly promised; Helen vows:

> "Joves lat hym nevere thryve,
> That doth yow harm, and brynge hym soone of lyve,
> And yeve me sorwe, but he shal it rewe,
> If that I may, and alle folk be trewe!"   2.1607–10

Yet when Criseyde needs precisely this kind of support against an all too real threat to her position, only the noble Hector gives it: "We usen here no wommen for to selle" (4.182). Whether or not Deiphebus and Helen play any part in her betrayal, their promises remind us that the Trojan council and people, who are willing enough to safeguard Helen, will sell Criseyde to the Greeks in exchange for the man whose treachery will destroy the city.

Such instances of dramatic irony as these are conventional in tragedy, and conventionally satisfying. Their usual effect, of special importance in *Troilus* because of Chaucer's interest in free will and predestination, is to measure the powers of human artifice against the dispositions of Fate or Providence. Dramatic irony requires the audience to play God for the moment; it calls on our knowledge of what for the characters is an unknown future. But Pandarus unwittingly prepares the just grounds for such ironies to be directed against himself by his insistence on the fun of manipulating the present. The same thing happens in the *Miller's Tale*, where "hende" Nicholas is too clever for his own good: a fictional Flood brings about his painfully real need for "water!"

---

much detailed knowledge of the Troy story does Chaucer expect them to have? Are they to know, for example, something we are never told: that Deiphebus and Helen will later marry? Are they to know what happened during the siege of Thebes, or what Oenone says in the bulk of *Heroides* 5, which Pandarus does not quote? Exactly this problem of allusion comes up in the *Legend of Good Women*; and as I have argued elsewhere (*Chaucer and Ovid* [New Haven: Yale Univ. Press, 1979], 98–116), Chaucer's meaning in the *Legend* clearly includes the significant omission of detail. What he does not tell us about Cleopatra, Medea, or Philomela is as important as what he does tell us. Whether Chaucer is indulging in private jokes or writing for a surprisingly sophisticated audience, his procedure in the *Legend of Good Women* justifies our reading *Troilus* with an eye to such subtleties.

Like Nicholas, Pandarus takes too much delight in his own ingenuity as he savors the process of artifice and shows his exhilaration as the stage manager. For example, as John L. Lowes pointed out long ago,[8] Pandarus pulls his niece "by the lappe" into Troilus's supposed sickroom (3.59), and the gesture foreshadows his later entrance into Criseyde's bedroom with her would-be lover in tow (3.742): the go-between probably intends the comedy of this symmetrical pattern, even if he is playing for an audience of only one—himself. The episode at Deiphebus's house also shows his gusto in arranging things, and creator's joy in the complications of his stratagem. Here the audience of the poem is implicated in Pandarus's drama, because we are let in on the secret knowledge that only he and Troilus have; and indeed, it would be hard not to share his pleasure at the incidental ironies of the scene. Deiphebus says that he would sooner help Pandarus than anyone but his most beloved brother Troilus (2.1410): Troilus, we know, is the man he is in fact about to help. The joke is underlined when Deiphebus asks Troilus "To ben a frend and helpyng to Criseyde" (1550); as the narrator remarks, "But swich a nede was to preye hym thenne, / As for to bidde a wood man for to renne" (1553–54). Pandarus tells the assembled company that he can "reherce" Criseyde's "cas unlik that she kan seye" (1656). No doubt he is correct, since she has hardly heard of the supposed "cas," and as Helen half implies (1680), only its inventor could possibly keep the whole story straight.

Chaucer is, however, not simply moralizing about the comeuppance due to someone who tries to copy God. In the details of the Deiphebus and Horaste episodes, simple dramatic irony turns into a complex exploration of illusion and reality, and of the relationship between them. We are told that Helen

> Shoop hire to ben, an houre after the prime,
> With Deiphebus, to whom she nolde feyne;
> But as his suster, homly, soth to seyne,
> She com to dyner in hire pleyne entente.
> But God and Pandare wist al what this mente.   2.1557–61

God knows more than Pandarus knows, of course, and so do we, though only because we have the unfair advantage of living after him. And one of the things we know is that Deiphebus, according to several versions of the Troy story, will marry Helen after the death of Paris.[9] This fact makes us aware, at the same

---

[8] "The Prologue to the *Legend of Good Women* Considered in Its Chronological Relations," *PMLA* 20 (1905): 840.

[9] This story does not appear in Dares, Benoît de Sainte-Maure, or Guido delle Colonne; but it is mentioned by Dictys and its outcome is described in grisly detail by Vergil in *Aeneid* 6. Chaucer alludes to this last passage in the *House of Fame* when he describes Aeneas' visit to the underworld and mentions "How he ther fond Palinurus, / And Dido, and eke Deiphebus" (443–44). And he clearly consulted it once again when he wrote Book 2 of *Troilus*: he takes the name Polyphete from the list of shades in the underworld (6.484), ten lines before Deiphobus's account of his death.

See McKay Sundwall's excellent note on this point, especially on the tradition of the story and its variant forms: "Deiphobus and Helen: A Tantalizing Hint," *MP* 73 (1975): 151–56.

time that we admire Pandarus's manipulative skill, of elements in the scene over which he has no control. Deiphebus, not Pandarus, is the one who suggests inviting Helen. His argument, that she can persuade Paris to help Criseyde (2.1449), seems disinterested; and we are given no reason at any point to doubt the generous nobility of his motives. But Pandarus's ruse, the wonderful cunning that manages to give Troilus a private audience with Criseyde, depends on Troilus's having shunted Deiphebus and Helen off into the garden together. Pandarus can then mislead everyone else and lure in his niece, by creating the false expectation that the other two will still be inside cheering up Troilus, and available as chaperons for her: "Come, nece myn, my lady queene Eleyne / Abideth yow, and ek my lordes tweyne" (1714–15; see also 1720). It is hard not to wonder, given all this complex trickery, what Deiphebus and Helen are really talking about during the hour (1707) they spend in the garden. After all, Pandarus himself argued to Criseyde that the best disguise for a secret amour was such friendship as we see "sisterly" Helen showing to her future husband: "Swych love of frendes regneth al this town" (379); indeed, Criseyde's first letter to Troilus promises, not to love him, "but as his suster, hym to plese, / She wolde ay fayn, to doon his herte an ese" (1224–25).[10]

If in this scene we feel the pull of another story, one that is out of Pandarus's control, there are also several points at which we feel the pull of foreshadowed history, which Pandarus tries to reduce to an efficacious illusion. At Deiphebus's house, for example, the assembled company all believe the real purpose of their meeting to be Criseyde's need for protectors against Polyphete. But we share the two insiders' knowledge that the whole business of Polyphete is simply an illusion, an excuse for the first meeting of Troilus and Criseyde. At several points Pandarus and the narrator conspire to rush through the strategic preliminaries as quickly as possible. The narrator is concerned to flee "prolixitee," and to "faste go / Right to th'effect" of the scene, the reason, ambiguously, "Whi al this folk assembled in this place" (2.1564–67); and he uses his haste as an excuse for omitting the "saluynges" of the assembled guests (1568), their extended praises of the absent Troilus (1595), and the process by which Deiphebus and his visitors promise to help Criseyde in any way they can (1622–24). Even Pandarus, much as he lingers lovingly over the details of his fabrication, promises to get on with it (1614) and not keep the group any longer than necessary.

Much the same thing happens in the Horaste episode, when differing ideas of what is real create comedy and comic awkwardness. The unfortunate assonance of Criseyde's response to pretended jealousy—"Horaste! allas, and falsen Troilus?" (3.806)—is funny only because we know that her defense, per-

---

Also see Edward Hanford Kelly, "Myth as Paradigm in *Troilus and Criseyde*," *PLL* 3, Summer Supplement (1967): 28–30.

[10] Priam's household is careful to maintain the courtesies of a happy family, but with a slightly suspect heartiness. Helen calls Deiphebus "My deere brother" (2.1675), Troilus calls Helen "my suster lief and deere" (2.1693). Troilus also offers to help Pandarus win the love of "my faire suster Polixene, / Cassandre, Eleyne, or any of the frape" (3.409–10).

fectly serious in itself, answers her uncle's illusory fabrication. Likewise, much of the comedy in Troilus's position comes from his need to act out, rather nervously, a seduction ploy that is not even of his own devising, while he confronts the real anger Criseyde feels at an accusation that he does not himself believe. At one point, his pretense nearly folds:

> What myghte he seyn? He felte he nas but deed,
> For wroth was she that sholde his sorwes lighte.
> But natheles, whan that he speken myghte,
> Than seyde he thus, "God woot that of this game,
> Whan al is wist, than am I nought to blame."   3.1081–85

Instead of saying, as he almost does, "It's all Pandarus's fault," Troilus escapes from an unbearable situation by fainting (1086–92). One can sympathize with his discomfort at having to make up a story to explain his supposed jealousy. He must do so in order to evade Criseyde's counterclaim that he is simply testing her (1154–55); indeed, she comes perilously close to guessing what is actually going on: "Wol ye the childissh jalous contrefete?" (1168). But he and the narrator share an understandable desire to get through the whole matter quickly, as an insubstantial if annoying diversion from the real business at hand:

> And for the lasse harm, he moste feyne.
> He seyde hire, whan she was at swiche a feste,
> She myght on hym han loked at the leste, —
> Noot I nought what, al deere ynough a rysshe,
> As he that nedes most a cause fisshe.   1158–62

Chaucer compounds the effect of this scene by tricking his audience. When Pandarus, instead of leaving the two lovers by themselves, retreats to the fireplace, "And took a light, and fond his contenaunce / As for to loke upon an old romaunce" (979–80), his action reminds us that we are doing exactly the same thing. We too are voyeurs, if only in the benign sense that all readers of literature are; we too are staying in the room, waiting—as we have waited for two and a half books—for Troilus and Criseyde to become lovers. We may laugh at Pandarus's impatience, when he tries to hurry his niece off to bed by praising a rainstorm as good sleeping weather (654–58); but his rush to get things under way is compelling. The immediate result of such impatience is an understandable lapse of attention as one reads the Horaste episode. Since the charge against Criseyde is illusory, her reply too takes on the distance of the fictive, which prohibits the possibilities of weightiness in a "real" scene about jealousy. One's first impulse might well be to skim through the scene as quickly as possible.

The phantom Horaste, however, foreshadows the unpleasantly real Diomede; and because we know what will happen later, we respond to the Horaste episode with a curious double vision. For Criseyde expresses sentiments whose weight she will soon enough make Troilus feel: "Ther is no verray weele in this world heere" (3.836). And her particular phrasing of this Boethian commonplace, inappropriate as it is in its immediate context, alters our reaction to the rest of Book 3. Man, she says, either realizes that joy is transitory, or he does not:

> "Now if he woot it nought, how may he seye
> That he hath verray joie and selynesse,
> That is of ignoraunce ay in derknesse?
>
> "Now if he woot that joie is transitorie,
> As every joie of worldly thyng mot flee,
> Than every tyme he that hath in memorie,
> The drede of lesyng maketh hym that he
> May in no perfit selynesse be."   824-31

The alternatives are certainly equally disagreeable: ignorant bliss, or the fore-knowledge that gnaws away at present happiness. Moreover, the first describes Troilus's position, and the second describes ours, as vicarious participants in the action. Criseyde has let slip one of the central moral questions of the poem, and her caveat must dampen our response to the "hevene blisse" (704, 1322) of sexual love that we are about to witness. Her untimely self-defense—like Pandarus's repeated, comic interruptions of the bedroom scene—counters our vicarious involvement with the pressure of an uncomfortable detachment.

It also compels us, in certain important respects, to question the substantial nature of reality itself. Part of this questioning comes from the sense that Criseyde's speeches are in the wrong place—one almost wants to tear them out of the book and paste them in somewhere in Book 5, where she could well use such defenses of herself. But Pandarus's ruse forces her to defend herself in Book 3; and the statement of a defense before it is necessary reduces it to the level of Pandarus's fabrications. Unfairly, our foreknowledge taints the sincerity of what Criseyde says in her own behalf. Her arguments seem exaggerated and false, both because they answer only a fictitious charge and because we can hardly keep from reading in ironic possibilities: "Now God, thow woost, in thought ne dede untrewe / To Troilus was *nevere yet* Criseyde" (1053-54; my italics). One inevitably looks for hints of the motives for her later betrayal, especially after Pandarus unwittingly forecasts what Troilus's response to it is likely to be: "This is so gentil and so tendre of herte, / That with his deth he wol his sorwes wreke" (904-5).

Such pressure toward reducing the real to the insubstantial is in fact perva-sive in the Deiphebus and Horaste episodes, and goes far to explain why one can so easily miss their central dramatic ironies. Since the whole business, in each case, is simply one of Pandarus's schemes, the consequences and attend-ant circumstances also, in our minds, become illusory. It seems to be for this reason that the narrator does not remind us to ask, when the Trojan council betrays Criseyde in Book 4, what has happened to the promises of support by Helen, Deiphebus, and the others. Since Polyphete's threat was merely an il-lusion, their promises too seem illusory. The characters themselves certainly drop the matter as quickly as we do: Polyphete is never again mentioned after he serves his purpose.

At the end of the Deiphebus episode there is yet another vanishing act, which raises the issue of illusion and reality in an extremely disturbing fashion. Troilus, in order to set up his assignation with the unsuspecting Criseyde, dispatches Deiphebus and Helen from his sickroom by asking them to look at

> The copie of a tretys and a lettre,
> That Ector hadde hym sent to axen red
> If swych a man was worthi to ben ded,
> Woot I nought who; but in a grisly wise
> He preyede hem anon on it avyse.   2.1697–1701

The situation is reminiscent of Pope's ironic contrast, in the *Rape of the Lock*, of the puff-paste *beau monde* with the mundane cruelties of the real world outside, where "hungry Judges soon the Sentence sign, / And Wretches hang that Jury-men may Dine."[11] Certainly the implicit contrast in *Troilus* is an analogous one: between the real, imminent execution of a nameless wretch, and the mere illusion of a threat to Criseyde's well-being. Indeed, Chaucer's purpose is even more complicated than Pope's. Both imaginary threat and real summary judgment are made to serve, in an undifferentiated fashion, Troilus's private ends. Fact and fiction, the real and the illusory, become interchangeable. For if the effect of the scene at Deiphebus's house is to give reality to the illusory, its concluding lines make the all too real seem an illusion. After Troilus has seen Criseyde, the letter from Hector has served its purpose, as Pandarus implies (3.191–92); and, like the request for assistance against Polyphete, the matter it concerns is quickly dropped:

> Now lat hire wende unto hire owen place,
> And torne we to Troilus ayein,
> That gan ful lightly of the lettre pace
>
> That Deiphebus hadde in the gardyn seyn;
> And of Eleyne and hym he wolde feyn
> Delivered ben, and seyde that hym leste
> To slepe, and after tales have reste.   3.218–24

Our distance from the Trojan past is disturbing at such points as this. Elsewhere it even keeps us from deciding whether an event described by Pandarus has actually occurred. At one point, indeed, he is clearly lying. He tells Criseyde that he has asked Hector and some other unnamed lords to support her against Polyphete (2.1481). But he cannot have spoken with Hector: after concocting his plot at Troilus's house, he goes directly to Deiphebus (1402), and from Deiphebus directly—"as streyght as lyne" (1461)—to Criseyde. (His lie is protected against discovery because he and Deiphebus have decided not to invite Hector, who has already shown himself to be a friend of Criseyde [1450–56].) Similarly, when Pandarus tells Criseyde how he discovered Troilus's

---

[11] *Rape of the Lock*, 3.21–22, in *The Poems of Alexander Pope*, ed. John Butt (New Haven: Yale Univ. Press, 1963), 227.

love for her, he describes a scene that we have not witnessed (2.506–53).[12] Boccaccio's Pandaro describes the same episode, and it may very well have taken place. But the second episode that Pandarus recounts (554–74), which we did witness in Book 1, certainly seemed to be the first time he knew anything at all about Troilus's plight; and he seemed to be merely improvising, when he made up "wordes ... for the nones" (1.561) to provoke Troilus out of his lethargy. Moreover, the scene he describes to Criseyde, even if it is a fiction, serves an effective rhetorical purpose. It shows her that Troilus is not a foolish lover, who easily talks about his sorrow and will later boast of his conquests, but one who is willing to die rather than reveal himself, and who demands all of Pandarus's skill at prying before he will uncover his secret.

Chaucer shows how hard it is to disentangle human motives, when the songs of Antigone and the nightingale, rational argument, and an eerie dream all delicately blur together to explain Criseyde's falling in love (2.598–931): conscious and unconscious thought, dream and waking reality contribute equally to her changing purpose. With an analogous result, Pandarus shows how hard it is, especially through the haze of history, to distinguish fact from fiction: his fabrications are lies that become true, or they describe events that may or may not have happened. Blurred outlines come to be expected in Pandarus's world; and when he, unknowingly, threatens our normal sense of chronology as well, the effect is astonishing. For the Deiphebus and Horaste episodes, though extraordinarily complicated, are conventional dramatic irony; but Chaucer also invents a third fabrication, one in which, remarkably, dramatic irony works in reverse. Instead of prefiguring the future, Pandarus in this one instance invents something that has already taken place.

He offers to carry a love letter from Troilus to Criseyde, tells Troilus what to write, and suggests that he

> "ryd forth by the place, as nought ne were,
> And thow shalt fynde us, if I may, sittynge
> At som wyndow, into the strete lokynge."   2.1013–15

Pandarus does succeed in steering his niece to the window (1185–86); and when Troilus rides by and she evidences "routh of his destresse" (1270), Pandarus "felte iren hoot, and he bygan to smyte" (1276), admonishing Criseyde that her lover's life is in her hands.[13] The self-conscious artifice of the scene, carried through in the best Ovidian manner, gives it a slightly precious quality. Its artificiality is heightened because, as one suddenly realizes, the scene has in fact occurred once before, though only Criseyde and the audience know that it has. The difference between Pandarus's fabrication and natural,

---

[12] My argument at this point, as at several others, is quite close to that of Donaldson, in *Chaucer's Poetry*, who maintains (1136) that "we do not know whether Pandarus's account of his discovering Troilus's love-sicknesses ... is in the realm of fact or merely a charming invention with which to please Criseide."

[13] Compare this scene as it occurs in the *Filostrato*, trans. Nathaniel E. Griffin and Arthur B. Myrick (Philadelphia: Univ. of Pennsylvania Press, 1929), 202–3.

accidental reality is emphatic. In this later scene Troilus follows Pandarus's orders to ride by "right in thi beste gere" (1012); in the earlier one, he is "an heven . . . for to see" (637) returning from the day's battle, his horse wounded, "his helm tohewen" and "sheeld todasshed" (638, 640). In the rehearsed scene Troilus rides by with "dredful chere" and debonair look (1258-59), self-conscious and aware that he is being observed. In its predecessor, his humble reaction to the people's praise is all the more charming because he does not know that Criseyde is watching him:

> For which he wex a litel reed for shame,
> Whan he the peple upon hym herde cryen,
> That to byholde it was a noble game,
> How sobrelich he caste down his yën.
> Criseÿda gan al his chere aspien,
> And leet it so softe in hire herte synke,
> That to hireself she seyde, "Who yaf me drynke?"   645-51

Chaucer thus puts time out of joint, almost as if he were for the moment recording events lived backwards. Like the remarkable "disruption of chronology"[14] in Book 5—where Chaucer jolts us back and forth between Troilus and Pandarus in Troy and Criseyde in the Greek camp—these two episodes contribute to a growing sense of lost moorings as the poem increasingly dislodges us from an assured perception of sequential reality; and they speed up the unsettling breakdown of normal distinctions between the illusory and the real. Chaucer also explores here some related distinctions between art and nature, distinctions that prove to be at the center of his meaning and define the purpose of Pandarus's fabrications. At the most basic level, the effect is certainly to value nature above art, naive innocence above sophisticated stratagems. Like the Man in Black in the *Book of the Duchess*, Troilus is most winning when he is most artless, riding by unawares or forgetting the speech to Criseyde that he has so carefully prepared (3.83-84). By comparison, Pandarus's artifice seems disagreeable. So does that of Troilus's rival, who is all art: in the *Filostrato* Diomede at least loves Criseida; Chaucer's character is simply an arch-seducer, coldly expert in the stratagems of love. The courtship in Book 5 echoes Troilus's in Book 2, but as tragedy or farce.[15] Artifice without sentiment now takes the place of love; and the difference in circumstances is underlined when Pandarus once more suggests that Troilus write a letter to his beloved (5.1292-95; cf. 2.1005-8). The expedients that once worked so well are no longer effective. Pandarus's stratagems may have fostered true love, while Diomede's are self-absorbed; but Book 5 in part erases such nuances and creates a revulsion against all artifice, and against a world that can demand and reward it.

---

[14] The phrase is from Robert Durling, who discusses its implications in Book 5; see *The Figure of the Poet in Renaissance Epic* (Cambridge: Harvard Univ. Press, 1965), 58-59.

[15] See Muscatine, *French Tradition*, 163-65.

Yet the two episodes at Criseyde's window remind us that human artifice is necessary, to the extent that the world must be engaged. For if Criseyde has already inclined toward Troilus on her own, there is no question that Pandarus's efforts, when the lover rides by the second time, bring her feelings into the open and commit her, in semipublic fashion, to look favorably on Troilus's suit. In fact, the need for the go-between's tricks becomes evident precisely when he picks up, amplifies, and makes effective the stratagems Troilus and Criseyde had thought up on their own and had used either fruitlessly or with naive simplicity. For the fabrication at Deiphebus's house has two ruses at its center. One is the precarious position of Criseyde and her property, "hire estat and . . . hire governaunce" (2.219), which she had previously used as the excuse for detaining her uncle and talking with him alone (213–19), so that she might unravel his teasing hints about Troilus's love. The other, which is to serve—as Pandarus explains to Troilus—as the "sleyghte, for to coveren al thi cheere" (1512), is the feigned illness trick, which Troilus has already attempted, with telling lack of success, back in Book 1 (491–97).[16] At Deiphebus's house Criseyde knows the real cause and cure of Troilus's sickness—"Best koude I yet ben his leche" (2.1582)—only because Pandarus has, in the meantime, told her. Without artifice, we must infer, nothing in the world can be accomplished.

Moreover, one can hardly ignore artifice, since pattern informs the web of history with significance. Diomede's courtship parodies Troilus's, just as Fate quotes Pandarus; and the artifices of Fate, the ways in which Providence reveals itself, offer figural models of our experience. They are usually opaque to us, or disregarded; as Troilus says of the fools who are lovers, just before he himself falls in love: "Ther nys nat oon kan war by other be" (1.203). Criseyde can blithely read the story of Thebes, unaware that the son of Tydeus will soon enter her life. She can innocently announce that she has just been reading "How the bisshop, as the book kan telle, / Amphiorax, fil thorugh the ground to helle" (2.104–5), oblivious of his moral relevance to her father's situation: like Calkas a seer, but one who chose despite his foreknowledge to die with tragic dignity. Examples of this sort are not encouraging. Yet to the extent that the world must be engaged, we inevitably struggle, however unsuccessfully, to understand such manifestations of pattern and to impose our own plans on our lives.

In sum, then, Pandarus's fabrications pull us in two directions at once. The more powerful, as the poem nears its end, is away from the world and from the concerns of earthly life. Pandarus pretends that the real world is an illusion until the pressures Fate exerts prove that he himself is the one who has dealt in insubstantial dreams. At their moment of highest bliss, the two lovers define in conventional terms the fragility of what the go-between has created:

> Or elles, lo, this was hir mooste feere,
> That al this thyng but nyce dremes were;
> For which ful ofte ech of hem seyde, "O swete,

---

[16] *We have slightly abbreviated the original essay here–RAS & CSC.*

Clippe ich yow thus, or elles I it meete?"   3.1341–44

Yet by the end of the poem such questioning takes on more than conventional force. For in fact Pandarus is correct, though for the wrong reasons: the real world *is* an illusion. Life is a dream from which Troilus is awakened when "His lighte goost ful blisfully is went / Up to the holughnesse of the eighte spere" (5.1808–9). The Trojan War, as much as Troilus's failed love, fades away to spectral outlines; and there comes to be little to choose between them, in value or in permanence. Against his intentions, the games Pandarus has played with his fabricated reality prepare us for Chaucer's Boethian moral.

Nonetheless, the effect of *Troilus* as a whole is curiously ambiguous, precisely because we must return to the earthly perspective from which we began—in down-to-earth terms because, unlike Troilus, we can reread his story and can temper the burden of knowing its ending with our delight in the artifices along the way. In this sense, Pandarus speaks to us as earth-dwellers by making the illusory seem real. If the dream of the *aubade* must be interrupted by an awakening from earthly life, its precarious self-assertion still retains its power over our imaginations. It is not by accident that Chaucer includes poetry in the general condemnation of the ending: "Lo here, the forme of olde clerkis speche / In poetrie, if ye hire bokes seche!" (5.1854–55).[17] Like the ending of the *Canterbury Tales*, the ending of *Troilus* moves beyond the world of human artifice to a realm where words cannot follow. But before it does so, it shows in full splendor our own human world of fabrications, illusions claiming and in part meriting the name of reality—of which the poem itself is not the least. Like those of Daedalus the master artificer, the airy fabrications of Pandarus and the poet must fail. Troilus's love cannot endure; Chaucer's poem awaits almost certain miscopying, mismetering, and misunderstanding (5.1795–98). But partly because of the threat of impermanence, which does after all mark our human situation, the two makers have succeeded in creating for us structures of artifice and poignant delight.

---

[17] Donaldson discusses the "exhausted calm" of these lines in "The Ending of 'Troilus,'" in *Speaking of Chaucer,* 99.

Come in Out of the Code: Interpreting the Discourse of Desire in Boccaccio's Filostrato and Chaucer's Troilus and Criseyde

ROBERT W. HANNING

Comparison of Boccaccio's IL FILOSTRATO and Chaucer's TROILUS AND CRISEYDE yields divergent representations of the role of interpretation in the perception and fulfillment of sexual desire. Troiolo's wooing of Criseida in IL FILOSTRATO exemplifies Pandaro's contention that all women have keen desires but must hide them behind a rhetoric of chastity in order to protect their reputation. Decoding Criseida's discourse of refusal as a "scudo" (shield) for her honor, the Trojan prince is received into the widow's bed, where her removal of her last garment symbolizes, and concludes, the drama of interpretation/decoding (i.e., stripping the text of misleading surface meanings) that constitutes the first part of IL FILOSTRATO. This drama is complicated, however, by the "proemio" of the poem, which suggests that interpreting the discourse of desire is in fact as much a question of imposing a favorable meaning on the text (and, by extension, the female object of desire) as it is of discovering a message hidden within it. In Chaucer's version of the story, Criseyde is represented from the beginning as a female "text" on which men— Troilus, Pandarus, the narrator—impose meanings that accord with their desires. The disappearance from Troilus and Criseyde's consummation scene of Criseida's symbolic act of self-uncovering creates a gap in the narrative which the Chaucerian text fills with not one but three emblems of desire, none given authoritative status, that compete to characterize the movement of the story, and the character of Criseida, to this moment of sexual and narrative climax.

Pandaro ... tosto il giovinetto
Troiol cercando, a lui n'andò con ella
e presentagliel con sommo diletto;
il qual, presala, ciò che scritto in quella
era, con festa lesse sospirando,
secondo le parole il cor cambiando.

Ma pure in fine, seco ripetendo
bene ogni cosa che ella scrivea,
disse fra sé:—Se io costei intendo,
amor la stringe, ma si come rea,

sotto lo scudo ancor si va chiudendo;
Ma non potrá, pur che forza mi dea
Amore a sofferir, guari durare,
ch'ella non vegna a tutt'altro parlare. —

E'l simigliante ne pareva ancora
a Pandaro, col quale el dicea tutto;
per che piú che l'usato si rincora
Troiol, lasciando alquanto il tristo lutto,
e spera in brieve deggia venir l'ora
ch'al suo martiro deggia render frutto.   *Fil* 2. 128–30[1]

(Pandaro ... straightway seeking the youth Troiolo, went with it [the letter from Criseida] to him and gave it to him with the greatest delight. Having taken it, he read what was written in it sighing with joy, his heart changing according to the words. But in the end, however, carefully repeating to himself everything she had written, he said to himself, "If I understand her, love constrains her, but like a guilty person, she still goes covering herself under a shield; but if love gives me the strength to suffer, she will not be able to keep herself for long from a very different kind of talk." And the matter also seemed like that to Pandarus, with whom he discussed everything. Therefore more than usual Troiolo was cheered, leaving somewhat his sad grief, and he hopes that the hour is destined to come soon which ought to yield up the fruit of his suffering.)

And Pandarus gan hym the lettre take,
And seyde, "Parde, God hath holpen us!
Have here a light, and loke on al this blake."
But ofte gan the herte glade and quake
Of Troilus, whil that he gan it rede,
So as the wordes yave hym hope or drede.

But finaly, he took al for the beste
That she hym wroot, for somwhat he byheld,
On which hym thoughte he myghte his herte reste,
Al covered she the wordes under sheld.
Thus to the more worthi part he held,
That, what for hope and Pandarus byheste,
His grete wo foryede he at the leste.   *T&C* 2.1318–30

These clearly related passages from Chaucer's greatest narrative poem and its Boccaccian antecedent attract the attention of the late twentieth-century reader

---

[1] In this essay, all citations from Boccaccio's *Il Filostrato* are from the edition of V. Pernicone (Bari: Laterza, 1937), as reprinted in Windeatt (1984). The translation is that of apRoberts and Seldis, which I have slightly modified in a few places.

because they so palpably reproduce the affective dynamics of reading—the in-
teraction between emotional response to, and interpretation of, a text. Con-
fronted with a letter from the object of his passionate desire, Troiolo/Troilus
must contend not only with his own volatile emotions—"his heart changing ac-
cording to the words" / "so as the wordes yave hym hope or drede"—but with
the antecedent problem of deciding what precise meaning to ascribe to the
words on the page before him, since the writer "still goes covering herself
under a shield [*scudo*]" / "covered . . . the wordes under shelde."

One of the more remarkable, but less attended to, aspects of the intertext-
uality of *Il Filostrato* and *Troilus and Criseyde* is the wide divergence between
their respective representations of how interpretation functions as a crucial ele-
ment in the discourse of desire. It is the aim of the present essay to consider
the issue of interpretation, as it affects the perception and fulfillment of sexual
desire, in the wooing and winning of Criseida/Criseyde by Troiolo/Troilus that
occupies the first half of the respective poems. What such a comparative study
reveals is that the interpretive process operates very differently, and is given a
very different valence, in the two works. In *Il Filostrato*, the key to the satisfac-
tion of Troiolo's desire is the accurate decoding of Criseida's language and be-
havior to reveal, beneath her apparent resistance to him, an oblique message
of reciprocal desire and encouragement. In *Troilus and Criseyde*, by contrast, the
female object of desire has become more ambiguous and complex, and the
activities of her suitors—Troilus, but also Pandarus and the narrator—are much
less exercises in decoding her desires than exercises in the construction and
imposition of meaning—on her and on the progress of the love affair—in accord
with their own.

The difference between these two interpretive paradigms is evident *in nuce* in
the two passages just quoted. The *Il Filostrato* version centers on Troiolo's straight-
forward decipherment of Criseida's emotional state—"love constrains her"—and
confident prediction of the outcome: "she will not be able to keep herself for long
from a very different kind of talk." Indeed, this last turn of phrase invites the
reader to decode Troiolo's utterance in a way that duplicates his decoding of
Criseida's. He predicts his ultimate sexual union with his beloved "under the
shield" of euphemism, using one kind of intercourse to stand for another.[2]

The interpretive procedure here governing both Troiolo's reading and our
own recalls the frequently prescribed medieval exegetical process of finding the

---

[2] Helen remarks on this euphemism in her letter to Paris, no. xvii of Ovid's *Heroides*.
Paris (xvi.283–84), seeking to persuade Helen to leave her home and husband for him,
writes, "Multa quidem subeunt; sed coram ut plura loquamur, / excipe me lecto nocte
silente tuo" ("Many things indeed come to my mind; but, that we may say more face to face,
welcome me to your couch in the silent night"). Helen replies (xvii.261–62), "Quod petis, ut
furtim praesentes ista loquamur, / scimus, quid captes conloquiumque voces; / sed nimium
properas. . . ." ("You ask that we speak of these things in secret, face to face. I know what it
is you court, and what you mean by speech with me; but you are over hasty. . . ."). Text and
translation quoted from Ovid, *Heroides and Amores*, tr. Grant Showerman, Loeb Classical
Library (1914; reprint Cambridge: Harvard Univ. Press, 1971). For further comparison
between the letters in *Il Filostrato* and their analogues in *T&C*, see John McKinnell, "Letters
as a type of the formal level in *Troilus and Criseyde*," in Salu, 80–83.

kernel of moral or philosophical truth beneath the outer husk, or *integumentum*, of a fable or poetic text. As Boccaccio would put it later in his career, in his mythographic encyclopedia, *De genealogia deorum*, "fiction is a form of discourse, which, under guise of invention, illustrates or proves an idea; and, as its superficial aspect is removed, the meaning of the author is clear" (xiv.9).[3]

By contrast, the Chaucerian text focuses much more on describing the effect of the letter on Troilus than on announcing his understanding of its meaning and promise. Absent is Troiolo's unambiguous declaration that love constrains Criseida; in its place we find a diffuse, equivocal rendering of the moment that stresses the tentativeness of Troilus's response:

> somwhat he byhelde
> On which hym thoughte he myghte his herte reste....
> Thus to the more worthi part he helde,
> ... what for hope and Pandarus byheste.

We are left to wonder, without sufficient evidence to decide, if it is the content of the letter, Pandarus's optimistic evaluation of it as he delivers it—he calls it "a charme ... the which kan helen the of thyn accesse"—or Troilus's own desire that generates his "hope" and diminishes "his grete wo"?

Il Filostrato's representation of the coding and decoding of female desire finds an important antecedent in the story of Troilus, Briseis, and Diomede woven into Benoît de Ste. Maure's twelfth-century *Roman de Troie*—specifically, in Benoît's account of how Diomede begins to woo Calchas's daughter as soon as she has left Troy for the Greek camp (13532-680).[4] Briseis's response to her new suitor's sudden protestations of love and promises of honorable service is equivocal: after offering several reasons why she must reject his offer—the risk to her honor and virtue; her grief; her uncertainty that she can trust him—she adds that she thinks highly of Diomede, that no damsel willing to love could reject him, and that, were she to give herself to love (which she reiterates she has no desire to do) she would "hold none more dear" than him. Diomede interprets this reply as a subtle encouragement; as Roberto Antonelli puts it, "he acknowledges both the 'courtesy' and the implied (consequential?) willing-

---

[3] Quoted from Giovanni Boccaccio, *Boccaccio on Poetry. Being the Preface and the Fourteenth and Fifteenth Books of Boccaccio's "Genealogia Deorum Gentilium,"* trans. Charles G. Osgood (1930; reprint New York: Liberal Arts Press, 1956), 48. The Latin text reads "fabula est exemplaris seu demonstratiua sub figmento locutio, cuius amoto cortice, patet intentio fabulantis"—Oskar Hecker, ed., *Boccaccio-Funde* (Braunschweig: George Westermann, 1902), 216. On *integumentum*, see further Winthrop Wetherbee, *Platonism and Poetry in the Twelfth Century: The Literary Influence of the School of Chartres* (Princeton: Princeton Univ. Press, 1972), 36-48. I am not arguing that the *Filostrato* itself should be read as an integument of a deeper truth, only that such exegetical reading is practiced on texts and people by characters in the work.

[4] Benoît de Ste. Maure, ed. Constans; the story of Troilus, Briseis, and Diomede comprises eight episodes between lines 13,065 and 21,782. The text is translated in N. R. Havely, *Chaucer's Boccaccio*, 167-83; for the translation of the passage under discussion, see 172-73. For other versions of the Troilus-Briseis story Boccaccio could have known, see Maria Gozzi, "Sulle fonti del *Filostrato*," *SBoc* 5 (1968): 123-209.

ness of Briseis ('Bien entendi as premiers moz / Qu'el n'esteit mie trop *sauvage*' [13650–51]); he will wait until she has 'merci'."[5]

The application of such an interpretive calculus to Boccaccio's Criseida begins in the dialogue between Troiolo and Pandaro at the beginning of Canto 2 of *Il Filostrato*. Once Pandaro knows that Troiolo loves Criseida, Pandaro's own kinswoman, he articulates two barriers to the satisfaction of his friend's desire (barriers of which Troiolo is also obviously aware): Criseida's personal virtue—"she is more chaste than other ladies and has scorned the things of love more" (2.23,3–4)—and the inherent subversiveness to honor of an illicit desire such as this (2.25,1–5) —

> "I ... see well that such loves are not proper for a worthy lady and what, furthermore, may come from it both to her and to hers if such a thing should ever come to the mouth of the people."

But Pandaro's prescription for these problems is neither despair nor withdrawal. It is rather to look beyond the apparently absolute binary opposition between honor and desire ("onor" and "amor," 2.25, 8) to perceive their real relationship—for women in general and Criseida in particular—and on the basis of this exegesis to construct a appropriate discourse for wooing Criseida. Since desire can take away a woman's honor and render her contemptible ("vituperosa," 2.25, 6), it would seem that honor preexists desire, and is threatened by its arrival, as by a serpent introduced into the garden. Pandaro in effect deconstructs this binary, substituting for it an integumental paradigm: desire is always already present in women, hidden by fear of shame which leads to the assumption of a facade of virtue.

> "I believe certainly that in desire every woman lives amorously and nothing else restrains her but fear of shame.... My cousin is a widow and has desires, and if she should deny it, I would not believe her."[6]

It follows that a lover such as Troiolo need not desist from seeking to satisfy his desire, as long as he respects the integumental (as opposed to the normative) importance of honor:

> "each lover, as long as he is discreet in deed and in appearance, can follow his high desire without any shame to those to whom shame and their honor hold importance."   2.26,4–8

---

[5] Roberto Antonelli, "The Birth of Criseyde—An Exemplary Triangle: 'Classical' Troilus and the Question of Love at the Anglo-Norman Court," in *The European Tragedy of Troilus*, ed. P. Boitani (Oxford: Clarendon Press, 1989), 40 (emphasis his). Antonelli translates and comments on the French text in note 51 (emphasis his):

"From her very first words, he well understood that she was not uncourtly"; I interpret "sauvage" ... as *external* to the court, to that which is *civilized* (also here, and especially by love; the meaning "reluctant" is not excluded, but is part of a much wider meaning which is also more precise.

[6] 2.27. On the sexual significance of Criseida's status as a widow, see Giulia Natali, "A Lyrical Version: Boccaccio's *Filostrato*," in Boitani, ed., *European Tragedy of Troilus*, 65–67.

Pandaro's analysis of Criseida's situation lays bare two important strands of the Boccaccian discourse of desire: a cynical assessment of the universality and strength of women's sexual desire (having its locus classicus in Ovid's *Ars amatoria*), which justifies wooing them, and a recognition of the formidable cultural restraints imposed on that desire, perceived as dangerous (restraints under powerful religious and social sponsorship in Boccaccio's own late medieval milieu), which necessitates that the wooing proceed with maximum discretion.[7]

From these assumptions follows a specific role for eloquence. Faced with Criseida's apparent virtue, Pandaro tells Troiolo, "believe me, I will find a way with my pleasing words to deal with this according to your needs" (2.23, 5-7). That way will be to mingle persuasions to love (the traditional rhetoric of the go-between) with assertions that he has cracked the "code" which conceals her desire and can assure her of secrecy when she indulges it with the Trojan prince.

Hence, in his subsequent wooing expeditions to his cousin, Pandaro counters her protestations of virtue not only by stressing Troiolo's desire for her and desirability as a lover, but by mocking women's pretended resistance to what they really all want (e.g., 2.112, 2-5), and by chiding Criseida to abandon her word games and pretended coyness (e.g., 2.39,1; 112, 5-7; 137,2). Criseida's response to this strategy proves the accuracy of Pandaro's decipherment of her: she is both susceptible to desire—indeed, driven by it—and an adroit practitioner of a discourse that simultaneously hides and encodes it. Smitten with Troiolo ("trafitta giá," 2.66, 2) by her kinsman's description of the prince's passion for her, Criseida hides her feelings behind a protective rhetoric of self-exculpation ("I am not cruel, as it seems to you, nor so devoid of pity," 2.65, 7-8) and accommodation, agreeing to *see* Troiolo (no more) in order to please Pandaro (who, as a respectable male relative, deserves her obedience), and in recognition of her suitor's status:

"Ah, I perceive where compassionate desire draws you [Pandaro], and I will do it because I ought to please you by it, and he is worth it, and let it suffice him if I see him."   2.66, 2-5

But she also stresses the importance of secrecy, in language that signals to Pandaro her eventual full capitulation, provided that he and Troiolo preserve

---

[7] See Ovid, *Ars amatoria*, trans. J. H. Mozley, Loeb Classical Library (1929; reprint Cambridge: Harvard Univ. Press, 1957), i.269-350, on the *furiosa libido* (281) of women. Ovid's *magister amoris* claims (e.g., *Ars* i.31-34, iii.57-58) that his advice on wooing should only be applied to the pursuit of courtesans, thus sidestepping questions of the dangers posed by female sexuality to patriarchal honor. On restraints imposed on fourteenth-century Italian women to prevent their indulging their dangerous (to husbands and lineage) desires, see, e.g., Charles de La Roncière, "Tuscan Notables on the Eve of the Renaissance," in *A History of Private Life*, 2, *Revelations of the Medieval World*, ed. Georges Duby, trans. Arthur Goldhammer (Cambridge: Belknap Press, 1988), 285-90.

her *scudo* of respectability: "but in order to avoid shame, and perhaps worse, pray him that he be discreet and do what will not be a shame to me, nor to him either" (2.66, 6–8).[8]

The circumstances surrounding the letter Criseida sends Troiolo offer the clearest evidence of her implication in a coded discourse of desire. Shortly before, she has seen Troiolo ride past her window, "and so suddenly was she taken that she desired him above every other good" (2.83, 5–6). Yet when Pandaro brings her Troiolo's letter, she pretends that honor prevents her from taking it (2.110–11). Again, after she has read in private of her suitor's desires, she responds passionately: "I wish that I were now in his sweet arms, pressed face to face" (2.117, 7–8). But the letter she sends Troiolo in reply is a master-piece of coded utterance, which manages simultaneously to reject his suit—on grounds of honor and reputation—and to encourage him to find a way to bring about consummation of their desire without threatening "l'onestá ... e la castitá mia" (2.121, 8).[9]

Troiolo's response to Criseida's letter, discussed at the beginning of this essay, shows that he has learned enough from Pandaro to be able to read it as an oblique discourse of desire. At this point an "interpretive community" has been established among the three principles of the narrative, and the way is thus finally clear to consummate the love affair.

The moment of consummation is accompanied by a symbolic act that sums up the interpretive impulse I have been tracing through the first part of *Il Filostrato*. The lovers have undressed, except for Criseida's "last garment"; now she asks Troiolo, "shall I strip myself? The newly married are bashful the first night" (3.31, 5, 7–8). He replies that he wishes to hold her naked in his arms, "and she replies, 'See how I free myself of it.' And her shift thrown away, she gathered herself quickly into his arms," after which "they felt the ultimate value of love" (3.32, 4–6, 8). It is hard not to see in this playful, provocative gesture by Criseida an acknowledgment of the decoding that has been prac-ticed on her by Pandaro and Troiolo, and an acknowledgment as well of her own active participation in stripping the code away from her desire.

It is worth recalling here that when Troiolo first sees Criseida in the temple, she has drawn back from her face her black mantle, and this gesture of expos-ing the body, the object of desire, allows Troiolo to gaze on her face and be smitten by the love in her eyes (1.27, 6–8). Hence the love affair, up to its con-summation, is bracketed by analogous gestures of "undressing" which equate

---

[8] Cf. David Wallace, *Chaucer and the Early Writings of Boccaccio* (Woodbridge: D. S. Brewer, 1985), 93: "for Boccaccio [in Fil], *cortesia* is an elaborate game in which a man must remain 'segreto' in order to avoid a public scandal. . . ."

[9] Francesco Bruni, *Boccaccio. L'invenzione della letteratura mezzana* (Bologna: Il mulino, 1990), 165–66, comments on "the apparent reserve of Criseida which in reality encourages the wooing, first of Troiolo, then of Diomede" (my translation). For an analogous letter of coded desire, see Helen's reply to Paris (Ovid, *Heroides*, xvii [see note 2 above]), which moves from the defense of her *pudor* (13–14), through the suggestion that Paris woo her in secret (153), to an all but open invitation to abduct her by force, to save her reputation (185–86).

the hiding of the desirable body in clothing with the hiding of desire itself behind facades of language.

Anticipating, and complicating, its role in the story of Troiolo and Criseida, the coded discourse of desire plays an important part as well in *Il Filostrato*'s framing fiction, which Boccaccio initiates in a prose Proemio to the poetic narrative, ostensibly a communication sent by "Filostrato" to his "Filomena, more pleasing than any other." This epistolary exercise appropriates the lyric convention of a lovesick poet addressing his absent, apparently unfeeling beloved in order to provide a frame that "decodes" the story to follow;[10] but the story-frame nexus thus established goes beyond this straightforward explicatory function to raise important questions about the complex relationship between fiction, experience, and the interpretational, or decoding, impulse.

Brought near to death by Filomena's departure from Naples, Filostrato faces apparently conflicting imperatives: the need to relieve his grief by giving voice to it and the need to protect his beloved's reputation by keeping secret his love for her. His solution is to hide his desire and grief, and their occasion, behind an "old story," and thus "make [it] into a likely shield [*far scudo verisimilmente*] for my secret and amorous suffering" (Pr. 27).

The story of Troiolo and Criseida meets Filostrato's need for both therapeutic utterance and discretion. And since he is sending it to Filomena, its "true and only inspiration" (Pr. 32), he undertakes as well to explain to her how she should read (or, more precisely, decode) it. There are, first of all, obvious parallels between "fact" and fiction: Troiolo's sorrow when Criseida leaves him; the beauty and many virtues of the Trojan widow, which Filomena should take as referring to herself (Pr. 34). But—and here the complications begin—there is also a major discrepancy between the signifying and signified levels, namely Filostrato's lack of success in love vis à vis Troiolo's possession of Criseida: "it is true that [in Troiolo's story] before his very bitter tears, part of his happy life is found in a similar style," although, Filostrato admits, "Fortune never was so favorable to me" (Pr. 30).

Filostrato's response to this discrepancy constitutes a complex, rather tricky exercise in interpretation. On the one hand, he excuses it in a somewhat overdetermined manner, arguing that 1) showing Troiolo's happiness fosters a better understanding of his [and Filostrato's?] subsequent misery [Pr. 30]; 2) even though Filomena never granted him the "amorous fruit" Troiolo obtains from Criseida, Filostrato has drawn "no less pleasure . . . from your eyes" [Pr.

---

[10] Filomena's departure for Sannio and Filostrato's subsequent rendering of the story of Troiolo and Criseida constitute an obvious parody of Beatrice's death and Dante's decision to write his *Commedia*. Note also the parallel between Dante's use of a lady other than Beatrice as his "schermo de la veritade," or "difesa" to hide the identity of his true love, and the theme of the *scudo* in *Il Filostrato*. (Dante, *Vita nuova*, ed. L. Magugliani [Milano: Rizzoli, 1952], 5, 20, 21, 23). For Boccaccio, textuality (Filostrato's story sent to Filomena, Criseida's letter sent to Troiolo) serves as a cover for sexuality; this may be his wry, subversive comment on Dante's allegorization and sublimation of his desire for Beatrice.

31]; 3) an accurate retelling of the "old story" of Troiolo entrains including some events not directly relevant to its narrator's situation (Pr. 35). (In fact, this protestation is a kind of private joke, since Boccaccio invented [as opposed to finding in earlier versions] precisely the part of *Il Filostrato* dealing with Troiolo's wooing of Criseida.)

On the other hand, Filostrato also suggests that an appropriate interpretation of the contradiction between his situation and Troiolo's lies in Filomenal's power:

> "if you are as perceptive as I believe you to be, you will be able to understand [from the discrepant parts] the greatness and the nature of my desire, what their limit is and what thing more than other they ask for, and if they merit any pity."   Pr. 35

It should be clear from this partial summary of the *proemio* that Filostrato's technique of using a story at once to reveal and hide his feelings of grief and desire for Filomena—not to say his use of the term *scudo* to describe the technique—establishes an analogy between Criseida (hiding her own desire behind a *scudo*-discourse of honor and virtue), the story of which she is a protagonist, and the situation described in the *proemio* itself. But it should also be clear that the analogy, and therefore the relationship between *Il Filostrato*'s narrative levels, is equivocal and many-faceted. For fiction can sometimes parallel experience—as when Filostrato equates his sorrow with Troiolo's and Criseida's beauty with Filomena's—and sometimes diverge from it, thanks to a narrative's autonomy (exemplified in details required for Troiolo's story but irrelevant to Filostrato's), which in turn points to a potential, if not inevitable, gap between experience and its recounting, between desire and the language it inspires.

Seen in this light, the exegetical, interpretive impulse becomes an instrument for closing the gap thus opened between language and desire. Filostrato self-interestedly attempts to control this impulse within Filomena by suggesting that she derive a clearer understanding of her own suitor's desires—and perhaps a willingness to show them "some pity"—from her reading of Troiolo's. That is, by a neat interpretive move of his own, Filostrato transforms his *scudo*-narrative into an exercise in persuasion, designed to convert imperfect analogy into implicit anagogy.

This last move has large consequences for our own reading of *Il Filostrato*. It sets up a decoding process that ultimately deconstructs the apparent binary opposition of Proemio (antecedent "truth") and story ("fiction constructed to encode the truth under a protective integument") by denying absolute priority to either in the textual system of *Il Filostrato*, and substituting instead a two-way flow of significance, and decoding energy, between them.

For example, if we follow Filostrato's advice to Filomena and read Troiolo's progress in the first half of *Il Filostrato* as the narrator's wish-fulfillment fantasy, and as an invitation to his beloved to align the fantasy with "reality" by her response of "pity," then we can use this interpretational model to decode all of the lyric, stilnovist rhetoric of the Proemio as a *scudo* for a desire which seeks more than to look upon its object once again. Regarded from this perspective, Filostrato's "very fervent desire which kindles all my other desires into such a flame to see you" (Pr. 18) becomes an obvious, metonymic euphemism for his desire for full sexual union, as does his plea that Filomena be moved by Troiolo's story to give thought to her "return" (Pr. 36).

Furthermore, Filostrato's decoding of the story he is about to tell is notoriously incomplete: he instructs Filomena how to see herself reflected in Criseida's virtues, and makes clear the parallel between the latter's grief-causing departure from Troy and the former's from Naples. But he is silent about how she should (or should not) apply to herself the behavior of Criseida in the last cantos of the story, i.e., her abandonment of Troiolo and acceptance of Diomede as a new lover.[11] This is a very loud silence indeed, and it invites Filomena (i.e., us as readers) to see a parallel between Filostrato's hope for her return and "Troiolo's vain hope in the base Criseida" (8.28, 7–8). That is, if she does not return to Naples she is a fickle, treacherous woman. (The way in which the story ends, with the narrator's warning "young men" [8.29, 1] to read the story of Troiolo as an admonitory mirror of their own potential betrayal by "Giovane donna, e mobile e vogliosa" [8.30, 1]—the appetitive, fickle woman of the European misogynistic tradition—supports such an implied reading.) To arrive at such an interpretation, however, entrains yet another re-interpretation of the Proemio, this time to discern beneath its refined discourse of yearning a current of resentment and accusation directed at the recalcitrant object of desire.[12]

The symbiosis of Proemio and story makes unavoidable a final judgment that the relationship between desire and its encoding in language is ultimately and always that of a regress. Behind the story of Troiolo and Criseida lurk the figures of Filostrato and Filomena. But these names are in turn obvious *senhals*. Desire is forever encoding itself in texts which can at best only approximate the extra-textual reality that prompts them. The inevitable gap between desire and language gives scope to the decoding impulse which is, however, itself motivated and fueled by desire, and as such tends more to impose meaning on texts than elucidate meaning already hidden there. In the case of *Il Filostrato*, its representation of female desire is a construct of male desire, designed to facilitate the latter's satisfaction or, in the absence of satisfaction, its vengeance.

A perfect emblem for this reading (or decoding) of *Il Filostrato* is to be found in Boccaccio's pastoral-etiological romance, *Ninfale fiesolano*, where the shepherd lad, Africo, disguises himself in women's clothing in order to surprise (and take by force) the nymph Mensola who is the object of his passionate desire. At the appropriate moment, Africo throws off his covering garment to reveal his maleness:

---

[11] Filostrato says of the "other things" in the story of Troiolo and Criseida that he has not applied to himself or to Filomena, "none pertains to me nor is set down there concerning me" (Pr.35); the repeated emphasis on "me" makes the exclusion of Filomena from the disclaimer all the more noticeable.

[12] Cf. the story of Joseph and Potiphar's wife in Genesis 39.7–20, of which Filostrato's implied accusation of Filomena appears to be a version, albeit with the genders reversed.

"and before he had completely undressed, the nymphs were all in the
water [bathing and playing]; and then, naked, he moved toward them,
showing everything he had in front."   239.1-4

The image of the male, member erect, lurking behind a female disguise the
better to satisfy his desire, catches well the dynamic of *Il Filostrato*; it is the
phallus—male desire wedded to male power in the world of gender relation-
ships—that constructs and encodes the discourse of desire in fictions. When
Africo throws off his garment, he recapitulates the gesture of Criseida at the
moment of sexual consummation; but his gesture reminds us that the expo-
sure/decoding of female desire in *Il Filostrato* is very much a matter of male
perceptions, which the Proemio of *Il Filostrato* seems designed to lay bare.[13]

At the beginning of this essay I contrasted the portrayal of interpretation, as
part of the discourse of desire, in *Il Filostrato* with its representation in *Troilus
and Criseyde*. The English work, while deriving its story from the Italian, dis-
mantles *Il Filostrato*'s network of acts (or symbols) of coding and decoding that
organizes the upward arc of the love affair between Troiolo and Criseida. In its
place, we find an emphasis on the limits of erotic interpretation in the face of
a complex reality, and especially on its tendency to become an exercise in con-
structing, rather than a process of demystifying, the object of desire.

Troilus and Criseyde jettisons *Il Filostrato*'s Proemio, and with it the framing
fiction of Filostrato's desire for Filomena that decodes, and is in turn decoded
by, the inset story of Troiolo and Criseida. In its place the English poem offers
a 56-line "prologue," more closely linked to the story it prefaces in both voice
(the narrator does not have a story of his own) and medium (it eschews the
prose of the Proemio). All the features of the Chaucerian prologue—the nar-
rator's status as a non-lover, telling a love story to which he hopes to do justice,
in the presence of an audience from whom he asks a prayerful, rather than an
interpretational, response—seem designed to distance the poetic occasion as far
as possible from the Boccaccian paradigm of desire shielding itself, cynically
and self-protectively, behind a decipherable discourse of respectability or
self-abasement.[14]

---

[13] The original reads:
　　E' nnanzi che spogliato tutto fosse,
　　le ninfe eran nell'acqua tutte quante;
　　e poi spogliato verso lor si mosse,
　　mostrando tutto cio ch'avea divante.
—Giovanni Boccaccio, *Ninfale Fiesolano*, ed. Armando Balduino, vol. 3 of *Tutte le opere*, ed.
Branca (trans. mine). Venus, whose idea it is that Africo disguise himself, also instructs him
to preface his unveiling with talk about things Mensola will find pleasant to listen to: "holy
things and affairs of the gods." Cupid, she says, will teach Africo "to say all the things that
will be pleasing and gracious to Mensola" (201.3, 7-8). That is, his language will also be a
"garment" to hide his rampant desire until the appropriate moment. Cf. Hollander,
Boccaccio's Two Venuses (New York: Columbia Univ. Press, 1977), who refers to Africo's
undressing as "a 'recognition scene'. . . which tells us what the 'argument' of the *Ninfale* is:
sexual pleasure. It offers a fitting emblem for the theme in Africo's phallus" (69).

[14] Consider, e. g.,

The latter part of Book 1 of *Troilus and Criseyde* presents a much more complicated relationship between Troilus and Pandarus (and a different role for the latter) than is the case in *Il Filostrato*. This substantial recasting embodies resistance to Boccaccio's representation of desire—Troiolo's, then Criseida's—seeking unsuccessfully to conceal itself from the worldly scrutiny, and interpretive powers, of Pandaro. Chaucer's poem reorients Pandarus's efforts toward convincing Troilus to stop pining and get to work (or, more precisely, let Pandarus get to work) winning the object of his desire. That is, much more than Pandaro, Pandarus must devote his persuasive powers to "wooing" Troilus before he can woo Criseyde. The goal of this wooing is to transform Troilus's lyric posture of static, hopeless longing into a narrative form of active quest for the object of desire. (As Pandarus himself puts it, "I hope of this to maken a good ende," [1.973] i.e., the happy end of a romance in which the man wins the woman.)

In accomplishing this task, Pandarus does not give Troilus a lesson in decoding female desire; *Troilus and Criseyde* suppresses completely the *ottave* (2.23–28) of *Il Filostrato* in which Pandaro explains to Troiolo that Criseida's virtue and the dishonorableness of the proposed affair are only apparent obstacles, given the real nature of feminine desire and its allegiance to honor only as a self-protecting, shame-preventing integument. Pandarus's strategy is rather to construct a matrix of significance for Troilus's desire that will galvanize the prince into action. He is quite open about this strategy; at one point, he tells Troilus,

> "I have right now of the
> A good conceyte in my wit, as I gesse,
> And what it is, I wol now that thow se."   1.995–97

Pandarus's "conceyte" is that Troilus's painful desire for Criseyde is a conversion experience, inflicted on him by the God of Love as recompense for Troilus's former mockery of Love's devotees. And now Troilus will be "the beste post, I leve, / Of al his lay," i.e., will show the zeal of the convert in pursuing the object of his heaven-sent desire (1.998–1008).

> For I, that God of Loves servantz serve,
> Ne dar to Love, for myn unliklynesse,
> Preyen for speed, al sholde I therfore sterve,
> So fer am I from his help in derknesse.   *T&C* 1.15–18

> But ye loveres, that bathen in gladnesse, . . .
> Remembreth yow on passed hevynesse
> That ye han felt. . . .
> And preieth for hem that ben in the cas of Troilus. . . .
> And biddeth ek for hem that ben despeired
> In love. . . .
> And biddeth ek for hem that ben at ese. . . , etc.   1.22–43

This "pope of love" is more concerned with heading off improper interpretation (or outright rejection) of his story than with propagating an authoritative, or persuasive, exegesis; cf. 2.21–49, 2.666–86.

Earlier in Book 1, the narrator has used the same religious imagery to explain to his audience the significance of Troilus's moment of enamorment: "Blissed be Love, that kan thus folk converte!" (1.308). Thus is established a link between Pandarus's activity as a go-between and the narrator's analogous mediation between his inherited story and its audience. That the paradigm shift from Boccaccian decoding to Chaucerian construction of desire governs, and harmonizes, the activities of poet and pimp is underscored at the end of Book 1, when the text describes Pandarus's incipient campaign to woo Criseyde for Troilus—"how he best myghte hire biseche of grace, / And fynde a tyme therto, and a place" (1.1063–64)—using the now-famous housebuilding simile (1.1065–71) drawn, as many have noted, from Geoffroi de Vinsauf's *Poetria nova*, where it is used to describe the construction of a poem.[15]

Just as *Troilus and Criseyde* omits the decoding of female desire as an element of Pandarus's first encounter with the lovesick Troilus, so in Book 2 it suppresses *Il Filostrato*'s demonstration of the correctness of such analysis. Gone is the Criseida who, while giving full scope to her passion for Troiolo, hides it behind a language of virtue and respectability that Pandaro, as he repeatedly reminds her, has penetrated. In place of this closed, self-validating system of hiding and seeking a guaranteed truth—all women have desires—*Troilus and Criseyde* offers a polycentric, ambiguous discourse focussed on a complex female "text," Criseyde, who is susceptible of [mis]construction from several perspectives, none certified correct by the poem that contains them all.[16]

As the interpretive uncertainties of this part of *Troilus and Criseyde* have been widely discussed, a brief summary of them, adapted to the needs of the present discussion, will suffice.[17] The narrator constructs Criseyde as sensitive, fearful, virtuous, prudent, and in general highly sympathetic. (The problems this causes him later in the poem, when he must chronicle her "untroth" to Troilus, are

---

[15] Cf. Geoffroi de Vinsauf, *Poetria Nova*, trans. Margaret F. Nims (Toronto: PIMS, 1967), 16–17:

> If a man has a house to build, his impetuous hand does not rush into action. The measuring line of his mind first lays out the work, and he mentally outlines the successive steps in a definite order.... Poetic art may see in this analogy the law to be given to poets.... As a prudent workman, construct the whole fabric within the mind's citadel....

On Pandarus's "housebuilding" and its implications for *T&C*, see Fyler, "Fabrications," 115–30 (*included in this volume*).

[16] On Criseyde as text, see Dinshaw, *Poetics*, Chapter One, 28–64 (*included in this volume*). Cf. E. T. Donaldson, "Criseyde and Her Narrator," in *Speaking of Chaucer*, 82–83: "Criseyde's character, if any, is a complex composite of emotional responses to her that the poem has evoked from the reader.... Psychologically, we are never allowed to form any very precise or consistent image of her; indeed we are actively prevented from doing so." Mark Lambert, "Criseydan Reading" (in Salu, 105), likewise contends that "there are few statements to be made about Criseyde's sensibility that will not themselves bring forth a throng of 'yes, but' qualifications: it is in good part because the reader must keep reinterpreting her that the entire poem shimmers as it does."

[17] See especially, besides the works mentioned in the preceding note, Alfred David, "Chaucerian Comedy and Criseyde," in Salu, 90–104, and Wetherbee, *Poets*, Chapter 6, "Character and Action: Criseyde and the Narrator."

well known.)[18] When Pandarus threatens to kill himself because of her resistance to Troilus's desire, the narrator rushes to her defense:

> Criseyde, which that wel neigh starf for feere,
> So as she was the ferfulleste wight
> That myghte be, and herde ek with hire ere
> And saugh the sorwful ernest of the knyght,
> And in his preier ek saugh noon unryght,
> And for the harm that myghte ek fallen moore,
> She gan to rewe, and dredde hire wonder soore.   2.449–55

Later, to head off suspicion about Criseyde's apparently erotic response to the sight of Troilus riding by outside her window—a response accepted by *Il Filostrato* as appropriate and inevitable (cf. *Il Filostrato* 2.83)—the narrator puts in his interpretive oar, shaping the story he is telling into a model romance of virtue triumphant on both parts, male and female:

> For I sey nought that she so sodeynly
> Yaf hym hire love, but that she gan enclyne
> To lyke hym first, and I have told yow whi;
> And after that, his manhod and his pyne
> Made love withinne hire herte for to myne,
> For which, by proces and by good servyse,
> He gat hire love, and in no sodeyn wyse.   2.673–79[19]

By contrast, Pandarus constructs Criseyde as a fragile and suspicious person of "tendre wittes" (2.267–73) and seeks, by marshalling people and events into an irresistible "proces," to coerce her into full compliance with Troilus's desire. Unlike his counterpart in *Il Filostrato*, Pandarus largely ignores the possibility that Criseyde might desire Troilus on her own. Instead, he appeals to a range of emotions that, in his eyes, render her manipulable. For example, her desire for approval and her capacity for guilt are Pandarus's target when he warns her that Troilus may die if she refuses to have mercy on him: "do what yow lest, to make hym lyve or deye.... If therwithal in yow ther be no routhe, / Than is it harm ye lyven, by my trouthe!" (2.322, 349–50).[20]

Criseyde's own comments and actions call into question both the narrator's and Pandarus's constructions of her. Her conversational give-and-take with Pandarus suggests considerably more self-assurance than he gives her credit for—indeed, the image of her grabbing him by the hood while he "in a studye

---

[18] See, for example, Wetherbee, *Poets,* 36–37; Donaldson, "Criseyde and Her Narrator," 68–70.

[19] On the narrator's immediate subversion of his construction by his reference, in the next stanza, to how Venus was helping Troilus in the affair—a nod toward determinism that ill accords with the notion of "proces and good servyse"—see Donaldson, "Criseyde and Her Narrator," 66–67.

[20] On Criseyde's desire for approval, see 2.188–89 where she says of Troilus "that alle pris hath he / Of hem that me were levest preysed be."

stood" and exclaiming, "Ye were caught er that ye wiste" (2.1180–83), suggests
the possible need for a reversal of assumptions about who is manipulating
whom in this part of the poem.[21] And her thoughts at the moment when
Pandarus threatens to die if she rejects Troilus betray neither panic nor other
emotional vulnerability (including excessive respect for her uncle):

> "Unhappes fallen thikke
> Alday for love, and in swych manere cas
> As men ben cruel in hemself and wikke;
> And if this man sle here hymself, allas!
> In my presence, it wol be no solas.
> What men wolde of hit deme I kan nat seye:
> It nedeth me ful sleighly for to pleie."   2.456–62

The words with which Criseyde responds to Pandarus—"A! Lord! what me is tid
a sory chaunce! / For myn estat lith now in jupartie, / And ek myn emes lif is
in balaunce" (2.464–66)—constitute a *scudo* for her calculating thoughts, but the
coded utterance cannot be cracked by using feminine desire as a cipher; the
relationship between word and meaning is much more complicated. The same
caveat applies to Criseyde's soliloquy weighing the pros and cons of becoming
involved with Troilus, after she sees him ride past her house and experiences
an erotic frisson ("who yaf me drynke" [2.651]). Her thoughts, even in the face
of the onset of desire, express a strong vein of cool, socially nuanced, and
strategically effaced self-appreciation that is equally distant from Criseida's
frank embrace of desire and secrecy, at this point in *Il Filostrato*, and from the
timidity ascribed to her by *Troilus*'s narrator, or the malleability counted on by
its Pandarus:

> "Ne me to love, a wonder is it nought;
> For wel woot I myself, so God me spede,
> Al wolde I that noon wiste of this thought,
> I am oon the faireste, out of drede,
> And goodlieste, whoso taketh hede,
> And so men seyn, in al the town of Troie."   2.743–48[22]

---

[21] Cf. Lambert ("Criseydan Reading," 113):
> Criseyde finds that this man [Pandarus] who thought he could trap her is himself quite
> trappable: returning from her reading of the letter, she takes Pandarus by the hood as
> he stands in a study. *She* is the one who can say, "Ye were caught er that ye wiste"
> (2.1182).
Lambert goes on to link this moment to Troilus's telling Criseyde she is "kaught" when they
are first in bed together (3.1207–8).

[22] Cf. *Il Filostrato* 2.69:
> "I am young, beautiful, lovely and gay, a widow, rich, noble, and beloved, without
> children and leading a quiet life. Why should I not be in love? If perhaps propriety
> forbids me this, I shall be discreet and keep my desire so hidden that it shall never be
> known that I have ever had love in my heart."

Troilus and Criseyde's discourse of desire, centered on a pervasively ambigu-
ous, multiply constructed Criseyde, is the proper context for the scene with
which this essay began: Troilus's reading of the first letter sent him by his be-
loved. *Il Filostrato* presents the full text of the letter (covering seven stanzas),
juxtaposing it to Criseida's confession of desire for Troiolo and thus making it
a paradigmatically coded utterance which Troiolo, having been schooled by
Pandaro, correctly reads as a self-protecting *scudo* for its writer's passion ("love
constrains her"). *Troilus and Criseyde* offers neither the letter's text nor its con-
fessional context, only a five-line paraphrase—Criseyde refuses to bind herself
to Troilus, "but as his suster, hym to plese, / She wolde ay fayn" (2.1224-25)—
about the sincerity of which the poem is silent (leaving the reader to wonder,
for example, if there is a quibble on "fayn").[23]

In fact *Troilus and Criseyde*'s emphasis, unlike that of *Il Filostrato*, is not on
the letter itself but on Pandarus's massive intrusion into, and construction of,
the surrounding scene. He thrusts Troilus's letter into Criseyde's bosom, offers
to write the reply if she dictates it—"so ye endite" (2.1162)—and even asks her
to let him have "the labour it to sowe and plite" (2.1204), an obvious reference
to his role as fabricator, rather than decoder, of the poem's discourse of desire.
But even more revealing is the continuation of this conversation between niece
and uncle. When Criseyde claims that she found writing her letter painful,
Pandarus replies with a proverb—"of thyng ful often looth bygonne / Comth
ende good" (2.1234-35)—which he then applies to Troilus's pursuit of her. The
implicit parallel between wooing and writing is made explicit via another
Pandaric proverb, "Impressiounes lighte / Ful lightly ben ay redy to the flighte"
(2.1238-39), which Pandarus accuses Criseyde of having taken too seriously in
resisting Troilus, so that "hard was it youre herte for to grave" (2.1241). That is,
Pandarus sees Criseyde as a *tabula rasa* on which he has been busily attempting to
write his message of, and program of acquiescence to, desire.

Thus the writing of letters in *Troilus and Criseyde* becomes less an exercise in
coding and decoding a discourse of desire than an emblem for the process of
imposing self-interested "messages"—suggestions, interpretations, counsels—on
others. This emblem replaces, and reverses, its analogue in *Il Filostrato*: Criseida
removing her last covering garment in order to experience the full pleasure of
fulfilled desire. In *Troilus and Criseyde*, not the removal of hindering integu-
ments but the inscribing of resistant surfaces characterizes the process (and dis-
course) of desire.

The disappearance from *Troilus and Criseyde*'s consummation scene of
Criseida's symbolic act of self-uncovering creates a gap in the narrative which
the Chaucerian text fills with not one but three emblems of desire offered to
characterize the movement of the story to this point. The first is an image of
male desire transformed into irresistible physical force—an image of rape.
Troilus, in bed at last with Criseyde, "in armes gan hire streyne, / And seyde,

---

[23] Cf. McKinnell, "Letters" [see n2 above], who speaks of "the possibility of a sinister
pun on *fayn*" (82).

/ 'Now be ye kaught, now is ther but we tweyne! / Now yeldeth yow, for other bote is non!' " (3.1205–08).[24]

This Troilan reading of the consummation scene is challenged, and under-cut, by Criseyde's reply to her lover's demand that she yield to him: "Ne hadde I er now, my swete herte deere, / Ben yold, ywis, I were now nought heere!" (3.1210–11). These lines offer a different interpretive key—female acquies-cence—to the moment and the story. In a way, they put Criseyde in charge of the affair; this is not (or not just) the house that Pandarus built, after all. But they also appear to assimilate *Troilus and Criseyde*'s Criseyde to *Il Filostrato*'s Criseida: feminine desire here reveals itself as, after all, the motor propelling the narrative.

To entertain this latter interpretation, however, is to founder in its difficulty. For unlike *Il Filostrato*'s depiction of Criseida, *Troilus and Criseyde*'s of Criseyde mystifies the moment of her yielding, hiding it behind a kaleidoscopic dis-course of events and images that defeats precise decoding: Pandarus's *suasoria*; Troilus's heroic appearance outside her house on his way home from battle; her own internal debate; Antigone's song; the nightingale that sang "peraunter, in his briddes wise, a lay / Of love" (2.921–22) outside her window; her dream of a considerably larger and more intimidating bird ripping out her heart and putting his in its place; and so on.[25]

The third emblem, embedded in *Troilus and Criseyde*'s consummation scene, that proposes itself as a key to the love story up to this point occurs two stanzas later:

> And as aboute a tree, with many a twiste,
> Bytrent and writh the swote wodebynde,
> Gan eche of hem in armes other wynde.   3.1230–32

This is an image of mutuality and symbiosis, a suggestion that the lovers have worked together to bring about the moment that satisfied their shared desire.

There is, of course, no way either to integrate or choose among these emblems; in arriving at its moment of highest aspiration, *Troilus and Criseyde*'s discourse of desire finds (or rather constructs) an interpretive impasse. This is the poem's genius: its recalcitrancy in the face of its reader's deepest exegetical impulses. One cannot but perceive in this fundamental characteristic of Chau-

---

[24] Troilus behaves as if he were following the advice of either Boccaccio's Pandaro (*Il Filostrato* 2.27, 3–6) or the Ovidian *magister amoris* (*Ars amatoria* 1.663–706), both of whom argue that women welcome rape. *See further the essay by Fradenburg above–RAS & CSC.*

[25] Lambert ("Criseydan Reading," 119) calls 3.1210–11: "the speech in the poem we most like Criseyde for making, and the statement in the poem which forces us most directly to acknowledge that things *have* been blurry, that we don't know, or at least seem unable to recall, just when, just how, with just what understanding of the situation, a central decision was reached." On the process in Book 2 by which Criseyde at least moves toward being in love, see Howard, "Experience," 173–92; and Jill Mann, *Geoffrey Chaucer* (Atlantic Highlands: Humanities Press International, 1991), 23–27, 105. For Mann's very different reading of the consummation scene, see 107–10.

cer's narrative a profound, negative reaction to the techniques of encoding and decoding desire that occupy a central place in the representation of love in *Il Filostrato*.

Gesture and Seduction
in Troilus and Criseyde*

JOHN P. HERMANN

TROILUS AND CRISEYDE frequently poses the question of its own readability. This essay responds by examining the role of gesture in the poem. Gesture, which expressively hovers between act and language, foregrounds language's self-division between muteness and communication, errancy and truth, unmeaning and meaning. Contradictory modern interpretations of gesture in the poem, typically asserted rather than argued, offer opportunities for rigorous reading to begin. These contradictions can serve to dislodge certain scholarly assumptions challenged by contemporary and medieval theories of meaning and powerfully belied by Chaucer's text. After a theory of resistance to the seductions of traditional medieval scholarship is framed, via structuralist theory, Boncompagno of Signa's ROTA VENERIS is offered as a check to modern interpretive reflexes. If modern gesture studies tend to view Boncompagno's incomplete taxonomy and systematic play as deficiencies, this essay exploits such qualities to open a plural reading of the gestures of seduction in Books 2 and 5. Since gestures in the poem are mediated by a narrator who differs from himself in important ways, this essay concludes by questioning the supposedly profound wisdom of the epilogue. To reduce undecidability to decidability in TROILUS AND CRISEYDE can, in certain important respects, only be provisional; to suspend, with a kind of negative capability, the ascription of meaning to this joyful and terrifying poem, I take as a precondition for its rigorous reading.

Recent work on gesture in Chaucer has added considerably to our ability to make sense of this important aspect of his artistry. Robert Benson's book on Chaucerian body language catalogues most of the gestures, allowing a synoptic overview for the first time, and furnishes a running commentary on their narrative function. Barry Windeatt's article offers a somewhat less complete treatment of the topic, since it limits itself to works which have a known literary source, but it does supply a set of observations on the role of gesture in delineating character. Finally, John Block Friedman's pioneering research into medieval affective physiognomy provides a useful supplement to the sturdy humoral physiognomic studies which Walter Clyde Curry conducted a half-century ago. As a result, those interested in Chaucer's use of gesture suddenly find

---

* Originally appeared in *Studies in the Age of Chaucer* 7 (1985): 107–35.

themselves with an embarrassment of riches. But no one has yet taken up the bristling theoretical problems involved in the study of Chaucerian gesture.[1] These are problems which strictly taxonomic or historical studies cannot solve, however much they might help to inform our readings. Such a critical lacuna is understandable, because literary gesture frustrates the traditional projects of medieval literary scholarship to an even greater extent than is customary with other, often recondite, medieval symbolic systems. The present essay offers a theoretical discussion of problems encountered in studying Chaucerian gesture, followed by a reading of gestures of seduction in Books 2 and 5 of *Troilus and Criseyde*.

1

A satisfactory definition of gesture is rather more difficult to come by than one might think. Windeatt uses the definition offered by Werner Habicht in his classic study: any expressive bodily movement or position which has meaning but does not serve a practical purpose. He faults Benson for examining Chaucerian gesture from the point of view of body-language, which he says is

> a less distinct and more psychological concept than traditional notions of gesture as certain acknowledged and definite physical signs, reactions, and movements.[2]

But are not textually uncertain and indefinite gestures what readers have found most interesting in the delicate negotiations between Pandarus and Criseyde or in the skillful seduction of Criseyde by Diomede? I prefer to base my definition upon a useful *summa dictaminis de arte amandi* in which Boncompagno of Signa discusses several varieties of lovers' gestures. His looser sense of gesture includes body language as well as the involuntary signs of affective physiognomy Friedman considers. For my purposes, gesture is any expressive bodily sign, such as a change in bodily position, a movement of the body, a change in hue, or even a sigh.[3]

Both Benson and Windeatt assemble lists based on their definitions, then comment on them. Their methodologies are framed by no acknowledged theoretical standpoint, and evidence or argumentation is seldom furnished to support a reading. Instead, assertions are made:

---

[1] Robert G. Benson, *Medieval Body Language: A Study of the Use of Gesture in Chaucer's Poetry*, Anglistica, 21 (Copenhagen: Rosenkilde and Bagger, 1980); Barry Windeatt, "Gesture in Chaucer," *M&H* n.s. 9 (1979): 143–61; John Block Friedman, "Another Look at Chaucer and the Physiognomists," *SP* 79 (1981): 138–52. Important reviews of Benson's book include Barry Windeatt, *SAC* 4 (1982): 144–46 and Edmund Reiss, *SoAR* 46 (1981): 100–101.

[2] Windeatt, *SAC* 4 (1982), 145.

[3] See the comparable definitions by Werner Habicht, *Die Gebärde in englischen Dichtungen des Mittelalters* (Munich: Verlag der Bayerischen Akademie der Wissenschaften, 1959), 8 and by Benson, 10. I discuss Boncompagno's *summa dictaminis* in Part III, infra.

As Pandarus tells Criseyde of Troilus' love, he swears that he is telling the truth, and "With that the teris bruste out of his yën." A moment later Criseyde too "began to breste a-wepe anoon." [C.S.] Lewis warns us against regarding Pandarus' tears as merely theatrical, and we must exercise the same caution in interpreting those of Criseyde. She is described as "the ferfullest wight / That myghte be," and her anxiety revealed by her tears is genuine. Criseyde is a complex character (Benson 90).

Why we must follow Lewis's warning or accept Benson's admonition that Criseyde's anxiety is not theatrical, but genuine, is never made clear. One might compare Windeatt's methodology in an analysis of two crucial scenes in Book 3:

> When Criseyde enters Troilus's sick-room and when Troilus is brought to Criseyde's bedside . . . in each case the character in bed is seized with such a sudden blushing in the presence of the other that Chaucer remarks that the blushing partner could not speak a word, even if his or her head were to be cut off. This thought of beheading appears equivalent to the modern wish to "fall through the floor," to escape from all consciousness of being looked at. Chaucer's introduction of these blushes emphasizes strongly his lovers' ability to appreciate the delicacy of their situation ("Gesture," 151, 152).

As with Benson's reading, meanings are assigned without any attempt to convince us that we should accept the interpretation set forth. Both read gestures in terms of an implicit theory of realism, and give covert support to that theory through an empirical and taxonomic scholarship. Windeatt's notion that the blushes function to emphasize the ability of the lovers to appreciate their delicate situation is oddly lacking in relevance to the perfervid critical debate surrounding the poem: the lines of interpretation are certainly more firmly etched—and differently drawn—than he appears to know.

The response made by Windeatt and Benson to their slippery topic is a kind of freewheeling taxonomy which appears to be ungrounded in theory, in traditional Anglo-American fashion. They seem comfortable in their roles as detached scientific observers, and conceive their enterprise as a rather unproblematic one: consequently, meanings are simply asserted rather than argued. Friedman avoids adopting such an investigative persona in his study, which uses a variety of contemporaneous sources in an attempt to ground his readings. Yet his historical research, which displays the heightened awareness of the importance of gestural conventions that Reiss called for, produces a noticeable critical tentativeness:

> Early in Book One of *Troilus*, Chaucer has Criseyde let her look fall a bit askance disdainfully. This gesture soon becomes a trait associated with her throughout the poem. At times her indirect gaze seems evidence of a perturbed emotional state; overall, it may be a sign of her own potentially disturbing indirectness. During the confrontation scene of Book Two she "gan hire eighen down to caste" in what may be only a gesture of modes-

ty but which still foreshadows later indirectness (Friedman 151).

Friedman had cited Caxton's *Book of Curtesye* and *The Babees Book* to demonstrate that looking directly upon one's interlocutor was a social virtue in the Middle Ages. The ruling assumption of his study is that paraliterary materials can help solve the problems of reading gesture. Rather than grounding the interpretation of gestures, however, sources simply add possibilities, in some cases making the interpretive horizon of a conclusive reading recede even further. Whether Criseyde's indirect gaze is a sign of modesty, perturbed emotions, or potentially disturbing indirectness cannot be determined by outside sources, which support each of these readings and, no doubt, others. But such a hydra-like multiplication of difficulties should not be seen as unwelcome. Friedman's interpretive hesitancy might be taken as a minor defeat for scholarship, but it bodes well for criticism.

The undecidability associated with reading gesture has much to tell medieval literary scholars about the validity of their methodological premises. In the work of Windeatt and Benson, the attempt to furnish a taxonomy is combined with an empirical and impressionistic criticism that never calls into question its own ruling assumptions. With Friedman, the tradition of affective physiognomy is shown to have undeniable relevance, but is unable to remedy the critical problems for which it was enlisted. Chaucerian gesture studies have arrived at an impasse, with a good deal of information present and doubtless forthcoming, but also with real problems in understanding the rules and limits of the game being played. The quest for a solution to these problems—although I would prefer to speak of finding ways of adding interest to the conversation—requires an examination of the theoretical constraints on reading gesture.

2

A word in a sentence, an image in a poem, a gesture, action, or speech performed by a person, a Sioux among the Sioux or a Parisian in Paris—each of these is a center of exchange for meanings, but is without meaning in isolation. The notion of structure is similar in all these contexts ... but it makes a great difference for literary criticism which context is taken as most important.[4]

This structuralist principle—that the atomistic approach to meaning is futile, since meanings are relational—by now has a familiar ring for most medievalists. The individual sound, or gesture, lacks sense apart from a system which invests it with meaning. On the phonemic level, one thinks of the difference between [sin] and [gin]. Or on the level of imagery, one realizes that the poetic descrip-

---

[4] J. Hillis Miller, "The Antitheses of Criticism: Reflections on the Yale Colloquium," in *Velocities of Change: Critical Essays from MLN*, ed. Richard Macksey (Baltimore: The Johns Hopkins Univ. Press, 1974), 143.

tion of a bird perched upon a barn functions differently within differing literary contexts.[5] Approaches which seek to attribute meaning to elements of language or literature in isolation fail to satisfy our interpretive desire. Consider, for example, the dream books which Freud's *Traumdeutung* replaced—yet which can still be found on bookstands—in which a given element is simply assigned a meaning by the oneiromancer. Freud's advance in the interpretation of dreams was a structuralist discovery *avant la lettre*, and is exemplary for other areas of research as well. In any system of signification, interpsychic or intrapsychic, it is the play of differences which constitutes the meaning of the individual element. As Ferdinand de Saussure first observed, although without drawing out the full implications of his insight, "in the linguistic system there are only differences, *without positive terms*."[6] What implications might this differential insight have for gestural study?

In the essay which furnishes my section headnote, J. Hillis Miller is concerned with the twin poles of interpretation: at one extreme are those who think that the literariness of a text inheres in its uniqueness as an individual work of art, and consider wider contexts of lesser importance. Such a mode of reading is opposed by those who argue that literature must be studied in terms of the context of "similar passages in other works by the author, or from books read by the author, or from the social and historical milieu in which it came into existence, or from the tradition to which it belongs" (Miller 141). The latter approach is a mirror image of the former. Taken only as "itself," the possibility of significant commentary diminishes. But when the work is read in terms of wider contexts, it tends to disappear into an instance of some privileged reality. Some might argue that this more inclusive reality is the base of Marxist theory, which generates the superstructure in an insufficiently questioned spatial trope.[7] Others might argue for the unconscious, "the fourteenth-century British mind," or even "the medieval mind." Even when the atomistic approach is avoided, one must understand the extent to which the structure invoked from within or without the text is itself figural, tending to reduce the force of meaning which outstrips any structure the interpreter might employ.[8]

In *Troilus and Criseyde*, we are never merely given gestures to decode, isolated elements which might then be read in terms of the interpretive conventions of realism or of Boncompagno's theory of gesture. The poem is mediated

---

[5] In assessing the significance of this image from PardT (VI. 397), it is helpful to know that the dove is associated with the Holy Spirit in Christianity. Such theological knowledge would probably not inform the reading of a similar image in a typical Romantic poem, however.

[6] *Course in General Linguistics*, trans. Wade Baskin (New York: McGraw-Hill, 1966), 120.

[7] See Christopher Norris, *Deconstruction: Theory and Practice* (London: Routledge, 1991), 81, 151. The defects of this founding metaphor of Marxist theory have been only partially remedied by the feedback mechanism that Louis Althusser and Pierre Machery have introduced, which leaves untouched the spatial figure it seeks to supplement.

[8] Jacques Derrida, "Structure, Sign and Play in the Discourse of the Human Sciences," in *Writing and Difference*, trans. Alan Bass (Chicago: Univ. of Chicago Press, 1978), 278–93.

by a narrator who interprets events and gestures in ways that have caused readers to question his reliability. It is this unreliable narrator who synthesizes individual gesture and wider context, and the poem gives us ample reason to be careful about taking him at face value. The narrator's blind spots and willful misreading of a text which points in directions opposed to his glosses serve to foreground the gestures of his characters without supplying any definitive way of knowing for certain what they mean. Yet our urge to interpret continues in spite of such difficulties. Or because of them.

It is this wayward narrator, differing significantly from himself at various points in the poem, who causes the gestures of his characters to take on such undeniable importance. We must attend not only to the gestures themselves, but to his manner of presenting them. Gestures in *Troilus and Criseyde* are not always translatable into some scholarly meta-language of paraphrase that recuperates their meaning. Indeed, gesture is often employed in life and literature to avoid being pinned down. The poem's gestural code is ambiguous from the standpoint of the narrator, author, and characters as well. The very attempt to eliminate the ambiguity of gesture, one comes to realize, runs curiously counter to its purposes, especially in literature, which frequently strives for a fertile suspension of meaning. In the case of *Troilus and Criseyde*, it is crucial to interrogate the status of the epilogue of an unreliable narrator who continually misreads his narrative: Is his final gloss privileged, or simply one more example of a meaning erroneously imposed upon a text which points in other directions? In what sense is the poem a warning to young women as well as young men? Is love between man and woman ever completely free of *fol amor*, or completely given over to a *caritas* focused solely upon God? And is the narrator's advice to turn completely away from earthly love in order to focus upon God really good advice for young people, or an adequate response to the narrative? Or is it emblematic of his rather overwrought reaction to Troilus's fate?[9]

A full account of gesture in *Troilus and Criseyde* is an interpretive limit, not an attainable end: it should be aspired to, but our eagerness for interpretive closure must not outstrip our respect for textual reticences. To arrive at a monovalent signified for the gestural signifier's bypassing of language is a hermeneutic richness which may only impoverish. A capacity for uncertainty in such matters may be preferable, allowing the possibility of a differential range of meanings for a given gesture, without insisting upon only one. Yet any serious reading of gesture begins with this hermeneutic desire for a one-to-one assignment of signifieds to gestural signifiers.

It is useful to foreground what might be termed the signification overload in gestures, an ambiguity that works to whet the reader's curiosity. The key issue is not detecting the signified for a given signifier, so much as juggling a plural-

---

[9] Bernard F. Huppé, "The Unlikely Narrator: The Narrative Strategy of the *Troilus*," in *Signs and Symbols in Chaucer's Poetry*, ed. John P. Hermann and John J. Burke, Jr. (Tuscaloosa: Univ. of Alabama Press, 1981), 179–94.

ity of signifieds which vie for acceptance. One response to this promiscuity of the signifier is to foreclose complexities by taxonomizing and ascribing meaning. But gestures tempt the reader to consider various interpretations within the range of possibilities offered by the text. Scholars have attempted to establish checks and limits upon the multivalency of gestures in the poem, but not to scrutinize the limitations of the critical methodologies which allow them to do so. To cast the light of scholarship upon *Troilus and Criseyde* may be only to cast darkness. Perhaps more needs to be said for the value of darkness in our encounter with the poem.[10]

3

In some ways, Boncompagno of Signa's medieval taxonomy of lovers' gestures is methodologically superior to more recent and, at first glance, more disciplined work on Chaucerian gesture. The *Rota Veneris*, a witty *summa dictaminis de arte amandi* of the early thirteenth century, has much to reveal not only about medieval gestures of love, but about how the modern reader of this fragment of a Western *ars sexualis* ought to construct a gestural hermeneutic. No genetic relationship between it and Chaucer's poem can be established. It is, however, the most valuable work extant for understanding lovers' gestures in medieval literature and deserves to be more widely known.[11]

Boncompagno begins his discussion by listing the four lovers' gestures: the nod, indication, signal, and sigh. He defines the nod in three rather diverse ways, as

> a sort of preambular herald of love which, through a certain inaudible gesture, reveals the secrets of hearts. Or: a nod is a certain symbol of love, which indicates what lovers have already achieved, or what they desire to

---

[10] Windeatt states his purpose in this way (143):
The present study aims to isolate instances of Chaucer's introduction of gestures into his retelling of received narratives and to trace the patterns of interest and emphasis these reveal in Chaucer. To do this it concentrates largely on those of Chaucer's works for which there is a known literary source in order to provide some check on what are Chaucer's own innovations. Innovation in description of human gesture must have natural limits, and in all writers' use of the same gesture will be a common core of similar observation.
The notions that commentary "traces" patterns from the text, that source study is capable of furnishing a "check" upon the play of gestural signifiers, and that all writers' use(s) of a literary gesture have a "common core" and "natural limits" are seemingly self-evident postulates. They deserve interrogation as the inaugural figures of a traditional scholarly discourse which attempts to police the text. On the recurrent visual metaphors of Western intellectual tradition which find their reflection in these scholarly tropes, see Jacques Derrida, "White Mythology: Metaphor in the Text of Philosophy," *Margins of Philosophy*, trans. Alan Bass (Chicago: University of Chicago Press, 1982), 207–71.

[11] Boncompagno da Signa, *Rota Veneris: A Facsimile Reproduction*, ed. and trans. Josef Purkart (Delmar: Scholars' Facsimiles and Reprints, 1975). The quotations which follow appear on pages 92–95.

do. Or: a nod is an indicator of true or false love, because through it, many people are often drawn into the snare of deception.

Winking the eye, for example, engenders in lovers "a certain indescribable joy, for which, very frequently, they are beside themselves." Nods also occur when a woman points to her throat with her index finger, lifts a scarf or headband to reveal the beauty of her hair, stretches out her arms to shift her dress, raises her head or lowers it, makes a movement of the hand, smiles, or walks with "a tortuous gait." Boncompagno admits to the incompleteness of his taxonomy when he states that "the nod assumes many forms, which I cannot enumerate because of its diversity of types." The indication is "a certain way of covertly revealing a secret, through which what we ought to do is indicated to us." An indication occurs when someone notices a woman and begins "to polish himself up more than was his wont." Unlike nods, which are "only accomplished by gesture," indications can make use of sound as well. Yet every nod is also an indication, since something is always indicated. Indications are well-nigh innumerable "and no one could fully do justice to their diversity." Furthermore, interpretive closure is difficult, since all indications are open to conjecture (*omne indicium est coniectura*).

The two remaining categories of lovers' gestures are the signal and the sigh. The signal reveals a secret, "as when a certain man or woman grows pale or blushes with a sudden motion, by which either joy or anger is indicated." This category explores the realm of affective physiognomy, whose importance Friedman has emphasized. Boncompagno does not discuss signals in general, but only those pertaining to love, "since the explanations of a signal are infinite." He adds that in a larger sense, signals are also indications, and vice versa. His final category of *amancium gestus* is the sigh, which is defined in the elaborate periphrastic style devoted to the nod. A sigh is "an innate passion of the soul arising out of a suspension of the mind." Or it is "a vehement passion of the mind arising out of extreme meditation." Or, finally, "a sudden and unexpected utterance of the mind resulting from the plight of the soul." Its etymology is related to the first of these definitions:

a sigh derives its name from the suspension of the mind (*spirituum suspensio*), since, when the soul relates to memory the happiness it once had or the immensity of its grief, or the immeasurable joy, or the contrary, or troubles to come, the mind is suspended, because the heart is fettered by the fact that the soul forgets its operative capacity. Thus, when the heart gradually begins to dilate again, the mind returns to its original state, and from this very return a certain sound arises, which is called a sigh.

However, sighs can also arise from bad manners, sickness, or the desire to deceive. Moreover, they can be classified as nods, indications, and signals as well and indicate "a great number of things." Since meaning depends upon context, which is not always clear, one can imagine the problems which might follow upon a faulty interpretation: one's beloved might be a heartless coquette, ill, or simply ill-mannered. Indeed, much of the humor of the *Rota Veneris*, just as with the *De Amore* of Andreas Capellanus, comes from imagining the folly of anyone who might try to put its advice into practice.

Although Boncompagno's remarks "seem to display lasciviousness," he says he is neither a libertine, nor wishes to be one. He refers to the Song of Songs which, if read literally, "could contribute more to the voluptuousness of the flesh than to the moral edification of the spirit." But wise men read such texts allegorically, and Boncompagno asks the reader to believe that he "did not say these things for any lascivious reason, but that, out of pure friendship, he conceded to the entreaties of his colleagues." Chaucer also, some critics argue, wrote the lascivious story of Troilus and Criseyde to reveal the deceptions of sensuality. But whether the glosses of Boncompagno and Chaucer should simply be reflected in the interpretations of modern readers is open to question.[12]

The *Rota Veneris* is not without an Ovidian irony frequent in medieval discussions of love. Its bubbling humor means that it can not be used in the same fashion as a modern scholarly discussion of gesture. On the other hand, Boncompagno's incomplete taxonomy and systematic play are interesting for these very reasons. Attention to the methodology which his treatise generates is of great value in approaching *Troilus and Criseyde*, since the difficulties which Boncompagno discovers in the interpretation of gesture are those of the modern reader as well. Boncompagno shows himself aware of the problem of interpretation not only by his wit, but by the play built into his system. Because he does not assign meanings in the manner of the modern scholar, his system can inform the construction of a hermeneutic adequate to the knotty gestures of seduction in *Troilus and Criseyde*.

4

At the beginning of Book 2, Pandarus rises to the swallow's sorrowful lay of the rape of Philomela, recalls his "grete emprise," and travels to his niece's palace. He finds Criseyde sitting in a tiled private room with two other women, listening to the story of the siege of Thebes. After they greet each other, Criseyde rises "and by the hond in hye / She took hym faste" (88–89) to a bench where they can talk in privacy. According to Benson, "Criseyde's warm greeting and the good humor with which they both treat her remarks about Pandarus's mistress reveal the affectionate familiarity of their relationship" (Benson 89). But this affectionate familiarity is soon put to the test. Niece and uncle make small talk about the *Thebaid*, a curiously apposite literary work. The story of the siege of Thebes is being read and discussed by Trojans who are

---

[12] Peter Dronke, "The Conclusion of *Troilus and Criseyde*," *MÆ* 33 (1964): 47–52; Anthony E. Farnham, "Chaucerian Irony and the Ending of the *Troilus*," *ChauR* 1 (1967): 207–16.

under siege themselves; moreover, this occurs within a poem directed to
Englishmen at war with France, a *mise en abîme* which has specific political rel-
evance. Pandarus's arrival coincides with the rubric indicating Amphiorax's fall
into hell.[13]

Their literary conversation does not continue for long, however, and Pan-
darus relies upon the paralanguage of gesture when he begins to communicate
his real message:

> "Do wey youre barbe, and shewe youre face bare;
> Do wey youre book, rys up, lat us daunce,
> And lat us don to May som observaunce."   2.110-12

These gestures are never enacted by the characters; they occur only within
Pandarus's discourse. None is catalogued by Benson, since he does not treat
discursive gestures, a methodological decision in keeping with his realist the-
oretical orientation. Making sense of the gestures that Pandarus recommends
depends upon the reader's grasp of their context. Taking off a headdress
would clearly have a different meaning if Criseyde were busy at her toilet and
the gesture were one recommended by her handmaiden. The gestures men-
tioned by Pandarus are rejected by Criseyde: God forbid that she should do
such a thing, she says. Her response, which even includes an accusation of in-
sanity, constitutes an endotelic interpretation of the gestural code—one, that is,
made within the narrative itself: "Is that a widewes lif, so God yow save?"
Criseyde detects the presence of what Boncompagno termed nods and indica-
tions. Such actions would be inappropriate, she tells Pandarus, since it would
better suit her to sit in a cave and read saints' lives. The actions he recom-
mends are more suitable to "maydens ... and yonge wyves" (119).

Criseyde's response is presented without comment by the narrator. Yet it is
quite unclear what the reader is to make of it. She tells Pandarus: "By God, ye
maken me ryght soore adrad!" (115). But why is she afraid? Concern for her
reputation? Or for her virtue? And why is she so vehement? A strong super-
ego? Or a strong id revealing itself in her excessive protestations? Is it even cer-
tain that she is vehement? Or is she making use of *urbanitas* and merely pre-
tending to virtue for the sake of guying it? Interpretation of Criseyde's reaction
to the gestures Pandarus recommends is made difficult by her comment that
it would suit her better to devote herself to her religious duties. In our first
reading we might feel justified in crediting her with an anchoress's desire for
sanctity. Since she does not display such religious leanings later in the poem,
however, it seems possible that irony is present. The scholar of gesture can
arrive at a single interpretation of the gestures Pandarus recommends only by
reducing the plurality of Criseyde's response.

Pandarus replies to Criseyde's objections by tantalizing her with the good
news he bears: "As evere thryve I ... / Yet koude I telle a thyng to doon yow

---

[13] David Anderson, "Theban," 109-33. On the infernal dimensions of the poem, see
Robertson, *Preface*, 482, 496.

pleye" (120–21). Although it is more than five times better than the lifting of
the siege, Pandarus does not want to tell her what it is, since it would make her
the proudest woman in Troy were she to know. Evidently, his impending rev-
elation of good tidings is not political but personal. Criseyde's response dis-
plays a splitting of desire and demand.[14] Unable to ask for a solution to the
enigma confronting her, gestures mark her conflict:

> Tho gan she wondren moore than biforn
> A thousand fold, and down hire eyghen caste;
> For nevere, sith the tyme that she was born,
> To knowe thyng desired she so faste;
> And with a syk she seyde hym atte laste,
> "Now, uncle myn, I nyl yow nought displese,
> Nor axen moore that may do yow disese."   2.141–47

Criseyde actively interpreted Pandarus's first stratagem, which relied on the
paralanguage of the gestural code. But this second ploy is met with downcast
eyes, silence, a sigh, and a verbal formula of submission to the communicative
ground rules established by her uncle. Pandarus's language has avoided direct
communication, and Criseyde responds with gestures that reflect his indirec-
tion. But it is easier to know what these gestures are meant not to communi-
cate than what their positive content might be. Context is helpful, but not de-
termining. Criseyde's downcast gaze is read by Benson as indicating that she is
"trying not to appear curious about the exciting news her uncle claims to have"
(Benson 89), while according to Friedman it "may only be a gesture of modesty
but ... still foreshadows later indirectness" (Friedman 151). Although numer-
ous studies of gaze and averted gaze have been conducted, it is finally impossi-
ble to decide whether this gesture is one of curiosity, modesty, concealment, or
submission, since internal and external evidence can be found to support each
of these readings.[15]

Suppose, for the sake of argument, that the medieval gestural system were
known in substantially greater detail. We would still not know the meaning of
this gesture in its context, although most medieval literary scholarship tries
vainly to keep skepticism at bay by refusing to question its goals and methodol-
ogies. Criseyde does not want to reveal her desire. Desire shows in the gaze, so
she husbands it carefully. Yet it shows in the custody of her gaze as well. Our
interpretation that she is trying to conceal her desire offers only a preliminary
reading. But to assign a meaning to Criseyde's gestures in this fashion is little
more than a mark of anxiety for interpretive closure. What, for example, are
we to make of the sigh that follows her downcast gaze? Should we associate it

---

[14] The mediation of desire by language is called by Lacan "demand"; see Anika Lemaire,
Jacques Lacan, trans. David Macey (London: Routledge, 1977), 161–75 and Jacques Lacan,
Écrits: A Selection, trans. Alan Sheridan (New York: Norton, 1977), viii.

[15] Michael Argyle and Mark Cook, *Gaze and Mutual Gaze* (Cambridge: Cambridge Univ.
Press, 1976), 58–82. *See further the essay by Stanbury in this volume–RAS & CSC.*

with mental fatigue? This is not a particularly charitable response, but Pandarus's subsequent remarks indicate that he thinks she is one of the "tendre wittes" (271). Yet Criseyde's suspicion shows critical intelligence, not slow-wittedness, since what can not be understood plainly in Pandarus's conversation is indeed due to guile. Should we then read her sigh as indicating her own guile in complying with Pandarus's wishes, given the difficulty of her solving the puzzle otherwise? Benson interprets it, along with her downcast eyes, as a sign of her effort not to appear curious (Benson 89). But to assign a monovalent meaning in such a fashion is to foreclose the textual richness of the poem. Such totalizing interpretations posit an author fully in possession of textual meaning, but authors as well as texts contain contradictions. The contradictions in Criseyde's character are resolved by readers who, thinking to do the text a service, betray the differences that set its textual play into motion. When Boncompagno said that "the explanations of a signal are infinite," he recognized this plurality in the course of a reading of gesture.

The outcome of Criseyde's gestures, which at the same time conceal and reveal her character, is an act of compliance. She decides not to displease her uncle, and in the ensuing conversation she carefully avoids mentioning what most interests her. As a consequence, Pandarus feels free to discuss Troilus, describing him as the friendliest man of great estate he ever saw, and the one who can offer the best friendship to those capable of benefiting from it. When he attempts to leave after this exercise in hyperbole, Criseyde urges him to stay by telling him she wants "to speke of wisdom" before he goes. Their companions withdraw, perhaps because speaking of wisdom seems boring to them. Or perhaps this idiom was a verbal signal for private conversation.[16] Pandarus concludes this parenthetical stage of their discussion by once again employing the language of gestures:

> "Now is it tyme I wende.
> But yet, I say, ariseth, and lat us daunce,
> And cast youre widewes habit to mischaunce!
> What list yow thus youreself to disfigure,
> Sith yow is tid thus fair an aventure?"　　　2.220-24

The widow's habit disfigures her and is certainly the wrong dress for an "aventure." Since Pandarus has been discussing Troilus at length, there would seem to be some connection between her widowhood and the good fortune that has befallen her. After more conversational indirection, during which Pandarus manages to discover that Criseyde is "withouten paramours," Criseyde finally asks him to "Lat be to me youre fremde manere speche" (248). He kisses her and asks her to take what he says for good:

> With that she gan hire eighen down to caste,

---

[16] John Hurt Fisher suggests that "wisdom" should be glossed as "serious business" in this context—see *The Complete Poetry and Prose of Geoffrey Chaucer* (New York: Holt, Rinehart and Winston, 1977), *ad loc.*

    And Pandarus to coghe gan a lite   2.253-54

Windeatt offers an interpretation of the literary and social context of these gestures:

> Pandarus begins his persuasions here with a cough; he is Chaucer's only character to cough outside the characters of the fabliaux. As she listens to her uncle, Criseyde is described as looking downwards, and when Pandarus has finished his exhortation he too hangs his head and looks down. In the averted looks Chaucer catches that embarrassed thoughtfulness and sense of awkwardness in over-solemn talk between relatives, but Criseyde's embarrassment seems social—she feels the awkwardness of her position ("Gesture," 152).

Benson (89) focuses upon the behavior of Pandarus:

> How skillful and spontaneous that cough is made to seem becomes evident when we compare it to Criseida's prearranged cough with which she signals Troilo in Boccaccio's poem. Panadarus' cough is both ceremonial and spontaneous. He is at the same time a devoted uncle, slightly hesitant to broach a delicate subject to his niece, and a self-conscious and theatrical go-between well aware of the dramatic potential of his situation. Even after he agrees to tell her, the seriousness of the matter gives him pause.

These persuasive interpretations are two possibilities out of many. Some critics might find them overly generous to Pandarus, who himself will worry in an elaborate euphemism that people will consider him "swich a meene / As maken wommen unto men to comen" (3.254-55). D. W. Robertson reads Book 2 as a "study in false 'curtesie,'... the activity of the unguided lower reason operating with its worldly wisdom in a sophisticated society" (*Preface*, 482). He sees Pandarus as anything but a devoted uncle. But Windeatt and Benson emphasize the realistic rather than the symbolic code in their readings. Should one privilege the final position of the frequently unreliable narrator, Pandarus's gestures can be read differently, as emblematic of the characters' awareness of the immorality of the sexual liaison about to be proposed. Windeatt's association of coughing with the fabliaux seems to undercut the role of gestures in effecting "the distinctively tender yet dignified internalization of his characters" ("Gesture," 160). The gestures of Criseyde and Pandarus are finally ambiguous; they allow contrary readings depending upon the critical model adopted by the interpreter.

    Pandarus then looks on her "in a bysi wyse," causing Criseyde to remark:

> "Lord! so faste ye m'avise!
> Sey ye me nevere er now?"   2.276-77

Criseyde's response can be read as signifying her discomfort, a well-documented reaction to a direct stare.[17] But her interpretation of his stare might

---

[17] Argyle and Cook, *Gaze and Mutual Gaze*, 74-75; 92-93.

also be read as ironic. Pandarus's cough might be related to his cunning, rather than his spontaneity or thoughtfulness as Benson and Windeatt claim. He tells her once again that good fortune is imminent, but also threatens her: if she is angry with him for what he says, or thinks that he lies, he will never again see her "with yë." Pandarus reads Criseyde's change in appearance at this threat in terms of the code of affective physiognomy:

> "Beth naught agast, ne quaketh naught! Wherto?
> Ne chaungeth naught for fere so youre hewe!"   2.302–3

Benson ignores Pandarus's endotelic interpretation:

> Bursting with curiosity following Pandarus' long preamble, Criseyde trembles and turns pale. These gestures are notable primarily for the way in which Chaucer includes them. They are static.[18]

The interpretation that she is curious rather than frightened is asserted without argumentation or consideration of alternative readings, including Pandarus's. The epistemological claim of direct access to the unitary mental state of a literary character which Benson's and Windeatt's readings are premised upon can be resisted by exploring the range of meanings for a given gesture. What can be made of Criseyde's reaction to Pandarus's threat? Is she afraid that Pandarus will commit suicide? Or that he will abandon her if she does not go along with his wishes? Or does her trembling and change of hue indicate her curiosity, as Benson maintains—is she bursting with anticipation?

Pandarus finally reveals that Troilus loves her and that she has the power to make him live or die. If she chooses to "late hym deye," Pandarus says he will cut his own throat with a knife. As usual in Chaucer, *eros* and *thanatos* follow close upon each other's footsteps. At this point "the teris breste out of his yën" (326). We have already considered Benson's warning not to read Pandarus's tears as theatrical. For Robertson, however, this is "obviously a carefully prepared bit of acting" (*Preface*, 484). Windeatt brings up the possibility of gestural duplicity only in order to de-emphasize it:

> [The] possibility of deception through contrived gesture is one part of Chaucer's interest in gesture as a sign of the inner life, but it is a qualification contained within what is his more preponderant overall impulse: to endow human feelings with gesture which intensifies the emotion but often surrounds it with an aura of dignity ("Gesture," 154).

The impressionistic aura he invokes is a rhetorical figure enlisted to support a critical position. What would happen if we were to follow Robertson in reading Pandarus's tears as contrived? There are ample grounds for doing so, since Pandarus frequently resorts to artifice in his role as go-between. Yet on what basis could we decide in favor of either the sincerity or insincerity of his tears?

---

[18] For Robertson, as for Pandarus, Criseyde's reaction indicates fear rather than curiosity: "Her fear, it should be noticed, is always self-centered and never actually involves the fear of violating any higher principles" (*Preface*, 483).

Critical readings of gesture premised upon the decidability of these questions should be resisted. To ignore the possibility of gestural deception is to ensure in advance the interpretation of Pandarus's tears as sincere. Counter-arguments do not prove their insincerity, but they can be deployed to show that interpretations of *Troilus and Criseyde* which attempt to arrest the play of the gestural signifier deserve rigorous scrutiny.

Pandarus tells Criseyde that he would never be willing to serve as Troilus's bawd—although that is what he appears to be doing—and offers a lengthy justification of the propriety of her loving Troilus, including the notion that doing so is friendship: "Swych love of frendes regneth al this town" (379). He informs Criseyde that her beauty is wasting with age, a topos of the literature of seduction already hoary with age in the fourteenth century. Then he pauses, and "caste adown [his] heed." Criseyde bursts into tears. She tells Pandarus that he ought to protect her from this kind of loving, then begins "ful sorwfully to syke" (428). In the *Rota Veneris*, the sigh is a powerful signal of passion or fear. But Boncompagno also argues that gestures are open to conjecture, and makes it clear that the code is manipulable. According to Robertson, "Criseyde feigns shock and astonishment" (*Preface*, 484). But how can we determine whether or not Criseyde has a flair for the theatrical without being thrown back upon the ambiguities of the gestural signifier? Such hermeneutic difficulties, although frustrating to the scholar reaching after certainty, constitute much of the pleasure of the text for the reader with critical negative capability. Different critical models will generate different values for individual gestures, and it is unlikely that any scholarly discourse can contain the play of the signifier.

Pandarus tells Criseyde that he has intended no "harm or vilenye," pledges suicide—by starvation, this time—and starts on his way "Til she agayn hym by the lappe kaughte" (448). According to Benson, this gesture merely indicates that Criseyde's "opposition to love is by no means unalterable" and that she is a complex character.[19] But in a Robertsonian reading, the comedy of manners of Book 2 is premised upon deception. Within such a critical frame, Criseyde's behavior is a bit of comic stage business, an almost vaudevillian shtick that is delightfully unsophisticated. Criseyde wants to accuse Pandarus of being false and to profess her own suicidal intentions as the shock of his lubricious suggestion sinks in. But she does not want him to leave.

---

[19] Benson, 90. Benson follows Norman Eliason's suggestion that "*lappe* may in Middle or Early Modern English mean 'hand'," but the relative scarcity of this reading makes it appear rather unlikely in this case. In 2.1181 Criseyde grabs Pandarus "by the hood." Eliason's recourse to Old Norse cognates is an example of scholarly erudition enlisted to limit implications of a word for the critic.

5

In Book 5, Diomede and Criseyde rely upon gesture to help negotiate the rapids of desire and seduction. But Troilus's gestures first draw the reader's attention. When the long-awaited exchange with the Greeks finally occurs, he bestows a ritual kiss upon Antenor and tries to "withholde of wepyng atte leeste" (76). The adverbial qualifier indicates that he can hope for little more than to avoid crying outright. This gesture of concealment posits an unprivileged internal audience—for whom it would not be a gesture at all—and a privileged audience of readers who grasp the significance of Troilus's restraint. Earlier, the narrator had claimed that Troilus

> gan his wo ful manly for to hide,
> That wel unnethe it sene was in his chere.   5.30–31

However, Diomede is able to detect his sorrow and divine its source without difficulty.

Troilus's gestures of concealment recall his facial dissimulation after being pierced by Criseyde's beauty at the feast of Pallas Athene in Book 1. But he performs positive gestures during his farewell, and fails noticeably to maintain his sang-froid as he begins his return to Troy:

> [He] caste his eye upon hire pitously,
> And neer he rood, his cause for to make,
> To take hire by the honde al sobrely.
> And Lord! so she gan wepen tendrely!
> And he ful softe and sleighly gan hire seye,
> "Now holde youre day, and do me nat to deye."
>
> With that his courser torned he aboute
> With face pale, and unto Diomede
> No word he spak, ne non of al his route.   5.79–87

These gestures are what Boncompagno's treatise would term love indications and signals. Troilus's glance at Criseyde, his solemn handclasp provoking her tender weeping, his secretive reminder that she return at the appointed time, his pallor, his indecorous silence before the Greek retinue—these gestures speak to Diomede, who is finely attuned to the eloquence of the lovers' silent language. He takes heed of these gestures

> As he that koude more than the crede
> In swich a craft.   5.89–90

In this liturgical (or catechetical) understatement, the narrator establishes Diomede's skill at the craft of love. According to a tradition dating from the eleventh century, the creed ends that portion of the mass, known as the mass of the catechumens, which the unbaptized had been permitted to attend in the days of the early church. Diomede is no novice at the rites of Venus. He is an adept at the craft of reading love gestures, the very art that Boncompagno expounds in his *Rota Veneris*. Like Boncompagno or the reader of *Troilus and Criseyde*, Diomede is an interpreter of gesture. The reader's hermeneutic desire is reflected in Diomede, who understands more than what is to be believed concerning this craft—or, alternatively, more than the rudiments. He has, that is, knowledge. Of course, Troilus also displays craft in the secrecy of his leave-taking. But he appears to know no more—or perhaps rather less—than the creed, since it does not occur to him that his gestures of concealment reveal his feelings as well.

That Diomede is a knowledgeable interpreter is made clear by his subsequent success. His interpretive skills allow him to enact his desire. This desire is mimetic, originating with Troilus's signs of desire for Criseyde.[20] Moreover, it gives evidence of a male sexual rivalry which parallels the military conflict between Greece and Troy. Diomede has read the gestures of the parting lovers as indicating that Criseyde will be without her lover. His interpretations are oriented towards action. Unlike the medieval or modern scholar, he pursues a goal of the loins rather than of the intellect. Diomede's most eloquent action is his seizing of Criseyde's reins, a conventional gesture of the sort whose importance Edmund Reiss has underscored.[21] On their journey to the Greek camp, Diomede puts his gestural interpretations to the test with a line of banter that culminates in an offer of service until death. This offer and Criseyde's response to it are remarkably rendered; they rival the depiction in Book 2 of conversations which hover between perilous ambiguities. As far as the narrator is concerned, Criseyde's reply to Diomede demonstrates her distraction:

> Criseyde unto that purpos lite answerde,
> As she that was with sorwe oppressed so
> That, in effect, she naught his tales herde
> But her and ther, now here a word or two.   5.176–79

Nevertheless, she thanks Diomede for his "travaile," "goode cheere," and offer of friendship—which she accepts. She proclaims her eagerness to do what is pleasing to him and her willingness to trust him. Her point-by-point response to his banter does not support the narrator's claim for either her sorrow or her inattentiveness. Moreover, her demeanor gives no indication of a heart that is breaking. When her father finally takes her in his arms, kissing her twenty times to welcome her,

> She seyde ek, she was fayn with him to mete,
> And stood forth muwet, milde, and mansuete.   5.193–94

Such gestural custody participates in a long-standing textual pattern. Throughout the poem, love has involved the composition of demeanor to mislead

---

[20] On the mimetic nature of desire, see René Girard, *Deceit, Desire, and the Novel: Self and Other in Literary Structure* (Baltimore: Johns Hopkins Univ. Press, 1965) and Jacques Lacan, *Écrits*, 5–6, 58, 67, 288–89.

[21] Reiss, 101. See also Robertson, *Preface*, 254, 394.

others, turning facial expression into a misleading sign written upon the body itself.

But is Criseyde heroically struggling to keep back her tears, as Troilus had been earlier, or is her composure evidence of her "slydynge corage"? Benson's reading of Criseyde's gestures makes a case for her innocence:

> Critics who question the depth of [Criseyde's] love for Troilus and who even see her as ready to betray him as soon as he is out of sight can offer no sensible explanation for the fact that she is the only one who weeps during the exchange sequence, that her separation from Troilus makes her "brighte face" grow pale, or that "Ful ofte a day she sighte ek for destresse." At every opportunity she stands and stares at the walls of Troy, and "tendrely she wepte, bothe eve and morwe." There is no justi-fication in the text for regarding these gestures as anything but honest ex-pressions of deep emotion (Benson 98–99).

Were literary characters and texts free from contradiction, one might acquiesce in the logical dichotomy this reading is founded upon: characters must be either faithful or faithless. But readers have often questioned the honesty and depth of Criseyde's reaction. The display of emotion in a public setting is already mediated by a complex code of signification, as is the attempt not to weep which reveals Troilus's love. To ascribe sincerity in this case is a critical judgment that evades the extent to which an emotional exchange between two people is always mediated by an elaborate cultural code. One can make the counter-argument that Criseyde's expression of emotion, followed within ten days by a falsely sworn oath denying her relationship with Troilus, is either not honest or not deep. But must Criseyde be free from contradiction? A theory of literary character based on the notion that she must deserve questioning. To resist interpretations of Criseyde's guilt or innocence by establishing counter-arguments is only to attempt to resist a criticism that ignores the extent to which characters differ from themselves as well as from each other.[22]

Criseyde betrays Troilus within ten days, and she begins her betrayal before alighting from her horse. When we next hear of her, she is gazing in sorrow at Troy's high towers, and decides to return the next night. The conclusion to her meditation—"Felicite clepe I my suffisaunce" (763)—is ambiguous. Does it mean that her happiness depends upon being with Troilus or upon doing what she pleases? Although she seems to be asserting her desire to return to Troy, we know she will never do so, since within "fully monthes two" she was "ful fer fro that entencioun." Indeed, even this statement by the narrator is overly gen-

---

[22] This deconstructive insight first appears in Montaigne's essay "De l'Inconstance de nos actions" (*Essais*, Livre II, Chapitre I): "Nous sommes tous de lopins et d'une contexture si informe et diverse, que chaque piece, chaque momant, faict son jeu. Et se trouve autant de difference de nous à nous mesmes, que de nous à autruy." Barbara Johnson reformulates it in a fine apothegm (*The Critical Difference: Essays in the Contemporary Rhetoric of Reading* [Baltimore: Johns Hopkins Univ. Press, 1981], x).: "The differences *between* entities . . . are . . . based on a repression of differences *within* entities."

erous: she appears quite far from that intention within a week and a half. Diomede immediately begins to plan how to bring Criseyde into his net as quickly as possible. He "leyde out hook and lyne" in order "to fisshen hire" even though he knows she has a lover in Troy. Indeed, his desire originated with the gestural signs marking Troilus's desire for Criseyde. He consoles himself that "he that naught n'asaieth, naught n'acheveth," the very proverb employed by Criseyde in Book 2. This example of symmetry goes unremarked by the narrator, who will attempt to defend Criseyde by blaming Diomede.

While his journey with Criseyde to the Greek camp had established Diomede as a shrewd interpreter of gestures, in their conversation on the tenth day it is his deployment of them which is emphasized. When Diomede arrives, feigning business with Calkas, Criseyde "down hym by hire sette" in a proxemic gesture of intimacy—"And he was ethe ynough to maken dwelle!" (849-50).[23] They speak "as frendes don" over spices and wine—the standard medieval hendiadys for Cinzano. Diomede first solicits Criseyde's thoughts concerning the war, although they do not appear to be his main interest:

> Fro that demaunde he so descendeth down
> To axen hire, if that hire straunge thoughte
> The Grekis gise, and werkes that they wroughte;
>
> And whi hire fader tarieth so longe
> To wedden hire unto som worthy wight.   5.859-63

It is difficult to decide which is more deserving of admiration in this passage: Diomede's tactical boldness in moving the conversation so deftly from international affairs to comparative anthropology on a first date, or the eloquent stanza break which punctuates his small talk. The sophistication of Diomede's conversational style also reveals itself in his use of gesture. The narrator tells us that Criseyde suffered love pangs for Troilus, but does so in a noticeably ambiguous manner:

> Criseyde, that was in hire peynes stronge
> For love of Troilus, hire owen knyght,
> As ferforth as she konnyng hadde or myght,
> Answerde hym tho; but, as of his entente,
> It semed nat she wiste what he mente.   5.864-68

To whom does "semed" refer: The narrator? Or Diomede? Does the last line mean that she knew Diomede's intent, but did not appear to? Or that she was ignorant of his designs? Is this an accusation veiled in irony, an excuse for her behavior, or a bit of reportage? And does the qualifying clause which deals with the extent of Criseyde's intelligence and ability refer to her manner of answering Diomede's question? Or to the extent of the pain she was capable of suf-

---

[23] For a guide to work on proxemics, see Mary Ritchie Key, *Nonverbal Communication: A Research Guide and Bibliography* (Metuchen: Scarecrow Press, 1977), 113-14.

fering for the absent Troilus? To come to a decision over these *insolubilia* is to reduce textual plurality to monovalency.

The upshot of Diomede's advice to Criseyde is that she should let Troy pass from her heart, since "er it be nyght" she will find someone to serve her better than any Trojan. The following stanza is given over completely to the language of gesture:

> And ... he gan to waxen red,
> And in his speche a litel wight he quok,
> And caste asyde a litle wight his hed,
> And stynte a while; and afterward he wok,
> And sobreliche on hire he threw his lok.   5.925–29

Such reliance upon the gestural code is unique in Chaucer: Diomede turns red, quavers in his speech, leans his head to one side, pauses, reawakens as if from a trance, and finally casts his gaze upon Criseyde "sobreliche." This overdetermined set of gestural signifiers occurs within a conversation that is tentative and provisional on several fronts. One possible interpretation is that Diomede is sincere: in this case, his blushes would indicate confusion, although of course he is no innocent. But why does he "throw" his look at her? Does the forcefulness of this gesture serve to contradict his seeming naïveté? Of course, previous indications that he is a ladykiller might also lead us to question his sincerity. According to Windeatt:

> The nature of Diomede, so strongly contrasted with Troilus, is correspondingly brought out by an added ability to look Criseyde quite confidently in the eye despite his intentions. To an otherwise closely translated passage expressing the apparent embarrassment of this new lover in Criseyde's presence, Chaucer adds the idea that Diomede is nonetheless still able to look "sobreliche" at the lady with a deliberateness that belies his seeming awkwardness ("Gesture," 153).

Windeatt emphasizes "deliberateness" rather than the "awkwardness" or "embarrassment" that would characterize readings based upon Diomede's sincerity. But is it certain that a womanizer cannot feel a moment of confusion at a crucial point in his seduction? Or that he might not also feel embarrassment when his intentions finally begin to surface? Should Diomede's gestures be read as indicating a genuine confusion that is then turned to his advantage? Or is his blush that of a sexual opportunist momentarily embarrassed at the crudity of his line? In the last case, the gestures which follow would indicate his difficulty in playing his role straight. Are all his gestures theatrical? Or only certain ones? How can one decide which of them are voluntary and which involuntary? Any reading which relies upon a mapping of inner states to gestural behavior runs into problems, for gestures tempt us to try out various interpretive alternatives without finally making any single interpretation decidable.[24]

---

[24] When Dido leads Aeneas around the ramparts of Carthage, her passion for the hero

Certainly Diomede's speech to Criseyde after this gestural pantomime, or spontaneous overflow of powerful emotion, or combination of the two, is no longer faltering. He asserts his claim to be as "gentil" as anyone in Troy, telling her that he would have been king had his father lived and that he still hopes to one day. After so placing himself socially, he tells Criseyde she is the first woman whose grace he has sought, and promises to serve her if she will allow him to speak of his sorrow on the next—and eleventh—day. She grants this request on the condition that he will not talk about love. The narrator claims that Criseyde had her heart fixed so firmly upon Troilus "ther may it non arace; / And strangely she spak" (954–55). But is her reply strange to the narrator or to Diomede? Criseyde says that she knows the Greeks will destroy her beloved Troy if they can, and that she is grateful to her father for rescuing her. She says she knows quite well that there are Greeks "of heigh condicioun," but that there are worthy Trojans too. She says she believes that Diomede could serve his lady in a way that would merit her thanks, then swears by Pallas Athene that she has never loved since her husband's death.

This is (of course?) a lie. Criseyde's reply takes up Diomede's claim to high social standing: "And that ye ben of noble and heigh kynrede, / I have wel herd it tellen, out of drede." She says her heart is in tribulation while she awaits the Greek defeat of the Trojans:

> "Peraunter, thanne so it happen may,
> That whan I se that nevere yit I say,
> Than wol I werke that I nevere wroughte!
> This word to yow ynough suffisen oughte."   5.991–94

Her fondness for periphrasis continues. She tells Diomede that she will speak with him the next day, so long as he doesn't talk about—well, what they have been talking about. She swears by Pallas Athene again: if she were to have "routhe" on anyone, it would be Diomede "by my trouthe." But her language finally breaks down in contradiction, and her reply concludes in the language of gesture:

> "I sey nat therfore that I wol yow love,
> N'y say nat nay; but in conclusioun,
> I mene wel, by God that sit above!"
> And therwithal she caste hire eyen down,
> And gan to sike.   5.1002–6

These gestures parallel those of Diomede earlier. It would be anachronistic, although not inappropriate, to recall the stylized gestures of early Hollywood. On the other hand, it might be argued that Criseyde is moved to some extent by genuine emotion. As with Diomede's gestures, one might easily develop a set

---

causes her speech to falter: "incipit effari, mediaque in voce resistit" (*Aen.* 4.76). Such knowledge of literary convention informs a reading of Diomede's stuttering, but is not capable of concluding one.

of parallel readings which emphasize either her confused sincerity or theatrical artifice. To any reader who would assert the artificiality of her gestural panto-mime, one might counter with the claim for her sincerity. And vice-versa. Neither pole of the dichotomy is finally the whole truth. Her sigh and down-cast eyes might indicate coyness, or innocence. Or perhaps they reveal her regret at the necessity of making a choice, since these gestures are followed by a prayer to let her see Troy again or else make her heart break. Once again, a plurality of responses is possible. Is it desirable for the reader to pick one inter-pretation, excluding the others? Or can only a willed critical blindness to alter-native readings supply a meaning for her downcast eyes and sigh? Diomede won't take no for an answer, begs her for mercy, takes her glove, and leaves in the evening when "al was wel." Criseyde's glove—"of whych he was ful feyn"—is synecdochic: the lady's gift is, of course, a conventional sign for the gift of her-self. With this gesture, Diomede's seduction of Criseyde is virtually completed.

This reading of the gestures of seduction in Books 2 and 5 has drawn out the implications of gestural plurality rather than seeking to limit it. Previous studies have arrived at contradictory conclusions, even as they have ignored the possibility of alternative readings. Gestures in *Troilus and Criseyde* both encour-age and discourage interpretation in a way that raises questions about the critical methodologies that have been applied to them. According to Benson (100):

> The gestures in the closing book of the *Troilus* lack the force of those in the earlier books largely because Pandarus, who is essential in bringing the lovers together and in controlling our perception of their relationship, is no longer needed there. In Pandarus Chaucer succeeded in creating a character in whom the colloquial style is virtually incarnate and for whom realistic and spontaneous gestures were necessary.

But gestures in Book 5 do have their own kind of force, and reliance upon a realist theory which allows the uncomplicated mapping of gestures to mental states is a critical seduction the reader would do well to resist. Source study and taxonomy are not adequate to the ambiguities of gesture in the poem, however valuable they have proven in other areas of Chaucer studies. Gestural interpretations vary according to the critical model employed by the reader: a critically neutral ascription of meaning for gestures is an enabling scholarly fiction which deserves challenge. The truth claims of the scholar-translator of the opening book of *Troilus and Criseyde* are canceled in the course of the poem, and the truth claims of scholars of Chaucerian gesture are undercut in a similar fashion by the poem.

Troilus and Criseyde offers two principal models for the interpretation of gesture. One is an aggressive hermeneutic associated with Diomede. It is suc-cessful, in a narrowly defined way. The narrator's is unsuccessful and marked by frequent misreadings. When he finally begins to understand where his story will lead him, he displays a shocked awareness of the deceptive nature of the world. This attitude is rather less profound than it is typically credited with being. The wisdom of the epilogue should not simply be identified with the wisdom of the poem itself. In *Troilus and Criseyde*, wisdom is founded upon the awareness of an excluded, painful desire, not upon a foundation of innocence as the moralizing narrator of the epilogue would argue. The entire text belies a virtue which is not earned through understanding the perils of a desire which it is the narrator's pleasure to elaborate. This unreliable and contradictory narrator is reflected in the undecidability of gestures in the poem. Were we to imagine the narrator in the position of the seducer, it seems likely that he would misinterpret the signs of Criseyde's interest. The labyrinth of interpretations that *Troilus and Criseyde* has spawned is an index of the plurality of the text, the joyfully puzzling game it establishes for the interpreter by supplying evidence for conflicting interpretations. To attempt to reduce this plurality for the sake of a monovalent interpretation of gesture is to succumb to the claims to knowledge traditionally made in scholarly discourse. Such a seeming hermeneutic richness impoverishes our response to the poem. In his discussion of the erotics of the plural text, Roland Barthes employed the term *jouissance* to indicate a pleasure both textual and sexual.[25] *Troilus and Criseyde* offers an exploration of the pleasures of sexuality as well as a warning against its dangers. These two levels do not co-exist harmoniously, but conflict. To attempt to reduce the force of either is to reduce its poetic force. And to refuse certainty in the face of the text's contradictions is perhaps not so much a reason for anxiety as for joy.

---

[25] Roland Barthes, *The Pleasure of the Text*, trans. Richard Miller (New York: Hill and Wang, 1974). The finest theoretical formulation of the plurality of the text may be found in Barthes' *S/Z*, trans. Richard Miller (New York: Hill and Wang, 1974). For the most rigorous critical meditation on undecidability, see Paul de Man, *Allegories of Reading: Figural Language in Rousseau, Nietzsche, Rilke, and Proust* (New Haven: Yale Univ. Press, 1979).

Ending a Poem Before Beginning It, or The "Cas" of Troilus

LEONARD MICHAEL KOFF

It is both a curious and fascinating feature of TROILUS AND CRISEYDE that its beginning is more conclusive than its ending. In the 56–line proem to Book 1, the narrator, as the "servant of the servants of love," announces his praiseworthy public task–to rehearse the story of Troilus's love for Criseyde, what he calls the "cas" of Troilus–and so establish our relationship with a narrative he sees illustrating one moral purpose and we see, or come to see, illustrating varied, complex and often contradictory ones. Indeed, in explaining the "cas" of Troilus in the proem to Book 1, the narrator is never more confident as a storyteller than he is there where he laments the substance of his poem–vulnerability to despair, to truth, to gossip, secrecy, and the wish for transcendence. Once the narrator begins to tell Troilus's tale, however, his ability to manage his "cas" falters and we, who are encouraged to ground our understanding of Troilus on experience itself, find we pull against the narrator's surefire use of an exemplary hero. Even Troilus is caught up in this cracking of smooth surfaces. Having seen Criseyde once, he breaks into full-blown Petrarchan song, the effect of which reveals how far he is from an amatory discourse that expresses real feelings and that can handle psychological and moral complexity.

There is no simple way to explain a literary work. But I hope this brief essay will help all readers of *Troilus and Criseyde* reconsider aspects of one critical commonplace that has made the *Troilus* accessible to us. That commonplace links the characterization of the poem's narrator with his effect on readers and can best be expressed, I think, in this way: the position that the narrator's "inexperience" puts us in as members of his audience ("For I, that God of Loves servantz serve, / Ne dar to Love, for myn unliklynesse" [1.15–16]) makes it possible for us to understand the *Troilus* because the narrator's amatory inexperience is, from our point of view, flattering. The narrator may not know love personally, but he assumes we do and on that pleasing assumption invites us to bring the *Troilus* to its conclusion, or series of conclusions. Just because *Troilus and Criseyde* rests on our experience, our past, it can exert a moral presence. The narrator says he has no amatory history; he does not exist anywhere within Love's radiance ("So fer am I from his help in derknesse" [1.18]). Yet as an outsider, the narrator tells a story we are eager to bring to life.

The narrator's distance from experience, given as the reason for his interpretive distance from the *histoire* he narrates, calls on us, as A. C. Spearing says, to use our "imaginations to resolve indeterminacies and apparent contradictions in the *histoire* and even to share with him in its production."[1] By *him*, Spearing means "Chaucer constructed in writing," that is, Chaucer's self-presentation in his own work, the speaking voice of the poem—in Émile Benveniste's terms, which Spearing borrows, the voice of *discours*.[2] To most readers of the *Troilus*, that voice has come to sound like a character in his own right, significant to us not because his experience of love can authenticate the story he tells, but because his readerly relationship to the *Troilus* is taken, for other characters in the work, and for people outside it, as a model of reading and understanding. That model is said to describe, for example, Pandarus's relationship to the two lovers in the poem,[3] and our relationship as readers in the real world to Chaucer's "litel bok."[4]

Like everyone, I can single out the narrator of the *Troilus* when I hear him, although he is for me the voice that demands my self-reflection. He functions to make me conscious of my experience of the work and the experience I bring to it. As such, he is a presence of mind in the poem. My aim in wanting to deepen a response to him is *not* to make him more stable than he appears to be, or more transparent than he is. I share Spearing's amusement (122) with arguments for the coherence of the "I" of the *Troilus* that "by a strange paradox" make the narrator more consistent than "those shifting and varying selves" named Troilus, Criseyde, or Pandarus. I do not wish to find in the "I" of the *Troilus* either genuine, meaning *real*, aspects of Chaucer the man, or self-conscious reflections of Chaucer the court poet. Rather I hope to delineate what Chaucer the man and the poet wants us to do with the *histoire* he narrates, and I assume he narrates the *Troilus for our sakes*.

The phrase that is the subtitle of this essay—the "cas" of Troilus—is Chaucer's, not mine.

> And preieth for hem that ben in the cas
> Of Troilus, as ye may after here,
> That Love hem brynge in hevene to solas.   1.29–31

The noun "cas" is used over 150 times in Chaucer, over 40 times in the *Troilus*.

---

[1] A.C. Spearing, "Narrative Closure: The End of *Troilus and Criseyde*," in *Readings in Medieval Poetry* (Cambridge: Cambridge Univ. Press, 1987), 120.

[2] Spearing, 119–20: "[The distinction is] between a sequence of events, real or imaginary (*histoire*), which could in principle be narrated in a variety of different media . . . and in an infinite number of different ways; and any specific discursive presentation of those events (*discours*)."

[3] See, for example, Carton, "Pandarus' Bed," 53: "The narrator's emotional involvement in the story begins to emerge in his opening hymn and pledge of devotion to lovers. His repeated denials of personal experience in love suggest a vicarious interest akin to Pandarus'."

[4] See, for example, Paul Strohm, *Social Chaucer* (Cambridge: Harvard Univ. Press, 1989), 62–63, on the projected fictional, actual, and implied audiences of the *Troilus*.

Used alone, as here in line 29, the word means a circumstance imagined as a predicament of fortune. Troilus's "cas" is his unfortunate situation. Chaucer also uses "cas" in the verb phrase "setten cas" (e.g., *T&C* 2.729) in a related sense to mean *suppose*. The phrase carries the idea that what is being supposed is a generalizing instance of something, a situation of engagement. "Cas" specifically means a legal case (in the portrait of the "Sergeant of the Lawe" in the *General Prologue*, 323, in the *Man of Law's Introduction*, 36, and in the *Physician's Tale*, 163); that is, a circumstance about which some determination can, or ought to be, made. Thus Troilus's "cas" is, for the narrator, a circumstance of fortune about which we can and should reason and from which we can draw lessons.

Chaucer does not use "cas" specifically to mean an *exemplum*, although after we hear, and hear described, Troilus's mocking behavior at the "observaunces olde" (1.160) for Pallas Athena—Troilus calls them "lewede observaunces" (198)—Chaucer draws our moral attention to Troilus's "exemplary" behavior.

> Forthy ensample taketh of this man,
> Ye wise, proude, and worthi folkes alle,
> To scornen Love, which that so soone kan
> The fredom of youre hertes to hym thralle.   1.232–35

As here, Troilus is forever being turned into an example of a lover, but not always, from our point of view, a consistent one. Seeing Troilus as a "cas" is difficult *simply because* his circumstances, despite the narrator, cannot be explained by the ends to which the narrator wishes to use him. The narrator does not see how he loses control of Troilus's *histoire* by inviting us to demonstrate assumptions about the nature of love the narrator believes we share with him, assumptions based on experience he himself has not had but which he believes will confirm his anatomy of love.

How exemplary is Troilus then? That depends on *when* we see him. Who in Chaucer's audience, for example, would scorn love as Troilus does? And in what sense would such "proude folkes" be "wise" or "worthi"? The tone of the narrator's commentary here is surely consciously naive; a certain doubleness attends it. We can hear both Chaucer and his moralizing narrator, the former encouraging a broader, less controlled exegesis than the latter: the narrator sees our submitting to the inexorable power of love, proving how disappointing experience is, and we see submitting to love proving how complex it may be. Both we and the narrator encourage Troilus's experience, though for different reasons.

As a "cas" brought to our attention at line 232, Troilus is distant and wrong-headed, his arrogance grounded in fear. Troilus's behavior does not acknowledge the binding power of love of which erotic love is a species. The narrator himself says as much in the apostrophe that characterizes Troilus's frame of mind ("O blynde world, O blynde entencioun!" [211]) and in the analogy he draws between Troilus and "proude Bayard" (218), an analogy that predicts with a certain philosophic assuredness Troilus's naturally inevitable humbling. Once Bayard feels the "longe whippe" (220), he remembers he is but a horse and subject to "horses lawe" (223). Likewise Troilus with respect to Love's law. We do not have to wait until Book 5 to see the kinds of self-misconceptions Troilus always displays, both before he is love's servant and after. We should add that the implicit darkness in the narrator's own analogy between Bayard's master's whip and love's humbling power seems to escape the narrator at this point. Troilus's sudden falling in love is benevolent humiliation for his scorning the harnass.

Applying the "cas" of Troilus to ourselves at line 232, where the narrator abstracts the "cas" of Troilus by comparing it to Bayard's, thus requires that we understand how Troilus's behavior describes a bachelor's fear, a deep and thoroughgoing resistance to love, and what is made to sound like a needful and transforming chastisement for an extraordinarily public show of disdain. Of course, the "cas" of Troilus is itself abstracted from Troilus's *histoire* so that we are in the realm of the morally theoretical at two removes. We would do well *not* to imitate Troilus. Doing so would narrow the fullness of our own psychological life and, in a figurative sense, bring down upon us the punishment of heaven. This last calamity is our fear reified absolutely.

Before we actually know anything about it, however, the "cas" of Troilus, as the narrator implies at line 29, is applicable in a straightforward way *because* it is for the narrator conceptually complete. In the proem to Book 1, the "cas" is a finished instance of a life whose theoretical arc can be lucidly traced and whose conclusions about love can be applied to ourselves without interpretive recovery. Troilus's "cas" is closed. We do not, for example, have to struggle in the proem to Book 1 with the difficult connection the narrator himself points out only two hundred lines into the *Troilus* between love's power to define our humanity and to command it.

> Yet with a look his herte wax a-fere,
> That he that now was moost in pride above,
> Wax sodeynly moost subgit unto love.   229–31

At line 35, the "cas" of Troilus is an "unsely aventure," an earthly one for which the only "solas" is heaven's consolation presumably after death.

We thus know the end of the *Troilus* and why it should matter to us very early on. And we perhaps expect the work, as we read it, to bear out the clarity of judgment with which the narrator introduces Troilus's *histoire*. We get application first and then text in a reversal of evidentiary procedure that seems to demand nothing of our critical skills, but everything of a compassion born of personal joy and disappointment.[5] Chaucer in the proem to Book 1 concludes the "cas" of Troilus by asking us to cooperate with a narrator in expressing

---

[5] On the relationship between rhetorical declamation and the structure of fiction, see Trimpi, *Muses*, esp. 306–20. Because Chaucer has consciously reversed interpretive expectations in the *Troilus*—we hear conclusions first and then the case—*Troilus and Criseyde* becomes a work through which we observe how fiction demonstrates "the capacity of fiction for ethical analysis and persuasion" (345).

compassionate understanding for those in Troilus's "cas," offered in the proem as typical of human experience.

To be asked to use a narrative for our moral growth is not an unusual request for a medieval author, perhaps any author, to make. It is surprising, however, for an author to make such a request *as soon as Chaucer does* and to make such curious and complex demands before any details of the "cas" are brought to our attention. These demands entail not only understanding the curve of Troilus's experience, but forgiving the errors of judgment we are told it illustrates. Dieter Mehl has explained what I too think Chaucer expects of his readers, what in particular they should ask of the *Troilus* and what Chaucer seems to forclose as questions or concerns about the narrative.[6] We are indeed, as Mehl says, part of the fictional audience the poem itself creates. But at the beginning of a work which *only the narrator has read before*, and which the narrator summarizes, whether or not we have read another version of the story of Troilus, or simply know about it (in whole or in part), we can hardly be expected to cooperate in its telling in Mehl's sense. Yet we are asked to show compassion for Troilus's "cas" and to hold a clear and generous perspective on Troilus that neither Troilus himself, nor the narrator both at the end of the work easily or convincingly manage: Troilus is simply too harsh with himself as seen on "this litel spot of erthe" (5.1815) from the "eighte spere" (1809);[7] and Chaucer is simply too busy concluding a poem whose artistic and moral complexity is not at all easily resolved.[8] It is only at the beginning of the work that we can be asked unambiguously to apply Troilus's "cas" to ourselves. We haven't yet heard it.

In asking us to use the *Troilus*, Chaucer introduces the two major issues that critics of the work have generally found difficult to resolve: first, the relationship between the conditions of despair (which Troilus feels) and the truth of love (to which Criseyde points him), and second, the connection between gossip and the wish for secrecy, on the one hand, and the experience of social freedom and the conviction of transcendence, on the other. These issues are difficult to resolve and I believe we are, like Troilus and Criseyde, meant to struggle with them. They constitute our points of engagement with the text, and Troilus's and Criseyde's points of engagement with their lives together. Yet the narrator easily resolves them in the proem to Book 1. *Troilus and Criseyde* is never clearer as a love story than at its beginning where we are invited to

---

[6] This is an important distinction that keeps Mehl's argument for the reader's cooperation with Chaucer from becoming an argument for a reader's subjective remaking of the text. See the "Afterword: 1979" (in Barney, 228–29) to Mehl's "The Audience of Chaucer's *Troilus and Criseyde*," in *Chaucer and Middle English Studies in Honour of Rossell Hope Robbins*, ed. Beryl Rowland (London: Allen & Unwin, 1974), 173–89, reprinted in Barney, 211–28.

[7] On the complexity entailed in an otherworldly perspective of this world, see Taylor, *Chaucer Reads*, 195.

[8] A. C. Spearing has carefully shown how difficult it is for Chaucer to conclude the *matere* of *T&C*—see 122–33.

end the work. After the proem, the *Troilus* becomes increasingly more difficult for us and the narrator both to read and apply perfectly.

Let's look at the proem in detail. From this 56–line beginning (divided into three sections), we can trace an unravelling of issues which leaves the narrator, us, and Troilus himself as a "cas" figuratively at loose ends. In the first section of the proem (1–21), the narrator announces his intentions as storyteller and lays bare his "personal" limitations. We have already noted his amatory inexperience, which constitutes his existence as the fictional "I" of the poem and our invited presence within it as readers of breadth and understanding. The narrator's guiding voice rests in the proem to Book 1 on his limitations as servant to those in love. These enable him in a neatly unruffled way to explain the story of Troilus. The narrator has in fact a finely distanced and bookish understanding of it, in keeping with his self-characterization as the pope, the *servus servorum Dei*, of the amatory community that serves the god of Love, a community from which his inexperience excludes him, though he everywhere encourages experience.

The narrator mentions the "double sorwe" of Troilus twice (1 and 54). It has, in the first section of the proem, an authenticating architectonic purity ("Fro wo to wele, and after out of joie" [4]) that can occasion tears ("Thise woful verse, that wepen as I write" [7]). These are philosophical tears, tokens of conclusion and distancing that show us how the narrator grasps the point of the story he is about to tell. The narrator's tears are even more removed and knowing than Troilus's laughter "in hymself" (5.1821) from the "eighte spere" at those who mourn him. Laughter in Book 5 is the sudden silent recognition of amatory distinctions based on final knowledge. Troilus's laughter is *seeing*, occasioned by, and depending on, an idea of himself on earth still caught, like us, in the play of "blynde lust" (1824). Troilus even imagines the earth "embraced" by the sea (1816) in a final global transmutation of passion, now made part of his visionary planetary structure. Troilus's laughter is not yet free of worldly entanglement, though we are meant to see it as the source of eventual freedom. By contrast, the narrator's tears in the proem to Book 1 are tears of pure conceptual sympathy extended to all lovers, including us. They are tears of scope and moral abstraction. Ironically, Troilus is closer to himself at the end of the poem than the narrator is to the story of Troilus—Troilus abstracted—at the beginning. The beginning of *Troilus and Criseyde* is thus a point farthest away from the overarching events of Troilus's life. No one has or achieves in the rest of the poem the narrator's perspective here.

As a result, the patterns of love in the proem to Book 1, where the poem begins for us and ends for the narrator, are virtually shaped love out of existence. Perhaps that has encouraged some readers to hurry over the proem. The narrator's commentary on the fortunes of Troilus seem formulaic at best, empty at worst. The oblique allusion to the idea of the wheel of Fortune—Troilus's emotional states (now sorrow, now joy, now sorrow) constitutes his circular and enclosed wheel—does not, for example, render Troilus's experience. The allusion merely summarizes it. Moreover, the narrator's self-conception as only the "sorwful instrument, / That helpeth loveres, as I kan, to pleyne" (1.10–11) is decidedly cool. His experience is not at the center of the poem. Ours is, through Troilus.

For lovers to "pleyne" in hearing the "cas" of Troilus implies that for them the *Troilus* provides an occasion to know the disheartening effects of love, which the narrator assumes we already do. But our responses are surely more complex than this. Part of our discomfort with the narrator stems from his narrowness with respect to our experience, despite the intimacy with which he addresses us ("er that I parte fro ye" [5]). The use of *ye* here rather than *yow*, a pronominal substitution unique in Chaucer,[9] reflects the narrator's wish to address informally the community of lovers in order to include us in his moral analysis. The narrator is counting on conceptual unanimity about the nature of love. For this reason, he can confidently see himself as the appropriate companion to woeful lovers and counterfeit, as he sees it, the clear moral purpose of his work.

> For wel sit it, the sothe for to seyne,
> A woful wight to have a drery feere,
> And to a sorwful tale, a sory chere.   12–14

Even the muse the narrator invokes in the proem to Book 1 is appropriate to his initial knowing view of his own poem. He calls on Thesiphone, one of the three Furies, to help him weep for a tormented Troilus, the guileless victim of love ("thow goddesse of torment, / Thow cruwel Furie, sorwynge evere yn peyne" [8–9]). There may be a sense, too, in the narrator's aligning himself with Thesiphone that judgment of Troilus's blind entanglement with the world echoes from the gods, and Thesiphone is their voice. She is thus both tormentor and vicarious sufferer for those she torments, a disturbingly helpless role that may account in part for her pain. A reference to Juno's having asked Thesiphone to drive Athamas mad is made as part of Criseyde's oath to be faithful to Troilus (4.1534–40). If she is false, Criseyde says, let her be driven mad too. Because Criseyde will be false, Thesiphone's divine errand is, by Criseyde's own words, just punishment for which, we should add, Thesiphone may herself weep. Chaucer's other reference to Thesiphone, where she is named with her sisters of the night, recalls her imitating compassion ("O ye Herynes, Nyghtes doughtren thre, / That endeles compleignen evere in pyne, / Megera, Alete, and ek Thesiphone"—4.22–24). Indeed, in his *Complaint unto Pity*, Chaucer calls pity "Herenus quene" (92), the queen of the Furies. Chaucer's complex sense of the Furies may derive from Dante's description of them (*Inf.* 9.37–51) as the handmaids of Persephone, the queen of everlasting lamentation, who tear their breasts with their nails and cry out. Compassion and self-inflicted echoing passion are here violently yoked.

If, then, Thesiphone helps the narrator speak for Troilus's torment and the punishment of his folly, the narrator means to align himself, not with lovers,

---

[9] Norman Davis, "Chaucer and Fourteenth-Century English," in *Geoffrey Chaucer: Writers and Their Background*, ed. Derek Brewer (London: Bell, 1974), 70.

but with those who know and judge them. By contrast, the narrator in the proem to Book 5 invokes the Fates, that is, the muses of ongoing individual fate. The narrator's invocation there reflects his entanglement with *histoire*.

> And to yow, angry Parcas, sustren thre,
> Committeth, to don execucioun;
> For which Criseyde moste out of the town,
> And Troilus shal dwellen forth in pyne
> Til Lachesis his thred no lenger twyne.   5.3–7

The invocation in Book 5 does not express the narrator's knowledge of effects and ends; the proem in Book 1 does.

Furthermore, if the story of Troilus "may don gladnesse / To any lovere, and his cause availle" (19–20), the narrator says in the proem to Book 1, let him have the thanks he owes me ("Have he my thonk" [21]) for writing—let him as a lover have my blessing—and let me only have the labor associated with writing what is morally useful ("and myn be this travaille!" [21]). Pandarus, in declaring himself Troilus's friend, makes a similar gesture of service: "Yef me this labour and this bisynesse, / And of my spede by thyn al that swetnesse" (1.1042–43). In ways delicately courtier-like, the narrator in the proem to Book 1, who has been pope and amatory "intimate," declares he is *nothing but* the servant of lovers. Our moral growth, the narrator implies, will be effected by our reading his work. At the beginning of the proem to Book 1, the narrator expects us to have appropriate experience vicariously as we read. At line 21, we do not yet know how unsatisfactory the narrator's moral assumptions will come to seem. In the proem to Book 1, the *Troilus* can thus for the narrator "don gladnesse / To any lovere, and his cause availle" *because* the narrator assumes that the experience we bring to the poem will confirm the moral truths of experience he sees the *Troilus* illustrating.

The phrase the narrator uses at line 20 ("his cause availle") is fascinating *just because* it does not point to amatory success. It implies that those hearing the *Troilus* can use it to help them feel confirmed in the reality of the sorrows they know. For the narrator, the phrase has a narrowing moral sense. The "double sorwe" of Troilus can "don gladnesse" because the *Troilus* will show that love is an inevitable disappointment. Because we are the privileged center of his focus, the narrator in the proem to Book 1 sees his story only allowing us to "pleyne."

In the first section of the proem, then, the narrator stakes his confident claim to knowing his story and judging it aright. In the second section (22–46), the narrator asks us, in the form of the bidding prayer, to respond charitably to examples illustrating the difficulties of love, Troilus's "cas" among them. Troilus's is the only "cas" actually mentioned in this section, though the narrator implicitly sets Troilus's "cas," singled out in lines 29–31, among other unnamed ones, all of which are seen as illustrating aspects of love's sorrow—vulnerability to despair, to truth, to gossip, to secrecy, and to a wish for the experience of transcendence. The remedy for such sorrow? Compassion we bring to the lives of others, fictional and real, who have failed to be invulnerable. Like the Host in the *Canterbury Tales*, the narrator assumes that we must have the "substance" of a tale already in us if we are going to understand it (VII. 2803-4). *Troilus and Criseyde* will teach us nothing if we do not already know it. Thus the work's circle of addressees is not considered bound by medieval time or place, but extended by a universal reach that creates for the narrator a community of like-minded persons. We are asked, for example, to remember the rocky course of our own experience (24-25) as if amorous instability were not only inevitable, but necessary to perceive that present joy ("ye loveres, that bathen in gladnesse" [22]) is merely tentative. This lesson Troilus learns. Moreover, we are asked to remember how wronged we felt when love displeased us (27) and to reflect on how unworthy we would have felt had we not experienced obstacles, or what seemed like obstacles, to the consummation of desire. The narrator says that love won too easily does not feel valuable enough. I suspect we concur. Troilus will learn this too.

Furthermore, we are also asked to have pity "on the adversite / Of othere folk" (25-26), as if adversity were both lamentable and wished for, a frustration we implore heaven to remove and a proof that we have correctly chosen someone to love since he or she is not governed by us. Such psychological contradictions are entirely unresolvable in real people and are seen by the narrator, who can rather finely delineate them, to exist in us by turns. We are even asked before we hear the story of Troilus to let it inform the judgment we make of our own behavior. How might we do this? Pray, the narrator says, for those who "ben despeired / In love" (36-37) permanently ("that nevere nyl recovered be" [37]).

The concept of despair is a subtle one and the narrator in the proem to Book 1 implicitly makes a set of distinctions about it that inform his narration of the entire *Troilus*. Those who despair of ever finding love, for example, can be said to "despeir of" it. They have fallen into "wanhope"; the *Parson's Tale* (693) uses "despeir of" in this way. Someone despairing of God's grace sees no sign of it, though it's there. Despair in this sense implies rejection of the power of love. Someone in love who feels at one time or another that love will not be acknowledged—one can fall into, and out of, despair—can be said to "despeir in" love. Those in this second group, including Troilus, feel love's pull, but not its realization. Troilus in the temple cannot, I think, be said to "despeir of" love. He simply scorns it. But when his eye falls on Criseyde (1.271-73) Troilus begins to "despeir in" love. His seeing Criseyde divides him from himself: he falls silent after his single exclamatory question that acknowledges Criseyde's presence (1.276-77), as if his breath had been taken away, and feigns a "pleyinge chere" (1.280); at the same time, he soars inwardly almost dove-like, moved by a holy spirit as yet untouched: "Therwith his herte gan to sprede and rise" (1.278). Only in Book 5 can Troilus be said to "despeir of" love. *Love* there means worldly love, not God's grace, which has rescued him. In lines 41-42 of the proem to Book 1, the narrator asks us to pray that God grant lovers like Troilus "soone owt of this world to pace, / That ben despeired out of Loves grace," not, of course, to pray that they literally die, but rather that they come to understand the sorrowful nature of worldly love, knowledge that brings a figurative death. In the proem to Book 1, Troilus's experience is described in the fullness of despair *because* the narrator sees him participating in the fullness of love.

It is not hard to understand how those who despair in love deserve our prayers. But the narrator also asks that we pray for those who have been gossiped about: "And ek for hem that falsly been apeired / Thorugh wikked tonges, be it he or she" (38–39). The phrase, "be it he or she," is difficult to attach to a noun. The slight syntactic problem here reflects Chaucer's recognizable handling of anaphoric reference.[10] The phrase can refer back *both* to "hem" and to "tonges." If the phrase refers to "hem," the narrator has just broadened his up-to-now generic reference to those in love. "Be it he or she" suddenly makes the pronoun "hem" more precise than it had been, calling attention to the gender of those who are injured by gossip and deserve our prayers. All readers are immediately asked to imagine a woman besieged because she loves. Such a woman merits our prayers too, though in ways that are different than the narrator reveals here. Criseyde, for example, may be injured by gossip, or fears she will. David Aers has explained this aspect of her social dependence.[11] Troilus too is a victim of the fear of being misunderstood. His hesitance to explain himself to Pandarus, for example—sometimes he cannot, sometimes he would not—suggests that Troilus sees Pandarus as misunderstanding him. As we know, he ultimately does, seeing Troilus's behavior as amusingly literary ("From haselwode, there joly Robyn pleyde, / Shal come al that that thow abidest heere. / Ye, fare wel al the snow of ferne yere" [5.1174–76]). We are thus asked in the proem to Book 1 to pray for those who may, like Criseyde and Troilus both (though she is unnamed here as somehow Troilus's equal as a lover), have their love spoken of and misunderstood. Our prayers, should we voice them, would express the hope that all besieged lovers find private, perhaps secret ways to triumph over "wikked tonges."

Before the phrase "be it he or she" defined "hem," each of us was surely projecting himself, or herself, into the position of Chaucer's addressee without the self-conscious regard to gender that comments about gender usually call into being. Suddenly gender matters, not only the gender of those in love, but the gender of those asked to understand the nature of love: its need for secrecy, its gift of freedom, its foretaste of transcendence. It will matter again in a surer way in the last stanzas of the *Troilus* ("O yonge, fresshe folkes, he or

---

[10] See David Burnley, *A Guide to Chaucer's Language* (Norman: Univ. of Okla. Press, 1983), 81, on anaphoric reference (one type of endophoric reference) in Chaucer. On pronominal distance, see page 17. On the methods of reference (both endophoric and exophoric) that create textual coherence in Chaucer, see page 81: "Reference, then, may be reference either back or forth within the text, referring to things already mentioned, or to things about to be discussed (endophoric reference), or, alternatively, it may be reference outside the text to a political, cultural, or other set of circumstances, or to features of the immediate physical situation (exophoric reference)."

[11] Aers, "Chaucer's Criseyde: Woman in Society, Woman in Love," in *Chaucer*, esp. 125.

she" [5.1835]), where the narrator directs men and women to leave "worldly vanyte" (1837) because both Troilus's "cas," which they have now heard, and Criseyde's case, which the narrator mentions without naming her in the proem to Book 1, and which the narrator, having developed, justifies and forgives (5.1772–85), proves that they should.

If the phrase "be it he or she" also refers back to "wikked tonges," the sex and social values of those who gossip also suddenly matter. The phrase gives us a passing reference to the historical world in which Troilus and Criseyde move. We can imagine lovers beset by faces close up. The phrase, "be it he or she," is loomingly iconographic. Pandarus, as we know, must find opportunities to speak in secret to Troilus and Criseyde, who are both shown leading lives in households that allow virtually no privacy.[12] With Pandarus's help, Troilus and Criseyde must find occasions to speak secretly to each other, although each values secrecy for different reasons. For Criseyde, secrecy brings safety from social censure, freedom even from a world of women, and protection from widening knowledge of her erotic expression. Criseyde, I would argue, would be true to the exchange of rings with Troilus *because* she promises herself to a lover whose basis for pledged fidelity is pure love service. Criseyde has nothing to fear from such a pledge as long as it remains secret. Criseyde subjects herself only to Troilus's *idea* of her in a portable place they can recreate between themselves. For Criseyde, the exchange of rings is really no exchange at all; Criseyde gives everything and nothing. For this reason, the exchange of rings, which guarantees the equality of their pledged fidelity, makes it possible for Criseyde to give Troilus a broach as a sign of her dependence (3.1370–71), dependence made safe by a joint exchange of rings *in play* ("And pleyinge entrechaungeden hire rynges" [3.1368]). Criseyde leaves the world of "wikked tonges" in highly contingent ways.

For Troilus, the secret world that Criseyde governs gives him a foretaste of transcendence as a realm exclusively his. Even Pandarus who shoves him into bed (3.1097) is literally and figuratively excluded from it. Pandarus never grasps the seriousness of Troilus's aim ("If she be lost, we shal recovere an other" [4.406]), though he recognizes Troilus's sorrow and feels powerless to help ("And dredeles, for hertes ese of yow, / Right fayn I wolde amende it, wiste I how" [5.1740–41]). Troilus subjects himself wholly to Criseyde who leads him to experience his own uninterfered with wish to serve. Thus Troilus's and Criseyde's play at marriage *in secret* entails an acting out based on shared values only grounded in themselves; an exchange of rings is the outward sign of a connection *only they see*.[13] Secrecy creates for Troilus the experience of

---

[12] On private space in the *Troilus* as self-consciously marked off areas of social intercourse, often shared only "for the nones," and the idea of private space that shapes feeling and conduct according to a "mental image of a more exclusive society [than the one in the *Troilus*, that is], the community of lovers," see Barry Windeatt, " 'Love that Oughte Ben Secree' in Chaucer's *Troilus*," *ChauR* 14 (1979–80): 116–31, at 121.

[13] Cf. Henry A. Kelly, *Love and Marriage in the Age of Chaucer* (Ithaca: Cornell Univ. Press, 1975), 230–42.

transcendence, love's projected world *in this world*, and for Criseyde the conditions under which she can give her heart to Troilus. Surely we can understand why we should pray that "wikked tonges" not sully such a sacred place.

At the end of the second section of the proem, the narrator asks that we also pray that love continue for those who "ben at ese" (1.43). Yet for the narrator even those enjoying love's happiness are subject to uncertainty. The narrator suggests that love as an active gift of Fortune may disappear. We are thus asked to pray that God grant "ay good perseveraunce" (44) and "sende hem myght hire ladies so to plese" (45). "Hem" now refers only to men and to the fear that their strength may lapse. Whatever momentarily comprehensive sense "hem" carried from line 39 has been at line 45 narrowed to one gender.

After our series of invitations to judge and forgive, the narrator says (in the third section of the proem) he will do likewise, taking his cue from us. He will pray for those who are love's servants—this implicitly includes Troilus—"as though I were hire owne brother dere" (51). At this juncture, the narrator's prayers for those who love entail a compassion that creates for him an *idea* of kinship, though the narrator as brother is no more an intimate of love than the narrator as servant. In the third section of the proem, the narrator is to all lovers as Pandarus will be to Troilus. The narrator thinks that praying for lovers (48), writing about their woe (49), and in this way demonstrating charity towards them (50) will "my sowle best avaunce" (47). For the narrator, the *Troilus* serves a narrowly ulterior, though altogether worthy, moral purpose, and it is in this light that he restates at the end of the proem a sure dedication to his literary enterprise. Here is the narrator of the *Troilus* at his most controlling:

> Now herkneth with a good entencioun,
> For now wil I gon streght to my matere,
> In which ye may the double sorwes here
> Of Troilus, in lovynge of Criseyde,
> And how that she forsook hym er she deyde.   52–56

In five lines, the narrator confines the scope of Troilus's "double sorwe" to this world and consciously narrows the context in which he himself placed Troilus's experience earlier in the proem to Book 1, and will place it in Book 5 by mentioning only Criseyde's betrayal of Troilus before *her* death. This makes the story of Troilus available to us as *histoire* that will not demand, from what the narrator says here, otherworldly categories of evaluation. Troilus's "cas" only demands compassion for a foregone conclusion and makes the *Troilus* a call to experience. As an instance of theoretical understanding, the narrator's anatomy of love closes Troilus's "cas" for him. But for us that closure opens it.

We have already mentioned the narrator's exemplary treatment of Troilus's behavior in the temple and seen how it reveals the narrator's loss of clear moral control *early* in the *Troilus* which critics see characterizing the narrator's relationship to Troilus's *histoire* at the end of the work. Indeed, we can see a continuing disjuncture between our response to Troilus throughout Book 1 and the narrator's implied response, which takes the idea of a courtly Troilus as if it were an uncomplicated manifestation of generic love. Moreover, Troilus too sees himself as a "cas" and, like us and the narrator, discovers that his relationship to himself is more complex than he first understood. In this way, he becomes part of the unravelling of issues the narrator in the proem to Book 1 thought were neatly tied. Though the narrator's remark has not often been taken to be accurate, Troilus's initial love behavior *is* "wonder nyce and straunge" (2.24), though I would not argue that Chaucer shows Troilus in Book 1 as a transparent courtly lover. C.S. Lewis's broad observation is correct: that Chaucer's "medievalization" of *Il Filostrato* entailed giving *Troilus and Criseyde* a doctrinal scope missing in Boccaccio that deepens our response to the work *because* Troilus is deliberately cast in the clarifying light of medieval erotic doctrine and psychology.[14] As such, what we see in Book 1 is a lover's experience with courtly discourse available to him in a completed form, discourse that is for Troilus itself "wonder straunge."

Let's look briefly at Troilus himself in Book 1, at his song, in particular, the one ascribed to Lollius. As the first formal voicing of Troilus's new feelings, his discovery through love of a turbulent interiority, Troilus's song displays none of the signs of mental life we notice *immediately* in Criseyde when she is alone and thinking. Derek Pearsall has shown us that Troilus's deciding in Book 5 whether he "kan nor may"—is capable of and willing to—"unloven" Criseyde (5.1696–98) resembles Criseyde's analysis of choice.[15] For Pearsall, Troilus in Book 5 takes us to "the marketplace of the will" (20). Troilus does indeed sound in Book 5 like Criseyde, whose mental world we are privileged to hear from the first. In Book 5, Troilus is an infinitely patient, spectral lover on the wall of Troy, haunted by what Criseyde meant. But in Book 1, where he is a scornful bachelor for whom the quasi-religious "observaunces olde" are dismissable child's play, Troilus is not a model for anyone. In Book 1, after he is caught by love, Troilus simply breaks into a full-blown courtly discourse, the effect of which unsettles him *because* he has as yet no ongoing inner life to which he can assimilate the effect of a discourse that unilaterally seizes him.

Like the narrator in the *Parliament of Fowls* ("The lyf so short, the craft so long to lerne"—1), Troilus must learn a genuine amatory mode. He does so only gradually, though he speaks one immediately. The true discourse of love, a "craft" like any other, takes practice to demonstrate. Chaucer's gloss in the *Parlement* ("al this mene I by Love"—4) clarifies what all readers surely mistake as Chaucer's self-conscious reference to the art of poetry. The clarification occurs when we see that the literary craft and the "craft" of love are analogous. Like the narrator of the *Parliament*, Troilus is an outsider in love matters, even after his eye pierces the "route" and lands on Criseyde (1.271–73) and his horns—first stag-like, then snail-like—are pulled in ("He was tho glad his hornes

---

[14] Lewis, "What Chaucer Really Did," 56–75.
[15] Pearsall, "Choices," 27–28.

in to shrinke" [1.300]) in figurative demasculation so that he can begin to learn love's terms. Troilus knows not love "in dede," though he would.

C.S. Lewis notes that Chaucer deletes Boccaccio's description of Troilus as a "lady-killer from the very beginning" (68). The change is absolutely essential for letting us see an innocent and arrogant Troilus fall in love and so observe his unexpected changes. Initially, Troilus scoffs at love. Then he sees Criseyde and is himself pierced ("Right with here look thorugh-shoten and thorugh–darted" [1.325])—notice how Chaucer has extended the convention of amatory archery, for Criseyde and Troilus both are pierced in the eye, the traditional seat of literary love. Then, shortly after his acknowledgement of Love's power over his servants (330–50)—all this is a kind of Bayard-speak since Troilus is now in harness—Troilus gives voice to full-blown Petrarchan song. Here is a sample of Troilus on the paradoxes of love.

> "And if that at myn owen lust I brenne,
> From whennes cometh my waillynge and my pleynte?
> If harme agree me, wherto pleyne I thenne?
> I noot, ne whi unwery that I feynte.
> O quike deth, O swete harm so queynte,
> How may of the in me swich quantite,
> But if that I consente that it be?"   407–13

Troilus also develops in the same song an image of himself in a rudderless boat blown "to and fro" by "windes two" (415–17), calling his contrary condition a "wondre maladie" (419). The description itself is sure-footed and almost effortlessly modulated, not in the least an unsteady description of emotional paradox. For this reason it has, like the rest of Troilus's song, a certain expected ring. Troilus is here demonstrating "loves craft" (379), as he proposed to himself to do, and he seems to have acquired it almost at once. His new amatory mode constitutes his verbal clothing, the sign of his profession, though it turns him inward, making him peculiarly self-conscious—in his own eyes *both* articulate and ineffective. Troilus's new discourse does not provide him with an easy public dress, despite its already perfected theatricality.

After he declares to the god of love that he's become Criseyde's "man" (434) and asks Criseyde, his "good goodly" (458), that she "on [him] rewe, er that [he] deyde" (460), Troilus speaks about himself. These first words *to himself* amplify images from his own song as if it had given him the conceptual key to his condition.

> "God wold I were aryved in the port
> Of deth, to which my sorwe wol me lede!
> A, Lord, to me it were a gret comfort;
> Than were I quyt of languisshyng in drede.
> For, by myn hidde sorwe iblowe on brede,
> I shal byjaped ben a thousand tyme
> More than that fool of whos folie men ryme."   1.526–32

Troilus "al stereless withinne a boot" (416) in his song is now provided a harbor, not his lady's grace, but a "port of deth" from which his "dere herte" may "help me" (535). The winds that blew Troilus "to and fro" in his song are now "hidde sorwe" blowing within. Troilus's words here are no less literary than his song, but his Petrarchan oxymorons are handled less formulaically than they were. The words *hot* and *cold*, for example, are not opposed to each other, but attached to appropriate natural objects ("But also cold in love towardes the / Thi lady is, as frost in wynter moone, / And thow fordon, as snow in fire is soone"—523–25). Troilus here projects his "despeir in" love unto the world in ways that movingly write him large. His yokings are more extreme here (death vs. life) than in his song, but less distant. They feel personal.

At the beginning of his speech, Troilus rehearsed how other lovers will mock him for scorning love. They will say, he says "to hymself" (506),

> "Loo, ther goth he
> That is the man of so gret sapience,
> That held us loveres leest in reverence."   514–16

Then Troilus drifts imperceptively—we really have no way to punctuate this—from third-person references to himself ("O thow woful Troilus" [519], *as if* he hears others addressing him and addresses himself at the same time *through them*, to first-person references ("God wold I were aryved in the port / Of deth" [526–7]). Within the space of one stanza, Troilus moves inward, letting language approach his feelings.

Earlier the narrator bookishly remarked, apparently not seeing the incapacitating effecting of Troilus's volatile discourse and behavior, that he doesn't know whether Criseyde did not understand Troilus, or feigned that she didn't, though in any case she seems, according to the text of Troilus's *histoire* which the narrator has consulted, not to care about him (492–97). But how indeed could Criseyde know anything about Troilus's love since Troilus *seems* not to have left his room? Moreover, even Troilus's declarations to others—to the god of love or Criseyde—are made to himself, wherever we imagine he is. Before Pandarus finds him "bywayling in his chambre thus allone" (547), Troilus's amatory mode, an extension of his Petrarchan song, is for him *secret* discourse, not because he chooses to keep it so as a matter of strategy until someone can help him reach Criseyde (380–83), but because his firm decision to learn "loves craft" only gives him its discourse already formed, though not yet brought to Criseyde's awareness. Chaucer has made Troilus's discourse the province of Troilus's already perfected fantasy and Pandarus, offering himself as "wheston" (631), finds Troilus appropriately enough in bed ("But longe he ley as stylle as he ded were" [723]).

Although Chaucer's extended translation of Petrarch's "S'amor non è" is the earliest evidence of Petrarch's Italian lyrics circulating outside Italy before the last quarter of the fifteenth-century,[16] Chaucer already sees in Petrarchanism an ease of performance that complicates the conjunction between language and

---

[16] Nicholas Mann, "Petrarch and Humanism: The Paradox of Posterity," in *Francesco Petrarca: Citizen of the World*, ed. Aldo S. Bernardo (Padua and Albany: Editrice Antenore and State Univ. of New York Press, 1980), 288.

the experience it is meant to describe. Observing that uneasy conjunction lies at the heart of Chaucer's artistic curiosity. Chaucer even adds a line to his translation of "S'amor non è": "For ay thurst I, the more that ich it drynke" (406). The line is completely in keeping with the spirit of Petrarch's literary paradoxes and reflects Chaucer's early and fluent assimilation of an "amorous" rather than a "medievalized" Petrarch,[17] whose identity he hides, perhaps because his audience would not know or trust this Petrarch, and whose song he makes historical by ascribing it to the venerable and, as we know now (though Chaucer believed otherwise), fictional Lollius.

With respect to Chaucer's *use* of Petrarch here, Donald R. Howard's nice distinction between soliloquy and inner speech in the *Troilus* is apposite.[18] The instance that illustrates that distinction for him is Criseyde's surrendering to feelings for Troilus she articulates by turns and in varying degrees of clarity and fullness. These are feelings that Antigone's song convinces Criseyde of *because* Antigone's song seems to address Criseyde's fears about loving Troilus (Howard 183). But Troilus sings to himself almost instantly and his Petrarchan song implicitly describes for him a different relationship between inner speech, soliloquy, and lyric argument. Unlike Criseyde, Troilus neither speaks in direct discourse nor dreams of eagles (2.925–31). He daydreams.

> He doun upon his beddes feet hym sette,
> And first he gan to sike, and eft to grone,
> And thought ay on hire so, withouten lette
> That, as he sat and wook, his spirit mette
> That he hire saugh a-temple, and al the wise
> Right of hire look, and gan it newe avise.   1.359–64

Troilus internalizes the incident in the temple with the same clear outline that had fixed him to one deep public moment. He changes nothing, investing the incident with compulsive desire that does not yet distinguish the sexual and the transcendent. Troilus subjects himself to a suddenly private wish he must come to grasp and make real, acknowledging in his daydreams his social good luck in loving Criseyde (368–69) and recognizing how his service will be seen by others and how he'll be esteemed for it (372–76). Because as yet he cannot bring to awareness his emotional turbulence—he has not forged its real language—his Petrarchan song about the paradoxes of love renders him a mystery to himself. Unlike Antigone's song, Troilus's song clarifies nothing. As lyric utterance, it does not create a bridge of discourse to Troilus's "inner speech," which exists untapped as the silent subtext to a scene and a language he keeps

---

[17] Mann, 296–97: "Petrarch's reputation outside Italy in the XVth century thus rested entirely on his Latin works. That these could so often be read and interpreted in an unenlightened way is the principal key to their success, for the *vulgus*, the mass of ordinary readers whom Petrarch so affected to despise, found in them all the conventional wisdom of the medieval morality."

[18] Howard, "Experience," 178.

reliving and repeating, as if repetition were an entrance in. Troilus's song is Troilus's point farthest from himself.

It is thus not surprising that the only locales available to Troilus in Book 1 are first the bed, and then the horse (1072–73)—the hermetic and the pictorial. Troilus has no middle place, neither the bedroom nor the hall. Here we see the distinction between private and public we touched on earlier, but now *within* the household. The bedroom is the socially private, a place reserved for two lovers whose intimacy is conducted in *their* discourse of love once they learn it (Troilus does by Book 3). The hall is the historically public, the realm of princely utterance and response. But in bed or on horseback, Troilus is silent to the world. Alone in bed, Troilus can only "pleyne," and Pandarus, who hears Troilus's complaints, devotes himself to teaching Troilus a behavior Pandarus believes Criseyde will understand.

When Criseyde sees Troilus in Book 2, she falls in love with a warrior lover, a figure she and Troilus fashion together. Troilus's calm ("he rood a pas ful softely"—2.627) reinforces his idea of self-control after battle. His horse bleeds. He does not. Seeing him thus (which is seeing Troilus's idea of himself), and imagining more, Criseyde lets Troilus sink into her with similar slowness ("so softe" [650]). Her memorable "Who yaf me drynke?" (651), first spoken aloud "to hireself" as she "gan al his chere aspien" (649), picks up the idea of thirst from the line Chaucer added to Troilus's song. Suddenly Troilus and Criseyde share an amatory discourse that permits them a secret world. They talk the same language whose coherence is both powerfully effecting and deceptive "because the relationship to reality" it and all conventions of discourse and behavior in the *Troilus* "propose is not direct, but mediated by desire."[19]

My point is that the "cas" of Troilus becomes troublesome almost immediately. We are not watching the degeneration of a lover in imagining an instance of one. Rather, we are witnessing the confident thread with which Troilus was explained in the proem to Book 1 unravelling *for the narrator*, and seeing Troilus deepen as a "cas" *for himself and for us*. The treatment of love in the *Troilus* thus reflects degrees of theoretical understanding as well as imagined historicalness. Our engagement with Troilus's discourse and behavior is initially as a literary style, or conflation of styles, made "historical." If Troilus is a Greek hero, his love behavior is "medieval." Its phases—awkward, comic, literary, perfectly staged—make it clear that for Chaucer's audience the present is not a thousand years. Indeed, Chaucer makes the past palatable, as Morton Bloomfield explains, so that we cannot "escape into the web of myth and cycle."[20] The misplacements of specific systems of discourse and value in the present only serve to anatomize it as a constellation of behaviors; in *Troilus and Criseyde*, the present is complex because it is deep and many. Setting the *Troilus*

---

[19] Karla Taylor, "Proverbs and the Authentication of Convention in *Troilus and Criseyde*," in Barney, 286–87.

[20] Bloomfield, "Distance," 17.

in the past, and in the theoretical, makes both history and theory idiosyncratic and allows us to amend them. We are invited to, and indeed it is precisely because the narrator can only bring his generic amatory categories to the work that we find room in the *Troilus* for our emotional complexity.

Meaning and Ending in a "Paynted Proces": Resistance to Closure in Troilus and Criseyde

ROSEMARIE P. MCGERR

Though it features many traditional medieval closure devices, the conclusion to TROILUS AND CRISEYDE does not resolve the questions raised by the poem. Instead, the ending reflects the poem's sustained ambiguity and emphasizes Chaucer's treatment of interpretation as an open-ended process.

Chaucer's exploration of how meaning relates to ending pervades every level of the poem. Through repetition of the words "mene" and "ende," along with their synonyms, the poem's discourse illustrates the difficulty of determining meaning. Ambiguity in the poem's use of religious terms links the issue of interpretation to the poem's treatment of love. Scenes in which characters try to read the meaning of someone's words or try to explain their own intentions highlight the interpretive processes central to the narrative and make us more aware of ourselves as interpreters of the poem. By alluding to medieval poetic theory, the poem also stresses the rhetorical nature of each character's discourse and so sets up a parallel between the verbal games played within the poem and the poem as a whole. We should therefore recognize the narrator's highly rhetorical conclusion as an attempt to determine the meaning of the love story for us. Despite its conventional appearance, the ending of the poem accentuates the ambiguous nature of the whole. Rather than asserting one interpretation of the value of human love, the poem as a whole encourages us to resist the illusion of closure in all of our reading experiences.

Much of the critical debate about *Troilus and Criseyde* has focused on the poem's conclusion. Though little consensus has developed on where the conclusion begins, how its parts relate to each other, or what the passage as a whole contributes to the poem, no reader can ignore the importance of the end to our understanding of this exquisite but unsettling poem.[1] Whether or

---

[1] The negative portrayal of the love story at the end of the poem strikes many readers as so different from the treatment in the rest of the poem that they consider the end an epilogue or palinode. Even Donald Rowe (*O Love!*), who argues for the poem's ultimate harmony, calls the conclusion the epilogue or (in his index) the retraction. For arguments about where the conclusion begins and the degree to which it has been considered distinct

not we agree with Talbot Donaldson's argument that the ending seems to be "the head of the whole body of the poem," we ought to recognize that the ending of the poem is of a piece with the ambiguities inherent in the rest of the work.[2] Simply in its interweaving of closing comments and narrative, the ending reflects the poem's overall sense of duality.[3] In addition, conventional as closing envoys may be in medieval poetry, the fact that *Troilus and Criseyde* has two envoys, with different standards for interpretation, indicates the complex nature of the poem's ending and meaning.[4] The end of the poem further contributes to the poem's general ambiguity with an almost parodic "piling on" of traditional medieval closure devices: the prayer to the Trinity that finally ends the poem comes after two exhortations to the audience, a prayer to God that the poem be understood, two stanzas recapitulating elements of the narrative, and the two envoys. Despite this "overdetermined" quality, moreover, the ending does not resolve the questions raised by the poem.[5] Chaucer clearly plays here with a conflict between conventional devices of literary closure and the notion of closure as artistic unity. Our perception of the poem's conclusion as conventional but inconclusive is crucial because it allows us to appreciate the many ways in which Chaucer encourages us throughout *Troilus and Criseyde* to resist closed readings and to confront the complex relationship of meaning to ending.

Two recent studies of *Troilus and Criseyde* that examine the poem's treatment of reading and interpretation provide support for my argument. In "Readers in/of *Troilus and Criseyde*," Carolyn Dinshaw argues that Chaucer "makes the act of critical reading a major preoccupation of the entire poem."[6] Dinshaw

---

from the body of the poem, see Steadman, *Laughter*, 149–52; and Kaminsky, *Critics*, 41–42, 65–68. Another relevant issue is the extent to which Chaucer may have revised this passage: see Steadman's chapter "The Revised Epilogue" (*Laughter*, 112–42); Charles Owen, *"Troilus and Criseyde*: The Question of Chaucer's Revisions," *SAC* 9 (1987): 155–72; and Kevin Cureton, "Chaucer's Revision of *Troilus and Criseyde*," *SB* 42 (1989): 153–84.

[2] Donaldson's assessment appears in "The Ending of *Troilus*," in *Speaking of Chaucer*, 92.

[3] Most critics agree that the poem's conclusion begins before 5.1800–27, the lines that relate Troilus's death and spiritual enlightenment. It is on the basis of this intermingling of what Steadman calls "incident and *envoi*" (*Laughter*, 143) that William Kamowski argues for emending the final fourteen stanzas of the poem: see "A Suggestion for Emending the Epilogue of *Troilus and Criseyde*," *ChauR* 21 (1986–87): 405–18.

[4] While the narrator addresses his "litel bok" in one envoy as "litel myn tragedye" and bids it "subgit be to alle poesye" (5.1786–90), he directs it in a second envoy to "moral Gower" and "philosophical Strode" (5.1856–58) for correction.

[5] Many readers would at least agree with Donaldson's argument that the poem ends in a paradox for which there is "no logical resolution," only a theological one ("The Ending of *Troilus*," 100). Other readers stress the poem's sustained ambiguity. Peter Elbow argues that Chaucer creates a dialectic "pulling mercilessly in two directions at once" (*Oppositions in Chaucer* [Middletown: Wesleyan Univ. Press, 1975], 171). In *The Strumpet Muse: Art and Morals in Chaucer's Poetry* (Bloomington: Indiana Univ. Press, 1976), Alfred David argues in a similar vein: *Troilus* is "a poem of Contraries" that "need not be resolved in the interest of logical consistency but should be frankly admitted as elements of [the poem's] texture and meaning" (29).

[6] *YJC* 1 (1988): 81–105; at 87 (*included in this volume*).

notes the parallel roles of the narrator and Pandarus as readers, shapers of texts, and translators of love into vicarious pleasure. Dinshaw also shows how the poem's references to its own future readers and a future text by the narrator work against his attempts to close interpretation of the poem; and she notes that Criseyde's choice of reading material (a romance instead of the saints' lives she claims she should be reading) suggests the difference between Chaucer's poem and texts that encourage closed readings. In another study, Karla Taylor argues for the importance of Dante's story of Paolo and Francesca as a context for Chaucer's treatment of love and poetry in *Troilus and Criseyde*.[7] Taylor suggests that Chaucer sometimes invites misreading in this poem in order to frustrate the desire for closure and emphasize the constant necessity of interpretation. As will become clear, my reading of resistance to closure in *Troilus and Criseyde* will intersect with these two assessments but will differ from them on two important points: I find the highlighting of problems of interpretation in *Troilus and Criseyde* to be both more pervasive than they argue and more closely bound up with the treatment of closure in medieval discussions of *dispositio* or rhetorical organization of texts.

In my view, Chaucer's exploration of how meaning relates to ending pervades every level of the poem and thus provides a backdrop for the poem's other concerns. On the most basic level, the poem practically teems with various forms of the words *mene* and *ende* and synonyms such as *purpos, entende, entencioun, entente, conclusioun, fyn, signifye, stynte, cesse, determyne,* and *diffyne*.[8] The exact numbers are not as important as the association of ideas created by the repetition and the fact that, on a broad range of topics, the narrator and characters express themselves in terms of means and ends:

> but what he mente,
> Lest it were wist on any manere syde,
> His woo he gan dissimulen and hide.   1.320–22

> To what fyn is swich love I kan nat see   2.794

> Not I how longe or short it was bitwene

---

[7] Taylor, *Chaucer Reads*. Though she offers only limited commentary on *Troilus and Criseyde*, Judith Ferster anticipates the arguments made by Dinshaw and Taylor about the depiction of reading as an on-going process in Chaucer's poems: see *Chaucer on Interpretation* (Cambridge: Cambridge Univ. Press, 1985).

[8] In almost every case, these words occur more often per line in *Troilus and Criseyde* than in any of Chaucer's other poems, including the *Canterbury Tales*. Sometimes these words actually appear more often in *Troilus and Criseyde* than in the CT, which is 2.35 times longer. For example, the words *mene, menest, meneth, menyng, menes,* and *mente* occur a total of sixty-five times in *Troilus and Criseyde*, while they occur forty-nine times in CT, and twenty times in BD, HF, PF, and LGW combined. The words *fyn, fynal,* and *fynally* occur a total of thirty-six times in *Troilus and Criseyde*, while they occur twenty-three times in CT and fifteen in BD, HF, PF, and LGW combined. The words in the group *cesse/cessed/cesseth* and the words *diffyne, signifiaunce,* and *signifye* all occur more often in *Troilus and Criseyde* than in all of the other poems combined. See Tatlock and Kennedy's *Concordance*.

> This purpos and that day they fighten mente   4.36–37

> To this entent he koude nevere fyne   5.776

The unusual emphasis on means and ends, meaning and ending, in the poem's discourse suggests that these ideas have a vital role in *Troilus and Criseyde*. The repetition also points to the way that Chaucer uses wordplay in this poem to emphasize the range of meanings inherent in individual words and the variety of words linked by meaning. As a result, the poem illustrates the difficulty of determining or closing meaning for any specific set of words or, put another way, of harmonizing the means and ends of language. Repeated phrases such as *the fyn of his entente* and *word and ende* and repeated rhymes such as *entente/ mente* and *mene/meene* help keep the complex relationship of words to meaning before us, requiring us to reinterpret the meaning of familiar words in different contexts and reminding us of the distance that can arise between a person's words and intent.[9]

If we recognize the significance of this wordplay on means and ends, we can also see that Chaucer calls attention to the ambiguity of language in ways that relate to the poem's dialectic of Christianity and courtly love. For example, along with its more conventional use of religious terms (such as *pray, grace, convert, sin, mercy,* and *heaven*) in a courtly love context, the poem plays very pointedly with the double phrases "God of Love" and "love of God."[10] The recurrence of these phrases throughout the poem, but especially in passages such as Diomede's "O god of Love in soth we serven bothe. / And for the love of God, my lady fre" (5.143–44), highlights the reader's need to judge what range of meanings for the words *god* and *love* might be available to Chaucer and his audience.[11] If not actually encouraging misreading, Chaucer makes it very difficult for us to determine the meaning of these phrases, as well as the many other references to God and love in the poem.[12] While we are probably

---

[9] Though *the fyn of his entente* appears only twice in the poem (3.125 and 3.553), its two appearances within close proximity and use of two terms referring to the end of one's words underscore its relationship to the poem's discussion of meaning and ending. For *word and ende*, see 2.1495, 3.702, and 5.1669. For the rhyme *entente/mente*, see 2.363–64, 2.1219–21, 2.1560–61, 3.125–26, 3.1185–88, 4.172–73, 4.1416–18, 5.867–68, and 5.1693–94; and for the rhyme *meene/mene*, see 3.254–56 and 5.104–5. In Chapter 8 of *Currency*, R. A. Shoaf comments insightfully on Chaucer's use of *entente* and *mene* as part of the treatment of mediation in this poem. As will become clear, parts of my argument complement his.

[10] While "God of Love" occurs eight times in the poem, "love of God" occurs thirty-four times and its variant "Goddes love" occurs twelve times.

[11] See Lee W. Patterson's "Ambiguity and Interpretation: A Fifteenth-Century Reading of *Troilus and Criseyde*," *Speculum* 54 (1979): 297–330, which discusses a fifteenth-century reader's interpretation of *Troilus and Criseyde* as a text that illustrates the difficulty of distinguishing between fleshly and spiritual love.

[12] Just how difficult this is can be inferred from the inconsistency shown by editors in using upper case in "God of Love." Why, in some modern editions, should the narrator and Pandarus refer to the "God of Love" (e.g., 1.421 and 1.932), while Antigone and Diomede refer to the "god of Love" (2.848 and 5.143)?

inclined to interpret "God of Love" as a reference to Cupid and "love of God" as either a reference to piety towards Jove or an anachronism when spoken by the poem's pagan characters, Chaucer complicates the picture for us considerably. At times, one could very well believe Chaucer to suggest that conventional expressions such as "for Goddes love," "by God," "God for-bede," "holy God," and "as help me God" become meaningless, both for the pagan characters and for the medieval audience. While these phrases sometimes add to the conversational tone of the dialogue, at other times the effect is almost parodic:

> "I? God forbede!" quod she, "be ye mad?
> Is that a widewes lif, so God yow save?
> By God, ye maken me ryght soore adrad!"   2.113–15

More important is the extent to which the poem interweaves pagan characters who use the discourse of Christian theology (as in Criseyde's comment, "by that God that bought us bothe two," at 3.1165) with a Christian narrator who uses pagan discourse, especially when he invokes pagan deities as muses and claims he serves the servants of the God of Love (1.15).[13]

This last phrase, with its allusion to the pope as *servus servorum Dei*, and the reference to "charite" just thirty-four lines later emphasize the true doubleness of the poem's use of *god* and *love*, which become examples of "amphibologies" (4.1406) or the "ambages" (5.897) that Diomede defines as "double wordes slye, / Swiche as men clepen a word with two visages" (5.898–99).[14] Book 3 further emphasizes the doubleness of *god* and *love* in Troilus's invocation of Cupid as both "Love" and "Charite" at 3.1254, in the proem's invocation of Venus in terms borrowed from descriptions of divine love by Boethius and Dante, and in the proem's use of ideas taken from the New Testament.[15] When the narrator describes Venus's influence as that "Thorugh which that thynges lyven alle and be" (3.16), we might hear an echo of the description of God by St. Paul in his famous speech to the philosophers of Athens: "In ipso enim vivimus, et movemur, et sumus" (Acts 17:28).[16] We might also hear an

---

[13] Morton Bloomfield ("Distance," in Barney, 79 and 88n7) argues that, except for the comment by Criseyde just quoted (which he believes contains a scribal error), Chaucer "never puts Christian sentiments" into the mouths of the pagan characters in this poem. Bloomfield also argues that references to grace, bishops, and saints' lives need not be seen as Christian. Nevertheless, language like this would call up Christian associations for Chaucer's audience, whether or not they judged the pagan characters as using the terms anachronistically. *For more on this matter, see the essay by Neuse later in this collection–RAS & CSC.*

[14] As David Wallace argues, Chaucer's "ambages" translates *ambage* in the *Filostrato*; but Chaucer may well have recalled Dante's use of *ambage* to describe the snares of pagan language at *Paradiso* 17.31, which echoes Virgil's use of *ambages* to describe the words of the Sibyl in the *Aeneid* 6.99. See "Chaucer's 'Ambages,' " *ANQ* 23 (1984): 1–4.

[15] Rowe (*O Love!*, 92–99) discusses the traditional duality of Venus as a symbol of both cosmic and sexual love. Rowe (97–98) also sees a link between the "blisful light" invoked in the proem and the depiction of God and Christ as light in the Gospel of John; but he does not discuss the other links I see. For other discussions of the Christian content of this proem, see Gordon, *Sorrow*, 30–33, and Wetherbee, *Poets*, 46–48.

[16] All quotations of the New Testament come from the Vulgate Bible: see *Biblia sacra*

echo of John 1:3: "Omnia per ipsum facta sunt: Et sine ipso factum est nihil, quod factum est." Even more important are the echoes of the chapter on love in the First Epistle of John just a few lines earlier in the proem:

> God loveth, and to love wol nought werne;
> And in this world no lyves creature
> Withouten love is worth, or may endure.   3.12–14

The First Epistle of John argues,

> Charissimi, diligamus nos invicem: quia charitas ex Deo est. Et omnis qui diligit, ex Deo natus est, et cognoscit Deum. Qui non diligit, non novit Deum: quoniam Deus charitas est.... Et nos cognovimus, et credidimus charitati, quam habet Deus in nobis. Deus charitas est: et qui manet in charitate, in Deo manet, et Deus in eo. (1 John 4:7–8, 16)

In Chaucer's ambiguous use of *love* in this poem, he encourages us to ask, "If God is *caritas*, is he also the God of Love?" Though the Vulgate Bible carefully distinguishes between *caritas* and *amor* and uses *diligere* rather than *amare* in order to express the love that is spiritual, writers in the Middle Ages did not always maintain these distinctions. For example, whereas the Wycliffite Bible regularly translates *caritas* as *charite*, it regularly translates *diligere* as *loven*.[17] Though a Christian, Boethius uses *amor* and *amare* to describe the love that orders the cosmos, in the same passage from the *Consolatio philosophiae* (2. met. 8) to which Chaucer alludes in the proem to Book 3; and Chaucer translates these Latin terms as *love* in his *Boece*. In Dante's *Commedia*, Francesca uses the same word (*amor*) for the passion that led to her damnation (*Inf.* 5.100–108) as the one the narrator uses to describe the divine love that orders the cosmos (*Para.* 33.145).[18]

Nevertheless, in the pilgrim's encounter with St. John in *Paradiso* 26, Dante suggests a distinction between *amor* and *caritate* that the rest of the canto links to the fallen nature of human language. Considered during the Middle Ages as the author of the Apocalypse, as well as the fourth Gospel and three epistles that bear his name, St. John was the New Testament writer most associated with the depiction of God as Love and Logos. In an examination of the pilgrim's beliefs about love, St. John asks the pilgrim to begin by identifying the end or goal of his journey (*Para.* 26.7–8). The pilgrim explains that God is the Alpha and Omega of the scripture that Love ("Amore") reads to him—terms that reflect the writings associated with St. John (*Para.* 26.16–18). When St. John asks the pilgrim for more detail about who directed his aim, the pilgrim

---

iuxta vulgatam Clementinam, ed. Alberto Colunga and Laurentio Turrado, 4th ed. (Madrid: Library of Christian Authors, 1965).

[17] See the passages quoted above in *The Holy Bible, Containing the Old and New Testaments, with the Apocryphal Books, in the Earliest English Versions Made from the Latin Vulgate by John Wycliffe and his Followers,* ed. Josiah Forshall and Frederic Madden (Oxford: Oxford Univ. Press, 1850).

[18] Quotations from the *Commedia* will be taken from the edition and translation by Singleton.

explains that it was the one who demonstrated to his intellect the first love ("il primo amore") of all eternal substances (*Para.* 26.37–39). In interpreting this answer, St. John says that it is the highest of all the pilgrim's loves ("amori") that draws him to God, and the saint asks about all the teeth by which this love ("questo amor") bites (*Para.* 26.46–51). In explaining that all things with the power to draw the heart to God have contributed to his love ("caritate") (*Para.* 26.55–57), the pilgrim reflects the arguments of St. Bernard, who describes himself as burning with love ("amor") for the Queen of Heaven at *Paradiso* 31.100–101 and whose prayer to the Virgin at *Paradiso* 33.15 Troilus echoes at 3.1263.[19] In this poem, therefore, as in the thinking of at least one medieval theologian, *amor* can lead to *caritas*. Nevertheless, Dante suggests that not all types of *amor* have this potential, for the pilgrim next argues that he has been drawn from an improper love ("l'amor torto") and brought to a proper one ("diritto") by God's creation and sacrifice (*Para.* 26.58–63). In addition, the pilgrim's examination is followed by an interview with Adam, in which they discuss mankind's fallen state in terms of changes in language, specifically in the names by which human beings refer to God (*Para.* 26.133–36). Dante reinforces the link between the discussions of love and language when the image of leaves ("fronde") that the pilgrim used to explain his love of all God's creatures at *Paradiso* 26.64 is transformed by Adam at *Paradiso* 26.137 into an image of a leaf ("fronda") which dies and is replaced by another. In this canto, then, Dante reminds us that the Fall ruptured both the spiritual integrity in which *amor* is *caritas* and the harmony of means and ends in language represented in St. John's depiction of Christ as the Incarnate Word.

In *Troilus and Criseyde*, however, Chaucer emphasizes the semantic ambiguity of the fallen world in order to reopen the question of how divine love relates to human love(s). Venus is the Alpha and Omega of Book 3's presentation of the love of Troilus and Criseyde, and the proem's suggestions of a parallel between *amor* and *caritas* are undercut by the end of the book, when Venus, as morning star, is called "Lucifer" (3.1417). Book 3 thus reminds us that, just as people sometimes call the archangel who became a power of darkness "Lucifer," what the poem calls "love" may not have the same nature as the "blisful light" invoked in the proem.[20] How, then, are we to know what *love*, or *charite*, or *God* means in this poem? If the narrator's desire to live in "charite" (1.49) links him with *caritas* rather than *amor*, does his description of Criseyde as "charitable" (5.823) link her with *caritas* as well? Does Pandarus mean *caritas* when he refers to "celestial" love (1.979)? And to which "God" should the lovers in the audience pray, so that the narrator will have the power to tell his tale (1.32–35)? The poem's foregrounding of such verbal amphibologies and the general problem of determining meaning takes on its most theological slant

---

[19] As Rowe notes (*O Love!*, 106), St. Bernard argues in *De diligendi Dei* and elsewhere that people can progress from carnal love to spiritual love through stages of liberation from materialism.

[20] Though patristic writings consider "Lucifer" to be Satan's name prior to his fall, medieval writers did not always recognize that distinction. See, for example, *Piers Plowman* 5.477 and 495.

in Troilus's lament about Criseyde's keeping her faith and word in Book 5: "God wot, I wende, O lady bright, Criseyde, / That every word was gospel that ye seyde!" (5.1264–65). For Chaucer's first readers, this anachronistic reference to the New Testament would certainly have emphasized the distance between the words of human beings and the Word of God or Logos. But Troilus's comment also points out a central paradox: while human words differ from the Word of God, the Word of God is made manifest through the Scriptures, which use the words of human beings.

Just as the poem's language highlights the difficulty of conclusive interpretation, the narrative repeatedly depicts characters trying to discover the meaning behind someone else's words or trying to explain their own intentions or ends. We watch, for instance, as Troilus and Criseyde attempt to interpret each other's letters and promises, as Criseyde tries to understand Antigone's song, and as Troilus tries to determine the significance of his dream. By giving us Antigone's interpretation of her song and Cassandra's interpretation of Troilus's dream, as well as the readings by Criseyde and Troilus, the poem points to the subjectivity involved in the hermeneutic process. The comments by Criseyde and Pandarus on the narrative she has been listening to when he arrives at the opening of Book 2 also illustrate the capacity of readers to interpret texts differently: whereas Criseyde describes the story of Thebes as a "romaunce" primarily about the murder of Laius by Oedipus (2.100–102), Pandarus describes the story as having twelve books, like an epic poem, and being about the siege of the city (2.107–108). By alluding here to the different forms in which the story of Thebes circulated in the late Middle Ages (the *Roman de Thèbes* and the *Thebaid* of Statius), Chaucer points not only to the interpretive significance of generic differences but also to the interminable rereading of texts in which *Troilus and Criseyde* itself participates.

In each case, the internal "reading" scene calls attention to our own role as interpreters of the text before us. Such is also the effect of the extreme "bookishness" of this poem. On the one hand, the characters exhibit great awareness of the physical properties of the texts they read: Criseyde refers to the rubricated passage ("lettres rede") at which her maiden stopped reading aloud in their copy of the story of Thebes (2.103–5), and Pandarus describes the letter he brings from Criseyde to Troilus as "al this blake" (2.1320). On the other hand, Troilus and Criseyde also conceive of their lives as texts to be interpreted or read by others. In Book 1, Troilus compares himself to the subject of a poem when he laments, "I shal byjaped ben a thousand tyme / More than that fool of whos folie men ryme" (1.531–32). Troilus portrays his experience of love in even more explicitly textual terms in Book 5: "Men myght a book make of it, lik a storie" (5.583–85). Criseyde also imagines how her actions will be read by others:

> "Allas, of me, unto the worldes ende,
> Shal neyther ben ywriten nor ysonge
> No good word, for thise bokes wol me shende."   5.1058–60

Troilus himself turns Criseyde into a text when he tells her, "Though ther be mercy writen in youre cheere, / God woot, the text ful hard is, sothe, to fynde!" (3.1356–57). The narrator reinforces the "bookish" nature of our own experience of Criseyde, when he challenges us to consult other books for verification of the details of her story (5.1086–90) and adds that the wide "publishing" of Criseyde's story is punishment enough for her guilt (5.1095–96). Since these comments occur just before the passage in which Troilus must begin to reinterpret Criseyde's promise to return, in order to reconcile her words with her actions, they highlight the parallel between the interpretive processes going on within the narrative and our own reading of the text.

An especially important instance of the narrative's presentation of attempts to determine meaning occurs at the opening of Book 3, when Troilus and Criseyde first have the opportunity to exchange words in person. After Troilus has overcome his embarrassment enough to declare himself devoted to Criseyde, Pandarus pleads with Criseyde to "make of this thing an ende" (3.118) and declare her "routhe" for Troilus (3.122–23). She, however, wants to know what Troilus's declaration really means before committing herself and so tells her uncle, "I wolde hym preye / To telle me the fyn of his entente. / Yet wist I nevere wel what that he mente" (3.124–26). Troilus does not wait for her to direct the request to him, but quickly tries to explain what he means ("What that I mene.... Lo, this mene I ..." 3.127–47): he means, he says, that they should become the ideal courtly love couple, she looking upon him with friendly eyes and agreeing to accept his pledge of service, he serving her patiently and diligently, no matter what the pain to him. Though Pandarus tries to interpret these words for Criseyde, asserting that they prove that Troilus desires nothing but her honor, Criseyde still does not pledge herself. Instead, after further consideration, she responds with carefully chosen words:

> "Myn honour sauf, I wol wel trewely,
> And in swich forme as he gan now devyse,
> Receyven hym fully to my servyse,
>
> Bysechyng hym, for Goddes love, that he
> Wolde, in honour of trouthe and gentilesse,
> As I wel mene, eke mene wel to me."   3.159–64

In spite of Pandarus's plea for Criseyde to bring the matter to an end, Criseyde's acceptance of Troilus's service is a conditional, open-ended one.[21] At its heart, moreover, is a chiasmus that expresses a desire for harmony or understanding between them in terms of meaning or intent: "As I wel mene, eke menen wel to me."

---

[21] Davis Taylor notes that, while Troilus prefers absolute statements of commitment, Criseyde "prefers conditional commitments," which "suggests that she sees love not as an absolute and eternal state but as one that depends on a particular person and time": see "The Terms of Love: A Study of Troilus's Style," as revised for inclusion in Barney, 235–36.

While the expression "mean well" suggests that good meaning or intentions will be the measure of their words, we recognize it as a phrase that becomes increasingly ironic as we move towards the conclusion that the narrator describes for us at the opening of the poem:

> Now herkneth with a good entencioun,
> For now wil I gon streght to my matere,
> In which ye may the double sorwes here
> Of Troilus, in lovynge of Criseyde,
> And how that she forsook hym er she deyde.   1.52–56

It is not just Criseyde's "meaning well" that becomes suspect, moreover. (As the narrator's exhortation suggests, *our* good intentions will also become an issue.) We hear reference to "meaning well" later in Book 3, when Pandarus assures Troilus, "For wel I woot, thow menest wel, parde" (3.337); but our confidence in this interpretation of Troilus's intent toward Criseyde is undermined by the speech that precedes this assurance. Here, Pandarus depicts his role in the love affair as a pander (3.253–56) and then traitor (3.271–73), or as the means to an end different from the one he has described to Criseyde. Though Troilus protests that Pandarus's actions should not be construed as "bauderye" (3.397) because Pandarus has acted out of "gentilesse" (3.402) rather than for "gold or for richesse" (3.399), the scene ends with the narrator declaring that both men considered themselves "wel apayed" (3.421), which suggests that Pandarus's reading of his role is more accurate than Troilus's. The idea that Troilus's intentions or meaning may be impossible to determine receives further emphasis when the narrator goes on to explain that Troilus could dissemble so well that no one could tell "by word or by manere, / What that he mente" concerning his affair with Criseyde (3.431–32).

We again hear a reference to "meaning well" in Book 3 when Criseyde must defend herself against the charge that she has shown favor to someone other than Troilus: "And she answerde, 'Swete, al were it so, / What harm was that, syn I non yvel mene?' " (3.1163–64). Though we may sympathize with Criseyde here because the charge is part of Pandarus's ruse to get Troilus into her bed, it is hard to read her response without remembering that, later in the narrative, the charge will be true. There, when Criseyde responds to Diomede's overtures in the Greek camp, the phrase reappears and resonates with irony:

> "I say nat therfore that I wol yow love,
> N'y say nat nay; but in conclusioun,
> I mene wel, by God that sit above!"   5.1002–4

Criseyde's response to Diomede is even more open-ended than her earlier response to Troilus and significantly omits any reference to Diomede's meaning well. Perhaps, as Troilus will eventually suggest, the hope of harmony between words and meaning has vanished. Troilus's desperate attempts to harmonize Criseyde's actions with her promises to return lead him finally to ask, "Who shal now trowe on any othes mo?" (5.1263 and 1681) and to interpret the brooch Criseyde has given to Diomede, Troilus's last gift to her, as a more accurate sign of her meaning than her words (5.1688–95). Though she argues that the "entente is al, and nat the lettres space" (5.1630), Troilus reminds us that physical signs (be they written or spoken words, objects, coughs, laughter, smiles, blushes, nudges, or tears) are what human beings invest with meaning.

Our reading of Criseyde's references to "meaning well" and her open-ended responses to both Troilus and Diomede is also shaped by the treatment of means and ends in the scenes that precede them. For example, Criseyde's resistance to the closure that Pandarus and Troilus hope to impose in Book 3 comes just after Chaucer has shown how literary form can work against traditional expectations of closure. The end of Book 2 divides a single scene of the narrative between two of its five major parts, which not only generates suspense and places the lovers' first meeting within the central book of the poem, but also calls attention to the artificial nature of narrative structure. In addition, Book 2 ends with a question: "O myghty God, what shal he seye?" (2. 1757). Such an ending associates at least this part of the narrative with the *demande d'amour*, a genre of medieval literature involving implicit or explicit open-endedness that generated debate about issues related to love. Book 2's question of what Troilus should say both encourages our active engagement with the poem and puts us in the same position as Troilus, who tries to choose his words while he awaits Criseyde's entrance (3.50–55). The question also serves as an effective means of focusing our attention on the issue of language and reinforcing the importance of this issue for the poem just as we enter its center.

Book 2 as a whole shapes our reading of Criseyde's references to meaning well and her resistance to defining relationships by deepening our appreciation of the difficulties involved in interpreting another's words. To begin with, the prologue to Book 2 treats the differences that arise in language owing to the effects of time (2.22–28), geography (2.36–42), and individual point of view (2.43–48) as relevant to both the narrator's interpretation of his Latin source and our interpretation of the narrative. Book 2 then goes on to present discourse as a game of reading to one's own advantage and blinding others to one's true intent. This becomes clear in the conversation between Pandarus and Criseyde in which he first tries to persuade her to accept Troilus as her courtly lover (2.85–595). As this passage develops, the poem offers us a detailed picture of the skill with which Pandarus works toward his end, assessing Criseyde's ability to read his meaning and varying his strategy to keep her resistance to a minimum. He begins by playing on her curiosity: " 'As evere thryve I,' quod this Pandarus, / 'Yet koude I telle a thyng to doon yow pleye'" (2.120–21). Criseyde's response plays on the close association of reading, speaking, interpreting, and advising in the Middle English words *reden* and *areden*.

> "For al this world ne kan I reden what
> It sholde ben....
> And but youreselven telle us what it is,
> My wit is for t'arede it al to leene.
> As help me God, I not nat what ye meene."   2.129–33

Criseyde's difficulty in reading Pandarus's words echoes her introduction in Book 1: Criseyde is "she that nyste what was best to rede" (1.96), as opposed to her father Calkas, the priest of Apollo, who defects to the Greek camp and is held in esteem by them as one who "hath konnynge hem to rede" (1.83). As Criseyde turns to Hector there, she turns to Pandarus here for interpretive assistance: "What is youre reed I sholde don of this?" (2.389). At the opening of Book 5, Criseyde will again be "she that nyste what was best to rede" (5.18), and there she will turn to Diomede.

Criseyde is not completely without skills in reading, however. The poem indicates that she knows how to play her uncle's game, even if she does not enjoy it. When she loses patience, she makes the game's confrontational terms explicit and pleads with Pandarus, "Lat be to me youre fremde manere speche, / And sey to me, youre nece, what yow liste" (2.248–49). At 2.386–7, the poem shows that she recognizes the need for a strategy to get at her uncle's true meaning: "Criseyde, which that herde hym in this wise, / Thoughte, 'I shal felen what he meneth, ywis.'" We also see that she recognizes Pandarus's attempts to interpret her promise to be kind to Troilus more broadly than she meant it: when Pandarus refers to the time when Criseyde will be completely Troilus's, she responds, " 'Nay, therof spak I nought, ha, ha!' . . . ; / 'As helpe me God, ye shenden every deel!' " (2.589–90). Nonetheless, the poem does not depict Criseyde as initiating the rhetorical games that the men around her play. Though she may not be as innocent of Pandarus's intentions as the narrator claims (2.1562 and 1723), her participation in the poem's wars of words, even in Books 4 and 5, is defensive: as the narrator says of Criseyde's first letter to Troilus, "Al covered she the wordes under sheld" (2.1327).

On the other hand, Chaucer characterizes Pandarus as a skilled rhetorician right from the start. Pandarus enters the poem speaking words for their effect, rather than because he means them: after hearing Troilus's lament, Pandarus asks his friend whether devotion or fear has brought him to this state, not because Pandarus truly believes that Troilus's behavior stems from devotion or fear, but because Pandarus knows that the question will anger Troilus and distract him from his sorrow. As the narrator explains, "Thise wordes seyde he for the nones alle" (1.561). This line will recur at 4.428, when Pandarus again uses words he does not truly mean in order to distract Troilus from his sorrow, this time over his loss of Criseyde in the exchange of prisoners. If we fail to admire Pandarus's rhetorical technique in persuading Troilus to pursue an affair with Criseyde, the allusion to the *Poetria nova* at the end of Book 1 encourages us to make the connection between Pandarus and poetic theory and helps us appreciate the rhetorical terms in which Pandarus, Troilus, and Criseyde perceive their discourse.

We should hardly be surprised that, in the poem offering his most extensive exploration of the relationship of meaning to ending, Chaucer uses his most extensive allusions to Geoffrey of Vinsauf's *Poetria nova*, the medieval rhetorical handbook that took earlier arguments for the importance of a text's conclusion and intent to new heights. At the end of Book 1, the narrator uses Geoffrey's famous comparison of the poet to an architect to describe Pandarus's preparation to persuade Criseyde that she should become Troilus's lover:

For everi wight that hath an hous to founde
Ne renneth naught the werk for to bygynne
With rakel hond, but he wol bide a stounde,
And sende his hertes line out fro withinne
Aldirfirst his purpos for to wynne.
Al this Pandare in his herte thoughte,
And caste his werk ful wisely or he wroughte.   1.1065–71[22]

In Book 2, Pandarus himself alludes to Geoffrey of Vinsauf's argument about
the primary role of a text's end or goal in determining its shape and meaning—
an argument similar to Donaldson's comment about the end of Chaucer's
poem being the head of the body. When Pandarus has finally agreed to tell
Criseyde the news about which he has been teasing her, he says,

"How so it be that som men hem delite
With subtyl art hire tales for to endite,
Yet for al that, in hire entencioun,
Hire tale is al for som conclusioun."   2.256–59

Pandarus plays on "ende" as intention as well as conclusion when he goes on
to assert that "th'ende is every tales strengthe" (2.260); but he reverses the
argument of the *Poetria nova* when he claims that, because of the nature of his
subject and his close relationship to his audience, he will not use any artistry or
"peynte" his tale (2.261).[23] We may not recognize this claim as already part
of Pandarus's "process"—his narrative or means of persuading Criseyde—until
the poem explicitly shows us Pandarus stopping to think through his rhetorical
strategy:

Than thought he thus: "If I my tale endite
Aught harde, or make a proces any whyle,
She shal no savour have therin but lite,
And trowe I wolde hire in my wil bigyle;
For tendre wittes wenen al be wyle
Theras thei kan nought pleynly understonde;
Forthi hire wit to serven wol I fonde."   2.267–73

Pandarus does not dispense with rhetorical art, as he suggests he will, but
instead chooses a style that he believes will give him most success in persuading
Criseyde to accept his argument. By appearing to reject artistry at the opening
of his "tale," he hopes to achieve the first objective of rhetorical discourse: to
capture the good will of his audience.

Though he tries to reassure Criseyde that he uses no artistry, Pandarus can-

---

[22] For Chaucer's source, see Ernest Gallo, ed. and trans., *The "Poetria Nova" and its
Sources in Early Rhetorical Doctrine* (The Hague: Mouton, 1971), 16–17. *See also the essays by
Hanning and Fyler in this volume–RAS & CSC.*

[23] Geoffrey argues that, while nature places the ending last, the true artist will bring the
end of the narrative to the beginning. See *Poetria nova*, lines 112–17, ed. and trans. Gallo,
20–21.

not help referring to his speech as a "proces" (2.292) and "tale" (2.305). His use of *proces* is especially significant, for its repeated appearance in the poem as a rhetorical term for a narrative, tale, discourse, or argument colors our interpretation of the other processes that occur in the poem and links them to the poem's treatment of the power of rhetorical language.[24] The fact that *proces* occurs twelve times in the poem, six in Book 2 alone, both underscores the extent to which language is perceived as rhetorical within the narrative and calls attention to the rhetorical nature of the text we are reading.[25] Criseyde's reluctance to take Pandarus's words at their face value manifests itself in her questions about his contemplation or reading of her (2.275–77) and in her thoughts after hearing her uncle's combination of flattery, protestation, exhortation, threat, and rhetorical flourish: "I shal felen what he meneth, ywis" (2.387). Her response to Pandarus's "clarification" of his argument shows that she understands the rhetorical nature of his words and the irony of his earlier discussion of ends: "Is al this paynted proces seyd—allas!—/ Right for this fyn?" (2.424–25). Here she effectively throws Pandarus's own terms—"peynte" (2.262), "proces" (2.292), and "ende" (2.260)—back in his face. Her response also lays bare the artifice of Pandarus's protestation of "good entencioun" (2.295) and does so in terms of his responsibility to offer her a good reading or advice:

> "Allas, what sholden straunge to me doon,
> When he, that for my beste frend I wende,
> Ret me to love, and sholde it me defende?. . . .
>
> Is this youre reed?"   2.411–13, 422

The fact that her response is made up of a series of exclamations and rhetorical questions, accompanied by tears, suggests that she has her own rhetorical skills; but Criseyde's questions also express her resistance to accepting this understanding of Pandarus's words as conclusive. She correctly perceives that the process in which Pandarus has involved her continues to develop: after again trying to determine the end of Pandarus's process ("Ye seyn, ye nothyng elles me requere?" 2.473), Criseyde warns Pandarus in terms that suggest she knows he may have yet a different end in mind:

> "And here I make a protestacioun,
> That in this proces if ye depper go,
> That certeynly, for no salvacioun
> Of yow, though that ye sterven bothe two,

---

[24] On the use of *proces* in the poem, see Siegfried Wenzel, "Chaucer and the Language of Contemporary Preaching," *SP* 73 (1976): 153–54; Stephen A. Barney, "Suddenness and Process in Chaucer," *ChauR* 16 (1981): 30–34; and Shoaf, *Currency*, 115–16.

[25] In addition to 2.268 and 2.292, the term occurs at 2.424, 2.485, 2.678, 2.1615, 3.334, 3.470, 3.1739, 4.418, 5.583, and 5.1491. The word occurs only six times in the CT, and five times in the BD, HF, PF, and LGW combined.

Though al the world on o day be my fo,
Ne shal I nevere of hym han other routhe." 2.484–89

As the poem makes clear, Pandarus's process continues, in spite of his repeated protestations of good intentions (2.580–81, 592) and in spite of Criseyde's intentions as well: Troilus eventually wins her love "by proces and by good servyse" (2.678).[26]

Our suspicions about Pandarus's means and ends grow as the poem gives us a "behind the scenes" view of the verbal magic that he works in order to arrange for a meeting between Troilus and Criseyde. With Troilus assenting to Pandarus's reading of the situation (2.1538–39), Pandarus uses "sleyghte" (2.1512) to "blende" (1496) the innocent players in the game; but the poem clearly indicates that the skills he uses are rhetorical.[27] Just as he spins a new account of his discovery of Troilus's love-sickness in order to persuade Criseyde that Troilus can speak well of love (2.506–74), Pandarus here takes on the role of master storyteller to achieve his ends: "He rong hem out a proces lik a belle" (2.1615). When Pandarus repeats his dramatic tale in Troilus's bedroom (to keep up the illusion that Troilus doesn't know why Criseyde is there), the poem describes Pandarus's rhetorical skill in the same dark terms that will describe the Pardoner's preparation to preach in the *Canterbury Tales* (1.710–13): "This Pandarus gan newe his tong affile" (2.1681).

The disjunction between a person's words and ends receives further emphasis and perhaps its most cynical expression in the account of Diomede's plans to win Criseyde's favors. With Diomede, the rhetorical process becomes a wholly self-serving one. Before speaking, he reads the parting of Troilus and Criseyde, "As he that koude more than the crede / In swich a craft" (5.89–90), and then plans his strategy in terms that remind us of Pandarus's:

"Certeynlich I am aboute nought,

---

[26] Criseyde makes the connection between Pandarus's process and the first night she spends with Troilus, when she asserts, "ye caused al this fare, / Trowe I, ... for al youre wordes white" (3.1566–67). When he is trying to persuade Criseyde to let Troilus into her bedroom that night, Pandarus himself uses the phrase "wordes white" to describe the kind of fair-seeming language that would appease Troilus, if he were just a jealous fool (3.901). The two references to "wordes white" thus frame the consummation scene, as if to call into question the value of the language used there.

[27] In discussing the artistic disposition of a poetic work, Geoffrey of Vinsauf comments on the magical quality of rhetoric and suggests its potential danger: rhetorical art "plays about almost like a magician . . . , and brings it about that the last becomes first, the future the present, the oblique direct, the remote near; thus rustic matters become polished, old becomes new, public private, black white, and vile precious" (*Poetria nova*, lines 121–25, ed. and trans. Gallo, 20–21). Two recent articles that explore the highly rhetorical nature of *T&C* have also stressed the intertwining of medieval poetics and classical rhetorical theory. In "Chaucer the Rhetorician: Criseyde and her Family," *ChauR* 20 (1985–86): 28–39, Marjorie Curry Woods shows how Chaucer's ambiguous characterization of Criseyde makes use of the discussion of character analysis in Cicero's *De Inventione*. In "Ethos, Pathos, and Logos in *Troilus and Criseyde*," *ChauR* 20 (1985–86): 169–82, E. F. Dyck shows how Chaucer makes use of a medieval rhetorical theory of persuasion that derives from Aristotle.

> If that I speke of love, or make it tough;
> For douteles, if she have in hire thought
> Hym that I gesse, he may nat ben ybrought
> So soon awey; but I shal fynde a meene,
> That she naught wite as yet shal what I mene."   5.100–105

Whereas Pandarus implicitly links his rhetorical skill with entrapment ("I / Shal wel the deer unto thi bowe dryve," 2.1534–35), the narrator makes the connection between rhetorical skill and entrapment clear in his description of Diomede

> withinne hymself ay arguynge
> With al the sleghte, and al that evere he kan,
> How he may best, with shortest taryinge,
> Into his net Criseydes herte brynge.
> To this entent he koude nevere fyne;
> To fisshen hire, he leyde out hook and lyne.   5.772–77

Diomede certainly sees his attempt to be Criseyde's "conquerour" (5.794) as a war of words: if he loses, he says to himself, "I shal namore lesen but my speche" (5.798).

These dark views of the power of words provide one background against which we read the references to meaning and ends in Books 3, 4, and 5. Nonetheless, the narrative counters this dark background by showing how the indeterminacy of language also generates great beauty and humor, as in the case of the lovers' metaphors and Pandarus's puns. In addition, the narrator suggests that intentions can communicate themselves in spite of words: Criseyde believes that Troilus understands her thoughts without her having to say anything (3.463–67). The poem also associates *dispositio*, the rhetorical organization of one's words, with the arrangement of history by divine providence:

> O god, that at thi disposicioun
> Ledest the fyn, by juste purveiaunce,
> Of every wight.   2.526–28[28]

Furthermore, "meaning well" cannot just be seen in an ironic sense in this poem without placing our own ends under suspicion, since the narrator requests "good entencioun" from us as readers in his opening remarks.

But that is precisely what the poem does. The poem encourages us to examine our role as readers, in part through its focus on reading and interpretation, in part through the narrator's references to his audience. The narrator encourages our engagement with the narrative: he asks us to listen with good intentions, to pray for lovers, and to correct his language (3.1331–36). In addition, he sometimes puts words into our mouths, or reads for us, as he does when he anticipates criticism about how Troilus pursued Criseyde's love (2.29–

---

[28] In Book 5, we hear twice that Fortune or Fate is under Jove's "disposicioun" (see 5.2 and 5.1543).

34) and how quickly Criseyde fell in love with Troilus (2.666–69). The narrator also effectively implicates us in the "process" of consummating the love affair, as if we and the narrator shared Pandarus's intent and artistic strategy: when Pandarus has made all his plans to bring Troilus and Criseyde together at his house, the narrator comments,

> This tymbur is al redy up to frame;
> Us lakketh nought but that we witen wolde
> A certeyn houre, in which she comen sholde.   3.530–32

Here, we become co-conspirators with Pandarus, like Troilus, who "al this pur-veiaunce / Knew at the fulle, and waited on it ay" (3.533–34). By referring to what we lack in terms of the building metaphor that links Pandarus's plans with the poetic *dispositio* described by Geoffrey of Vinsauf, the narrator suggests that our role is akin to those of the other poet-figures in the poem. Are our ends fully accomplished in Book 3, like Pandarus's (3.1582)? Do we share responsi-bility for the process of entrapment that we read, or are we mere observers of events caused by some other power? The questions take on greater significance when we compare the poem's picture of Pandarus "reading" the romance of Troilus and Criseyde by the fire (3.978–80) with the poem's picture of Provi-dence disposing the ends of history and with the questions about Providence raised in Troilus's meditation on free will. Though the narrator appears to fol-low Geoffrey of Vinsauf's advice and gives us a providential perspective on the action of the tale by announcing its end during his prologue, the poem keeps our perspective double and makes us suspicious about the narrator's means and ends, just as we are of Pandarus's.

Even before the narrator refers to his own tale as a "proces" (3.470), the parallel between Pandarus and the narrator becomes clear. In addition to the many other ways in which the narrator and Pandarus mirror each other, the narrator's comments about his tale's end at 2.1564–66 and 1595–96 echo those of Pandarus at 2.256–62, 1614, and 1622 and suggest a shared interest in focus-ing the audience's attention on the announced end of the process. While this approach seems to follow the poetic theory outlined by Geoffrey of Vinsauf, the parallel between the narrator and Pandarus calls attention to the manipula-tive nature of the rhetorical process, including the way that its end is present-ed. Chaucer therefore leads us to wonder if we can interpret the narrator's true end from his means, especially if the means are ambiguous. Instead of being co-conspirators, perhaps we are the narrator's victims; but, if the poem does not allow us to believe that Criseyde is fully innocent of Pandarus's tricks, cer-tainly we cannot claim total innocence as readers.

In fact, the narrator fears we will subvert his end by exercising our power as readers to close the book ourselves: at 5.1032, he says that he will come to the point quickly, "lest that ye my tale breke." Perhaps he feels that, like Paolo and Francesca, we will choose to ignore the end of the text before us and "rewrite" it according to our own ends. In addition, throughout the poem, the narrator suggests the power of poetic tradition by asserting that he is trapped into fol-lowing his sources, just as Criseyde is trapped, first by Pandarus and Troilus, then by Diomede. The parallel becomes especially clear in the ambiguous metaphor used at 3.1191–2: "What myghte or may the sely larke seye, / Whan that the sperhauk hath it in his foot?" While this question certainly relates to Criseyde, enclosed at this point in Troilus's arms, we discover that our first interpretation is not the only one possible, for the rest of the stanza discusses not her inability to escape, but the narrator's:

> I kan namore, but of thise ilke tweye, —
> To whom this tale sucre be or soot, —
> Though that I tarie a yer, somtyme I moot,
> After myn auctour, tellen hire gladnesse,
> As wel as I have told hire hevynesse.   3.1193–97

Nevertheless, the narrator's reluctance to condemn Criseyde for her unfaithfulness (5.1050, 1098–99) reminds us of the power he has to question the texts he reads and the power we have to keep an open mind about all of the issues raised by the poem.

Since the parallel that the poem sets up between Pandarus and the narrator encourages us to wonder about the relationship of the rhetorical language of the poem to the pandering and persuasion within the narrative, we ought to react with suspicion when the narrator attempts to "close" our reading of the poem with his anaphora on "Swich fyn":

> Swich fyn hath, lo, this Troilus for love!
> Swich fyn hath al his grete worthynesse!
> Swich fyn hath his estat real above,
> Swich fyn his lust, swich fyn hath his noblesse!
> Swich fyn hath false worldes brotelnesse!   5.1828–32

Driving home the point that courtly values end in disillusionment, the narrator uses the same particularly dramatic rhetorical flourish we have seen earlier in the poem.[29] With the summary of the poem in the next two lines, moreover, we learn that we have come full circle. We are now at the end of the story described at the opening of the poem and now should see what the narrator really meant when he discussed his intentions at the opening of the poem. As the narrator goes on to admonish young men and women to cast their sights on heaven instead of the transitory world and to set their hearts on God, the only lover who will never be false, the narrator suggests that his intent all along was to serve the Christian God and bring lovers to solace in a Christian heaven. Here, at the end of his tale, he makes explicit that he considers *charite* the only true form of love.

Then, in a final example of anaphora, the narrator exhorts us to look back at the poem from this point of view and recognize the false values illustrated in it:

> Lo here, of payens corsed olde rites!

---

[29] Earlier examples of anaphora include 2.344–47, 3.29–32, 4.759–63, 5.43–49, etc.

Lo here, what alle hire goddes maye availle!
Lo here, thise wrecched worldes appetites!
Lo here, the fyn and guerdoun for travaille
Of Jove, Appollo, of Mars, of swich rascaille!
Lo here, the forme of olde clerkis speche
In poetrie, if ye hire bokes seche!   5.1849–55

In condemning the ancient poetic tradition in which his poem has thus far par-
ticipated, the narrator counters the closure of the earlier envoy. He therefore
submits his book to two Christian assessors, Gower and Strode, as if to convert
his own poem to a proper Christian end. Following his own advice, the narra-
tor then sets his heart on Christ and beseeches him of the mercy that courtly
lovers conventionally ask of their ladies.

While we might agree that this ending appears to accord with Christian doc-
trine and medieval conventions of closure, we may also be tempted to echo
Criseyde and ask, "Is al this paynted proces seyd, allas / Right for this fin?"
For modern readers, certainly, and I suspect for many medieval readers as well,
this change of perspective on Troilus's experiences seems incongruent with
what has come before; for this ending tries to erase the ambiguities about
means and ends and the tensions between *amor* and *caritas* that generate ques-
tions throughout the poem.[30] This ending instead asserts that only one mean-
ing, one conclusion, should be in our minds. We must therefore have misinter-
preted the narrator when he argued that love "is a thing so vertuous in kynde"
(1.254), when he admonished, "I yow rede / To folowen hym [i.e., Love] that
so wel kan yow lede" (1.258–59), and when he asked, in reference to the
lovers' night of bliss, "Why nad I swich oon with my soule ybought, / Ye, or
the leeste joie that was theere?" (3.1319–20). We now understand, even more
than we did with our double view of the plot, how ambiguous the narrator's
language was when he described the heaven, the bliss, and the love that Troilus
and Criseyde shared. We have a right, therefore, to feel betrayed or at least
manipulated by this narrator, for he now appears to be even more like Pan-
darus than we suspected.[31]

But is the narrator's condemnation of pagan love and poetry the true "end"
of the poem? Does the poet have another "end" or purpose in mind? As Dyck
argues, reading the poem in terms of the rhetorical theory available to Chaucer

---

[30] Cf. Larry Sklute's argument in *Virtue of Necessity: Inconclusiveness and Narrative Form in
Chaucer's Poetry* (Columbus: Ohio State Univ. Press, 1984) that the poem's "second"
conclusion is an "overconclusion" that "overwhelms the moral implications of the first
ending" and "undercuts our sense of the poem's genre" because it "denies the magnificent
tragic meaning about the ultimate pain of the human condition" (83). He also argues that
this "overconclusion" creates "an inconclusiveness in the poem's form" (84).

[31] As Bloomfield argues, "The reader . . . , unless he is extraordinarily acute, remains in
ignorance [of the narrator's belief that the only true love is the love of the Eternal] until he
finishes the whole work" ("Distance," 20). Bloomfield also notes that the narrator at times
"plays down his own Christianity" and at others expresses "the Christian point of view"
(ibid., 19).

suggests that the poet and narrator's "means and ends may not be the same, and ... the poet (but not the narrator) may be exploring the meaning of rhetoric for poetry."[32] The conclusion that the narrator gives us does require us to look back on the narrative from the perspective of the outcome of the love affair and from a Christian point of view of *contemptus mundi*. In looking back, however, we should recall that these ideas have been with us, at least implicitly, since the outset of the poem, and they have not led us to close the book on the love story or the love portrayed. We must also remember that the narrator's rejections treat as closed issues ones on which medieval theologians themselves did not agree. For most readers, therefore, the effect of the narrator's concluding admonitions is to make us feel acutely the tension between earthly and heavenly values: "Instead of turning us from the world, Chaucer only attaches us to it more strongly than ever before, though with a greater understanding of what it is we love."[33] If anything, the retrospective view we receive reminds us that we have not left our earthly perspective behind, in spite of the narrator's suggestions that casting up our hearts to heaven (5.1825) will allow us to shed our blindness and share Troilus's new view of the world. Unlike Troilus, we have not yet escaped the elements to join the immutable world, but remain in a world in which the relationship of spiritual and temporal values is not clear. We may, like the narrator, appeal to a divine Alpha and Omega whose view transcends ours and provides true closure; but we must do even this in ambiguous terms.

It is this recognition of our own dual natures, our own embodiment of contraries like *amor* and *caritas*, with the resulting ambiguity in our words and ends, that is the true "end" of the poem. In spite of the intense concern for meaning and ending exhibited in the process of the poem, *Troilus and Criseyde* ultimately makes clear the difficulty of determining meaning and the need for resisting the illusion of closure in our pursuit of understanding. Again, Shoaf's assessment is apt:

> if and when the book is understood, what will be understood, in part, is the process of understanding itself, or the increasingly self-conscious assumption of a position always resignable because contingent upon mutable signs—signs fraught with temporality (*Currency*, 150).

That the manipulations of this narrative ultimately disturb us indicates that *Troilus and Criseyde* works: the poem remains open, in spite of the narrator's piling on of closure devices. As a result, *Troilus and Criseyde* is not the comfortable reading experience many readers expect it to be, for Chaucer experiments with a narrative mode that encourages us to read actively, to ask questions, to worry about the whole process of signification, and to reconsider the ultimate end of the reading experience in which we are engaged.

---

[32] "Ethos, Pathos, and Logos in *Troilus and Criseyde*," 171.

[33] David, *The Strumpet Muse*, 33.

Troilus and Criseyde:
Another Dantean Reading

RICHARD NEUSE

This essay aligns itself with a number of discussions published in the last fifteen years that view TROILUS AND CRISEYDE from a Dantean perspective; it parts company with these to the extent that they treat the COMEDY's subtextual presence as an ironic commentary on the Trojan love affair. The stress on irony as the poem's dominant mode is traced to Bloomfield's idea, in his 1957 essay "Distance and Predestination in TROILUS AND CRISEYDE," of a gulf between the Christian narrator and the pagan world of his narrative. The idea is shown to be problematic in light of the pervasive Christian references especially in the speeches of the (pagan) characters. This curious stylistic feature suggests that TROILUS AND CRISEYDE realizes the COMEDY's "agenda" of intimating the spiritual compatibility, inseparability, even, of paganism and Christianity, and it allows for an unironic reading of the parallels between the Trojan lovers and the lovers reunited in Dante's Earthy Paradise. The real difference between the pairs of lovers is that one belongs to tragedy, the other to comedy. In TROILUS AND CRISEYDE the lovers experience sexual love as a cosmic force, but eventually are defeated by a world ruled by political passions and war. Instead of Dante's final "paradisal" vision Troilus receives one that, though still paradisal in the Dantean sense, leaves him sadly disillusioned with "this wrecched world adoun." His tragedy leaves both poet and reader impaled on the cleft stick of an unresolved conflict between a this-worldly and an other-worldly Christianity.

This reading of *Troilus and Criseyde* follows in the steps of a number of precursors, especially Monica McAlpine, R. A. Shoaf, Winthrop Wetherbee, and Karla Taylor,[1] who in recent years have shown the importance of the *Comedy* to an understanding of Chaucer's poem. My excuse for offering yet another discussion along the same lines is a persistent doubt concerning the essentially ironic role these scholars assign to the *Comedy* in the textual economy of the *Troilus*.

---

[1] See McAlpine, *Genre*; Shoaf, *Currency*; Winthrop Wetherbee, *Poets*; and Taylor, *Chaucer Reads*. Perhaps I should add that of these four McAlpine's, though not explicitly "Dantean" in its approach, is decidedly so in numerous details and in the general tenor of its insights. Finally, I should mention a very interesting article by James I. Wimsatt also broadly Dantean in orientation: "Medieval and Modern in Chaucer's *Troilus and Criseyde*," *PMLA* 92 (1977): 204–16.

At the risk of glossing over some important differences among them, I would characterize their approach as one in which the recurrent echoes of the *Comedy* are seen as ironic reminders of another, sublime world of values by comparison with which Chaucer's Trojan world falls pitifully short.

Though some scholars have argued that parallels with and allusions to the *Comedy* already serve a similarly ironic function in Chaucer's "source," the *Filostrato*,[2] I think this idea is especially congenial to discussions of the *Troilus* because it fits so well with the general view of the poem established by Morton Bloomfield's justly influential article "Distance and Predestination in *Troilus and Criseyde*,"[3] according to which the text constantly underscores and plays upon the moral-spiritual distance between the Christian poet-narrator—and his audience—and the pagan world of his poetic fiction.

Bloomfield, it will be remembered, sees the narrator of the *Troilus* as a "historian" who "meticulously maintains a distance between himself and the events in the story" (75–76),[4] a distance most notably in the religious sphere. "Troilus, Pandarus, and Criseyde are pagans," he writes.

> The great barrier of God's revelation at Sinai and in Christ separates Chaucer and us from them. Chaucer portrays them consciously as pagans, for he never puts Christian sentiments in their mouths.... They ... can attain to the truths of natural law—to the concept of a God, a creator, and to the rational moral law but never to the truths of revealed religion (79–80).

It is this very contention as well as the corollaries that have been drawn from it that I want to call into question, and in doing so I hope, incidentally, to move the *Troilus* back into the orbit of tragedy where I think it belongs.

Chaucer, then, I suggest, does not invoke the *Comedy* as a way of defining a vantage point superior to that of the Greeks and Trojans. To the contrary, it is my contention that in the *Troilus* he follows what might be called the *Comedy*'s agenda of rewriting history so as to demonstrate that in their concrete manifestations pagan and Christian are often hard if not impossible to distinguish and do not constitute an automatic moral or spiritual hierarchy. In conjunction with this I will argue that like the *Comedy* the *Troilus* contains an untraditional idea of sexual love. What links the two most emphatically is that in both, erotic love possesses a powerful religious, even theological, dimension. I will deal with this matter later on and here will merely restate it in rather different terms. In both poems, I suggest, love—its nature, its meaning, its place in the scheme of things—becomes a central enigma. And as something which involves separation and loss, love also becomes the most arduous moral and intellectual test a

---

[2] On this, see Nicholas Havely, "Tearing or Breathing? Dante's Influence on *Filostrato* and *Troilus*," *SAC: Proceedings* 1 (1984): 51–59.

[3] See the "List of Frequently Cited Works" above.

[4] Like Bloomfield, Lee Patterson (*Chaucer and the Subject of History* [Madison: Univ. of Wisconsin Press, 1991], chapter 2, "*Troilus and Criseyde* and the Subject of History") treats the author of the *Troilus* as a "historian" but unlike Bloomfield he does not attach any significance to the fact that he is dealing with a pagan past.

person can undergo. The "resolution" of this enigma, of this test, will mark one poem as a comedy, the other as a tragedy.[5]

My primary evidence for disputing the notion of a self-enclosed pagan world in the *Troilus* is a curious feature of its dialogue that to the best of my knowledge has been either neglected or overlooked. I am referring to the very considerable number of oaths, interjections, asseverations, and asides of a plainly Christian character that are sprinkled throughout the speeches of the pagan characters. In a footnote Bloomfield cites the oath " 'by that God that bought us bothe two' " (3.1165) with which Criseyde assures Troilus of her pure "entente." He attempts to dispose of this rather spectacular exception to his rule by citing the variant reading "wrought" in R. K. Root's text. Modern editions, like Barney's in the recent *Riverside Chaucer* and B. A. Windeatt's, favor "bought" (meaning, of course, "redeemed"); in any case, however, it is misleading to imply that this oath is the sole exception to the alleged rule, and "by that God that wrought us bothe two" is assuredly still an expression a fourteenth-century English audience would feel to be unmistakably Christian.

To illustrate just how extensive is the characters' use of Christian (by which I also designate Biblical) references would require either tedious tabulation or an amount of quotation well beyond the space at my disposal. Accordingly I will rely on the reader's willingness to look beyond the limited evidence I can provide here.[6] Many of those references, further, are altogether unobtrusive to the point of seeming mere verbal tics or fillers. Nonetheless, I would insist that they all contribute to a pattern whose larger significance in the narrative I will attempt to establish.

Criseyde is especially prone to refer to the Christian God (especially when talking with Pandarus). In her response to Pandarus's suggestion that she put her book away and do observance to May, this is made pretty unmistakable by other Christian references (which I have likewise italicized):

> "I? *God forbede!*" quod she, "be ye mad?
> Is that a widewes lif, *so God yow save?*
> *By God,* ye maken me ryght soore adrad!
> Ye ben so wylde, it semeth as ye rave.
> It sate me wel bet ay in a cave
> *To bidde and rede on holy seyntes lyves;*
> Lat maydens gon to daunce, and yonge wyves."

---

[5] As one who has been overly impressed by an ironic idea of the *Troilus*—see my *Chaucer's Dante: Allegory and Epic Theater in* THE CANTERBURY TALES (Berkeley: Univ. of California Press, 1991)—I am glad to offer the present essay as a kind of palinode.

[6] The reader of Shoaf's edition is helped by the fact that unlike the manuscripts and a number of modern editions like Root's and Windeatt's, it consistently capitalizes all references to the Christian God.

Throughout this essay, I use italics to mark the passages under consideration in *Troilus and Criseyde*.

"As evere thryve I," quod this Pandarus,
"Yet koude I telle a thyng to doon yow pleye."
"Now, uncle deere," quod she, "telle it us
For Goddes love; is than th'assege aweye?"
I am of Grekes so fered that I deye."   2.113–24

Of course, a pagan could theoretically use some of the expressions I have
italicized, though surely not "so God yow save," and a pagan would hardly
think of sitting in a cave and reading saints' lives, but the real point is after all
that the italicized language is what people in fourteenth-century England might
well use in talking with each other.

My next example, still from Book 1, again enforces the specifically Christian
character of the references precisely by their juxtaposition with the pagan. Told
that Pandarus has won Criseyde's love for him, Troilus exclaims:

"*O Venus deere,*
Thi myght, thi grace, yheried be it here!"

And to Pandare he held up bothe his hondes,
And seyde, "*Lord*, al thyn be that I have!
For I am hool, al brosten ben my bondes.
A thousand Troyes whoso that me yave,
Ech after other, *God so wys me save*."   2.972–78

Here the Christian reference in line 978 (and presumably in 975) follows so in-
conspicuously and yet unmistakably the impassioned apostrophe to Venus that
I am prepared to suggest that Chaucer is at least partly dealing in subliminal ef-
fects. Without being (fully) conscious of it, the reader is seduced into accepting
perhaps not just the compatibility but even the interchangeability of pagan and
Christian, first of all on the level of a kind of verbal automatism. The proof of
this would seem to be that even careful readers, as I suggested earlier, do not
seem to have noticed their more or less continuous juxtaposition.

Here is a brief list of interjections and the like following Troilus's just-quoted
prayer to Venus and also illustrating the juxtaposition of pagan and Christian
references. Pandarus (to Troilus): "for the love of Marte" (988), "God toforn"
(992), "pardee, God woot" (995), "God help me so" (1004), "God shilde us fro
meschaunce" (1019), "by that Lord that formede est and west" (1053); Troilus:
"Depardieux" (1058), "blisful God prey ich with good entente" (1060), "and
thow, Minerva, the white, / Yif thow me wit my lettre to devyse" (1062–63);
Pandarus (to Criseyde): "By God" (1107), "helpe me God" (1126); Criseyde (to
Pandarus): "For love of God" (1131), "by God" (1138); Pandarus (to Criseyde):
"for Goddes love" (1200); Criseyde: "Depardieux, ... God leve al be wel! /
God help me so" (1212–13).

Turning to Book 3, we find the same pattern. Before he removes the candle,
here is Pandarus addressing the lovers, whom he has helped put in bed to-
gether: "*for the love of God*, syn ye ben brought / In thus good plit, lat now no
hevy thought / Ben hangyng in the hertes of yow tweye" (1138–40; my em-
phasis). Then, after the lovers have cleared up their "misunderstanding" and

Criseyde has asked Troilus's forgiveness for pain she caused him,

> This Troilus, with blisse of that supprised,
> *Putte al in Goddes hand*, as he that mente
> Nothyng but wel; and sodeynly avysed,
> He hire in armes faste to hym hente.   1184–87

The italicized phrase is of course the narrator's, but presumably intended to express Troilus's thought or state of mind. Juxtaposed with his clasping her in his arms, its effect is certainly comic, but for all that the language implies that (the Christian) God has a hand in this affair. Troilus himself is in no doubt about the matter as he goes on to address Criseyde:

> "Now *wolde God* I wiste,
> Myn herte swete, how I yow myght plese!
> . . . .
> Here may men seen that *mercy passeth right*;
> . . . .
> And *for the love of God*, my lady deere,
> Syn *God hath wrought me* for I shall yow serve,
> . . . .
> N'y wol nat, certein, breken youre defence;
> And if I do, present or in absence,
> *For love of God*, lat sle me with the dede."   1277–1301

These examples must suffice, but I should note that our Christian narrator shares his characters' penchant for repeated and often seemingly redundant references to the deity. Earlier, for instance, describing Troilus riding by in the street below Criseyde's window, he exclaims:

> *God woot* if he sat on his hors aright,
> Or goodly was biseyn, that ilke day!
> *God woot* wher he was lik a manly knyght!   1261–63

Describing Criseyde's reaction, he exclaims again:

> *To God hope I*, she hath now kaught a thorn,
> She shal nat pulle it out this nexte wyke.
> *God sende mo* swich thornes on to pike!   1272–74

This habit of invoking God's participation in the events of his pagan story, of which I have given just a limited sample, blossoms into the narrator's full-scale *participation mystique* in the lovers' first night in bed together. "O blisful nyght," he exclaims

> of hem so longe isought,
> How blithe unto hem bothe two thow weere!
> Why nad I swich oon with my soule ybought,
> Awey, thow foule daunger and thow feere,
> And lat hem in this hevene blisse dwelle,
> That is so heigh that al ne kan I telle!   3.1317–23

Peter Dronke has pointed out echoes in this passage of the Church's Easter-night liturgy, which begins *O vere beata nox*, and he has remarked upon the "strong undercurrent of language relating to the Redemption" in Book 1.[7]

An example of what Dronke has in mind is the already-cited oath "by that God that boughte us two" (3.1165) that Criseyde uses in telling Troilus he has no reason for jealousy. Throughout the entire account of the lovers' night together, as Dronke has suggested, there are verbal hints pointing to an implicit equation between their erotic passion and Christ's passion on the cross. And this would account for the narrator's hyperbolic, perhaps shocking, exclamation, "Why nad I swich oon with my soule ybought, / Ye, or the leeste joie that was theere?"

This, I take it, is a deeply serious statement, not made for any shock value, least of all for the kind of "ironic humor" D. W. Robertson, Jr. finds in the use of religious imagery in Book 1.[8] When the narrator tells us that Criseyde forgives Pandarus his deception of the night before, he uses an interjection, "What, God foryaf his deth, and she al so / Foryaf, and with here uncle gan to pleye" (3.1577–78), which Shoaf glosses as "God forgave those responsible for his crucifixion." Flippant and blasphemous though the interjection may be, for that reason it will hardly qualify as the skeptical irony of Robertson's Christian moralist.[9]

That the lovers' association with the Crucifixion extends well beyond their night of erotic joy is evident in the scene in Book 4 when they have learned of the parliament's decision to exchange Criseyde for Antenor.

> Tho woful teeris that they leten falle
> As bittre weren, out of teris kynde,
> For peyne, as is *ligne aloes* or *galle*.
> So bittre teeris weep nought, as I fynde,
> The woful Mirra thorugh the bark and rynde.   4.1135–39

Combined with the terms italicized, the simile of Myrrha "weeping" through the bark becomes a powerful, if submerged, allusion to the Crucifixion. Myrrha, after incest with her father, gave birth to Adonis when she had been metamorphosed into a myrrh tree. In the gospel narratives, finally, Jesus on the cross receives a "mixture of myrrh and aloes" (John 19.29), "vinegar mingled with gall" (Matthew 27.34), or "wine mingled with myrrh" (Mark 15.23).[10]

---

[7] See Peter Dronke, "The Conclusion of *Troilus and Criseyde*," *MÆ* 23 (1964): 47–52, at 50–51.

[8] See Robertson, *Preface*, 487: the religious imagery serves "to suggest the values the hero inverts and, at the same time, to furnish opportunity for ironic humor" (487).

[9] Though he forgets that Criseyde is here forgiving Pandarus, not Troilus, Rowe (*O Love!*, 105), takes seriously the idea of her Christ-like mercy. On a blasphemous reading of the phrase, Criseyde is like God in that both knew perfectly well beforehand what they were getting themselves into. Blasphemy, it may be helpful to remind ourselves, by no means has to be the expression of an irreligious attitude, as the mystery plays and the *Miller's Tale*, for example, make clear.

[10] Rowe (*O Love!*, 146, 148) notes two other echoes of the Crucifixion in Troilus's words to Criseyde, at 1.422–23 and 4.1209–10.

In the fourteenth century, and since, the great literary model for the representation of erotic love with an intensely religious dimension is Dante's, in the *Vita Nuova* and *Comedy*. It is Dante's "affair" with Beatrice, as especially Monica McAlpine and Winthrop Wetherbee have shown, that serves as a model for the love relationship in *Troilus in Criseyde*.[11] To be sure, the love between Dante and Beatrice lacks the element of physical intimacy that is of such obvious importance in the *Troilus*. But it seems clear from the *Comedy* as well as the *Vita Nuova*[12]—though this is obviously not the place to argue the matter—that theirs is definitely an erotic love. Beatrice, that is to say, is not loved and desired as an abstract ideal—whether Platonic, moral, theological, or whatever—but as a genuine "other" who, though dead, is nevertheless somehow "embodied." At the same time, their reunion in the Earthly Paradise, after Beatrice's death, and the progression of their love relationship from that point on, is marked by an increasing religious awareness that gradually erases the old antithesis between pagan and Christian.

A striking example of this is furnished by Canto 8 of the *Paradiso*, where Dante and Beatrice suddenly find themselves in the sphere of (the planet) Venus, something the Pilgrim realizes when he sees that Beatrice is even more beautiful than before (8.14–15). The canto itself opens with the suggestion that the ancients made gods of Venus and Cupid because they feared erotic passion, *folle amore* (8.1–9 and 22). But as the mention of Beatrice's increased beauty (in the eyes of the Pilgrim) makes clear, the poet is not concerned to demystify love, but rather to suggest that Christianity has corrected the ancients' ancient error and Christians need not fear the influence of Venus' rays, and this is shown by the blessed spirits in her sphere, ranging from the Wife of Bath-like Cunizza to the harlot Rahab.[13]

I have already discussed examples of a similar interpenetration of pagan and Christian in an erotic context in the *Troilus*. At this point I want to draw attention once more to one of those seemingly casual phrases which in the course of its frequent use by the characters and narrator, gathers to itself a new and unexpected semantic charge. The phrase is "for (the) love of God" or "for Goddes love."[14] In the mouth of the pagan characters and juxtaposed with references to their gods, it undergoes a kind of insensible assimilation to the god of love (six times so named in the *Troilus*), raising the possibility that the biblical deity, in Dantean spirit, includes rather than banishes the pagan gods of love. The reiteration of the phrase, in other words, might serve as a subliminal reinforcement, as it were, of the claim made in the hymn to Venus at the beginning of Book 3, that "God loveth, and to love wol noght werne" (3.12).

That there *is* powerful opposition to that possibility the narrator is keenly

---

[11] See McAlpine's sensitive comments in *Genre*, 152ff. Wetherbee, *Poets* (145, 146, 172, 178), draws attention to parallels between the two.

[12] See Robert Harrison, *The Body of Beatrice* (Baltimore: Johns Hopkins Univ. Press, 1988). Chaucer's possible knowledge of the *Vita Nuova* cannot be discussed here.

[13] See *Para.* 9.13ff. and 112ff.

[14] By my count, there are 42 uses of this phrase out of a total of 319 references to God (excluding, in other words, all those to pagan gods).

aware, as witness his impassioned speech after the lovers, still in bed, have ex-
changed various gifts, including rings:

> *Lord,* trowe ye a coveytous or a wrecche,
> That blameth love, and halt of it despit,
> That of tho pens that he kan mokre and crecche
> Was evere yit yyeven hym swich delit
> Nay, douteles, *for also God me save,*
> So perfit joie may no nygard have.

> They wol seyn "yis," *but Lord!* so that they lye,
> Tho besy wrecches, ful of wo and drede!
> Thei callen love a woodnesse or folie,
> But it shall falle hem as I shal yow rede,
> They shal forgon the white and ek the rede,
> And lyve in wo, *ther God yeve hem meschaunce,*
> And every lovere in his trouthe avaunce!

> As *wolde God* tho wrecches that dispise
> Servise of love hadde erys also longe
> As hadde Mida, ful of coveytise,
> And therto dronken hadde as hoot and stronge
> As Crassus dide for his affectis wronge,
> To techen hem that coveytise is vice,
> And love is vertu, though men holde it nyce.   3.1373–93

Who are these avaricious despisers of love? The mention of Midas and Crassus
might recall the fifth terrace of Dante's Purgatory, where their stories are re-
cited, along with those of a number of others, by the penitents, precisely "To
techen hem that coveytise is vice" (*Purg.* 20.101–17). The line following this
one, however, seems to imply that not just the avaricious, but the generality of
mankind, consider love foolishness rather than virtue.

In the perspective of the *Troilus,* as of the *Comedy,* love is *like* a religion.
Troilus's conversion to love in Book 1 is compared by Pandarus to the conver-
sion of heretical "clerks" to the true faith (1.988–1008). As the Crucifixion ref-
erences we have noted might imply, it requires a "death of the self," and as the
narrator's just-quoted outburst implies, it may require a stance antithetical to
the common ways of the world. In any case, it is far from the shallow "religion
of love" C. S. Lewis ascribes to the tradition on which the *Troilus* is supposed
to draw.[15] That is evident, too, from the Dantean character of the spontane-
ous hymn Troilus utters in bed with Criseyde after the sexual consummation:

> "O Love, O Charite!

---

[15] See *The Allegory of Love: A Study in Medieval Tradition* (1936; reprinted New York:
Galaxy Books, 1958). Like Lewis, commentators usually "know" that they are dealing with
an erotic "pseudo-religion" whose conventions and sentiments are familiar if not to every
schoolboy at least to every student of medieval literature.

Thi moder ek, Citherea the swete,
After thiself next heried be she

. . . .

Benigne Love, thow holy bond of thynges,
Whoso wol grace, and list the nought honouren,
Lo, his desir wol fle withouten wynges."

3.1254-56; 1261-63

Troilus's language conveys the thrill of a deeply personal discovery. It suggests that he has experienced a force that has transformed him ("fro cares colde") and his entire sense of the world. He begins by attributing this transformative power to Cupid and his mother Venus (doubling as a planet), as well as to Imeneus (Hymen). And then, in the second stanza (1261-67), which adapts to Cupid or "Benigne Love" what St Bernard in *Paradiso* 33 attributes to the Virgin Mary, Troilus's intensely personal feeling for Criseyde becomes at the same time, Dante-fashion, the basis for a powerful moral and philosophical vision.[16]

The intertextuality with the *Comedy* here is especially significant. One reason St. Bernard's prayer occupies the climactic place it does in the poem is that the saint's devotion to Mary parallels—dare we say prefigures?—the poet-pilgrim's to Beatrice. And what Troilus attributes to "Benigne Love" is after all due to Criseyde, who in his letter to her (5.1419-20) is seen as "his agent of salvation, his Mary or Beatrice" (Wetherbee 80). Like Beatrice, Criseyde throughout is associated with light and bliss (Rowe 96-100) and has the "eyen brighte" (4.310) or "clere" (3.129; 1353; 5.566) that provoke the narrator's claim:

But for to speken of hire eyen cleere,
Lo, trewely, they writen that hire syen,
That Paradis stood formed in hire yën   5.815-17

—lines that recall especially the *Paradiso*, where the Pilgrim sees so consistently in and through Beatrice's eyes that she is prompted to remind him that "not only in my eyes is Paradise" (*Para.* 18.21: "non pur ne' miei occhi è paradiso").[17]

Despite the bad press, then, that Criseyde has had, for the most part, among the commentators,[18] she has the essential attributes of a "Beatrice figure." What, I can hear the reader object, of her eventual betrayal of Troilus? It seems to me altogether too much has been made of this, especially by those who read backwards from it to the Criseyde of the earlier books and find her an essentially faithless, frivolous, or unstable type from the outset. Furthermore, the

---

[16] For an illuminating commentary on Troilus's hymn, see Wetherbee, *Poets*, 80ff. But where Wetherbee finds a "confusion of earthly and divine in Troilus's view of love" (85) I find, rather, *fusion* in the Dantean manner. McAlpine's remarks (*Genre*, 158) on the consummation scene are as usual very illuminating and highly relevant to the general argument of this essay.

[17] The allusion is noted in Windeatt's edition, *ad loc.*

[18] A notable recent exception is Dinshaw, *Poetics* (*included in this volume*).

term "betrayal" seems needlessly melodramatic and hyperbolic. Being, the narrator says, "slydynge of corage" (5.825), she may be said to *slide* into the affair with Diomede, hardly the calculated act of betrayal, say, her father Calkas commits (1.71ff.). Indeed, the narrator, who appears so anxious to excuse her offense, fails to mention what seems the most important extenuating circumstance, namely that in being sent to the Greek camp in exchange for Antenor Criseyde has reason to feel betrayed herself.[19]

Even remembering Criseyde's statement to her uncle early in the poem, "I am of Grekes so fered that I deye" (2.124), the reader may still feel that my last point is illicitly outside the scope of the text. I will return to this point in a moment, but first I will concede that Criseyde, like any humanly conceived character, is a Beatrice with limitations and defects. What I am intent on guarding against in "defending" her is the impulse to locate the "cause" of the love tragedy in some pseudo-Aristotelian character flaw of either protagonist or in their kind of love. The love tragedy of Shakespeare's *Romeo and Juliet* seems a particularly useful parallel to *Troilus and Criseyde* in this respect. In both cases the ultimate precipitate of the tragedy is rather specific and palpable, to wit, the family feud in Verona and the war between the Greeks and Trojans.

In referring to these as the "precipitate" of the tragedy I mean to differentiate them from the tragic *idea* in either work. In the case of the *Troilus* that idea has less to do, directly, with the lovers as individual characters than as representatives of what I am inclined to call simply *another way* of love, life, religion. For all their exaltation and all their suffering, neither Troilus nor Criseyde has the stature of Romeo and Juliet, say, who at a crucial moment take matters in their own hands and assert a heroic will as well as a personal grandeur that makes them anything but passive victims of their elders' bloody folly. Troilus and Criseyde, to the contrary, without incurring any blame for it, conform their wills to the political and military imperatives of the world around them.

Commentators have repeatedly made the point that Troilus—whose name means "little Troy"—represents his city and that his love affair mirrors the eventual fate of his city. I want to take this idea seriously, but in quite a different sense from the way it has usually been developed. Thus I accept Eugene Vance's description of Troy as a city of lovers and Troilus and Criseyde as their preeminent representatives. But whereas Vance sees this as the very *cause* of the city's downfall,[20] I suggest, to the contrary, that we are meant to see it positively, as a sign of its unique distinction. Riming with *joy* (e.g., 5.1546–47), it is a place of Arnoldian sweetness and light, of song and the social graces, of brotherly and parental love (as witness Troilus's tender apostrophe to the city, his father, mother, and brothers: 4.1205–7), a place, in other words, where love in the widest possible sense prevails and people eagerly help each other in need.

In the *Troilus* there are, at the same time, recurrent references to another, very different city, namely Thebes. In briefest outline I propose that the two

---

[19] As Shoaf (*Currency*, 108) says: Criseyde "will, in fact, be sold."

[20] See Eugene Vance, *Mervelous Signals: Poetics and Sign Theory in the Middle Ages* (Lincoln: Univ. of Nebraska Press, 1986), chapter 9.

cites, Troy and Thebes, comes to be seen as more or less starkly opposed paradigms of history. Thus Thebes incarnates the story of the contested kingdom, of an interminable Oedipal struggle, of sibling fighting against sibling,[21] of the earthly city perennially doomed by its penchant for violence and the *libido dominandi*. Readers will have no trouble recognizing here the traditional paradigm of history in the West, enshrined as it is in its sacred as well as profane historiographic monuments.

Now, it is of course true that for all their differences, Troy in *Troilus and Criseyde* looks like another Thebes in the making. It, too, is besieged and doomed to destruction. But there the parallel between the two stops. Despite the siege, the ladies gathered in Criseyde's house to listen to a reading of the *Thebaid* evidently see no connection between the fate of Thebes and the impending fate of Troy (of which they are obviously ignorant). For them Statius's poem is a *romance* (2.100) rather than a solemn epic exemplum or *memento temporis acti* and *futuri*.

By this ingenious gesture reducing Statius's monumental epic to the status of a courtly entertainment, the author of the *Troilus* wittily establishes the claim of his own five-book tragedy as itself a new epic discourse (prophetic of the novel waiting in the wings to displace the epic altogether) whose paradigm is eros, the various civilized forms people have of dealing with each other, rather than the ancient tale of war and fratricidal strife. Unlike Statius's Thebans "burdened by an almost paralyzing sense of" their past history, in Wetherbee's incisive formulation (117), the Trojans show as little interest in the war outside their walls as the narrator himself, who insists both at the beginning and end of his poem (1.140ff.; 5.1765ff.) that it does not belong in his narrative plan.

Allusions to the Theban war, far from serving to satirize the Trojans heedless of coming disaster,[22] are, on the contrary, themselves subjected to varying degrees of irony. This is particularly evident when Cassandra is asked to explicate Troilus's dream of the boar (5.1234ff.). Not only does she resort to the totally simplistic device of identifying the boar with Diomede (on "genealogical" grounds), but in the process she also gives a confused and irrelevant capsule summary of the entire *Thebaid*. To her Statius's epic does represent the master narrative of history. Like a pagan Old Testament,[23] she endows it and its prophecies (5.1494) with a kind of scriptural authority able to resolve life's mysteries (5.1485–1512).

It fits with the picture we get of Troy and its way of life that Troilus dismisses Cassandra as "thow sorceresse, / With all thy false goost of prophecye!" (5.1520–21) and that her prophecies are doomed to fall on deaf ears. The dismissal of Cassandra also fits with what I have called the new epic discourse of

---

[21] One of these, Antigone, makes an unexpected appearance in Troy, having undergone a significant metamorphosis into Criseyde's Trojan niece and singer of a Trojan love song: see 2.826ff.

[22] As alleged by Anderson in his "Theban History in Chaucer's *Troilus*," esp. 109, 120, 132.

[23] Some medieval commentators appear to have viewed the *Thebaid* in that light; cf. Anderson, "Theban," 116.

the *Troilus* and its attitude to war (cf. 5.1765-71). When the narrator does stray into that sphere the result tends to be burlesque. Thus Hector's death is elaborately anticipated (5.1548-54), but the actual event is presented as grotesquely unheroic when Achilles kills him unknowingly, almost accidentally, while Hector is dragging a king by the "aventaille" (1558-61). In the epic scheme of the *Troilus* Hector's death has no "historical" significance.

Like Hector, Troilus receives high praise as a warrior until the very end but also dies ignominiously at the hands of Achilles. But this is in the epilogue, after the farewell to "litel myn tragedye" (1786), when the latter's implications are starting to become clear, as signalled—again, unobtrusively!—by that odd exclamation:

> But weilaway, save only Goddes wille!
> Despitously hym slough the fierse Achille.   1805-6

By way of a very brief epilogue, I would like to conclude with the suggestion that Troilus's posthumous ascent to the eighth sphere and derisory vision of "This litel spot of erthe" (5.1815), though itself inspired by the *Paradiso*,[24] may be seen as a kind of counterpart to the Pilgrim's final vision in *Paradiso 33*. The two visions, the Pilgrim's and Troilus's, might well serve as symbolic epitomes, not of opposed metaphysical systems, and certainly not of Christianity and paganism, but of a comic and a tragic hero's final perspectives, the one with his heaven-conquering love, the other with his greatly diminished sense of what love avails "in this wrecched world adoun."

---

[24] Canto 22.133-54, as well as by Arcita's ascent to the eighth sphere in Book 11 of the *Teseida*.

Sweet Persuasion: The Subject of *Fortune in* Troilus and Criseyde

LARRY SCANLON

The role of Fortune is a traditional problem in TROILUS AND CRISEYDE scholarship. A fuller appreciation of that role can come from exploring the complex political value Fortune had in medieval culture. Returning to Boethius's PHILO-SOPHIAE CONSOLATIO, we find Fortune figures the limit of ruling-class hegemony, that is, the point where the common interest that holds members of the ruling class together breaks down. As both personification and deity, Fortune figures that limit by simultaneously establishing a subject position (that of a deity), and declaring that this subject position (as a personification) is fictional. In TROILUS AND CRISEYDE Chaucer uses Fortune's double value to complicate his analysis of the social construction of sexual desire. By framing Troilus's loss of Criseyde in the fourth book as a downturn of Fortune, Chaucer can present Troilus as trapped in the very circuit of patriarchal power he struggles to escape.

Cassandra's brief exegetical turn in Book 5 of the *Troilus* is one of the many bits of extra business Chaucer adds to Boccaccio's *Il Filostrato* and his other sources. Troilus asks her to interpret his dream, in which Criseyde kisses a boar. For a soothsayer, her response is oddly mediated through textual tradition:

> She gan first smyle, and seyde, "O brother deere,
> If thow a soth of this desirest knowe,
> Thow most a fewe of olde stories heere,
> To purpos, how that Fortune overthrowe
> Hath lordes olde; thorugh which, withinne a throwe,
> Thow wel this boor shalt knowe, and of what kynde
> He comen is, as men in bokes fynde."   5.1457–63

This appeal to "olde stories" is odd as a form of prophecy. Nevertheless, it clearly alludes to another work of Boccaccio's, one considered more important by his immediate posterity than *Il Filostrato*, the *De casibus virorum illustrium*. The *De casibus* was precisely a collection of "olde stories," which demonstrated how "Fortune overthrowe / Hath lordes olde." Indeed, as Willard Farnham suggested over half a century ago, in a work now largely forgotten, Cassandra "composes" in the lines that follow "a brief *De Casibus* ... of the rises and falls in that line of princes from which Diomede is descended, beginning with

Meleager" (149)–the figure whom the boar symbolizes.[1] Boccaccio mentions
Meleager in the first book of the *De Casibus*, a book which is dominated by the
Theban story, and other accounts of internecine conflict in ancient Greece.
Cassandra characterizes the operation of Fortune as specifically political, the
overthrowing of lords, and the term "overthrowe," echoes the phrase *revoluti-
onum Fortune*, which Boccaccio uses to sum up the chapter where he discusses
Meleager.[2] Moreover, this specifically political dimension of Fortune takes us
all the way back to Boethius, who links it to tragedy, the very mode which Boc-
caccio and the other earlier Italian humanists revived, and which Chaucer
brought to England.[3] In Book 2 of the *Consolatio*, Philosophy asks, "Quid
tragoediarum clamor aliud deflet nisi in discreto ictu fortunam felicia regna
vertentem?" which Chaucer translates as "What other thynge bywaylen the
cryinges of tragedyes but oonly the dedes of Fortune, that with an unwar
strook overturneth the realms of greet nobleye?"[4]

This essay will offer a brief reassessment of Fortune's role in *Troilus and
Criseyde*, concentrating on its politics. I have two goals. The first is mainly nega-
tive and corrective. Too much criticism of this poem has considered Chaucer's
many invocations of Fortune a straightforward gloss on the poem's narrative,
which make it an "exemplum of false felicity."[5] These readings treat the figure
as distinct from the rest of the poem, an entirely external principle which im-
poses an unproblematic moral standard on it.[6] Such an approach impoverishes
both the poem and the cultural complexity of this figure. Recovering the
figure's political dimension will restore its rhetorical complexity. This is my sec-
ond, more positive goal: I want to demonstrate the extent to which Fortune's
figuration and its politics are interdependent, and the contribution this interde-
pendence makes to the poem's thoroughgoing analysis of the social construc-
tion of desire. As the recent work of David Aers, Carolyn Dinshaw, Stephen
Knight, Arlyn Diamond and others has made clear, this social analysis is

---

[1] Willard Farnham, *The Medieval Heritage of Elizabethan Tragedy* (1936; reprint New York:
Barnes & Noble, 1956), 149.

[2] Giovanni Boccaccio, *De Casibus Virorum Illustrium*, ed. Branca, I.xii.9 (66). Subsequent
citations are from this edition; book, chapter and sentence numbers will be given in the text.

[3] Renate Haas, "Chaucer's *Monk's Tale*: An Ingenious Criticism of Early Humanist
Conceptions of Tragedy," *HumLov* 36 (1987): 44–57.

[4] Boethius, *Philosophiae Consolatio*, ed. Ludwig Bieler, *Corpus Christianorum, Series Latina*,
94 (Turnholt: Brepols, 1957), 2 Pr. 2.12. Subsequent citations will be from this edition. Book,
chapter and sentence numbers will be given in the text. I cite Chaucer's *Boece* from *The
Riverside Chaucer*, 2 Pr. 2.67–70.

[5] Steadman, *Laughter*, 127.

[6] This reading is usually associated with D.W. Roberston, Jr. (see esp. "Chaucerian
Tragedy," *ELH* 19 [1952]: 1–37) but it has also been propounded by others who do not
consider themselves Robertsonian, and it considerably predates Robertson. It occurs as early
as Howard Rollins Patch, "Troilus on Predestination," *JEGP* 17 (1918): 399–422. For two
recent versions, see John V. Fleming, *Classical Imitation and Interpretation in Chaucer's
"Troilus"* (Lincoln: Univ. of Nebraska Press, 1990), esp. 216–45; and Katherine Heinrichs,
" 'Lovers' Consolations of Philosophy' in Boccaccio, Machaut, and Chaucer," *SAC* 11 (1989):
93–115.

self-conscious, rhetorically sophisticated and complex.[7] The contribution Fortune makes to it is no less so. But this complexity is neither the static complexity of the organic form of the New Critics, nor the only slightly more dynamic, universalized textuality of most post-structuralism. It is rather the complexity of history, "bound up with specific social and ideological systems," and articulated within the rhetorical space of the poem.[8]

The notion that the figure Fortune always delivers the same, unchanging dismissal of human history, irrespective of its context, begins with a reductive reading of the *Consolatio*, the work which bequeathes the figure to the Middle Ages. Philosophy introduces the figure in Book 2 as a preliminary step to lead Boethius out of his despondent state, and toward a rational acceptance of it. "When Fortune smiled on you," she tells him,

> Solebas enim praesentem quoque, blandientem quoque virilibus incessere verbis eamque de nostro adyto prolatis insectabare sententiis. Verum omnis subita mutatio rerum non sine quodam quasi fluctu contingit animorum; sic factum est ut tu quoque paulipser a tua tranquillitate descisceres. Sed tempus est haurire te aliquid ac degustare molle atque iucundum, quod ad interiora transmissum validioribus haustibus viam fecerit. Adsit igitur rhetoricae suadela dulcedinis quae tum tantum recta calle procedit cum nostra instituta non desirit cumque hac musica laris nostri vernacula nunc leviores nunc graviores modes succinat.
>
> 2 Pr. 1.5–8

> you manfully scorned her and attacked her with principles drawn from my deepest wisdom. But every sudden change of fortune brings with it a certain disquiet in the soul; and this is what has caused you to lose your peace of mind. Now is the time for you to take some gentle and pleasant remedy which may prepare you for stronger medicine. I shall use the sweet persuasion of rhetoric, which is suitable enough if it does not contradict the truths of philosophy, and I shall add the grace of Music, a servant of mine whose songs are sometimes happy and sometimes sad.[9]

The "sweet persuasion of rhetoric" turns out to be an exploration of the figure of Fortune's wheel, through which Philosophy conveys the complete arbitrariness of human history. This purely rhetorical consolation will prepare the way for the more philosophical consolations to follow. By the end Boethius realizes

---

[7] Aers, *Chaucer, Community,* 117–52; Diamond, "Politics"; Dinshaw, *Poetics,* 28–64 (*included in this volume*); Stephen Knight, *Geoffrey Chaucer* (Oxford: Basil Blackwell, 1986), 32–65. See now also Lee Patterson, *Chaucer and the Subject of History* (Madison: Univ. of Wisconsin Press, 1991), 84–164.

[8] Aers, *Community,* 118.

[9] Boethius, *The Consolation of Philosophy,* tr. Richard Green (Indianapolis: The Bobbs–Merrill Co., 1962), 21. All subsequent translations will be from this edition. Page numbers will be given in the text.

even bad fortune is good, for it teaches one the ephemeral nature of all ex-
ternal goods, and realizes further that his very fixation on his misfortune was
a symptom of his philosophical naivety. The preliminary role the figure For-
tune plays in this process has usually been read in entirely literal terms.
Boethius's movement beyond his fixation on Fortune is usually assumed to take
him beyond the rhetorical as well, into a supra-rhetorical realm of philosophical
understanding. It is further assumed that this lesson passes into medieval lit-
erary culture fully and invariantly formed. Every time the figure appears it de-
livers this lesson, and every character who bewails his or her misfortune does
nothing more than reveal their philosophical immaturity.

This view is problematic in respect both to the *Consolatio* itself, and in rela-
tion to its use in medieval culture. The desire to derive some invariant lesson
from the *Consolatio* that will serve as a master-key to all the subsequent works
it influences reduces it from a dialogue to something approaching a catechism.
It is clear that the notion of Fortune represents a preliminary stage, but it is
considerably less clear that the dialogue ever completely escapes that stage. For-
tune's apparent injustice continues to bother Boethius, and while Philosophy
gets him to see that this question is actually "the greatest of all mysteries" (in-
volving among other things, "the simplicity of Providence, the course of Fate,
unforeseeable chance, divine foreknowledge and free will") she cannot ulti-
mately resolve it. He must be content with the knowledge that the intricacies
of Divine Justice are simply unavailable to the limited consciousness of human
beings (4 Pr. 5-6; 89-96).

The openendedness of this conclusion leaves philosophic space for Fortune
in spite of its purely figural and rhetorical status. To the extent philosophy can-
not make the Divine Good intelligible in its own terms, human understanding
is thrown back on rhetorical stopgaps like the figure of Fortune and her wheel.
Nor does the more ratiocinative consolation Philosophy herself offers ever
cease to be rhetorical. As a personified abstraction, Philosophy is a rhetorical
convention. If it is true, as Seth Lerer rightly observes, "the dialogue itself
gradually moves to philosophical monologue," the monologue is not offered in
the unmarked, ostensibly neutral, authorial voice we usually associate with
philosophical exposition.[10] It is offered instead in the voice of a rhetorical
projection, whose relation to Boethius's authorial voice is ambiguous from the
beginning, and is only made more ambiguous by the fact that the voice he
identifies as his own within the dialogue is the one her monologue silences.

Yet these ambiguities become an insurmountable problem only if we deny
the inherently paradoxical rhetorical goal the *Consolatio* announces in its very
title. It is a text to designed to *console*, that is, to do a certain kind of work in
the world. The spiritual transcendence it offers Boethius does not allow him to
escape the world. On the contrary, the *Consolatio* enables him to come to terms
with it. In this respect the later philosophizing is no less a matter of "sweet per-

---

[10] Seth Lerer, *Boethius and Dialogue: Literary Method in* THE CONSOLATION OF PHILOSOPHY
(Princeton: Princeton Univ. Press, 1985), 167.

suasion" than the earlier poetic figurations.[11] Philosophy's shift to rational argument simply replaces one form of rhetoric with another. But this more transcendent rhetoric is still tied to the world by virtue of the task of consolation it aspires to perform there. Its radically paradoxical task ties it as well to the more preliminary, but equally paradoxical figure of Fortune.

The Middle Ages clearly understood and valued Fortune's figural complexity. As Derek Pearsall astutely observes:

> The paradox of Boethius's influence upon the Middle Ages ... is that the illusions of Fortune's power that Philosophy so authoritatively dispels proved more potent and resilient as images than the rational arguments demonstrating their non-existence. Medieval literature is full of portraits of the awesome goddess Fortuna, and particularly fond of demonstrations of the remorseless and arbitrary power of her Wheel.[12]

For later medieval culture, there is no better illustration of the image's potency than Boccaccio's *De casibus*, which uses Fortune as the central organizing principle in an encyclopedic exploration of the falls of illustrious men from Adam to contemporary princes. Often mistakenly assigned to the tradition of the *De contemptu mundi*, the work is in fact much more closely related to the *Fürstenspiegel*, the Mirror of Princes. Boccaccio's Prohemium, whose opening sentence echoes the opening Thomas Aquinas's *Fürstenspiegel*, *De regno ad regem Cypri*, clearly locates itself in the *Fürstenspiegel* tradition, announcing as its purpose the moral correction of princes and acknowledging "the enormous volumes of our betters in this matter" (1 Pr. 4).[13] For Boccaccio the rhetorical effect of Fortune is not simply to console, but also to empower. It enables him to speak to princes in their own language, making his moral correction that much more persuasive (1 Pr. 6).

---

[11] Lerer, *Boethius and Dialogue*, 147–49.

[12] Derek Pearsall, *The Canterbury Tales* (London: George Allen & Unwin, 1985), 281.

[13] Boccaccio's sentence begins:

Exquirenti michi quid ex labore studiorum meorum possem forsan rei publice utilitatis addere, occurrere preter creditum multa; maiori tamen conatu tamen in mentem sese ingessere principum atque presidentium ...

I was wondering how the labor of my studies might perhaps add to the benefit of the state, and many things occurred to me beyond belief, but the obscene desires of princes and rulers in general were forced upon my mind with particular energy.

Aquinas's work, formerly known as *De regimine principum*, begins:

Cogitandi mihi quid offerrem regiae celsitudini dignum, meaeque professioni congruum et officio, id occurrit potissime offerendum, ut regi librum conscriberem. . . .

As I was turning over in my mind what I might present to your Majesty as a gift at once worthy of your Royal Highness and befitting my profession and office, it seemed to me a highly appropriate offering that for a king I should write a book on kingship.

See *De regimine principum, Ad regem Cypri*, ed. Joseph Mathis (Torino: Marietti, 1948), 1. The translation is that of Gerald B. Phelan, *On Kingship*, rev. with introduction and notes by I. Th. Eschmann (Toronto: PIMS, 1949), 2. The first clause is a Ciceronian formula, from the opening of *De oratore*.

Nevertheless, to understand fully the political charge Fortune held for medieval court audiences, it is necessary to return to the *Consolatio* and examine the dramatic circumstances in which its sweet persuasion is offered. As a senator condemned for treason, deprived of his property and imprisoned, what Boethius faces is expulsion from the ruling class. If this dilemma affects him most directly, it also implicates the ruling class as a whole. For it presents the possibility that the hegemonic power in which each member has some share can suddenly and unpredictably turn against him. The *Consolatio*'s dramatic situation marks the ideological limit of the internal unity of the ruling class. Fortune figures that limit, and figures it in such a way as to reduce its threat. For although the image of Fortune and her wheel speaks to the contingency of material power, it understands such contingency as absolutely random, and denies it any coherent historical specificity. It assumes an invariable baseline against which increases or losses are measured, an immutable *status quo*, which in application will turn out to be the existing class structure.

Speaking in Fortune's voice, Philosophy declares,

Haec nostra vis est, hunc continuum ludum ludimus: rotam volubili orbe versamus, infima summis summa infimis mutare gaudemus. Ascende si placet, sed ea lege, ne ut cum ludicri mei ratio poscet descendere iniuriam putes. An tu mores ignorabas meos? Nesciebas Croesum regem Lydorum Cyro paulo ante formidabilem mox deinde miserandum rogi flammis traditum misso caelitus imbre defensum? Num te praeterit Paulum Persi regis a se capti calamitatibus pias impendisse lacrimas?

2 Pr. 1.9–12

Here is the source of my power, the game I always play: I spin my wheel and find pleasure in raising the low to a high place and lowering those who were on top. Go up, if you like, but only on condition that you will not feel abused when my sport requires your fall. Didn't you know about my habits? Surely you had heard of Croesus, King of Lydia, who was a formidable adversary to Cyrus at one time and later suffered such reverses that he would have been burnt had he not been saved by a shower from heaven. And you must have heard how Paulus wept over the calamities suffered by Perses, King of Macedonia, whom he captured (24).

Like any metaphor which defines social experience as a game, this one has an aspect that is profoundly conservative. By necessity, it assumes a stable, non–ludic ground against which the play of the game can be defined as play. The balance of the passage strongly suggests that this ground is constituted by the social position of any participant the moment before he joins the game. In effect, then, the figure of Fortune's wheel posits a stable class structure to which one can always retreat. The figure further suggests one has already to be a part of the ruling class—in late Antique terms, a landowning free man—in order to get into the game in the first place. The two royal exempla Fortune cites reinforce this impression. The kind of ascent she clearly has in mind is one which begins from a certain base of social privilege and acquires more.

The *status quo* which underwrites Fortune's game also underwrites Philosophy's Stoic antidote, the internal self-possession which enables one to see through Fortune's illusions. For if we ask what exactly is possessed in this state of self-possession, we will see it can be nothing other than the equilibrium that exists in the moment before Fortune's game begins—in other words, one's social position. To suggest that some element of one's social position is innate, self-possessed, is simply to ratify the bias already built into any society ruled by an aristocracy of birth. In the figure of Fortune an aristocratic class can at once recognize the flux of historical existence, and affirm its own privilege as a locus of stability beyond such flux.

Furthermore, the recognition enables the aristocracy to evade its own role in producing that flux. Great men who fell from the top of Fortune's wheel were usually given a good push by would-be great men below them. Fortune completely deflects such intra-class conflict, whose motivations are clearly identifiable and highly specific, onto to its own random, indefinite figural space. It establishes a rhetorical common ground to which the ruling class can appeal even at that moment when it is most divided. Thus Paulus can weep for Perses at the very moment he captures him. Here is the subtlety, at once rhetorical and ideological, which Fortune's ostensible simplicity conceals. As a figure, Fortune seems entirely threadbare. It consists of nothing more than a perfunctory indication of gender and the single image of the wheel, whose sole function is to register, in an abstract and completely dehistoricized fashion, the variability of political power. Yet that is precisely the point. The figure designates a specific interest at work in the process of history and simultaneously denies its specificity. It allows history to be understood at once as receptive to sentient action, and as entirely given. It serves perfectly the ideological needs of an aristocratic ruling class, which must continually struggle to maintain its privilege, but wishes also to understand that privilege as a given.

One of the reasons Fortune has been so resistant to modern understanding is precisely because it is both rhetorical and ideological. It cuts across the tendency of modern thought to distinguish rhetoric, which it treats as dispersive and liberating, from ideology, which it treats as controlling and constraining. Fortune clearly provides a form of ideological control. That control is dispersive to the extent that it is irreducibly double, forever split between Fortune's rhetorical sweetness, the ideological common ground it establishes, and the intra-class conflict that common ground signifies. Paradoxically, then, this is a dispersiveness continually closing in upon itself. Fortune figures historical conflict in order to lessen it.

The paradox can be stated in even more specifically post-modern terms. Fortune's cutting across of the distinction between rhetoric and ideology occurs on the issue which for recent theory has been most crucial to both. This issue is the production of subjectivity. Semioticians have come to regard subjectivity as the central effect of discourse, while Marxist theorists of ideology since Althusser have come to regard it as the central effect of ideology.[14] The semiot-

---

[14] For the issue of subjectivity in semiotics, see Kaja Silverman, *The Subject of Semiotics* (New York: Oxford Univ. Press, 1983), esp. 3–53, and 194–236. For Marxist accounts, see

ic account of the subject privileges its dispersiveness; the Marxist account, its ideological coherence. Fortune hovers between these two poles. At once personification and deity, it foregrounds the production of subjectivity as both a discursive and an ideological process. As a personification, Fortune literally enacts the power of all rhetorical structures to produce subject positions. But its original status as pagan god also makes it ideological, invoking divinity's function as the ultimate anchor of belief. In Althusser's terms, divinity is the "Absolute Subject," the principle which enables one to assume the identity of a believer, the specular structure in which individuals recognize their own ideological subjectivity.[15] It is precisely in the gap between Fortune as mere personification and Fortune as divinity that the figure finds its ideological power. To the extent Fortune is a rhetorical effect it offers its audience nothing less than rhetorical control over divinity—a discredited divinity, to be sure, but a divinity nonetheless. It suggests that structures of belief are rhetorically produced and subject to rhetorical manipulation—that believers have the power to reshape the sources of their beliefs.

The possibility of such power counterbalances the radical disempowerment the figure signifies. This is a rhetorical and ideological power which anticipates in a different guise, one of Marx's most fundamental insights: "the ideas of the ruling class are in every epoch the ruling ideas."[16] But Fortune anticipates this insight in the manner in which, as most Marxists have come to recognize, power actually manifests itself, not as a monolithic bloc, but as a hegemony that "once achieved, must be constantly and ceaselessly renewed, reenacted" (Hall 54). Fortune participates in that process in a performative and self-reflexive fashion, reiterating the continual need to maintain the struggle for hegemony while it also portrays hegemony as an irresistible given. Fortune is about much more than the pallid and predictable moralizing David Aers has justifiably, if intemperately, described as a sophisticated form of "thumb sucking" (*Community*, 147). It is about power. Its paradoxical figurations of power relations were crucially important to a culture which characteristically understood such relations in textual and rhetorical terms. This is the figural logic Fortune brings to *Troilus and Criseyde*.

Carolyn Dinshaw has recently argued that the Christian morality the narrator offers in the final stanzas of the *Troilus* constitutes a "markedly gendered" response to the erotic desires the narrative concentrates in the figure of Cri-

---

Louis Althusser, *Lenin and Philosophy and Other Essays*, trans. Ben Brewster (New York: Monthly Review Press, 1971), 127–86; Stuart Hall, "The Toad in the Garden: Thatcherism Among the Theorists," in *Marxism and the Interpretation of Culture*, ed. Cary Nelson and Laurence Grossberg (Urbana: Univ. of Illinois Press, 1988), 35–73; and James Kavanagh, "Ideology," in *Critical Terms for Literary Study*, ed. Frank Lentricchia and Thomas McLaughlin (Chicago: Univ. of Chicago Press, 1990), 306–20.

[15] Althusser, *Lenin and Philosophy*, 177–83.

[16] Karl Marx and Friedrich Engels, *The German Ideology*, trans. C. J. Arthur (New York: International Publishers, 1970), 64.

seyde. Without in any way gainsaying the piety of this closing gesture, we can nevertheless see that it also comes as a defense against "the seemingly uncontrollable feminine" which the "narrator's amatory participation in the preceding narrative" unleashes. His vicarious enjoyment of this feminine continues up to the point where it "threatens to destroy masculine lives and masculine projects"—that is, until Criseyde forsakes Troilus.[17] In other words, the opposition between the carnality of the narrative and the spirituality of its moral—an opposition which so many critics have taken to be irreconcilable—is subtended by a continuous "masculine control of the feminine," which remains continuous throughout (48). As the conclusion of this narrative of masculine desire, the transcendence the moral offers is not simply the spiritual transcendence of the carnal, but also a more specifically male transcendence of the sinful desire for a female body. While Troilus's laughter from the hollowness of the eighth sphere obviously signifies his renunciation of his desire for Criseyde, it requires no similar renunciation either on the part of the narrator, or the masculine reader for whom he speaks. On the contrary, the very gap between Troilus's spiritual laughter and his earlier desires protect the narrator from ever having to acknowledge his own participation in such desires. They can be assigned entirely to the earlier Troilus, whom, like the discredited Criseyde, the narrative has now left definitively behind.

The poem both enacts and critiques this continual reimposition of narrative control. For if the poem tirelessly seeks to control Criseyde, it seeks just as tirelessly to expose the ways she herself is controlled. Crises in patriarchal order inform the narrative throughout. The most central of these is the double breakdown in the exchange of women, that power structure which necessarily undergirds any aristocratic society (Dinshaw 56–58). The first is the abduction of Helen, which initiates the war and provides the poem's premise. The second, of course, is the irregular exchange of Criseyde for Antenor. As it brings the love affair with Troilus to an end, this brutal assertion of patriarchal power exposes some of the affair's pretensions. The illicitness of his secret love leaves Troilus no grounds on which to resist the demands of the state. On the other hand, the parallel between Helen and Criseyde exposes the pretensions of the social order to whose interest it must give way. For the *raison d'état* here is based ultimately on Paris's illicit abduction of Helen.

Nevertheless, Troilus cannot for that reason claim any privileged status for his love for Criseyde. For the structures of patriarchal power inform that love from the moment he first catches sight of Criseyde, and move it forward at every stage, through Pandarus's double role as Criseyde's fatherly protector and Troilus's procurer, and through his active complicity in Pandarus's designs. When Troilus offers Pandarus one of his sisters in return for Pandarus's aid in enabling him to sleep with Criseyde, he only exposes a contradiction that has been inherent in the pursuit of his desire from the beginning. On the one hand Criseyde is a God—as Troilus literally addresses her when her first sees

---

[17] Dinshaw, *Poetics*, 39–47 (*included in this volume*).

her (1.276)—upon whom all his happiness and indeed even his life depends. On
the other hand, she is a social subordinate, whose powerlessness he and
Pandarus exploit at every turn. His idolatrous psychic submission to her cannot
be separated from the position of social superiority from which it is enacted.
It should be viewed as a form of rhetorical empowerment; by making her the
source of all his desire he makes the source of his own subjectivity a "Subject"
over which he has social control.

Given the rigor with which the poem strives both to control the feminine
and to critique that control, it seems less crucial to assign the poem a unified
meaning than to understand the exact contours of its doubleness. Fortune
must figure prominently in any such consideration precisely because of its
intermediate status. Both the narrator and the characters frequently exploit it
to define both Troy's political fate, and the progress of Troilus and Criseyde's
affair—uses which look forward to the transcendent moralizing which closes the
poem. But the sweetness of the figure's persuasion has more in common with the
textual pleasure of the earlier part of the narrative. Fortune's gender, a dormant
feature in most of medieval tradition, intensifies its figurations of power in this
poem where social conflict is specifically the conflict between men about the
control of women, Fortune's gender recalls the specific nature of this conflict,
even as the figure fulfills its usual role of dehistoricizing conflict. This paradoxical
heightening of specificity gives the figure greater ideological power, for it makes
the dehistoricizing the figure performs that much more forceful.

Although invocations of Fortune are scattered throughout the poem, they
are most concentrated in Book 4, which begins with the announcement

> From Troilus she gan hire brighte face
> Awey to writhe, and tok of hym non heede,
> But caste hym clene out of his lady grace,
> And on hire whiel she sette up Diomede.   8–11

Book 4 marks the moment where the patriarchal social order which had made
Criseyde available to Troilus takes her from him. Figuring this disruption as a
shift in Fortune enables the narrative to begin to recuperate Troilus's loss and
move toward its final transcendence, but the figure also enables the recupera-
tion to be staged precisely as a continuation of Troilus's entrapment in the
patriarchal. His lament in lines 260–336, which occurs shortly after the "par-
lement" which decides Criseyde's fate, provides the most spectacular instance
of this double process.

The lament is eleven stanzas long and consists of a series of seven apostro-
phes. He begins with an apostrophe to Fortune that is four stanzas long,
followed by a two-stanza address to Love, then five single-stanza addresses to
his "goost," his eyes, Criseyde, other lovers, and Calkas. As Jonathan Culler has
demonstrated, apostrophe is the rhetorical figure which makes most prominent
and problematic the power of language to produce subject positions. For in it
speaking subjects make subjectivity the source of other subject positions, which

they impose on the world around them.[18] In this rapid series, Troilus at-
tempts to exert ideological control over his impending material loss, projecting
his own subjectivity on those who are escaping his control. If the lament marks
his desperation, its energy also marks the force of his struggle.

He addresses Fortune not purely as a personification but also as a deity:

> "Have I the nought honoured al my lyve,
> As thow wel woost, above the goddes alle?
> Whi wiltow me fro joie thus deprive?"   267–69

At first glance, this clear reference to one of the "payens corsed olde rites,"
might encourage us to read this lament as part of what John Fleming calls
Chaucer's "critique of pagan idolatry."[19] The problem is that appeals to For-
tune as an explanatory principle are hardly restricted to Troilus or even the
other inhabitants of pagan Troy. They are made just as frequently by the nar-
rator, who, as I have already mentioned, uses an extended discussion of For-
tune to open this book. In this context, the insistence here on the figure's
status as a deity has exactly the opposite effect. It exposes the narrator's com-
plicity with the very pagan world he will attempt at the end of the poem to
leave behind. That complicity consists in recognizing the ideological power
pagan deities still retained for Christian culture, even when reduced to rhetori-
cal figures. More specifically, it consists in recognizing the extent to which rhe-
toric's "sweet persuasion" can manage the ideological world it inhabits. If, in
the figure of Fortune, pagan culture deified the shifting essence of political
power, Troilus's address to that figure will lead him to its patriarchal source.

"Why ne haddestow my fader, kyng of Troye, / Byraft the lif, or don my
bretheren dye?" he asks, adding that "If that Criseyde allone were me laft, /
Nought roughte I whider thow woldest me steere" (4.276–77, 281–82). This
declaration that he values Criseyde beyond his patrilineage does more than
simply express the intensity of his desire. It reveals the extent to which that
desire enacts itself precisely as a conflict with the Law of the Father, as an at-
tempt to wrest control of a woman outside the normal channels of exchange.
This characterization will surface twice more in this lament, first in the invoca-
tion of Oedipus two stanzas later, and in the final, abrupt attack on Calkas.

The reference to Oedipus occurs in the apostrophe to Love. Love is more
idealized as a deification than Fortune, and Troilus's shift of address here
begins an idealization of his love for Criseyde that will continue through to the
penultimate stanza of the lament. Oedipus is the archetypal transgressor
against the exogamous Law of the Father. Troilus's vow that he will end his life
"as Edippe, in derknesse" (4.300), actually moves him away from his immediate
confrontation with the demands of his own patrilineage, and encloses his trans-
gressive desires in the memorialization of a mythic past. The next three stanzas,

---

[18] Jonathan Culler, *The Pursuit of Signs: Semiotics, Literature, Deconstruction* (London:
Routledge, 1981), 135–54.

[19] Fleming, *Classical Imitation*, 74.

which address his spirit, his eyes, and Criseyde amplify this memorialization. Frozen in his disappointment, he thus becomes a sepulchral monument for future lovers, "that heigh upon the whiel / Ben set of Fortune" (4.323–24).

This return to Fortune is elegaic, a distinct contrast to the reproachful tone with which he began. The repose he achieves in this stanza would seem to offer an appropriate moment of closure, his rhetoric having moved him beyond the agitated state from which he began. The repose is illusory, however, for the final stanza is yet to come and its confrontation with patriarchal power is the most direct and bitterest in the entire lament.

> "O oold, unholsom, and myslyved man,
> Calkas I mene, allas! what eileth the,
> To ben a Grek, syn thow art born Troian?
> O Calkas, which that wolt my bane be,
> In corsed tyme was thow born for me!
> As wolde blisful Jove, for his joie,
> That I the hadde where I wolde, in Troie!"   330–36

The dehistoricizing pretense of Fortune has been dropped. Troilus now confronts his tormentor face to face. But he still uses the rhetorical power of the apostrophe to express his aggression. He withholds Calkas's name until the second line, as if he cannot bring himself to utter it until he has stigmatized the discursive position he addresses as "oold, unholsom, and myslyved." Where the language of the preceding stanza was fluid the language in this one is choppy and abrupt. In the entire preceding stanza there are two caesurae. In this one there are five in the first three lines alone. In the question he addresses to Calkas, "what eileth the / To ben a Grek, syn thow art born Troian" lies the dilemma he can't escape.

The relation between birth and nationality (which etymologically, of course, means "birth") is a patriarchal one. Patriarchy's imposition of its own form of order on the process of birth is what produces political groupings like "Grek" and "Troian." Calkas is a father who has violated the very structure which underlies his paternal power. Yet this violation does not so much invalidate patriarchy as demonstrate that its power is never exhausted by the structures that sustain that power. Transgressions like Calkas's treason are as characteristic of patriarchy's will to power as the structures he violates. For this reason, the fantasy of violence with which Troilus closes this stanza, and the lament as a whole—"That I the hadde where I wolde"—returns him to the very circuit of patriarchal power he is trying to escape. For even if he got Calkas where he wanted him, his attack would only be one more instance of the male conflict over women which constitutes that circuit. Thus, while this stanza radically historicizes Troilus's dilemma, exposing in its address to Calkas the specific source of his suffering, the stanza only ends by strengthening the dilemma.

Cassandra's miniature *De Casibus* recapitulates his entrapment in fuller terms. As Monica McAlpine has observed, the identification of Meleager with the boar he killed suggests that "boars and boar-killers both belong to the same race" and that "Diomede's 'kynde' and Troilus's 'kynde' cannot really be separated."[20] The same transgressive desire for patriarchal power drives both the Theban story and the Trojan story. The only differences are that the Theban story is longer and its transgressions more extreme. Both of these facts simply underline patriarchy's capacity to survive its own transgressions, and its indifference to the particular individuals who wield its power. So long as Criseyde is possessed, it doesn't matter whether it is Troilus or Diomede who does the possessing. Troilus's violent rejection of Cassandra's explanation only reaffirms his complicity in the cycle of violence she has adumbrated, as does his subsequent decision to seek death in battle.

Fortune's figurations of his entrapment render this fact inevitable, and anticipate the final displacement of this Troilus by his own later, disembodied laughter and the narrator's moralizing. Accordingly, it would seem that Fortune's ultimate effect in this poem is to produce ideological control, to undergird the poem's final transcendence with a clear-eyed political recognition of the inevitability of patriarchal power. To this extent my reading of Fortune's politics runs counter to other readings of the poem's politics such as Aers's, Dinshaw's, and Knight's, which stress its critical element more heavily. Nevertheless, I see my account as less a counter-instance than an extension of these readings. For the issue at stake here is not whether the poem contains a self-reflexive critique, but how it is to be understood. Is this self-reflexiveness the responsibility of Chaucer alone, or does he merely sharpen capacities for self-reflexiveness already present in the culture at large? The self-reflexiveness of Fortune would suggest that the latter is the case. It may be that *Troilus and Criseyde* provides such rich ground for the analysis of medieval ideology precisely because Chaucer reproduces it so faithfully.

---

[20] McAlpine, *Genre*, 172.

The Lover's Gaze in Troilus and Criseyde

SARAH STANBURY

Troilus and Criseyde fall in love through the eyes, Troilus with Criseyde at the Festival of the Palladion, and Criseyde with Troilus when, in Book 2, she watches him ride past her window as he returns from battle. In these paired scenes, Chaucer dramatizes the experience of falling in love through imagery drawn from medieval optical science and shaped by gendered social taboos and entitlements on looking. The visual imagery gives us a confusing and even deceptive picture of the lover's will. In Book 1 Troilus falls in love through visual rays, which penetrate his eye to wound his heart. Chaucer's use of the image of the lover's eyebeam, which is drawn both from the poetic tradition of "Love's Fatal Glance" as well as from medieval optical science, gives him a brilliant tool with which to allow Troilus—penetrated by love's arrows—the appearance of passivity, even as he chooses to love. Similar complexities in agency occur when Criseyde falls in love in Book 2, though without the uses of amatory iconography. Criseyde's position unseen at the window, gazing on a male body, suggests at first that she chooses to love. Further examination of the scene's complex lines of sight, however, suggests that Criseyde's gaze is interrupted by her identification with Troilus, who is the object of the crowd's admiring gaze. Through her identification with him and her sense of passivity as one who is looked on rather than looking, she is able to relinquish her will and feel that she has had no choice but to love him.

> No man knows so, as that strong arguments may not be brought on the other side, how he sees; whether by reception of species from without, or by emissions of beams from within; And yet no man doubts whether he sees or no.
> —John Donne, Sermon No. 10, 1630[1]

In *The Imaginary Signifier*, his classic study of psychoanalysis and cinema, Christian Metz describes the double movement of the gaze. The object seen, separated by distance, nevertheless seems bound to us by an almost tangible thread, one that integrates the polarities of active and passive looking:

---

[1] *Sermons*, vol 9, ed. Evelyn M. Simpson and G. R. Potter (Berkeley: Univ. of California Press, 1958).

All vision consists of a double movement: projective (the "sweeping" searchlight) and introjective: consciousness as a sensitive recording surface (as a screen). I have the impression at once that, to use a common expression, I am "casting" my eye on things, and that the latter, thus illuminated, come to be deposited within me. . . . A sort of stream called the look, and explaining all the myths of magnetism, must be sent out over the world, so that objects can come back up this stream in the opposite direction (but using it to find their way), arriving at last at our perception, which is now soft wax and no longer an emitting source.[2]

Metz's account of visual intersubjectivity, which he applies to an exploration of cinematic voyeurism, refers to the psychology of vision, and bears only superficially on modern optical science. From the point of view of medieval studies, however, this passage is extraordinary for its articulation of a medieval theory of vision. Up to Kepler's theory of the retinal image in 1604, a major point of debate in classical and medieval optics concerned the operation of the visible species or visual ray, Metz's "stream," down which the look is projected and up which impressions of objects return to the eye. Even though Ockham, in the fourteenth century, argued against the existence of species, either projective or introjective,[3] medieval optical theory in general debated not so much whether species or visual rays existed at all, but rather their form and source of generation. Grosseteste (ca. 1168–1253), for instance, argued that the visual species was a substance, similar—according to David Lindberg—to "the old visual fire of the Platonic tradition"; this "species" joined, like Metz's stream, with an emanation from the object viewed to complete vision.[4] Grosseteste writes:

Nor is it to be thought that the emission of visual rays [from the eye] is only imagined and without reality, as those think who consider the part and not the whole. But it should be understood that the visual species [issuing from the eye] is a substance, shining and radiating like the sun, the radiation of which, when coupled with the radiation from the exterior shining body, entirely completes vision. . . . Therefore true perspective is concerned with rays emitted [by the eye].[5]

With his extensive knowledge of ancient and medieval optical texts, Bacon

---

[2] Christian Metz, *The Imaginary Signifier: Psychoanalysis and the Cinema*, trans. Celia Britton, Annwyl Williams, Ben Brewster, and Alfred Guzzetti (Bloomington: Indiana Univ. Press, 1982), 50.

[3] For a concise summary of Ockham's discussion of vision, see David C. Lindberg, *Theories of Vision from Al-Kindi to Kepler*, The Chicago History of Science and Medicine, ed. Allen G. Debus (Chicago: Univ. of Chicago Press, 1976), 141–42; for a fuller discussion see Katherine H. Tachau, *Vision and Certitude in the Age of Ockham: Optics, Epistemology and the Foundations of Semantics, 1250–1345*, Studien und Texte zur Geistesgeschichte des Mittelalters, vol. 22 (New York: E.J. Brill, 1988), 130–35.

[4] Lindberg, *Theories of Vision*, 101.

[5] Grosseteste, *De iride*, quoted from Edward Grant, *A Source Book in Medieval Science* (Cambridge: Harvard Univ. Press, 1974), 389.

in the mid-thirteenth century stressed the non-materiality of the visual species and the operations of its intromission, rather than its projection out from the eye; yet his important synthesis did not abandon the theory of extramission, the visual ray sent out from the pupil.[6] Bacon makes his position clear on the debate about the intromission or extramission of visual species in his remark, "But many have denied that something issues from the eye to complete the act of sight, positing that vision is completed only by intromission and not by extramission.... However ... this opinion is false...."[7] Species emanating from things "must be aided and excited by the species of the eye," which alters the eye to allow it to receive the entering visual impression.[8]

The history of theories of the visual rays is extraordinarily complex.[9] Here I have briefly mentioned some of the medieval arguments about visual rays in order to locate the scientific matrix of a familiar conceit in medieval erotic poetry: the lover's gaze that penetrates as an arrow or visual ray, usually through the eye, to wound the heart. This is the agency of affective visual linkage described in "Merciles Beaute," a roundel ascribed to Chaucer, in which the beloved's gaze sends a dart that penetrates to wound the heart:

> Your yen two wol slee me sodenly;
> I may the beautee of hem not sustene,
> So woundeth hit thourghout my herte kene.   1–3

In this poem the implied visual ray connecting eye and object of desire takes the shape, of course, of Cupid's arrow, which functions in this lyric similar to the wounding look in the *Knight's Tale*: after casting his eye on Emilye, Palamon explains why he cried out: "But I was hurt right now thurghout myn ye / Into myn herte" (I.1096–7).

Chaucer's most complex development of the imagery of the lover's gaze, however, occurs in *Troilus and Criseyde*, first through the detailed accounts of visual emanations when Troilus falls in love with Criseyde at the temple in Book 1, and second through the description of her reciprocal visual and amatory gesture, falling in love with him when she watches him ride by her window in Book 2. In Book 1, erotic imagery is even explicitly situated within an optical metalanguage. Troilus is first shot by the God of Love's arrow; then his eye (emitting a kind of phallic and amorous "species") penetrates the crowd to

---

[6] See Lindberg 112–14.

[7] *Roger Bacon's Philosophy of Nature: A Critical Edition, with English Translation, Introduction, and Notes, of De multiplicatione specierum and De speculis comburentibus*, 1.2, ed. David C. Lindberg (Oxford: Oxford Univ. Press, 1983), 33; see also 1.5, 75.

[8] *The Opus maius of Roger Bacon*, pt. 1.1, dist. 7, chap. 4, ed. John H. Bridges (Oxford: Clarendon Press, 1900; reprint Frankfurt, 1964), 2:52; cited in Lindberg, *Theories of Vision*, 115.

[9] Indeed, even in a somewhat metaoptical permutation (the evil eye), belief in visual rays have a complex and widespread history; French folklorist Arnold von Gennep even chose, as a parable of the researcher buried under thousands of sources, a story about a scholar studying the evil eye. For this parable and other essays on the evil eye, see *The Evil Eye: A Folklore Casebook*, ed. Alan Dundes (New York: Garland, 1981).

smite Criseyde, "and so depe it wente / Til on Criseyde it smot, and ther it stente" (1.272–73); and then (the narrator says in an unambiguous reference to the mechanics of visual species) Troilus has "felte dyen," felt himself slain by the "subtile stremes" (1.305) of her eyes, within which love has his dwelling place.

The connection between the imagery of love's fatal glance and medieval optical theory is not a new one, and it has been remarked *en passant* in a number of studies of medieval love poetry.[10] Less fully explored or explained, however, is the basis for this persistent imagistic coupling: why should this erotic metaphor so frequently be grounded in medieval faculty psychology? The most immediate answer to this question is that the optical species that emanate from and penetrate the eye can simply be said to essentialize the experience of love at first sight, or even of simple looking. The gaze seems to fracture the boundaries of the private self—as Roland Barthes writes in his essay, "Right in the Eyes": "By dint of gazing, one forgets one can be gazed at oneself. Or again, in the verb 'to gaze', the frontiers of active and passive are uncertain."[11]

I would also like to argue that this erasure of boundaries between active and passive, the simultaneous double movement Christian Metz describes between the gaze as projective and introjective and that medieval amatory imagery describes through penetrating and emanating "species" or visual rays, sends as well an extraordinary smoke-screen over questions of agency.[12] One of the most persistent features of the image of Love's Fatal Glance is the recurrent representation in this image of a mechanical reversal, in which the experience of looking is instantly perceived to be an experience of being looked upon; this is the central visual process, for example, in "Merciles Beaute" ("your eyen two wol slee me sodenly"). The poet's sense of execution by the woman's two eyes describes as much the effect his gaze on her has on himself as it describes the moment at which his look is returned. Like Palamon, he is instantly a victim, a feminized and passive recipient of a martial blow or even phallic penetration of the body ("so woundeth hit throughout my herte kene"). Nevertheless, it is his gaze entirely that arranges this scene of desire and destruction. In the

---

[10] See, for example, Ruth H. Cline, "Hearts and Eyes," *RPhil* 25 (1971–1972): 263–97; Lance K. Donaldson-Evans, "Love's Fatal Glance: Eye Imagery in Maurice Scève's *Délie*," *Neophilologus* 62 (1978): 202–11; Robert Baldwin, " 'Gates Pure and Shining and Serene': Mutual Gazing as Amatory Motif in Western Literature and Art," *Ren&R* NS 10, 1 (1986): 23–48; and Lee Patterson, " 'Rapt with Pleasaunce': Vision and Narrative in the Epic," *ELH* 48 (1981): 455–75.

[11] Roland Barthes, *The Responsibility of Forms: Critical Essays on Music, Art, and Representation*, trans. Richard Howard (New York: Hill & Wang, 1985), 238.

[12] Writing on the image of the entranced gaze, Patterson argues ("Rapt with Pleasaunce," 458) that the image signals discursive absence or suspension of consciousness: "The Gaze implies a nostalgic evasion of understanding, a lowered state of consciousness that is figured by a trance-like stupor that must be broken, both to disarm its dangerous seductions and to unlock the riches its object contains." I would agree that medieval representations of the lover's gaze also share in this evasion of understanding, but I would argue that evasion is accomplished through a slippage or transference in agency.

Knight's Tale, similarly, the lover's eye sends the arrow or ray that smites his own heart: Emilye, as far as we know, never even looks up to see Palamon and Arcite gazing on her from their tower.

In both of these texts, "Merciles Beaute" and *The Knight's Tale*, the one who looks is male, and his gaze, following a highly conventionalized masculine trajectory, is the gaze of desire on a woman. This is not to imply that in medieval poetry representations of a lover's gaze belong only with male characters. In the lengthy discussion of amatory optics in Chrétien's *Cligés*, for instance, *both* Soredamours and Alexander say that love has pierced them through the eyes to the heart.[13] Nevertheless, in medieval narrative the sight lines of desire are most often projected by a male viewer. A growing body of research in psychoanalytic theory, non-verbal communication, feminist film theory, and art history has demonstrated that in Western culture this aggressive masculine eye dates from at least the classical era. It is usually a male line of sight, for instance, that positions the Renaissance nude, the Hollywood blond (and, according to feminist film theory, controls the diegesis of classical Hollywood cinema in general), and the programmatic top-to-toe description of the beautiful woman in poetry.[14] An exploration of medieval representations of the lover's look needs to explore as well the way tropes of visual desire have been shaped by contemporary attitudes toward masculinity and femininity.

In the remainder of this article I would like to look at a medieval representation of this paradigm of desire, the penetrating lover's gaze in Books 1 and 2 of *Troilus and Criseyde*; and I would like to look at the way it functions both as an index in a system of gestural codes and as a contextualized sign revealing something to us about Troilus and Criseyde's sense of self—the shaping of their desire, their relationship to public opinion, their active or passive will. The expressions and practice of will by Troilus and Criseyde (and also by Pandarus

---

[13] *Cligés* 470–523; 689–857, in *Arthurian Romances*, trans. D. D. R. Owen (London: Dent, 1987), 97–98, 100–101.

[14] The social and political ramifications of the gaze have recently been so intensively investigated that we might now speak of "gaze" studies as a discipline. For explorations of gender, some of the most rigorous inquiries into the processes of spectatorship have been developed within feminist film theory and in discourses about the intersections between film theory and psychoanalysis. For just a few of these studies see, for instance, Kaja Silverman, *The Acoustic Mirror: The Female Voice in Psychoanalysis and Cinema* (Bloomington: Indiana Univ. Press, 1988), 1–41, 141–86; Jacqueline Rose, *Sexuality in the Field of Vision* (New York: Verso, 1986), 167–213; *Feminism and Film Theory*, ed. Constance Penley (New York: Routledge, 1988). For a highly theoretical application of discourses of the gendered gaze to literary texts, see Barbara Freedman, *Staging the Gaze: Postmodernism, Psychoanalysis, and Shakespearean Comedy* (Ithaca: Cornell Univ. Press, 1991); and for essays that discuss the politics of the gendered gaze in medieval literature, see Hope Weissman, "Aphrodite/Artemis // Emilia/Alison: The Semiotics of Perception," *Exemplaria* 2 (1990): 89–125; Gayle Margherita, "Desiring Narrative: Ideology and the Semiotics of the Gaze in the Middle English *Juliana*," *Exemplaria* 2 (1990): 355–74. I have also explored female spectatorship in medieval texts in several other essays: "Feminist Film Theory Seeing Chrétien's *Enide*," *Literature and Psychology* 36 (1990): 47–66; "The Virgin's Gaze: Spectacle and Transgression in Middle English Lyrics of the Passion," *PMLA* 106 (1991): 1083–93; and "The Voyeur and the Private Life in *Troilus and Criseyde*," *SAC* 13 (1991): 141–58.

and even the narrator) offer some of the most teasing and enigmatic questions posed by this poem; for *Troilus*, staged, as Derek Pearsall writes, in the "marketplace of the will," is a poem in which agency repeatedly seems to slide out of control.[15] In its use of the iconographic motif of the lover's gaze, *Troilus* adopts a system of imagery that lends itself, through its imagistic and even physiological basis on visual rays with self-reflexive agency and action (at least according to medieval scientific theory), to mechanical reversals that problematize issues of agency. Who, in fact, is looking? And does that look (with its rays or arrows) have power over the body of the other, or is it simply an elaborate conceit for a kind of erotic solipsism?

The first appearance in *Troilus* of conventional amatory iconography is the moment in Book 1 in which Troilus, who has been gazing over ("scoping," one might say) the women attending the festival of the Palladion, suddenly is struck by the arrow of the God of Love.[16] He raises his brow as if to indicate his superiority to those who sigh and feast their eyes on any particular woman, and at that moment the angered God of Love shoots his arrow through (it seems) Troilus's exposed pupil:

> And with that word he gan caste up the browe,
> Ascaunces, "Loo! is this naught wisely spoken?"
> At which the God of Love gan loken rowe
> Right for despit, and shop for to ben wroken.
> He kidde anon his bowe nas naught broken,
> For sodeynly he hitte hym atte fulle.   1.204–9

Stricken by the God of Love's arrow, Troilus's initial self-possession and self-sufficiency in regard to love are quickly reconfigured to represent him as a victim to love.[17] He is penetrated, feminized, made passive in a dramatic erotic reversal, a process that becomes even more fully specified as he feels himself victimized by Criseyde's gaze. After he watches Criseyde's "mevynge and hire chere" and her glance "a lite aside," gestures that communicate both

---

[15] Criseyde's choices, according to Pearsall ("Choices," 20) are staged in "the marketplace of the will, that place of mysteriously complex transactions in which the self, seeking to maximize its chances of obtaining the things that it perceives as valuable, maneuvers at the same time to preserve and embellish that image of the self which is the very formative cause of the sense of identity." For discussions of will and agency, see also Donald R. Howard, who argues that we understand Criseyde's lack of freedom, the contingencies of her choices, because we enter into her consciousness ("Experience," 173–92); and Evan Carton, "Pandarus' Bed."

[16] See the discussion of Troilus's predatory gaze in David Aers, "Masculine Identity in the Courtly Community: The Self Loving in *Troilus and Criseyde*," in *Community*, 119–21.

[17] Discussions of how Troilus falls in love also have pointed to the problematized agencies of his will. See esp. Aers, who explores the psychoanalytic and cultural construction of the courtly lover; see also Benson, *Chaucer's T&C*, 129–33; and for a discussion of the portrayal of Troilus as a victim of the God of Love in Book 1, see Ian Bishop, *Troilus and Criseyde: A Critical Study* (Bristol: Univ. of Bristol Press, 1981), 25–29.

her isolation and her self-possession, he feels himself again penetrated by her gaze:

> And of hire look in him ther gan to quyken
> So gret desir and such affeccioun,
> That in his hertes botme gan to stiken
> Of hir his fixe and depe impressioun.   295–98

Criseyde, in possession of her glance ("a lite aside"), seems also possessed of the visual ray, the "species" that penetrates the lover. Troilus, the narrator explains, had been unaware that love was located in the radiation of her eye beams:

> Lo, he that leet hymselven so konnynge,
> And scorned hem that Loves peynes dryen,
> Was ful unwar that Love hadde his dwellynge
> Withinne the subtile stremes of hire yën;
> That sodeynly hym thoughte he felte dyen,
> Right with hire look, the spirit in his herte.   302–7

In an apostrophe to Criseyde's eyes in Book 3, Troilus describes them as nets (3.1355), an image of entrapment; and subsequent to his first impaling by the God of Love's arrow, Troilus throughout the text will continue to be entrapped, as Stephen Barney has argued, for a persistent pattern of imagery will depict him as without will—penetrated, tied up, wishing for death at the foot of his bed.[18] Shot in Book 1 by the God of Love's arrow, then victimized by Criseyde's look, "right with hire look thorugh-shoten and thorugh-darted" (325), Troilus, this pattern of imagery indicates, is acted upon rather than acting.

Yet is he? Earlier I suggested that the optical imagery medieval poets use to describe how love enters through the eyes sends a smoke-screen over subjectivity. If we look more closely at the ocular dynamics of Book 1, we can discern similar inconsistencies in their system of imagery. Following the statement that the God of Love has struck Troilus, the narrator departs on an eight-stanza discourse on love. When he returns to Troilus at the festival of the Palladion, it is to specify and dramatically redirect the source of the visual ray that emanates when Troilus looks on "this lady, and now on that":

> And upon cas bifel that thorugh a route
> His eye percede, and so depe it wente,
> Til on Criseyde it smot, and ther it stente.   271–73

Troilus is wounded by the God of Love, that is to say, the moment that his eye strikes Criseyde; even though he seems victimized, that victimization occurs through his own action: *his* gaze pierces the crowd and smites Criseyde.

Yet the dominant visual imagery of the scene at the temple insists, as we

---

[18] Barney, "Troilus Bound" (*included in this volume*).

have seen, that Criseyde's gaze, projected by the "subtile stremes" of her eyes, has instead victimized Troilus. Following the account of Troilus's penetrating stare and of his own visceral reflex (sighing, his heart spreading and rising), Criseyde's gesturally evocative stance and sideways look make him aware of *her* look:

> for she let falle
> Hire look a lite aside in swich manere,
> Ascaunces, "What? may I nat stonden here?"
> And after that hir lokynge gan she lighte,
> That nevere thoughte hym seen so good a syghte.   290-94

This oft-remarked passage, which in a simple and masterful stroke depicts Criseyde's isolation, her assertive sense of herself, her humor (and also Troilus's awareness of and vulnerability to her contradictory tissue of strength and need), casts the terms of his falling in love in relation to her "look a lite aside;" yet that glance, defined by its angularity, occupies a curious place in the scene's complex construction of lines of sight. Does she even look on him? Most readers of this scene have assumed that she does. But that reading is, I think, coerced by the narrative's representation of Troilus's own desire. "Hire look in him" that incites his desire ("gan to quyken") in the following stanza can refer as much to the look "a lite aside" by which Criseyde declares herself enfranchised. *His* gaze, penetrating through the crowd, smiting Criseyde, incites his desire, catches her sidelong glance, and then leads him to fabricate in his heart her "fixe and depe impressioun." The rest of the scene is marked, in fact, by a precise attention to spatial configurations that define distance. Troilus beholds her "from afer"; she pleases him; he watches her, looking at her again and again.

One can argue, rightly I think, that the use in Book 1 of ocular iconography affords Chaucer a flexible tool for depicting intersubjectivity, the experience, central to the ethics of the Western love tradition, of loss of boundaries.[19] The way the gaze can appear to dissolve boundaries is expressed in a beautiful passage in Jean-Paul Sartre's *Being and Nothingness*. Sartre describes, through terms evocative of Troilus's sense of Criseyde's glance, the revelation of the Other as a look:

> I am possessed by the Other; the Other's look fashions my body in its nakedness, causes it to be born, sculptures it, produces it as it *is*, sees it as I shall never see it. . . . He makes me be and thereby he possesses me, and this possession is nothing other than the consciousness of possessing me.[20]

---

[19] For a history of empathy in Western philosophy and poetry, see Karl F. Morrison, *"I Am You": The Hermeneutics of Empathy in Western Literature, Theology, and Art* (Princeton: Princeton Univ. Press, 1988), esp. 43–136.

[20] *Being and Nothingness: An Essay on Phenomenological Ontology*, trans. Hazel E. Barnes (Secaucus: Citadel Press, 1956), 340.

Troilus, possessed by Criseyde's gaze, is created in it. This constructed self, Troilus as lover, shaped by the imagined gaze of the other, is what the rest of the poem (at least in part) is about.

Yet the dramatically angled representation of intersubjectivity at the scene at the temple also obscures, through the reversals entitled by the optical imagery of love, issues of agency. When Troilus is shot by the God of Love, that moment has a complex syntactic parallel in Criseyde's glance "a lite aside," for each of them casts a glance that proclaims self-sufficiency. Troilus raises ("castes up") his eyebrows "ascaunces [as if to say], 'Loo! is this naught wisely spoken?' " (1.204–5); Criseyde casts her look aside, "ascaunces [as if to say], 'What, may I nat stonden here?' " (1.292–93). The response to each of these private proclamations of self is overtly parallel: that is, the private gesture is intercepted, Troilus's by the God of Love, Criseyde's by Troilus, and the independent will is ambushed by love's arrows. Yet the parallel is inexact, for Troilus (shooting himself with arrows from his own eyes) sees Criseyde, whereas Criseyde never explicitly notices Troilus in this scene. In her little spot at the temple, she is set apart, untouched and unaware of the potent and aggressive agency with which she has been credited. Troilus's gesture of self-possession ("is this not wisely spoken?") is conterminous with his imaginary appropriation of Criseyde's body; Criseyde's gesture of self-possession ("may I not stand here") is conterminous with Troilus's appropriation, in his heart's bottom, of *her* very sense of self.

After Troilus returns to his palace, he sits on the foot of his bed and makes a mirror of his mind:

> Thus gan he make a mirour of his mynde,
> In which he saugh al holly hire figure.   365–66

In his imagistic reconstruction of Criseyde, Troilus in a sense studies the image implanted within him by the "subtile stremes" of her eyes. Mirroring her image, his mind becomes a reflecting surface, a passive screen on which her image is recorded. Yet this image, I would like to suggest, also obscures agency. The image printed on Troilus's mirroring mind is his picture of her, garnered by his own secret and desiring gaze through the crowd. The reflecting mirror, which perhaps develops a conceit similar to the image of the eye as a mirror for the heart in Chrétien's *Cligés*, may more properly be described as a kind of lens. Troilus, a lot less passive than the image implies, makes a mirror of his mind in which he can reconstruct and study the image that his own gaze has encompassed.[21]

---

[21] For a discussion of the eye, the heart, and the mind as a mirror, see Herbert Grabes, *The Mutable Glass: Mirror-Imagery in Titles and Texts of the Middle Ages and English Renaissance*, trans. Gordon Collier (New York: Cambridge Univ. Press, 1982), esp. 83–90; see also Patricia Eberle's argument that the title, *Le Mirouer aus Amoureus* [The Lover's Glass], that Jean de

In presenting a picture of Troilus's gaze as one with assertive and even pred-
atory operations, I realize I may be giving a somewhat mechanistic and even
sinister reading of the way Troilus falls in love. Nevertheless, the ocular
dynamics of this scene allow an apparent vaporization of boundaries and per-
mit Troilus to see himself as acted upon, even at the very moment that he acts.
The optical imagery of visible species or rays provides a brilliantly flexible
metaphorics for the scene's representation of obscured or even disappearing
subjectivity. Medieval optics, even as it debated extramission or intromission of
species, was grounded on a model of the material or at least kinetic relation-
ship between eye and object. Chaucer uses this imagery to literalize the
moment at which the self is reconfigured by desire for the other, the moment
in which active and passive become obscured. What I have tried to suggest, in
addition, is that the very blurring of boundaries gives Troilus in Book 1 extra-
ordinary power. "Thorugh shoten and thorugh darted" by her look, as he
believes himself to be, he is free to gaze on her, to imagine her, and ultimately
to win her.

Yet that victory seems hardly unilateral. As Book 2 unfolds, point of view shifts
to present Troilus through the eyes of Criseyde. The most graphically drama-
tized reversal of this sort occurs, of course, in the scene when she looks down
on him from the window in her chamber as he, returning home from war
weary and bloody, rides past. The scene is a pivotal one, because—in careful
symmetry with the scene in the temple in Book 1 where Troilus falls in love
through the eyes—it marks the point at which Criseyde, visually framing an
object of desire, falls in love with Troilus.[22] It also marks a point where we are
given access to Criseyde's thoughts, and hence has led to considerable debate
as to how we should understand her—either as self-conscious and modest;[23] as
assertive or self-possessed;[24] as suffering from "insufficiency of will";[25] as a

---

Meun proposed for *The Romance of the Rose*, took its significance from developments in
thirteenth century optics, and that his image of the mirror in the *Roman* should actually be
understood as an optical instrument or lens ("The Lover's Glass: Nature's Discourse on
Optics and the Optical Design of the *Romance of the Rose*," *UTQ* 46 [1977]: 248–53).

[22] Bishop, 61–64, discusses the pairing of these scenes and suggests that they set up a
kind of dialectic; the first, in the temple, represents Troilus as a victim to the God of Love,
whereas the second represents Criseyde as innocent witness (since the chance sighting in the
first window scene in Book 2 itself parallels a planned sighting in 2.1247). Rowe (*O Love!*,
51–52) also discusses the paired sightings, arguing that each book focuses on the different
types of love each character in turn experiences. Benson (*Chaucer's T&C*, 129–41) also
discusses the paired scenes through Chaucer's departures from Boccaccio, and argues—in
contrast to Howard's assertion in "Experience," that the reader temporarily *is* Criseyde—that
Chaucer distances us from Criseyde's mind and heart in Book 2 (135).

[23] A. J. Minnis, *Chaucer and Pagan Antiquity* (Totowa: Rowman and Littlefield, 1982), 90.

[24] A. C. Spearing, *Chaucer: TROILUS AND CRISEYDE* (London: Edward Arnold, 1976), 47–48.

[25] Sheila Delany, *Chaucer's HOUSE OF FAME: The Poetics of Skeptical Fideism* (Chicago: Univ.
of Chicago Press, 1972), 116; Wood (*Elements*, 137) advances a similar position.

mirror of Troilus's desire;[26] or instead as an eye that offers us a principal center of consciousness.[27]

Most of the questions critics have asked of the scene refer to questions asked generally of Criseyde's role in the narrative as a whole: is she victim or prime mover? Object or subject? These questions collectively express uncertainty about her positioning as a woman; the uncertainty readers express about the location of centers of consciousness in the narrative reflects their doubts about Chaucer's sympathy with a woman's position and also about where they are to align their sympathies. The fascination readers have with Criseyde (one that verges on enamorment) may be motivated in part by their discomfort with the process of identification in the narrative; for in a text that invites us to identify with either or both Troilus and Criseyde, the reader's position has to be an uneasy one. When we ask whether Criseyde is active or passive, agent or victim, and active or acted upon in Book 2 when she looks down on Troilus out the window, that question is also self-referential, for it positions us, spectators of a spectacle, defining how we see her in part through the terms of our willingness to take her (as object of desire) or to share in the drama of her subjectivity and ultimate treachery.

In the scene in Book 2 where she looks out the window on Troilus, the agencies of spectatorship would, at least on first analysis, seem to showcase Criseyde by positioning her as subject of the gaze, giving her a place of visual authority that parallels the distanced, scopophilic gaze of Troilus in Book 1. Criseyde's unimpeded look on Troilus violates social prohibitions on a woman's unrestricted gaze, and would seem to emphasize her access to visual authority, positioned above him, and his reduction to objectified status.[28] The account emphasizes his position as object, not only of her gaze, but of a collective look:

> This Troilus sat on his baye steede,
> Al armed, save his hed, ful richely;

---

[26] Muscatine, *French Tradition*, 164. Benson argues, in contrast, that Chaucer imbues Criseyde and her choice to love with deliberate uncertainty and forces interpretation of her actions onto the reader (135).

[27] Bishop, 11.

[28] Except to comment on the relationship between this scene and its sources in Boccaccio, only a few readers have discussed the window in Book 2; see, for instance, Linda Tarte Holley, "Medieval Optics and the Framed Narrative in Chaucer's *Troilus and Criseyde*," *ChauR* 12 (1986): 26–44; John B. Friedman's comment that although Criseyde in the scene at the window "dominates him spatially and emotionally, she is herself yielding to love at the same moment" ("Pandarus' Cushion and the 'Pluma Sardanapalli'," *JEGP* 75 [1976]: 520); Benson, 133–41; and my brief discussion of these scenes in "The Voyeur and the Private Life in *Troilus and Criseyde*," 146–48. Readers have, however, focused attention on the narrator's subsequent assertion that Criseyde's love was "not sodeyn" and on the meaning of this statement for Criseyde's decision-making; see esp. Howard, 173–92; Wood, 136; Bishop, 63; and Donaldson, *Speaking*, 66. Wood (*Elements* 136) argues that "Criseyde adheres a little more closely [than Boccaccio's Criseida] to a standard literary pattern for enamorment: *Visio, cogito,* and *passio*"; I argue, in contrast, that the trajectories and positionings of *visio* are themselves complex and determining.

And wownded was his hors, and gan to blede,
On which he rood a pas ful softely.
But swich a knyghtly sighte, trewely,
As was on hym, was nought, withouten faille,
To loke on Mars, that god is of bataille.

So lik a man of armes and a knyght
He was to seen, fulfilled of heigh prowesse;
For bothe he hadde a body and a myght
To don that thing, as wel as hardynesse;
And ek to seen hym in his gere hym dresse,
So fressh, so yong, so weldy semed he,
It was an heven upon hym for to see.   2.624–37

In his treatment of the scene, Chaucer departs from Boccaccio by framing
point of view with Criseyde's gaze and by making her look both accidental and
unreciprocated. In contrast, Boccaccio in the *Filostrato* describes a planned as-
signation, one that gives Troilus control over the visual interchange:[29]

> She was standing at one of her windows, and was perhaps awaiting what
> happened; neither harsh nor forbidding did she show herself toward
> Troiolo when he looked at her, but at all times over her right shoulder
> she gazed toward him modestly. Troiolo turned away from there delight-
> ed at that, giving thanks to Pandarus and to God.[30]

In this rewriting of Boccaccio Chaucer would seem to give power and visual au-
thority to Criseyde. His positioning of the visual trajectories (Criseyde looks
out from above; Troilus rides past, eyes cast down) gives her gaze a controlling
interest in the ocular hermeneutic.[31]

The potency of Criseyde's gaze as she looks down through the window is
even further suggested by the affinities of this scene with an iconographic
scheme that appears widely in medieval literature and the visual arts and that
gives to Chaucer's scene of Criseyde at the window a cultural scrim that is even
eschatological in its promises. In a number of representations of marriage, of
profane love, and even of the Annunciation, a window is used as a frame or
partition across which lovers look.[32] Of particular applicability to the Chauce-

---

[29] The textual pairings are clearly illustrated in the *vis-à-vis* edition by Windeatt (183),
who notes Chaucer's changes: "At this point B's Criseida debates with herself whether to
love (69–78), after which she sees Troiolo from her window (82). But Ch inserts T's first
ride-past before Criseyde's soliloquy starts (687)."

[30] *Il Filostrato* 2.82, trans. apRoberts and Seldis, 94–95.

[31] For a provocative study of role-reversals in *Troilus* in general, see R. E. Kaske's essay
on role reversals in the *aubes*: "The Aube in Chaucer's *Troilus*," in Schoeck and Taylor,
2:167–79.

[32] The image may derive from a line in Canticles 2:9: "Behold he standeth behind our
wall, looking through the windows, looking through the latices," a line that was glossed in

rian scene is an episode from Dante's *Vita Nuova* 35.[33] A lady, whom Dante later comes to recognize as Temptation, looks down on him through a window, encompassing such compassion in her gaze that Dante is swept into a false love.

What is suggested by the use of the window in Dante's image, as well as in representations that sacralize the lover's gaze, is the power of the look—and particularly of the woman's look—to cross boundaries. The window sets the boundary between self and other, inside and outside, domestic interior and the exterior plane; it is a metaphor for the eye, the window of the soul; it is also a mirror and lens through which we discover ourselves in the other. Criseyde's look down on Troilus through a window frames both her and the object of her gaze, as Linda Holley has argued;[34] it also frames the gaze. That is, the iconography of the window centralizes the gaze—here controlled by Criseyde—in an erotic visual interchange. Strategic prop, cultural sign, and embodied architectural referent, the window frames the look that crosses it.

Yet in the window scene in *Troilus*, there is no interchange. Or more precisely, the interchange does not occur as a shared gaze between two lovers, as in the scene in Boccaccio or in the many medieval representations of lovers exchanging a look through a window. In the scene in Book 2 the visual interchange involves the crowd; it is the roared approval of the crowd, in fact, that causes Troilus to cast down his eyes in embarrassment, a gesture that is not lost on Criseyde:

> For which he wex a litel reed for shame,
> Whan he the peple upon hym herde cryen,
> That to byholde it was a noble game,
> How sobrelich he caste down his yën.
> Criseÿda gan al his chere aspien,
> And leet it so softe in hire herte synke,
> That to hireself she seyde, "Who yaf me drynke?"   2.645–51

The visual dynamics in this scene set up a complex interchange in which Criseyde is not the single spectator, her eyes fixed on or fixing a static subject, but rather a spectator of a drama whose ocular interactions in effect determine how she sees the scene. Even though, as Holley argues, the scene is technically framed through her point of view by use of a window frame,[35] the scene's de-

---

medieval commentaries as describing the mutual gaze of Christ and his bride; for sources see Robert Baldwin, "Mutual Gazing," 30–31. A well-known commentary on Canticles 4.9 by Gilbert of Hoyland reverses genders to exploit the intersubjective tensions of the gaze (*Sermons on the Song of Songs*, trans. Lawrence C. Braceland [Kalamazoo: Cistercian Publications, 1979], 2, sermon 30, 363): "Do not hesitate, O bride, to aim such weapons at your Spouse. Use devout glances as darts . . . pierce him with wound after wound. Happy are you if your arrows are fixed in him . . . aim at him the arrows of a pure gaze. . . . For no sound health is there where there are no wounds inflicted by the loving gaze of Christ. One gaze challenges another; therefore try to wound him with your view from afar."

[33] Dante, *Vita Nuova*, trans. Mark Musa (Bloomington: Indiana Univ. Press, 1973), 74.

[34] Holley, "Medieval Optics," 31.

[35] "We understand the development of Criseyde's thought if we watch her seeing: Her

scriptive details are actually framed through eyes that are *not* hers. The descrip-
tion is laden with references to acts of sight: "he was to seen" (632); and "and
ek to seen hym in his gere hym dresse" (635); "it was an heven upon hym for
to see" (637); "But swich a knyghtly sighte, trewely / As was on hym, was
nought, withouten faille, / To loke on Mars, that god is of bataille" (628–32).
Certainly Criseyde shares in this gaze; yet her exact placement at the window
is only fully located later, when she withdraws. Her gaze, that is, participates in
and is in part constructed by the gaze of a crowd that even seems masculinized
by its exteriorized positioning, outdoors, jostling in the world while she looks
out from a feminized interior space. The masculine animus of this collective
gaze is even further suggested by the narrator's assertion that "men myght"
find arrows in Troilus's shield.[36]

Criseyde's position as a spectator is thus vastly more complex than the scene
immediately suggests. Even though Criseyde technically controls point of view
and frames the scene through her line of sight, her own response to Troilus is
actually subject to a complex set of specular oscillations; finely mediated by a
social interchange, a gaze (the crowd's) and response (Troilus's lowered eyes)
that is transacted on the street below her, her look incorporates her doubly as
viewer and as the object seen. Troilus is not, in fact, so much the object of her
scrutiny as he is the object of a collective look; and his blush and lowered eyes,
so suggestive of the conventional blush and lowered gaze of a woman that is
looked upon, are a gestural response not to Criseyde's gaze, but to the crowd's
adulation. Nevertheless, it is *his* blush and lowered look that in effect sweep her
away. Her position as spectator, one that initially appears to violate taboos on
women's looking and to adopt a male posture of master of the gaze, like
Troilus in Book 1, is subtly undermined by a complex set of ocular trajectories
that deflect and restructure the dynamics of control. Even though she chooses
to love ("and leet it so softe in hire herte synke" [650]), her choice is contin-
gent on a process manipulated proleptically outside her scope of vision (Troi-
lus's infatuation, Pandarus's announcement of Troilus's love) and simultaneous-
ly within it (the crowd's adulation of Troilus); and also by a blush so fortuitous-
ly placed as to project her own sense of herself. Troilus's blush reveals *her*
sense of sudden exposure; his blush, we might say, is really her own.

That Troilus's gesture, waxing red for embarrassment, both mimics and ini-
tiates a reciprocal gesture is immediately specified. Her own recognition of her
infatuation precipitates *her* blush: "For of hire owen thought she wex al reed"
(2.652). At this point, furthermore, she withdraws her eyes in shame, as if the
dynamics of visual control had completely reversed and she were the object of

---

uncle offers a 'peynted proces' through words; she sees the lover for herself; she makes a
mirror of her mind, turning him in the light of her hopes and fears"—Holley 31.

[36] For a history of gendered nominals in English and an argument that Chaucer was well
aware of the double meaning of "man," see John Fyler, "Man, Men, and Women in
Chaucer's Poetry," in *The Olde Daunce: Love, Friendship, Sex, and Marriage in the Medieval
World,* ed. Robert R. Edwards and Stephen Spector (Albany: SUNY Press, 1991), 154–76.

someone else's gaze. Unseen though she remains, she has become objectified by her own consciousness, the mutual "shame" both she and Troilus experience effected through a recognition that they are constituted as objects of someone else's scrutiny.

Where and with whom that scrutiny ultimately resides is a final question I would like to explore, for it brings us to the issue of identification, and of how we as readers participate in the set of visual exchanges in this scene. One way to frame questions of identification is to ask: Whose fantasy it this? Criseyde—at least overtly—controls the look; yet her look, so strategically accidental, encompasses Troilus's greatest moment. He returns home from war in triumph, his body displayed like Saint Sebastian's, his shield full of arrows; and the woman to whom he has pledged his heart just happens, at that moment, to be watching. For at least some male readers, Criseyde's gaze is projected within the structure of a carefully orchestrated masculine fantasy. Her look at that particular moment not only causes her to fall in love, but even turns her into an object of male desire, the woman in the grandstand at the tournament, looking down on her knight at his most heroic moment.

A.C. Spearing, fascinated by the contradictory elements of Criseyde's character, which seems to shift between shyness and self-possession, argues that she becomes incomprehensible as the final Book of *Troilus* proceeds: "there is, then, a real mystery in Criseyde; she is a mystery even to herself; and Chaucer's narrative method encourages us to realize that mystery without ever dissolving it."[37] One could argue that her "mystery" and even incomprehensibility are present as early as these scenes of amatory optics in Books 1 and 2, and that they are shaped by Chaucer's play with shifting centers of consciousness.

Later Criseyde will complain that she suffers a visual infirmity, a lack of Prudence's third eye, the one that can see the future; and perhaps her position in Books 1 and 2 is also empowered, even eroticized, by lack, by the ocular subversions that diffract her gaze or that, as in Book 1, give the illusion of empowering it. She is, she claims, her "owen woman"; yet that possession of selfhood is defined by what it means to be a woman within a patriarchal culture (and text) that repeatedly structures her sight through an exteriorized or even collective desire. Even as subject of the gaze, looking down on the spectacle of a body offered up for display and situated such that no one even knows she is looking, she becomes finally a spectacle to herself. The reversal even definitively disrupts her look. Unable to sustain her gaze with knowledge of its implicit reciprocities, she pulls in her head, cocooning herself within interior space, while Troilus rides by, "whil he and alle the peple forby paste."

---

[37] Spearing (n24 above), 50.

Inferno 5 *and*
Troilus and Criseyde *Revisited*

KARLA TAYLOR

This essay explores how Dante and Chaucer inflect the gender expectations of literary love in order to examine their effects. Lyric and romance traditions shape the intertextual background against which the COMMEDIA and TROILUS AND CRISEYDE depart from conventional representations of women; methodologically, I use grammatical and syntactic analysis to reveal the degree to which female subjectivity is represented and voiced in each text. The representations of Francesca, Beatrice, and Criseyde depend on an understanding of the gendered conventions they both appropriate and invert or resist. Dante's deliberately outrageous reversal of gender roles with Francesca and Beatrice departs less from convention than Chaucer's apparently unresisting reliance on the traditional female roles with which he portrays Criseyde. By voicing Francesca's subjectivity through the male lyric voice, Dante creates it as inauthentic; and he finally reinscribes Beatrice into the romanesque tradition of the "daungerous woman" used instrumentally to develop his own authentic subjectivity. But Chaucer, by foregrounding acts of representation so as to suggest their representing subjects, probes critically at the uses and effects of these conventions. Although Criseyde is often the object represented– lyric's cruel lady or romance's "daungerous woman"–because she is also sometimes the representing subject, she cannot be entirely confined by the roles she herself puts on. Chaucer's focus on the acts and effects of representation reveals an interest that Dante lacks in the difficulty of female subjectivity.

I have argued elsewhere that Chaucer's *Troilus and Criseyde* borrows plot and language from Dante's Paolo and Francesca episode in *Inferno* 5 in order, not to imitate, but to controvert Dante's effort to reconcile politics and religion with eros in his great love poem.[1] In this essay I would like to revisit *Inferno* 5 and *Troilus and Criseyde* from another angle. My argument here does not proceed from the contested issue of influence, which is not essential to my more modest purpose of comparison. Rather, I am interested in the ways in which each text, with differing results, treats conventional gender expectations in

---

[1] See Karla Taylor, "A Text and Its Afterlife: Dante and Chaucer," *CL* 35 (1983): 1–20, and *Chaucer Reads*, esp. 50–77 and 203–8. I wish neither to rehearse nor to retract my previous arguments; this essay should be regarded as a supplement to them.

order to expose to critical scrutiny the habitual, and thus usually unexamined, moves of lyric and romantic literary love.

1

That love in *Inferno* 5 is gendered cannot be doubted. The focus throughout is on the women in love stories ancient and modern, from the definitions of the souls in the second circle as "le donne antiche e ' cavalieri" ("the ladies and knights of old"—*Inf.* 5.71) and "la schiera ov' è Dido" ("the troop where Dido is"—*Inf.* 5.85) through Francesca's double narrative of love and death, spoken to the unheard accompaniment of Paolo's hovering silence.[2] Nor can it be doubted that Dante directs his gaze equally at the genres and typical languages of literary love. The cranes to which the souls are compared sing lays ("i gru van cantando lor lai," *Inf.* 5.46),[3] and the doves to which Paolo and Francesca are likened are drawn from Guido Guinizelli's touchstone canzone of the Italian tradition, "Al cor gentil ripara sempre amore / come l'ausello in selva a la verdure" ("Love always repairs to the gentle heart, as the bird in the wood to the verdure").[4] The "freddo tempo" ("cold season"—*Inf.* 5.41) of the canto's other bird simile suggests (although I would not wish to press such slender evidence too hard) the bleak winter landscape of Dante's own *rime petrose*.[5] Furthermore, the canto's literary agenda is not unrelated to its gendered representation of love.

Dante combines the two issues most obviously in Francesca's altered retelling of the prose Lancelot, which she blames for her downfall in her second, more romantic, narrative. In the book she and Paolo read, when the go-between Gallehault brings Lancelot into Guinevere's private presence, he is so bashful that the queen seizes the initiative and kisses him.[6] Lancelot's diffidence suggests how love frequently paralyzes manly prowess in Old French romance; Chrétien, for instance, repeatedly worries at the relationship between the ideals of love and prowess, each indispensable and each compatible with the other only by the most extraordinary (or better: fantastic) effort. Perhaps the clearest example of this tension is Erec's chivalric lassitude after his marriage to Enide in

---

[2] Throughout my essay I use Singleton's translation of the *Comedy*.

[3] These could be the short romantic narratives of the Northern French tradition, typified by Marie de France's lais, as well as the melancholy Provençal lyrics for which Renato Poggioli argues; see "Tragedy or Romance? A Reading of the Paolo and Francesca Episode in Dante's *Inferno*," *PMLA* 72 (1957): 313–54, at 318. Poggioli concludes (358) that literature is as much the subject of *Inferno* 5 as love.

[4] For the text of Guinizelli's poem, see *Poeti del duecento*, ed. Gianfranco Contini, 2 vols. (Milan: Ricciardi, 1960), 2:460–64.

[5] See, for instance, the winter setting of #77—*Dante's Rime*, ed. and trans. Patrick Diehl (Princeton: Princeton Univ. Press, 1979), 167–71.

[6] See Paget Toynbee, "Dante and the Lancelot Romance," in *Dante Studies and Researches* (1902; reprint Port Washington: Kennikat, 1971); and Anna Hatcher and Mark Musa, "The Kiss: *Inferno* V and the Old French Prose *Lancelot*," *CL* 10 (1968): 97–109.

Erec et Enide. Erec's knightly rehabilitation requires Enide's silence (or so he thinks; in fact, she repeatedly breaks her vow of silence to save him). In his essay on *Inferno* 5, Renato Poggioli touches on the ways in which love diminishes the male hero; it makes Lancelot a coward and a butt of comedy, and it renders Paolo silent.[7] Like Erec's, Paolo's diminishment comes about because his female beloved talks too much—although I think attributing it to female speech is rather an aspect of representation than precisely a causal explanation.

Francesca does not transmit the Lancelot romance as she found it, but changes it to suit the high romantic heroism by which she wishes to define herself. Her memory influenced by desire, she reverses the gender roles so that Lancelot kisses Guinevere—and Paolo kisses her:

> "Quando leggemmo il disïato riso
>   esser basciato da cotanto amante,
>   questi, che mai da me non fia diviso,
> la bocca mi basciò tutto tremante."   *Inf.* 5.133–36

"When we read how the longed-for smile was kissed by so great a lover, this one, who never shall be parted from me, kissed my mouth all trembling."

Lancelot, in her version, has a stature ("cotanto amante") he lacks in the original scene, while Guinevere is reduced to the bodily fragment most appropriate both to kissing and to its periphrastic courtly representation. The passive of "esser basciato" is telling, for while Francesca clearly identifies herself with Guinevere, it suggests that she also imagines her experiential model as seen from without. The grammar, that is, creates the perspective of an observer rather than that of the agent or recipient of the action. Indeed the only interiority in the passage aligns Francesca with Lancelot's desires ("il disïato riso," "the longed-for smile") rather than Guinevere's. If this is Francesca's ideal of romance, then she apparently wishes to be, or to be seen as, the object rather than the agent of desire.

In the last two lines of the passage I have quoted above, Francesca shifts to her own past and its imitation of the transformed romance scene. Again she does not conceive of herself as an agent in love; instead Paolo is the subject of the verb "basciò" as well as the reference of the phrase "tutto tremante." His agency sits ill with his silence throughout her discourse. It also jars with his inadequacy as a latter-day Lancelot; the "questi" ("'this one here'") with which Francesca designates him lacks the qualitative intensifier of his model's "cotanto amante," "so great a lover." Francesca herself appears in the sentence only as the indirect object, "mi," which is an ethical dative linked to the direct object "la bocca," the mouth. She thus reproduces her bodily fragmentation of Guinevere, with the effect that she seems to see herself from without rather than re-experiencing the kiss from within as a participant.

---

[7] "Tragedy or Romance," 354–55.

In a poem in which people assert their truest identities by what and how they love, Francesca's grammar of love is odd.[8] Her self-assertion as Guinevere's peer is also a self-diminishment: in the process of asserting her identity, she fragments and objectifies herself. This is clearly a product of the female beloved adopting the perspective of the male in the male-anchored discourse of romance, yet the model she alters in order to fit it to her imitation is not so simple. That is, Francesca also diminishes the Lancelot romance. By reverting to the baldest conventions by which romance depicts male action and female passivity, her gender reversal elides whatever capacity the original may have had to probe at those conventions. Instead Francesca simply reproduces habitual and unexamined assumptions about proper gender roles in love. Dante may not present genuine female subjectivity directly, but by focusing on problems of representation—not only his own to his readers, but also Francesca's to her listeners and to herself—he exposes some of the difficulties for authentic identity that arise when a resilient, male-anchored discourse provides the means of conceiving and expressing even the female self.

Francesca's name associates her with the romanesque literature of Northern France, and I have begun with the influence this tradition exerts on her second narrative. However, her first narrative owes more to the lyric traditions of Provence and Italy; and here her self-diminishment appears in the guise of self-magnification. In this version as well, Francesca reverses conventional gender roles to become a ventriloquist, for in her famous anaphora she adopts the resolutely male voice of the troubadours and their Italian successors:

> "Amor, ch'al cor gentil ratto s'apprende,
>   prese costui de la bella persona
>   che mi fu tolta; e 'l modo ancor m'offende.
> Amor, ch'a nullo amato amar perdona,
>   mi prese del costui piacer sì forte,
>   che, come vedi, ancor non m'abbandona.
> Amor condusse noi ad una morte.
>   Caina attende chi a vita ci spense."   *Inf.* 5.100–107

"Love, which is quickly kindled in a gentle heart, seized this one for the fair form that was taken from me—and the way of it afflicts me still. Love, which absolves no loved one from loving, seized me so strongly with delight in him, that, as you see, it does not leave me even now. Love brought us to one death. Caina awaits him who quenched our life."

Because a woman speaks these lines, Poggioli denies any connection between *Inferno* 5 and the lyric literature of love, especially Dante's own contributions.

---

[8] I also want to stress that the grammar of "la bocca mi basciò" is perfectly ordinary; this is indeed the point. Dante here and elsewhere probes the capacity of ordinary ways of speaking to inform individual speakers, and to circumscribe the possibilities of their understanding of self and others. I thank Ralph Williams for his help with the grammar.

He quotes Francesco De Sanctis on the gendered voice of both Provençal and stilnuovistic lyrics; in this poetic tradition, De Sanctis wrote,

> man fills the stage with himself; it is he who acts, and speaks, and dreams; while woman remains in the background, named and not represented ...; she stays there as man's shadow, as a thing he owns, as an object he has wrought, as the being issued from his rib, devoid of a separate personality of her own.[9]

Poggioli is quite right to rehabilitate De Sanctis on this point, at least for the chanson and canzone.[10] But I draw a different conclusion from the gender reversal: Francesca's first version of her fatal love story is lyric, and Dante means her assumption of the lyric voice of love to be outrageous.

Her self-magnification in this first version is created by its characteristically lyric voicing. The personification of love as an abstract force preempts human agency, as does the automatism of love's process. To say that people are seized by love, and that they cannot resist mirroring another's love (or seizure, as the case may be), suggests a void in moral as well as grammatical agency, as if they were not the doers of their own deeds. Elsewhere in the *Commedia* Dante revises the syntax (moral and grammatical) of love without purging its lyricism; Francesca's grammatically reflexive "Amor, ch'al cor gentil ratto s'apprende" becomes Virgil's transitive "Amore, / acceso di virtù, sempre altro accese" ("Love, kindled by virtue, has ever kindled other love"—*Purg.* 22.10–11), for instance. In the metaphor developed throughout the *Commedia*,[11] souls are reflective bodies that radiate the love they receive back outward onto others, according to their capacity to mirror the divine. Paolo, however, appears only as the figment of Francesca's desire. In the context of the controlling metaphor, Francesca's reflexive, lyric love might be called absorptive. She looks into the mirror, and sees only an image of herself being loved. She is, in sum, a lyric Narcissus.

But her Echo lacks even a voice. Francesca weeps and speaks ("piange e dice," *Inf.* 5.126), but Paolo only weeps: "Mentre che l'uno spirto questo disse,

---

[9] Originally published in 1869 in *Francesca da Rimini secondi i critici e secondo l'arte* (see *Lezioni e saggi su Dante*, volume 5 of *Opere di Francesco de Sanctis*, ed. Carlo Muscetta [Turin: Einaudi, 1955]); I quote from Poggioli's translation in "Tragedy or Romance," 353.

[10] This is the "major" genre of the medieval lyric tradition; other genres, like the *alba*, are voiced less restrictively or at least differently. On the voice of women characters in the *alba*, see Jonathan Saville, *The Medieval Erotic Alba: Structure as Meaning* (New York: Columbia Univ. Press, 1972), esp. 113–174 and 216–37. On gender in medieval lyric and love literature generally, see E. Jane Burns, "The Man Behind the Lady in Troubadour Lyric," *RN* 25 (1985): 254–70; Simon Gaunt, "Poetry of Exclusion: A Feminist Reading of Some Troubadour Lyrics," *MLR* 85 (1990): 310–29; the essays in *The Voice of the Trobairitz: Perspectives on the Women Troubadours*, ed. William D. Paden (Philadelphia: Univ. of Pennsylvania Press, 1989); and Toril Moi's work, e.g., "Desire in Language: Andreas Capellanus and the Controversy of Courtly Love," in *Medieval Literature: Criticism, Ideology, and History*, ed. David Aers (New York: St. Martin's Press, 1985), 11–33.

[11] Particularly in the central cantos of *Purgatorio*, 15–25.

/ l'altro piangëa" ("While the one spirit said this, the other wept"—*Inf.* 5.139–40). "Paolo and Francesca" are inseparably linked, it seems, and most critics write as if they could be certain that her story is his too. It may be, but the assumption is unwarranted. You don't know, and he doesn't say. Perhaps his story would be different. Francesca's adoption of the lyric voice silences Paolo, and puts him in the position conventionally filled by the female beloved in the chanson/canzone. This position (well described by De Sanctis above) is characteristically alien; moreover, the absence of the female voice is an enabling factor, or perhaps even the necessary condition, for transforming the women of lyric into the typical conventions of their representation: the cruel lady whose gelid mercilessness freezes the lover's blood in midsummer; or Caesar's untouchable white doe in Petrarch's *rime sparse* (190), or the disembodied fragments scattered throughout the collection; or the idealized figure of all virtue found so often in medieval love lyrics. Positive or negative, these lyric images are not so much women as markers, or vessels to be filled by the desires (and fears) of their male speakers. Frequently, what appears to be erotic desire for the female beloved turns out to be poetic desire for a bravura literary performance. Literary desire is, after all, more susceptible of self-fulfillment: Laura won Petrarch poetic fame and his laurel wreath. The female site of desire, that is, becomes an occasion for the male poet to achieve a fulfillment that has little to do with women or love. Similarly, Paolo's silence enables Francesca's narcissism, which is lyric narcissism: the first person in these lyrics cannot be authentically plural, and the other is present only to reflect the speaker.

And the outrage? All of what I describe above would be unmarked, and perhaps scarcely noticeable, had Dante done what Francesca does to the Lancelot romance: stick to the conventional gender assignations, and thus give her words to Paolo. But Dante makes his audience sit up and take notice by lending lyric words to a woman. I do not argue here that Dante condemns egotism as the peculiarly feminine vice of women in love and in love literature. Rather, the reversal renders visible the profoundly destructive usurpation of genuine selfhood—anybody's selfhood—underwritten by the conventional words of love.

Dante's treatment of gender in *Inferno* 5 is central to his poetic ambitions in the *Commedia*. These are figured through his replacement of Francesca with Beatrice, who appears in person in the Earthly Paradise (*Purg.* 30). The figurative language surrounding her encompasses both genders: as a magnificent admiral, the avenging angel Michael, and the goddess Minerva, she differs markedly from Virgil's idealized courtly representation of her in the allegory of intercession he narrates in *Inferno* 2. An Aeneas to Dante's Dido,[12] Beatrice is also a figure for Christ. Announcing her advent, Dante compares the event

---

[12] See *Purg.* 30.46–48: "Men che dramma / di sangue m'è rimaso che non tremi: / conosco i segni de l'antica fiamma" ("Not a drop of blood is left in me that does not tremble: I know the tokens of the ancient flame"). Dante translates *Aeneid* 4.23 ("Agnosco veteris vestigia flammae") and assigns Dido's words to himself. His trembling is the first parallelism in this canto between himself and Paolo ("tutto tremante," *Inf.* 5.136).

to the rising sun and the second coming. The company of souls addresses her with the grammatically feminine "Veni, sponsa de Lebano" ("Come, spouse from Lebanon"—*Purg.* 30.11), and with "Benedictus qui venis" ("Blessed are you who come"—*Purg.* 30.19)—where the second-person verb is linked to a grammatically masculine, and therefore outrageous, appropriation of the eucharistic language designating Christ.

Beatrice differs from Francesca especially in her treatment of her male beloved. Though she is "the bearer of blessedness," she scarcely resembles the ethereal merciful lady of lyric tradition. She is fierce. And she refuses to allow Dante to reproduce the behavior sanctioned by either the lyric tradition or Francesca's appropriation of it. With her first words, she tells Dante to stop weeping; he may not imitate Paolo either. The pressure of Dante's need to differentiate himself and Beatrice from the lovers of *Inferno* 5 causes him to break the rules of decorum and name himself:[13]

> "Dante, perchè Virgilio se ne vada,
>   non pianger ancor, non piangere ancora;
>   chè pianger ti conven per altra spada."   *Purg.* 30.55–57

"Dante, because Virgil leaves you, do not weep yet, do not weep yet, for you must weep for another sword!"

The contrast to Francesca—who acknowledges Paolo only with dismissive locative demonstratives, and not at all as a being separate from herself—could not be starker. There can be no question that Dante means, through Beatrice, to correct Francesca's versions of love and self. (Whether he actually succeeds in creating a woman with a voice genuinely different from his own and from his poetic and soteriological desires is a different issue, to which I'll return.) When Dante subsequently dissolves in tears, becoming (like Paolo) "colui che di là piagne" ("he who weeps yonder"—*Purg.* 30.107), it is not possible to understand his anguish either as Francesca's self-magnifying nostalgia or as whatever Paolo's weeping might be. And Dante's effort, through Beatrice and her difference from Francesca, to rescue the lyric and erotic for his epic of salvation cannot be separated from his treatment of gender.

2

What Chaucer really did to Boccaccio's *Il Filostrato* in *Troilus and Criseyde*, according to C. S. Lewis, was to "medievalize" it.[14] Insofar as Lewis's observations concern love and love literature, to medievalize is in large measure to

---

[13] Dante refers to the rules at lines 62–63; he had stated them in *Convivio* I.ii.3. There are, of course, other reasons for naming oneself in a confessional autobiography; see Singleton's commentary on line 63 (2:2:743–44).

[14] In "What Chaucer Really Did," 56–75.

Frenchify—to restore the language and assumptions of both the northern ro-
manesque and the southern lyric traditions whose absence make *Il Filostrato* so
"modern."[15] But enlarging the role of aristocratic French love literature in no
way requires that Chaucer endorse it, and indeed I regard *Troilus and Criseyde*
as an anti-romance. The poem does not celebrate the discourses of love uncrit-
ically, but rather voices them through its various speakers in order to probe the
causal relations among their social situation, their role in informing individual
consciousness, and their often destructive consequences. By setting lyric,
romantic, and unromantic voices next to one another, Chaucer gives his audi-
ence the opportunity to discover the fabrications involved in any version of
love.

Readers sometimes respond to Criseyde alone in Book 2 (lines 596–931) as
egotistical and narcissistic. This reading, I think, reflects the difference between
her practical weighing of the advantages and disadvantages of love affairs—her
sense that circumstances are crucial—and the romantic ideology of love that sur-
rounds her and increasingly constrains both her actions and her sense of self.
She speaks and thinks from outside the conventional discourses of love, and
such negative judgment measures mainly the power with which the lyric and ro-
mantic modes voiced by Troilus, Pandarus, and the narrator have already
defined her. Unromanticism looks bad to the romantic.

But the collision of competing perspectives on love invites analytic thinking
rather than categorical judgment. Structurally, Chaucer often embodies these
competing perspectives through doubled representations of the same or similar
events. So, for instance, Troilus seems to fall in love twice, once allegorically
when the God of Love shoots him to avenge his mockery of lovers (1.204–10),
and then more naturalistically when he catches sight of Criseyde and feels the
powerful pull of erotic attraction (1.267–80). (These two passages may also be
read as a sequence, but the difference in representative style is unmistakable.)
Criseyde sees Troilus twice through her window; the first time (2.610–65) is un-
planned; and the second (2.1247–88), since Pandarus arranges it precisely in
order to cause her to love Troilus, identifies the view from the window as a
characteristic scene of romance.[16] Troilus tells Pandarus that he loves Cri-

---

[15] I include here also the Italian progeny of the Provençal tradition, especially Petrarch's
lyric poetry. For the suggestion that Chaucer "Petrarchized" Boccaccio, see Richard Waswo,
"The Narrator of *Troilus and Criseyde*," *ELH* 50 (1983): 1–25, at 23. For Boccaccio's insuffi-
cient *gentilesse* as a cause of Chaucer's adaptations, see David Wallace, "Chaucer and
Boccaccio's Early Writings," in *Chaucer and the Italian Trecento*, ed. Piero Boitani (Cambridge:
Cambridge Univ. Press, 1985), 141–62, at 159.

[16] *Il Filostrato* contains one window scene, the second. Lavinia sees Aeneas through her
window at the beginnings of French romance in the *Roman d'Eneas*, ed. J. J. Salverda de
Grave, 2 vols., CFMA (Paris: Champion, 1925–29), 8047–72. The window scene becomes a
standard romantic representation of women falling in love; see also Chrétien's *Yvain*, ed.
Mario Roques, CMFA (Paris: Champion, 1964), lines 1339–1506. For a suggestive discussion,
based on French romances, of women's private space as a place of "reverie, openness,
expectation, and confidence," and windows as boundaries crossed by the gaze, see Danielle
Régnier-Bohler, "Imagining the Self," in *A History of Private Life*, 2, *Revelations of the Medieval*

seyde in Book I; later, responding to Criseyde's question "Kan he wel speke of love?" (2.503), Pandarus spins a more conventionally romantic version of the same event.[17] Chaucer may not get at the unrendered reality of falling in love—the putative truth behind the surface of the text—but by including such doubled representations, he makes us aware of the element of fabrication in each of them. Chaucer doesn't pretend to present reality itself, but rather stresses the representation of it by literally re-presenting crucial scenes, with differences, in his poem. He thus encourages us to consider the possible agendas, whether intended or not, these fabrications might further.

Chief among such agendas is the transformation of Criseyde, initially a distant figure in widow's weeds, isolated from the "olde daunce," into the willing object of Troilus's lyric love and into a character in Pandarus's book of romance.[18]

In Book I, Troilus's lyric conception of Criseyde dominates. We see little of her except as filtered through his imagination (and that of Pandarus as well, who "for the nones" puts on the assumptions of lyric love).[19] After glimpsing her at the temple of Athena—a moment underwritten by the lyric tradition to which Dante and Petrarch also belong—Troilus retires to his chamber and the anguished imaginings of *amor lonh*, the love for a distant, indifferent lady. He creates a Criseyde that derives rather more from literature than from the woman herself—who, since she is unaware of his feelings, could scarcely have chosen to disregard them. Troilus's Criseyde is the classic Cruel Lady of lyric. Her power to grant or withhold mercy is also the tyrant's capricious power over life and death in Troilus's complaint:[20]

"But now help, God, and ye, swete, for whom
I pleyne, ikaught, ye, nevere wight so faste!
O mercy, dere herte, and help me from
The deth, for I, while that my lyf may laste,
More than myself wol love yow to my laste.

World, ed. Georges Duby, trans. Arthur Goldhammer (Cambridge: Belknap, 1988), 345–48, at 345.

[17] Pandarus's fictionalized version follows at 2.506ff. Part of his concern in fictionalizing is to assure Criseyde that Troilus does not have loose lips. For the role of Pandarus's stories here and elsewhere, see Fyler, "Fabrications" (*included in this volume*).

[18] For a more thorough discussion of Pandarus's and Troilus's treatments of Criseyde as acts of reading, see Dinshaw, "Reading Like a Man: The Critics, the Narrator, Troilus and Pandarus," in *Poetics*, 28–64 (*included in this volume*). See also Aers, "Chaucer's Criseyde: Woman in Society, Woman in Love," in *Chaucer*, 117–42; and "Masculine Identity in the Courtly Community: The Self Loving in *Troilus and Criseyde*," in *Community*, 117–52. For an account that sees Dante's influence at work, see Shoaf, *Currency*, 107–57. I also wish to acknowledge a general debt to Muscatine's description of the differing styles of the three main characters of *Troilus and Criseyde* in *French Tradition*, 124–61.

[19] On Criseyde as "a mere image serving Troilus' fantasy life," see McAlpine, *Genre*, 127.

[20] Pandarus later calls Criseyde's continuing resistance to Troilus a tyrant's game: "But ye han played the tirant neigh to longe" (2.1240). Perhaps not surprisingly, political metaphors are common in hierarchical conceptions of love.

> And with som frendly look gladeth me, swete,
> Though nevere more thing ye me byhete."   1.533–39

The distinction between woman and representation is apparent in Troilus's most succinct definition of the Cruel Lady:

> "But, O thow woful Troilus, God wolde,
> Sith thow most loven thorugh thi destine,
> That thow beset were on swich oon that sholde
> Know al thi wo, al lakked hir pitee!
> But also cold in love towardes the
> Thi lady is, as frost in wynter moone,
> And thow fordon, as snow in fire is soone."   1.519–25

Troilus addresses himself, focusing on his own interiority; Criseyde is present only in the third person. The last three lines of the stanza could have been drawn from Petrarch; in fact they follow Boccaccio.[21] It's worth noting that Chaucer has transposed a concept from the Romance languages into a wholly native lexicon. He is artistically involved in the Englishing of Continental love discourses—though not, I think, in endorsing them.

Whatever one might say about the objectification involved when Troilus substitutes for Criseyde these highly wrought images with their impeccable literary lineage, his lyricism has little design on Criseyde herself. It dictates to her no particular behavior; it requires of her no response; demands of her no conformance to the images of Troilus's desires and fears. Instead, in the navigational metaphor woven throughout Book I, the port Troilus longs for and fears is not Criseyde, but death.[22]

It takes Pandarus to translate Troilus's words into action; and he does this by first relocating the reference of these lyric images, and then transposing love lyric into the narrative genre of romance. Having finally learned whom Troilus loves, Pandarus counters the Cruel Lady with its equally conventional opposite, and tries to persuade Troilus that Criseyde, as the vessel of all virtue, is instead the granter of pity. From her external appearance and good manners, Pandarus moves easily to a more inwardly defined nobility of character at 1.880–96, and concludes:

---

[21] See *Il Filostrato*, 1.53, lines 5–8:
"Ma quella per cui piangi nulla sente
se non come una pietra, e così stassi
fredda com' al sereno intero ghiaccio
ed io qual neve al foco mi disfaccio"

"But she for whom you weep feels nothing, like a stone; and stays as cold as ice under a clear sky, and I am unmade like snow in fire."
I have used Windeatt's parallel text edition; translation mine.

[22] See the *Canticus Troili*, 1.400–420, a translation of Petrarch's sonnet "S'amor non è," where it's not entirely clear what the absent port might be; death is more clearly the destination at 1.526–27 ("God wold I were aryved in the port / Of deth") and 1.606 (". . . streight unto the deth myn herte sailleth").

> "And also thynk, and therwith glade the,
> That sith thy lady vertuous is al,
> So foloweth it that there is some pitee
> Amonges alle thise other in general;
> And forthi se that thow, in special,
> Requere naught that is ayeyns hyre name;
> For vertu streccheth naught hymself to shame."   1.897–903

Troilus's port of death becomes Pandarus's "good port"—unmistakably Criseyde—and moreover a destination Troilus has already attained: " 'Stond faste, for to good port hastow rowed' " (1.969). The shift in reference implicates Criseyde firmly in the love story to come in a way Troilus's lyric images of her had not. And Pandarus's syllogism of virtue prescribes behavior for her (and for Troilus, too) that will eventually ensnare her in romance conventions of the feminine. It requires, in a word, action: though for her action, within the scaffolding of Pandarus's house of romance, will be for the most part reaction. That is, while I do argue that Pandarus's romance brings Criseyde into the poem more fully in her own person, I do not wish to preempt the far more complex issues of her autonomy and (in grammatical and moral terms) her agency.

In their conversation in the first part of Book 2, Pandarus edges Criseyde into her role as romantic heroine. The Ovidian metaphor of love as war implicitly underwrites the scene; Pandarus besieges her, and she defends herself, just as Greeks beset Trojans and Trojans defend themselves in the real war at the margins of the poem. Pandarus and Criseyde are equally skilled at the art of conversation, though he has the advantage of prosecuting the offense. He assumes from the outset that she will be unwilling to hear, much less accept, his suit on Troilus's behalf, and his strategy to overcome her reluctance is clever: first he makes her want to know what he has come to tell her; then—by withholding, delaying, and threatening to leave without telling her—he increases the urgency of her desire to know. Having created in her a powerful but generalized desire, he then tries to relocate its object in Troilus.

But Criseyde is also adept; wishing neither to seem too eager nor to commit herself to anything before she knows what it is, she conceals the strength of her desire to hear Pandarus's message:

> Tho gan she wondren moore than biforn
> A thousand fold, and down hire eyghen caste;
> For nevere, sith the tyme that she was born,
> To knowe thyng desired she so faste;
> And with a syk she seyde hym atte laste,
> "Now, uncle myn, I nyl yow nought displese,
> Nor axen more that may do yow disese."   2.141–47

But Pandarus's sidestepping attack eventually makes her confess how much she wants to know:

> "Now, my good em, for Goddes love, I preye,"

> Quod she, "come of, and telle me what it is!
> For both I am agast what ye wol seye,
> And ek me longeth it to wite, ywys;
> For whethir it be wel or be amys,
> Say on, lat me nat in this feere dwelle."   2.309–15

Although she does not commit herself to a positive response, her concession here is a small defeat, for it invites Pandarus to press his suit. She has signalled her willingness at least to hear it.

And so Pandarus springs his trap: "The noble Troilus, so loveth the, / That, but ye helpe, it wol his bane be" (2.319–20). Without allowing Criseyde a response, he adds two things designed to channel it in the direction he wishes: he threatens to join Troilus in death if she refuses the suit, and he imposes the lyric opposition between the Cruel Lady and her merciful counterpart to define Criseyde. She can choose which she'll be, but Pandarus loads the choice: in courtly terms, virtue accrues only to the latter, and who would choose vice?[23] Criseyde, still defending herself adroitly, asks only for advice, as if it were not already clear what course he recommends. Pandarus then acknowledges the reluctance he has assumed all along as her response—the "daunger" of line 384— only to counter it with the classic carpe diem threat: " 'To late ywar, quod beaute, whan it paste'; / And elde daunteth daunger at the laste" (2.398–99).

When Criseyde at last bursts into her tearful reproach against the faithlessness of the world, and of Pandarus in particular (2.409–27), the rejection is no victory for the capacity of a female object of desire to define her own, autonomous desires:

> And she began to breste a-wepe anoon,
> And seyde, "Allas, for wo! Why nere I deed?
> For of this world the feyth is al agoon.
> Allas! what sholden straunge to me doon,
> When he, that for my beste frend I wende,
> Ret me to love, and sholde it me defende?"   2.408–13

Delay, and the theatricality of the lament, suggest that Criseyde is playing a role rather than expressing her inmost response to the news that Troilus loves her. It suggests, moreover, that she has lost, for she has accepted the terms in which Pandarus has framed her alternatives. Her reluctance is now the "daunger" of the virtuous courtly lady, a quality defined not only by initial resistance but also by eventual capitulation.[24]

Daunger, a central fabrication of aristocratic love literature, is not quite the same thing as resistance or reluctance. A trace acknowledging that women's desires aren't necessarily compatible with those of the men who love them, and

---

[23] See lines 337–50 for Pandarus's contrast between vicious cruelty and virtuous pity.

[24] For the way Criseyde exploits, for self-protection, the courtly conventions for virtuous female behavior offered by Pandarus, even as they also come to limit and define her options, I have been greatly influenced by Elizabeth G. Allen's unpublished Senior Essay, "Chaucer and Henryson: The Mirror of Fiction," Yale College Department of English, 1988.

that the beloved might thwart the desires of her lover, it is also a translation device. Daunger assumes the woman's reluctance, but stages it as only temporary. Daunger thus converts resistance into something more manageable, and incorporates the anxiety-provoking possibility of female difference, thus tamed, into the male-anchored system of aristocratic love. It provides a rationale, still very much alive today, by which a man may hear a woman's "no" as "yes."[25]

Beyond its function effectively to negate genuine female subjectivity, daunger also provides the space in which to stage the drama of male self-discovery. Although it allows the lyric poet as well to define his unique subjectivity, I will focus (since Troilus's lyric imaginings have given ground in Book 2 to Pandarus's romantic narrative) on daunger's centrality to romance. Though by no means a universal convention, the lady's daunger—along with physical obstacles like imprisonment—is coextensive with delay and deferral, the characteristic narrative movement of romance. Her initial refusal gives the romantic hero the opportunity to prove himself worthy of her love, which he does by going out on a sometimes vastly dilated aventure. But questing itself is usually as much the point as its ostensible goal, the lady's favor, for worthiness is defined by the traditional martial values of chivalric prowess: courage, loyalty to one's lord and fellow knights, invincibility in battle (that is, superiority to other knights). Daunger thus becomes a means by which the twin ideals of chivalric romance— love and prowess—reciprocally strengthen one another. (The reciprocity of love and prowess is the chief fantasy of the genre, and shown in the most interesting romances to be constantly at risk.) The conventional attribute of romance ladies, then, has far more to do with masculine identity than with feminine anything.

In providing the space for discovering and developing masculine identity, daunger redirects the focus of feminine resistance (of whatever quality). When conceived as daunger, the lady's reluctance is not so much a problem—that which thwarts the hero's desires—as it is the obstacle he needs in order, inevitably, to overcome it. Where it appears, her daunger is what makes him the hero. Its deferrals allow him to show his superiority to all other men, and thus daunger is also the means by which romances establish their hierarchies of male worthiness. In this process, one notes, the woman and her resistance (again, of whatever quality) tend to disappear.[26]

---

[25] A wonderful, and baldly stated, example may be found in Walter Map's "Dissuasio Valerii ad Ruffinum philosophum ne uxorem ducat" (A Dissuasion of Valerius to Rufinus the Philosopher, that he should not take a Wife), a tract against marriage circulated separately and then included in the satirical compendium De Nugis Curialium (Courtier's Trifles), written ca. 1180–90:

Finally, amongst so many millions, did ever one woman sadden a constant and earnest suitor by a permanent denial? Did she consistently silence the suppliant's words? No, her answer has some taste of favour in it, and however hard it is, it will always contain in some nook of its wording a concealed stimulus to your petition. Every one of them refuses, none goes on refusing.

Cited from De nugis curialium, ed. and trans. M. R. James, rev. C.N.L. Brooke and R.A.B. Mynors, Oxford Medieval Texts (Oxford: Clarendon Press, 1983), Dist. iv, c. 3 (308–9).

[26] The woman's disappearance might be exemplified in Pandarus's treatment of Cri-

But the male focus of daunger does not prevent it from affecting the women of romance as well. As one of two defining feminine virtues, it prescribes their behavior. Its deferral waylays the danger of erotic overeagerness; indeed one of the chief differences between Boccaccio's Criseida and Chaucer's Criseyde is that the former uses daunger only as a very temporary cover to mask her swift, powerful desire to begin the love affair. She is thus "loose," which is to say insufficiently courtly. Daunger's delay also prevents the virtuous woman from succumbing prematurely to the wrong man, insuring rather that she will hold out for the fully proven hero. At this point, daunger has no further role. A prelude to its own opposite, it is virtuous only if it eventually yields. Not to relinquish it at the proper moment would brand the lady as pitiless, and pity is the second defining virtue for romance women. Daunger tames potentially genuine female resistance into something more easily manageable: fear of the social opprobrium that descends upon overeager women, for instance. It has both individual and social effects: it translates an inward, subjective sign of female autonomy into an objective, externally defined code of behavior; and it converts resistant women into the instruments by which men discover and prove themselves to others.

The quality of Criseyde's reluctance in her conversation with Pandarus is hard to gauge because it is always tactical. Criseyde adopts the conventional feminine roles of Pandarus's romance, but her unspoken mental maneuverings show her awareness of these roles precisely as conventions. They don't necessarily express Criseyde's subjectivity; she also exploits them for her own ends. Even though the role of the daungerous woman presupposes her eventual surrender, adopting it also wins Criseyde time to consider Pandarus's suit in her own terms. Since these terms differ from the romance conventions of Pandarus's persuasion, Chaucer gestures toward a female autonomy not wholly confined by the strictures of romantic love, without, however, actually representing it.

In the following scene Criseyde, weighing her options alone, is genuinely ambivalent. The delicate interplay of her mental debate shows that she is not simply the daungerous woman of Pandarus's romance. Attraction, and political considerations, pull her even as her hesitations make her shy away from Troilus and love generally. More important, Criseyde, even alone, wavers between conceiving of herself as the object and as the subject of desire. She sees herself through the eyes of others as "oon the faireste" woman in Troy (2.746). And she is aware of herself as the object of Troilus's desire: "I woot for me is his destresse" (2.719), she thinks; or later, in more objectified terms:

---

seyde's daunger at 2.1372–93; here Criseyde herself may be immoveable, but daunger (via Pandarus's comparison of it to an oak) converts her very implacability into complaisance:

> "And reed that boweth down for every blast,
> Ful lightly, cesse wynd, it wol aryse;
> But so nyl nought an ook, whan it is cast;
> It nedeth me nought the longe to forbise.
> Men shal rejoissen of a gret empryse
> Acheved wel, and stant withouten doute,
> Al han men ben the lenger theraboute."

"I thenke ek how he able is for to have
Of al this noble town the thriftieste,
To ben his love, so she hire honour save."   2.736–38

In conceiving of herself as the object of another's desire, she thinks in the terms of romance; her thoughts also share Francesca's grammatical subordination of self to the agency of another. But this is only part of the story; in the rest, Chaucer leaves Dante behind.

For Criseyde also sees herself as the genuine subject of her own desires, capable of choosing whether or not to love, rather than as the object constructed by daunger:[27]

[She] was somdel astoned in hire thought,
Right for the newe cas; but whan that she
Was ful avysed, tho fond she right nought
Of peril, why she ought afered be.
For man may love, of possibilite,
A womman so, his herte may tobreste,
And she naught love ayein, but if hire leste.   2.603–9

And:

"What shal I doon? To what fyn lyve I thus?
Shal I nat love, in cas if that me leste?
What, par dieux! I am naught religious.
And though that I myn herte sette at reste
Upon this knyght, that is the worthieste,
And kepe alwey myn honour and my name,
By alle right, it may do me no shame."   2.757–63

Nor does the narrative context belie her subjectivity. When Troilus passes under her window, Chaucer represents the view as seen through her eyes; she is the implicit subject of the verbs of perception in lines 610–51 (if not often the grammatical subject; most of the verbs are infinitives).

But the narrative context both confirms Criseyde's agency and shows how difficult it is to escape the discourses of love that would entrap her anyway. She is open to the influence of Antigone's love lyric; its very presence suggests that it has penetrated Criseyde's consciousness, even though she initially queries it ("Who made this song now with so good entente?"—2.878) and remains finally noncommittal ("Criseyde unto that purpos naught answerde"—2.897). She seems aware, with the song as with other conventional utterances about love, that it matters who speaks them. And the autonomy of the seeing subject in the window scene, which I have just used to argue for Criseyde's genuine subjectivi-

---

[27] Her agency, or power to choose, is implicit in the Augustinian structure of moral choice that provides the framework for her deliberations; see Donald R. Howard, *The Three Temptations: Medieval Man in Search of the World* (Princeton: Princeton Univ. Press, 1966), 121–35; for a negative evaluation, using the same framework to stress sin rather than choice, see Robertson, *Preface*, 477–97.

ty, is thrown into question by Pandarus's fabricated duplicate later in Book 2. The re-presented window scene confirms the conventionality of the original as well, and suggests that the private chambers of Criseyde's mind are furnished by the very romances she also sees as inimical to her freedom to choose. And, with the same re-presentation, Chaucer shows us the difficulties poets face when, with the best of will, they try to represent female subjectivity. Here two problems are entangled—that of genuine female subjectivity itself, and that of representing it within the traditional discourses of poetic love.

One of Criseyde's chief objections to love, as it is practiced, is that it constrains not only behavior but also her sure sense of her own subjectivity (the first problem above). Outside the terms of romance, she thinks, "I am myn owene womman" (2.750); but if she chose to love, she would also yield to the discourse that subjects her to the actions and desires of another:

> "Allas! syn I am free,
> Sholde I now love, and put in jupartie
> My sikernesse, and thrallen libertee?"   2.771–73

As Criseyde is absorbed more fully into Pandarus's romance, she retains a sense of her autonomy even though her choices and actions accommodate his manipulations. When Troilus voices his fulfilled desire in words that cast Criseyde as prisoner and prey, she reminds him that she is more than the object of his pursuit. She has also chosen to yield:

> This Troilus in armes gan hire streyne,
> And seyde, "O swete, as evere mot I gon,
> Now be ye kaught, now is ther but we tweyne!
> Now yeldeth yow, for other bote is non!"
> To that Criseyde answerde thus anon,
> "Ne hadde I er now, my swete herte deere,
> Ben yold, ywis, I were now nought here!"   3.1205–11[28]

Because Criseyde retains a sense (however constrained) of her own autonomy for so long into the romance, it is especially painful when, now in the Greek camp, she uses the objectifying discourse of love to reduce herself to its

---

[28] I follow Aers, who quotes the last two lines here to make the point beautifully (*Community*, 130–31):

> So while Criseyde, trained to be a woman in a knights' community, characteristically accommodates to the language of the male, imported from the public sphere, she simultaneously draws on her own resources to resist its implications: "Ne hadde I er now, my swete herte deere, / Ben yold, ywis, I were now nought heere!" (III, 1,210–11). The resistance is in the deft way she takes responsibility for her own presence in bed with him. In doing so she reminds him that she is not here simply because she is "kaught", but because she is a human agent who, whatever the gross pressures brought against her, had made decisions "er now" without which, "I were now nought heere". Continually the poem works thus to negate man's traditional denial of subjectivity to women, brushing its culture and its own sources strongly against the grain, a mark of its idiosyncracy, lasting significance, and greatness.

conventions of women. Her lament in Book 5 shows that her sense of autonomy, of herself as subject and agent, has become more tenuous and intermittent. She forthrightly acknowledges her choice (under great pressure) to shift her "truth" to Diomede: "For I have falsed oon the gentileste / That evere was, and oon the worthieste!" (5.1056–57). Thereafter, her grammatical agency and her moral courage become obscured by her powerful sense of subjection to the actions and opinions of others. First she shifts to the passive voice, an impersonal construction, and the objective case as she imagines (quite correctly) her fate in literature:

> "Allas! of me, unto the worldes ende,
> Shal neyther ben ywriten nor ysonge
> No good word, for thise bokes wol me shende.
> O, rolled shal I ben on many a tonge!
> Thorughout the world my belle shal be ronge!
> And wommen moost wol haten me of alle.
> Allas, that swich a case me sholde falle!"   5.1058–64

The next stanza is filled with obscurities of voice and agency:

> "Thei wol seyn, in as muche as in me is,
> I have hem don dishonour, weylaway!
> Al be I nat the first that dide amys,
> What helpeth that to don my blame awey?
> But syn I se ther is no bettre way,
> And that to late is now for me to rewe,
> To Diomede algate I wol be trewe."   5.1065–71

The prepositional dative of "in me" deflects both grammatical and moral agency from Criseyde; and though the next line indirectly acknowledges that she "dide amys," the misdeed is couched in the third person as she seeks protection among the multitudes. It's not clear who voices the next line: is Criseyde still paraphrasing the hostile women's reproaches? or does she retract, in her own voice, the evasion of agency in the syntax of the preceding line?

The end of her lament captures the difficulty of Criseyde's subjectivity in small:

> "And gilteles, I woot wel, I yow leve.
> But al shal passe; and thus take I my leve."   5.1084–85

It's grammatically possible that "gilteles" modifies "I"—Criseyde—instead of the more likely "yow"—Troilus—although it is a stretch to read "I woot wel" as something Criseyde would say when characterizing herself, for it would require Criseyde to see herself from without. But such self-objectification characterizes the syntax of the lament thus far, and would correspond well with its blurred agency as she hovers between denial and acknowledgement of responsibility.

And further: such self-objectification is the plot of romance for its women characters. *Troilus and Criseyde* includes (among many others) the story of Criseyde's diminishing subjectivity, and her growing complicity with the pressures that shape her experience. It includes, in addition to the story of her Trojan present, also that of her medieval future in literature, for her negated subjectivity allows her to become the figure Chaucer found in the medieval Troy tradition: the exemplary Faithless Woman.

Chaucer's concerns with conventional gender representations result in a critique of the discourses of love far more radical than Dante's in the *Commedia*. For after her initial fierceness toward Dante, Beatrice relents, her hardness revealed as daunger; and she becomes the gracious guide of his heavenly flight. She is reinscribed, then, into the conventional plot of romance, so that her religiously shaded daunger presages her eventual pity and grace. Dante is certainly concerned with the errors he perceives in the discourses of love—primarily their diminishment of human moral agency and their promotion of an inauthentic subjectivity—but he does not fundamentally depart from their conventional treatment of women. His poetic project, to redeem the erotic and to reconcile it with equally redeemed politics and religion, creates Beatrice as the Daungerous Woman writ large across the heavens, her initial resistance the means by which he proves his worthiness. She is the instrument by which he becomes the hero of his epic journey of Christian self-discovery. Dante uses the gender reversals of *Inferno* 5 and *Purgatorio* 30 to rewrite conventional representations of the feminine into another system, whose purpose, though perhaps more divine, is still to voice his own redeemed subjectivity.

But Chaucer is not the hero of his own poem, and he is genuinely interested in the difficulties of female subjectivity and of representing it. He voices the discourses of love through the variously limited characters of *Troilus and Criseyde*. He re-presents the same or similar scenes to show the fundamental fictiveness in the way all of the poem's people—the representing poet included—conceive of love. And he shows, through Criseyde's capacity for theatrical self-representation according to romance conventions she also knows to be more or less other than her feelings and thoughts, that the discourses of love inform even how people conceive of themselves. *Troilus and Criseyde* explores the destructive effects of the discourses of love that lead people to treat one another as if they really were the symbols ("hevene blisse" or "this false world") and exempla (the Daungerous Woman, or the Faithless Woman) that populate love literature. What is destroyed? Criseyde's theatricality, along with her awareness of its role-playing, presupposes a representing subject not necessarily coextensive with its own representations, which are the fictive shapings of something else. Chaucer may not be able directly to capture that something else—the possibilities of female subjectivity, and of voicing it—with the clarity with which he shows the constraints on it. Like Criseyde herself, who resists the notion that she can be "kaught" without her assent, these possibilities remain elusive. But by focusing on a poet's difficulty of representing them, with tools forged by the tradition out of which he writes, Chaucer can at least gesture toward the voices that tradition excludes. By such indirection, *Troilus and Criseyde* offers at least the possibility of alternatives. The rest is up to us.

Troilus *and the* Filostrato: *Chaucer as Translator of Boccaccio*[*]

DAVID WALLACE

The sequence of passages studied below explores various aspects of Chaucer's practice as a translator of Boccaccio. Some of what follows may not seem particularly exciting—it sounds more like technical talk in a poetry workshop than smart talk in a Chaucer seminar—but it does establish some groundrules that test or authenticate larger speculations (such as those essayed elsewhere in this volume). It is now indisputably evident that Chaucer was an extremely gifted Italianist; few writers in the English-speaking world have ever understood Italian poetry better. Chaucer's translating of Boccaccio, in which eight-line Italian stanzas rhyming ababababcc must be rendered as rhyme royal (ababbcc), reveals enormous technical intelligence; it is only through such detailed, local observation that we realize quite how intelligent a poetic practitioner Chaucer really was. Local decisions concerning syntax, phrasing, and meter are, of course, fundamental to the greater strategy of the poem; the changing or shifting of a single adverb or pronoun can be of enormous, long-term consequence. Such observation of stylistic and technical matters provides many points of departure for (can hardly be held apart from) critical exposition. Now, equipped with Windeatt's edition and Havely's crib, everyone who aspires to write on the TROILUS can look between the Italian and English stanzas and deduce what Chaucer is actually doing to IL FILOSTRATO.

Chaucer made more use of Boccaccio than of any other writer in any language and chose Boccaccio's *Filostrato* as the source of *Troilus and Criseyde*, his most ambitious extended narrative.[1] It is curious that Chaucer nowhere mentions Boccaccio by name. Perhaps this is because the study of Boccaccio might reveal too many of Chaucer's social and artistic secrets. The *Filostrato* and the *Troilus* are clearly attempting to find a middle way between popular and illustrious precedents: both are fundamentally indebted to native narrative traditions

---

[*] Originally appeared in *Chaucer and the Early Writings of Boccaccio*, Chaucer Studies xii (Woodbridge, Suffolk: Boydell & Brewer, Ltd., 1985), Chapters 5 and 6.

[1] The passages discussed in my essay are taken from Chapters 5 and 6 of my *Chaucer and the Early Writings of Boccaccio*. References to the *Filostrato* follow the edition by Branca, vol. 2. For a helpful survey of work on the *Filostrato*, see Benson, *Chaucer's T&C*, 13–38. For a useful table showing the main parallels between the *Troilus* and the *Filostrato*, see *The Riverside Chaucer*, 1024–25.

(Boccaccio to the *cantare*, Chaucer to metrical romances) while both aspire to follow in the footsteps of Dante and the great *auctores* of antiquity. Such equivocation in matters of source and style may be associated with, taken as symptoms of, equivocal social loyalties: both poets move from mercantile origins (which are never definitively repudiated) towards a more learned and court-centered culture; their fictional worlds are played out somewhere between the court, the cloister, and the customs house.

The *Filostrato* represents an early phase of Boccaccio's development and receives its chief narrative impetus from the lower levels of literary inspiration that were available at Naples.[2] Although Boccaccio treats of a classical subject he makes little use of classical texts: his fascination with pagan antiquity—so impressively developed in the *Filocolo*—is barely awakening. And yet Chaucer chose to employ this relatively unsophisticated poem as the source of his great *tragedye*.

It is at once apparent that it was the *Filostrato*'s simple virtues that were most to Chaucer's liking. Boccaccio does occasionally attempt to embellish his narrative with sophisticated rhetorical figures and with ingenious verbal configurations.[3] He sometimes smoothes the flow of his verse by alliterating and makes considerable use of anaphora. *Troilus and Criseyde* is not one of Chaucer's most stylistically elaborate works:[4] Chaucer had no truck with Boccaccio's most ostentatious verbal effects (which he may well have ascribed to artistic immaturity). Fortunately, however, the Italian poem unravels its story-line straightforwardly enough, for the most part; and its author speaks with becoming candor even when considering complex possibilities:[5]

> E qual si fosse non è assai certo:
> o che Criseida non se n'accorgesse
> per l'operar di lui ch'era coverto,
> o che di ciò conoscer s'infignesse;
> ma questo n'è assai chiaro ed aperto,
> che niente pareva le calesse
> di Troiolo e dell'amor che le portava,
> ma come non amata dura stava.   1.48

> And seyde he hadde a fevere and ferde amys.
> But how it was, certeyn, kan I nat seye,
> If that his lady understood nat this,
> Or feynede hire she nyste, oon of the tweye;

---

[2] See Wallace, *Early Writings*, 23–38.

[3] See, for example, *Filostrato* 3.59.1–2; 3.65.1–2; 4.65.4; 6.19.7–8; 3.94; 4.60; 4.107.

[4] See Payne, *Key*, 191.

[5] To draw attention to the *Filostrato*'s contribution to the language of the *Troilus*, I have underlined equivalent phrases in the Italian and English texts; ideas paraphrased or recast from the Italian are not underlined. Such a simple expedient is intended only as an approximate, initial guide to Chaucer's imitations.

> But wel I rede that, by no manere weye,
> Ne semed it as that she of hym roughte,
> Or of his peyne, or whatsoevere he thoughte.   1.491–97

The argument of Boccaccio's stanza divides neatly into two parts; its contents are formally announced by the first and fifth lines: first reporting what is not known about Criseida's feelings for Troiolo, it then tells us what is known. Chaucer compresses, abbreviates and amends Boccaccio's argument, but upholds its formally articulated bipartite structure. Chaucer's opening line is taken up in completing an idea developed in his previous stanza; compression is further necessitated by Chaucer's employment of rhyme royal, which contains one line fewer than the *ottava*. Having allowed himself six lines in which to translate the Italian stanza, Chaucer elects to drop Boccaccio's third line and to compress the sense of Boccaccio's couplet into a single line. Although Boccaccio's first and fifth lines do not contribute to the development of the narrative action, Chaucer decides against cutting either of them. He reduces Boccaccio's fifth line to a half-line format familiar from the English romances and fills up the rest of this line with a simple, intensifying phrase which yields his third "b" rhyme. Neither this phrase nor the phrase "oon of the tweye" with which it rhymes advances the narrative action. But Chaucer, like Boccaccio, recognizes the useful function played by such phrases in ballasting the narrative and in regulating its rate of development.

One significant shift between these stanzas remains to be noted: whereas Boccaccio chronicles events by employing impersonal, third-person constructions, Chaucer speaks in his own person, drawing attention to his authorial role. Such a shift is typical:

> E spesse volte insieme s'avvisaro
> con rimproveri cattivi e villani   8.26.1–2

> And ofte tyme, I fynde that they mette
> With blody strokes and with wordes grete   5.1758–9

The phrase "I fynde" has counterparts in both the *cantari* and the English romances. In his next five stanzas Chaucer departs from the Italian in order to discuss the scope and limitations of his authorial activity with his audience. On rejoining the Italian work he again injects a personal note into Boccaccio's flat chronicling of events:

> L'ira di Troiolo in tempi diversi
> a' Greci nocque molto sanza fallo   8.27.1–2

> The wrath, as I bigan yow for to seye,
> Of Troilus the Grekis boughten deere.   5.1800–1

By cutting the phrase "in tempi diversi" and the tag "sanza fallo," and by opening a parenthetic space between "ira" and "di," Chaucer wins room for the insertion of a casual aside: that is, he employs thoughtful and painstaking art to create an impression of casualness and ease; such an impression is furthered later in the book by the rhyming tag "as I kan heere" (5.1804). Although Boccaccio makes fewer personal incursions into the narrative,[6] he too cultivates a comfortable narrative manner by employing a battery of convenient tags and phrases. Some of his parenthetic asides seem strikingly "Chaucerian" in form and mood:

sì come suole
spesso avvenire a chi sanza difetto
riguarda in fra le cose c'ha per mano   8.5.5–7

as it is wont
often to happen to he who, without erring,
looks into matters that he has in hand

Chaucer passes over this generalized appeal to experience, but seizes on Boccaccio's next usage of the *topos* to fashion a fine epigrammatic couplet (8.7.2–4; 5.1637–8). Three stanzas earlier, he had followed yet another employment of the *topos*, this time suggesting a detached attitude towards the behavior of lovers:

come suole esser degli amanti usanza   8.2.4

And as thise loveres don ...   5.1572

It is perhaps surprising to hear Boccaccio sounding and inspiring such a typically "Chaucerian" note.[7] But in "Parte" 2, he offers a more elaborate employment of the *topos* which, in uniting author and auditors, again seems strongly reminiscent of the "Chaucerian" manner:

Ma come noi, per continua usanza,
per più legne veggiam foco maggiore,
così avvien, crescendo la speranza,
assai sovente ancor cresce l'amore;
e quinci Troiol con maggior possanza
che l'usato sentì nel preso cuore
l'alto disio spronarlo, onde i sospiri
tornar più fier che prima e li martiri.   2.85

Chaucer apparently makes no use of this stanza or the stanzas which surround it: in 2.977–9, he adopts an idea from 2.81.2–4, but then appears to ig-

---

[6] Most of Boccaccio's authorial posturing is confined to the rubrics that punctuate his narrative at frequent intervals; in these rubrics he habitually refers to himself impersonally as "l'autore."

[7] On Chaucer's characteristic and frequent appeals "to *common* human experience," see Jill Mann, "Chaucerian Themes and Style in the *Franklin's Tale*," in *The New Pelican Guide to English Literature*, ed. Boris Ford, 1, *Medieval Literature. Part One: Chaucer and the Alliterative Tradition* (Harmondsworth: Pelican, 1982), 133–53, at 137.

nore the Italian text until 2.981 brushes with 2.89.1. Further on in Book 2, however, we find:

> But as we may alday oureselven see,
> Thorugh more wode or col, the more fir,
> Right so encrees of hope, of what it be,
> Therwith ful ofte encresseth ek desir;
> Or as an ook comth of a litel spir,
> So thorugh this lettre, which that she hym sente,
> Encressen gan desir, of which he brente.
>
> Wherfore I seye alwey, that day and nyght
> This Troilus gan to desiren moore
> Thanne he did erst, thorugh hope ...   2.1331–40

The first four lines of Chaucer's first stanza intelligently imitate the phrasing and structure of 2.85.1–4; his fifth offers a parallel exemplum; the couplet connects all this with the immediate facts of the narrative action. The second stanza sees Chaucer returning emphatically ("Wherfore I seye alwey") to the task of storytelling. It also sees him realigning his narrative with his source text: having employed phrases from 2.129–30 in the stanza ending at 2.1330, he links up with 2.131 in 2.1338–44, the second stanza quoted above:

> Crescea di giorno in giorno più l'ardore
> e come che speranza l'aiutasse   2.131.1–2

It was, apparently, this notion of hope kindling ardour which reminded Chaucer of the *topos* of 2.85. Such appeals to experience are commonplace in medieval literature: but Boccaccio's employment of the *topos*, uniting the experience of author and auditors, clearly had a particular attractiveness for the English poet. In all their writings, Chaucer and Boccaccio seem especially concerned to excite pity and compassion from their readers, and to unite author, readers, and protagonists in a common bond of sympathy: such an aim is explicitly stated at the opening of the *Troilus* (1.22–51) and in the opening periods of both the *Fiammetta* and *Decameron*.

The *Filostrato* further qualified itself as a suitable source for Chaucer by the fertility and dense abundance of its ideas: every stanza offers two, three, four or more motifs for elaboration. Here, for example, Boccaccio develops three distinct ideas:

> Era contento Troiolo, ed in canti
> menava la sua vita e 'n allegrezza;
> l'alte bellezze ed i vaghi sembianti
> di qualunque altra donna nulla prezza,
> fuor che la sua Criseida, e tutti quanti
> gli altri uomin vivere in trista gramezza,
> a respetto di sé, seco credeva,
> tanto il suo ben gli aggradava e piaceva.   3.72

The ideas developed in this stanza might be summarized as follows: Troiolo was content, and led his life in singing and joyfulness; he paid no attention to female beauty, excepting that of Criseida; compared with his life, which so delighted him, he believed the life of other men to be miserable. Chaucer was so impressed by these ideas that he allocated a stanza to each of them (3.1716–36). Boccaccio's first idea, developed over two lines, is diligently rendered by two lines of English. Chaucer improves upon Boccaccio's bald opening phrase "Era contento" by employing the courtly, French-derived phrase "In suffisaunce": but he upholds Boccaccio's choice of the verb *menare* ("to lede") and imitates "in canti" with "in singynges," a phrase found nowhere else in his writings. He then expands his translation of *Filostrato* 3.72 by transferring details from *Filostrato* 2.84, an earlier account of Troiolo's courtly behavior:

> Troiolo canta e <u>fa</u> mirabil <u>festa</u>,
> <u>armeggia</u> e <u>dona</u> e <u>spende lietamente</u>,
> e <u>spesso</u> si rinnuova e <u>cangia vesta</u>   2.84.1–3

> In suffisaunce, <u>in blisse</u>, <u>and in singynges</u>,
> This <u>Troilus gan</u> al <u>his lif to lede</u>.
> He <u>spendeth</u>, <u>jousteth</u>, <u>maketh festeynges</u>;
> <u>He yeveth frely ofte</u>, <u>and chaungeth wede</u>   3.1716–19

The last three lines of this stanza and the first three of the next add two characteristic Chaucerian emphases: Troilus's love makes him highly companionable (1720–22) and famous (1723–5). Chaucer then proceeds to develop Boccaccio's third idea:

> And, as in love, <u>he was in swich gladnesse</u>,
> That in his herte <u>he demed</u>, as I gesse,
> <u>That ther nys lovere in this world at ese</u>
> <u>So wel as he</u>; and <u>thus gan love hym plese</u>.   3.1726–29

Chaucer's third stanza offers an exquisite poetic realisation of Boccaccio's second idea:

> The goodlihede or <u>beaute</u> which that kynde
> In <u>any other lady</u> hadde yset
> Kan nought the montance of a knotte unbynde,
> Aboute his herte, of al <u>Criseydes</u> net.   3.1730–33

Boccaccio's third line proposes a somewhat vague and hazy ideal of feminine beauty which restricts itself to externals: Chaucer, with the phrase "goodlihede or beaute," characteristically concerns himself with both moral and aesthetic qualities.[8] For the remainder of his stanza, Chaucer takes no pains to introduce fresh ideas: he is content simply to elaborate the strain of imagery set in

---

[8] For a detailed account of such qualities in Chaucer, see J. D. Burnley, *Chaucer's Language and the Philosophers' Tradition*, Chaucer Studies ii (Cambridge: D.S. Brewer, 1979).

motion by his first four lines. In this and in dozens of other amplifications, Chaucer shows great respect for Boccaccio's text, and particularly for his powers of invention: indeed, it often appears that Chaucer wished to do the *Filostrato* justice by giving its ideas room to breathe. Sometimes, however, he found Boccaccio's powers of narrative compression most congenial:

> Ed el similemente ebbe in pensiero
> ancor più volte di volervi andare,
> di pellegrino in abito leggero,
> ma sì non si sapeva contraffare
> che gli paresse assai coprire il vero,
> né scusa degna sapeva trovare
> da dir, se fosse stato conosciuto
> in abito cotanto disparuto.   8.4

> And ofte tyme he was in purpos grete
> Hymselven lik a pilgrym to desgise,
> To seen hire; but he may nat contrefete
> To ben unknowen of folk that weren wise,
> Ne fynde excuse aright that may suffise,
> If he among the Grekis knowen were;
> For which he wep ful ofte and many a tere.   5.1576–82

Dropping "similemente," Chaucer compresses Boccaccio's first two lines into one: "ebbe in pensiero" is neatly rendered as "he was in purpos grete," and "ancor più volte" simply translated as "ofte tyme"; the force of "di volervi andare" is sharpened by "To seen hire," and saved for the beginning of the third line. For the rest of the stanza, Chaucer keeps pace with Boccaccio's ideas: the phrasing of "he may nat contrefete" is indebted to "non si sapeva contraffare"; the phrase which follows gives concrete expression to the anxiety vaguely alluded to in Boccaccio's fifth line. The polysyllables of Boccaccio's final line are impressively sonorous but add little to the narrative: Chaucer rejects them, sealing his stanza with impressive and independent finality; his monosyllables stand like a bulwark against the feverish thinking which has gone before.

Chaucer's translation of *Filostrato* 7.29 provides a typically impressive example of his resolution to build climactically towards a memorable couplet. Here, as often, the autonomy of Boccaccio's couplet is much eroded by enjambment and elision:

> "Oh me, Criseida, qual sottile ingegno,
> qual piacer nuovo, qual vaga bellezza,
> qual cruccio verso me, qual giusto sdegno,
> qual fallo mio o qual fiera stranezza,
> l'animo tuo altiero ad altro segno
> han potuto recare? Oh me, fermezza
> a me promessa, oh me, fede e leanza,
> chi v'ha gittate dalla mia amanza?"   7.29

> "<u>O</u>, my <u>Criseyde, allas</u>! <u>what subtilte</u>,
> <u>What newe lust, what beaute</u>, what science,
> <u>What wratthe of just cause have ye to me</u>?
> <u>What gilt of me, what fel experience</u>,
> Hath fro me raft, <u>allas</u>! thyn advertence?
> <u>O trust, O feyth, O depe aseuraunce</u>,
> Who hath me reft Criseyde, al my plesaunce?"   5.1254-60

Chaucer's translations of Boccaccio's terms here are so intelligent and precise that they might almost have served as a glossary for a fourteenth-century English reader of the *Filostrato*. Chaucer translates "sottile ingegno" by forming a noun from the adjective "sottile" which corresponds to the sense of the substantive "ingegno": *subtilte* invariably has associations with mental ingenuity in Chaucer. "Newe lust" crisply translates "piacer nuovo"; "beaute" translates "bellezza." Chaucer drops "vaga" (one of Boccaccio's favorite adjectives)[9] to introduce "science" (one of Chaucer's favorite nouns)[10] and to create a threefold pattern of appeal which matches and balances that of the stanza's penultimate line. Chaucer flattens the two-fold appeal of Boccaccio's third line into a single question, but his phrase "wratthe of juste cause" splendidly combines the sense of "cruccio" and "giusto sdegno." "Gilt of me" neatly renders "fallo mio"; "fel experience" intelligently interprets "fiera stranezza," its choice of adjective being particularly apt.[11] Up to this point—the end of the fourth line—Chaucer has kept pace with Boccaccio's stanza. Boccaccio's object, verb, and complement have not yet been reached; if Chaucer is to secure the relative autonomy of his couplet, he will need to compress these into his next line. Chaucer achieves such compression with great assurance: his choice of "raft" as verb and "advertence" as object is quite inspired.

Of the three qualities which feature in Chaucer's penultimate line, "feyth" directly translates "fede" while "trust" and "depe aseuraunce" correspond more loosely to "fermezza / a me promessa" and "leanza." The couplet, once again, brings a subtle shift of emphasis from Chaucer. Whereas Troiolo continues his appeal to Criseyde, Troilus's appeal drifts away from any fixed point of address. Troilus, momentarily, speaks into a void. This subtle shift is beautifully accompanied by a modulation between the first four syllables of the fifth line and the first four of the seventh; the verb *reven* is employed again to fine effect.

I would like to draw attention to one last detail of this particular Chaucerian translation: whereas Troiolo opens his apostrophe with "Oh me, Criseida,"

---

[9] The adjective *vaga*, which has a broad range of application, appears forty-four times in the *Decameron*; the phrase "vaga bellezza" appears at 3.8.25; 4 Intro 31; 10.8.78.

[10] *Science* is featured forty-five times in Chaucer's writings (including nineteen times in the *Boece*). In the *Troilus* it appears only twice (1.67; 5.1255). In speculating that "science" may have drawn Criseyde's attention away from him, Troilus is probably thinking of the influence of Calkas, "That in science so expert was . . ." (1.67).

[11] ME *fel* derives from OF *fel*, "fierce, savage"; its range of meaning corresponds closely to that of the Italian *fiera*.

Troilus begins "O my Criseyde." The change is slight. It may be that Chaucer's text had "mia" for "me," or that Chaucer misunderstood: but it seems highly likely that Chaucer would have recognized "Oh me" (and its variant forms)[12] as an exclamation approximating to the English "allas"; and, in fact, we find that two of Boccaccio's usages of the exclamation in this stanza bring forth an "allas!" from Chaucer. I think it probable that Chaucer consciously decided to insert the possessive adjective "my" into 5.1254; if we juxtapose the opening of his previous stanza with its Italian counterpart,[13] we may deduce what provoked him to do this:

> "La tua <u>Criseida</u>, oh me, <u>m'ha ingannato</u>,
> <u>di cui io più che d'altra mi fidava</u>,
> <u>ella ha</u> altrui <u>il suo amor donato</u>   7.26.1–3

> "My lady bryght, <u>Criseyde, hath me bytrayed</u>,
> <u>In whom I trusted most of any wight</u>.
> <u>She</u> elliswhere <u>hath</u> now <u>here herte apayed</u>."   5.1247–49

This juxtaposition elicits a most striking contrast: whereas Troiolo disassociates himself from Criseida in speaking (to Pandaro) of "la tua Criseida," ("your Criseida"), Troilus speaks of "my lady bryght." With such a change, Chaucer repudiates Troiolo's repudiation of his beloved. Chaucer's wish to emphasize the continuing selfless devotion of Troilus to Criseyde also accounts, I would suggest, for the reappearance of the possessive adjective in 5.1254. It accounts for the suppression of the self-referential quality of Troiolo's "fermezza / a me promessa" (7.29.6–7). It may also account for the translation of "altrui" (7.26–3, "another person") as if it were "altrove" ("elsewhere") in 5.1249. The thought that Criseyde may have bestowed her love "elliswhere" is painful but comfortingly vague; it shields Troilus from the more painful admission that Criseyde has taken another man.

In incorporating ideas from *Filostrato* 3.78 into his *prohemium* to Book 3, Chaucer packs more words into his seven lines than Boccaccio can fit into eight. Skillfully compressing each of Boccaccio's first three ideas, Chaucer gains the effect of *anaphora* on "Ye." Having disposed of Boccaccio's first five-and-a-half lines in just over three lines, Chaucer is able to rearrange and develop the ideas introduced by the Boccaccian relative adverb "onde" in a more leisurely fashion:

> Tu <u>'n unità</u> <u>le case</u> e le cittadi,
> <u>li regni</u> e le province e 'l mondo tutto

---

[12] The form "oh me" occurs once in the *Commedia* (*Inf.* 28.123) and "omè" five times. The form "oimè" occurs frequently in the *Decameron*, and in the *Canzoniere* too (but not as frequently as Petrarch's imitators lead one to expect).

[13] The Italian counterpart is 7.26. Chaucer makes no use of 7.28. In 7.27 Troiolo interprets his own dream; Chaucer saves this stanza until 5.1513–19 and makes Cassandra the interpreter.

tien, bella dea; tu dell'amistadi
se' cagion certa e del lor caro frutto;
tu sola le nascose qualitadi
delle cose conosci, onde il costrutto
vi metti tal, che fai maravigliare
chi tua potenza non sa ragguardare.   3.78

Ye holden regne and hous in unitee;
Ye sothfast cause of frendshipe ben also;
Ye knowe al thilke covered qualitee
Of thynges, which that folk on wondren so,
Whan they kan nought construe how it may jo
She loveth hym, or whi he loveth here,
As whi this fissh, and naught that, comth to were.   3.29–35

This juxtaposition reminds us that whereas the mature Chaucer is a skilled and experienced versifier, the youthful Boccaccio has yet to discover his métier as a prose writer. Boccaccio's respect for the restraints of poetic form is somewhat limited: his first main verb here arrives with a sudden thump ("tien"), and his positioning of "onde" is particularly awkward. It is ironic that *Troilus and Criseyde* has so often been discussed as if it were a novel (and especially ironic that Meech should have contributed to such a discussion):[14] for much of Chaucer's translating of the *Filostrato* is analogous to a movement from prose to verse.[15]

Chaucer's choice of the *Filostrato* as the source of his great *tragedye* is unlikely to have been a happy historical accident. Chaucer's knowledge of Italian was, as we have seen, extraordinarily good: he knew just what he was choosing (and, presumably, paying for) in adopting Boccaccio's poem. The author of the *Filostrato*, Chaucer would have realized, shares his reverence for Dante: but he also shares his fondness for a tradition of stanzaic narrative that draws much of its peculiar vigor from popular, oral-derived origins. Chaucer's discriminating adherence to the style and conventions of the English romances was, it would seem, a matter of deliberate choice.[16] In the final book of the *Troilus* Chaucer leans especially heavily upon the conventions of romance: it is as if he wishes

---

[14] See Meech, *Design*, vi. In approaching Boccaccio's "*Filostrato* and other works of his contributory to the *Troilus* as materials for Chaucer's transforming art" (vii-viii), Meech ignores anything that Chaucer may have learned or adapted from the *Filostrato* as a *stanzaic poem*.

[15] Chaucer's rendering of the *Filostrato* often brings an increase in expressive vehemence and intensity: see Barry Windeatt, "The 'Paynted Proces': Italian to English in Chaucer's *Troilus*," *EM* 26–27 (1977–78): 79–103. It is important to emphasize that Chaucer often achieves such intensification by compressing loose Italian arguments into single lines: for example, in translating *Filostrato* 4.50 in 4.435–41, he achieves expressive vehemence but avoids enjambment.

[16] John Burrow, *Ricardian Poetry* (London: Routledge and Kegan Paul, 1971) observes (29) that "Gower stands off from the [popular English romance] traditions so generously represented in the work of Chaucer."

to push his protagonists (brought to imaginative life by his artistry) back into the world of artifice.[17] To this end, he elects to follow Boccaccio's summary, *cantare*-like account[18] of Troiolo's death, emitting a cry ("weilawey") and a pious exclamation ("save only Goddes wille!") that are quite typical of an English romancer:

> ... e dopo lungo stallo,
> avendone già morti più di mille,
> miseramente un dì l'uccise Achille.   8.27.6–8

> But weilawey, save only Goddes wille!
> Despitously hym slough the fierse Achille.   5.1805–6

This couplet provides one ending to the story of Troilus; the remaining nine stanzas provide another which bears witness to Chaucer's highest artistic pretensions.[19] The very last of these stanzas sees Chaucer turning to Dante: it is the *Commedia*, Chaucer suggests, that stands before him as his pattern of versification, of style, and of Christian propriety:

> Quell' uno e due e tre che sempre vive
> e regna sempre in tre e 'n due e 'n uno,
> non circunscritto, e tutto circunscrive   *Para.*14.28–30

> Thow oon, and two, and thre, eterne on lyve,
> That regnest ay in thre, and two, and oon,
> Uncircumscript, and al maist circumscrive,
> Us from visible and invisible foon
> Defende, and to thy mercy, everichon,
> So make us, Jesus, for thy mercy digne,
> For love of mayde and moder thyn benigne.
>   Amen.   5.1863–69

---

[17] The set-piece descriptions of Diomede, Criseyde, and Troilus in conventional romance terms in 5.799–840 inevitably distance us from these characters. This distancing effect is continued when the narrative proper resumes in 5.840; Diomede, pressing on with his seduction, is said to be "as fressh as braunche in May" (5.844; and see 5.847, 848, and 854).

[18] Discussed and translated in Wallace, *Early Writings*, 93.

[19] This brief account of the ending of the *Troilus*, which necessarily concentrates upon stylistic register, may be supplemented by the fine article by Bonnie Wheeler, "Dante, Chaucer, and the Ending of *Troilus and Criseyde*," *PQ* 61 (1982): 105–23. For an excellent new account of religious aspects of the ending, see Benson, *Chaucer's T&C*, 190–204.

Notes on Contributors

Stephen A. Barney teaches at the University of California, Irvine. He edited *Troilus* for the *Riverside Chaucer*. Among his books are *Allegories of History*, *Allegories of Love* and *Word-Hoard: An Introduction to Old English Vocabulary*. A group of his studies in Chaucer is forthcoming from Colleagues Press.

C. David Benson was educated at Harvard and Berkeley. He has taught at Columbia, Colorado, and Connecticut. He is the author of the *Medieval History of Troy*, *Chaucer's Drama of Style*, and *Chaucer's TROILUS AND CRISEYDE*. He is the editor of *Critical Essays on Chaucer's TROILUS AND CRISEYDE* and (with Elizabeth Robertson) *Chaucer's Religious Tales*.

Sheila Delany teaches at Simon Fraser University near Vancouver. She writes on Chaucer, medieval culture, and gender studies. Her translation of Osbern Bokenham's fifteenth-century legendary is just out from the University of Notre Dame Press (1992); her study of Chaucer's *Legend of Good Women* is forthcoming from the University of California Press (1993).

Carolyn Dinshaw teaches at the University of California at Berkeley. She is the author of *Chaucer and the Text: Two Views of the Author* (1988) and *Chaucer's Sexual Poetics* (1989).

Robert R. Edwards is Professor of English and Comparative Literature at The Pennsylvania State University. He is the author of *The Dream of Chaucer* (1989), *Ratio and Invention* (1989), *The Poetry of Guido Guinizelli* (1987), and *The Montecassino Passion and the Poetics of Medieval Drama* (1977); and coeditor of *The Olde Daunce: Love, Friendship, Sex and Marriage in the Medieval World* (1991). He is the editor-in-chief of *Comparative Literature Studies*.

Louise O. Fradenburg teaches medieval English literature in the University of California at Santa Barbara. She has published numerous articles on Chaucer; recently she published her book, *City, Marriage, Tournament: Arts of Rule in Late Medieval Scotland* (1992).

John M. Fyler is a Professor of English at Tufts University, and has been an ACLS and Guggenheim Fellow. He has published a book on *Chaucer and Ovid* (1979), and a number of articles on Chaucer and other medieval texts; he also edited the *House of Fame* for the *Riverside Chaucer*. He is currently interested in theories of language in the Middle Ages and medieval biblical commentaries.

R. W. Hanning is Professor of English and Comparative Literature at Columbia University. Author of *The Vision of History in Early Britain* (1966) and *The Individual in Twelfth-Century Romance* (1977), he has published articles on Chaucer in *Studies in the Age of Chaucer, Signs,* and several other journals and collections.

John P. Hermann teaches both medieval literature and contemporary criticism at the University of Alabama and has chaired the Critical Theory Group there since 1982. His publications include *Signs and Symbols in Chaucer's Poetry* (1981), and *Allegories of War* (1989), as well as articles in *Chaucer Review, Studies in the Age of Chaucer, Annuale Mediaevale* and *Philological Quarterly.*

Leonard Michael Koff teaches English and humanities at the University of California, Los Angeles. He is the author of *Chaucer and the Art of Storytelling* (1988).

Rosemarie P. McGerr is a visiting associate professor of Comparative Literature at Indiana University-Bloomington. Her publications include articles on the *Canterbury Tales,* the *House of Fame,* and concepts of literary closure in the Middle Ages. At present, she is completing a book on resistance to closure in Chaucer's narrative poems.

Richard T. Neuse teaches in the University of Rhode Island. He has published widely on poetry of the English Renaissance as well as on Middle English poetry. His recent book is *Chaucer's Dante: Allegory and Epic Theatre in THE CANTERBURY TALES* (1991).

Larry Scanlon is assistant professor of English at the University of Wisconsin-Madison. His book, *Narrative, Authority, and Power: The Medieval Exemplum and the Chaucerian Tradition,* is forthcoming from Cambridge University Press. He is currently at work on his next book, provisionally entitled *Text and Taboo in the Later Middle Ages.*

Sarah Stanbury teaches English at The College of the Holy Cross. She is the author of *Seeing the Gawain-Poet: Description and the Act of Perception* (1991) and co-editor with Linda Lomperis of *Feminist Approaches to the Body in Medieval Literature* (1992). Her articles addressing the gaze have recently appeared in *PMLA, Studies in the Age of Chaucer,* and *Literature and Psychology.*

Karla Taylor received her Ph.D. from Stanford University in 1983, taught at Yale University, and is presently Associate Professor of English and Director of Graduate Studies in the English Department at the University of Michigan, Ann Arbor. She is the author of *Chaucer Reads THE DIVINE COMEDY* (1989) and various articles on Chaucer, Dante, and Middle English literature.

David Wallace is Paul W. Frenzel Chair in Medieval Studies and Professor of English at the University of Minnesota. His most recent publication is *Boccaccio, DECAMERON* (1991).